MY DESTINY THE SEA

Volume I

Aged 14

Frederick William Sweetingham

All rights reserved.

My Destiny the Sea, by Frederick William Sweetingham was first written by FW Sweetingham between 1945 and 1950. The epilogue was added by his wife, Adelaide post Frederick's death in 1954.

***

This edition:

ISBN: 978-1-923454-18-7 – Volume I - Paperback
ISBN: 978-1-923454-19-4 – Volume II - Paperback

Preamble and edits to the original manuscript within this edition are copyright © Mark Sweetingham, 2025

Published 2025 by the Book Reality Experience, an imprint of
Leschenault Press, Leschenault, Western Australia

Cover Design by Brittany Wilson | Brittwilsonart.com

All source material has been fully acknowledged and used with permissions where applicable. Should you feel any material within is in breach of copyright please contact the publisher in the first instance.

The author asserts that no Artificial Intelligence methods, techniques or tools have been used within the researching or production of this biography.

Without in any way limiting the author's [and publisher's] exclusive rights under copyright, any use of this publication to "train" generative artificial intelligence (AI) technologies to generate text is expressly prohibited. The author reserves all rights to license uses of this work for generative AI training and development of machine learning language models.

Recommended citation: Sweetingham, FW 2025. My Destiny the Sea, Vol 1. The Book Reality Experience, Leschenault, Western Australia.

Dedicated to my dear wife

Adelaide Theresa

with devoted love.

Imagery Acknowledgements

All imagery is courtesy of the Mark Sweetingham archive with the exception and kind permission of:

Volume I

Cover Images:

Frederick William Sweetingham, courtesy of Clive Sweetingham

Isle of Wight Map, AJL Westbrook

Interior Images:

Frederick William Sweetingham, courtesy of Clive Sweetingham

Isle of Wight Map, AJL Westbrook

HMS Powerful, courtesy of WF Mitchell. In: Brassey's Naval Annual, 1896 – https://archive.org/details/CASGA_120403/page/n27/mode/2up

HMS Encounter moored in Hobart on Regatta Day, January 1912, Hobart's Big Aquatic Carnival. The Weekly Courier, January 25, 1912, p22. Courtesy of the State Library and Archives of Tasmania.

Arrival of the HMS Drake in the Derwent River, Hobart, February 1912, New Flagship of the Australia Station, The Tasmanian Mail, February 8, 1912, p5. Courtesy of the State Library and Archives of Tasmania.

Boomerang presented to FW Sweetingham of HMS Drake in Sydney, 1912, courtesy of Smith & Singer Fine Art

Inscription on barometer wedding gift from the WO's Mess, Whale Island, courtesy of Susan Elliott

Wedding gift from the WO's Mess, Whale Island, courtesy of Susan Elliott

Table of Contents

Preamble i

    Publisher's Note iii

    Author's Note v

Part 1 - Early Life

    CHAPTER I

        The Isle of Wight 1

    CHAPTER II

        Parents, Early Home Life, Education & Recreation. 8

    CHAPTER III

        I Leave the Beautiful Isle of Wight 13

    CHAPTER IV

        I Enter the Nautical School at Greenwich 15

Part 2 - I Join The Royal Navy

    CHAPTER V

        I Join Her Majesty's Ship St Vincent 21

    CHAPTER VI

        I Join a Sea-going Man of War 24

    CHAPTER VII

        Sailing Ship Days 31

    CHAPTER VIII

        I Join the Gunnery School 43

    CHAPTER IX

        We Commission HMS Powerful for Foreign Service 48

    CHAPTER X

        The Powerful Joins the British Naval Force in China 55

    CHAPTER XI

        Wei-hai-wei 68

Part 3 - The Boer War

CHAPTER XII

Homeward Passage Abruptly Halted in South Africa 79

CHAPTER XIII

The Investment of Ladysmith 89

CHAPTER XIV

Events Elsewhere in South Africa 98

CHAPTER XV

The Ongoing Defence of Ladysmith 102

CHAPTER XVI

The Siege Lingers As We Await Buller's Troops 109

CHAPTER XVII

The Battle of the Tugela Heights and the Relief of Ladysmith 112

Part 4 - Growing Experience In The Royal Navy

CHAPTER XVIII

Return to Portsmouth. 123

CHAPTER XIX

Life as a Staff Gunnery Instructor. 131

CHAPTER XX

Life in Destroyers and Torpedo Boats 153

CHAPTER XXI

Back to the Mediterranean on HMS Aboukir 168

Part 5 - Birth Of The Australian Navy

CHAPTER XXII

I Join HMS Drake 177

Chapter XXIII

War Clouds and Political Strife 197

Part 6 - The Beginnings Of World War I

Chapter XXIV

The First Days of World War I 213

CHAPTER XXV

Chasing the Goeben and Breslau in the Mediterranean 221

CHAPTER XXVI
>   The Navy's Part in Home Waters...225

CHAPTER XXVII
>   Deployment of the British Army..229

CHAPTER XXVIII
>   Naval Action off Heligoland...232

CHAPTER XXIX
>   Capture at Sea and Contraband Cargoes..236

CHAPTER XXX
>   Exploits of the German Raider Emden...241

CHAPTER XXXI
>   Ongoing Patrol Work at Gibraltar..246

CHAPTER XXXII
>   Battles of the South American Station...249

Part 7 Naval Action In Home Waters

CHAPTER XXXIII
>   The Dover Patrol and the North Sea Strategy..255

CHAPTER XXXIV
>   German Raids on the East Coast of England...259

Chapter XXXV
>   The Battle of Dogger Bank..262

Chapter XXXVI
>   The War on Commerce..267

Preamble

The partially torn label glued to the ageing cardboard box told that the manuscript had previously journeyed to F.W. Cheshire Pty. Ltd., Booksellers and Publishers of 338 Little Collins Street, Melbourne.

Fortunately, the manuscript, hand-typed on yellowing foolscap paper, was not as badly devoured by silverfish as the accompanying memo from Mr Julian Smith recommending the manuscript not worthy of publication, but noting its potential interest to naval historians.

The box had subsequently resided in Hobart, Tasmania for several decades. It was tucked away with other family keepsakes in the possession of John Frederick (Peter) Sweetingham. Peter was born in 1915 in Portsmouth, England and passed away in 1998 in Hobart.

I was in Hobart for his funeral and amongst many conversations Peter's wife Joan, my mother, I decided to take the box with its contents back to Fremantle, Western Australia for safe-keeping. I did, but it was several years before I found the time to carefully sift through the contents in the box.

As I began to read the narrative, I was transported to a bygone era by an author with vivid and detailed observations of events, both historically significant and trivial, with intriguing insights and opinions of my grandfather who died three years before I was born.

Those who have lived through the latter half of the 20th Century and into the new millennium consider it to have been a time of unprecedented change; but on reflection it seems to me no more dramatic than the changes that occurred during the life of Frederick William Sweetingham - born at Freshwater on the Isle of Wight in 1877, died in Hobart, Tasmania in 1954.

The narrative ends somewhat prematurely in 1918, apparently due to the author's ill health. But the pen was picked up by his wife, Adelaide, who describes more adventures to round out a biography of her husband's life.

The manuscript was originally handwritten by Commander Sweetingham in his twilight years, in his study in 'Puget House' in the village of Lindisfarne, Tasmania; overlooking a majestic view of Hobart across the Derwent River. It was later typed, double spaced, onto foolscap paper by his youngest daughter Mary. I recall as a very small boy seeing this same cardboard box tucked away next to an old Remington typewriter in her home in South Hobart.

I began the process, much as Mary did some 50 years earlier, to transfer as faithfully as I could the deteriorating document to the hopefully more durable electronic media of my era. The process of scanning nearly 1,000 pages of flimsy foolscap typescript and checking the fidelity of the optical character recognition software has been time consuming process. In fact, it has taken me nearly 2 decades. I have been joined in this process by my cousin Douglas Wilson, eldest son of Thelma Sweetingham - Fred's eldest daughter.

In proof reading, we have applied just the mildest editorial touch so the reader can enjoy the story in the style and voice in which it was told.

Mark Sweetingham, Fremantle, Western Australia
January 15, 2025

The Manuscript

Doug Wilson and Frederick Sweetingham (1952)

Publisher's Note

Some names and identifying details have been changed to protect the privacy of individuals. Please be aware, that when these accounts were written, language that is no longer acceptable now, was mainstream. **It is included for accuracy and not for offense.** With special thanks to Clive Sweetingham for the portrait in the frontispiece.

Author's Note

During this work, my aim has been to fit in all the facts and events experienced in chronological form. For one, however, who has kept no diary this has proved a difficult task. I trust therefore that the reader will be pleased to overlook any inconsistency in this narrative.

Frederick William Sweetingham

Part 1

Early Life

CHAPTER I

The Isle of Wight

---ooOoo---

It is not improbable that my parents had formed an early impression as to my destiny and had agreed that it should be in ships upon the great oceans for, at the tender age of eleven months, I took my departure alone to sea off the coast facing the English Channel. The incident occurred on the foreshore at Freshwater, a small place situated on the south-west coast of the Isle of Wight. My nursemaid had taken me there in a perambulator for the usual daily outing, and upon reaching the esplanade, which sloped down to the sea, she met a young Coast Guardsman who had attracted her attention. The young man presented a very smart appearance in Naval Uniform and carried a brightly polished telescope under his arm, which indicated that he was on duty at the time. Doubtless, these two young persons had met on previous occasions, for after an exchange of greetings, the perambulator, with occupant, was abandoned on the spot and the couple proceeded nonchalantly along the shore with presumably little concern for the infant left all forlorn.

A strong gusty wind was blowing directly off shore and by the time the maid and her companion had strolled for some distance, a heavy squall caught the perambulator and set it in motion down to the sea at increasing velocity. The vehicle was strongly built and fitted with a square wooden back which formed a perfect sail as it careered into the water. Indeed, the whole outfit behaved in a most seaworthy manner from the moment it became afloat. The little craft remained delightfully on even keel and maintained a steady course to seaward without the slightest deviation. As to the manner in which my outward-bound voyage was interrupted and how the homeward course was set, there is nothing tangible to record. Nevertheless, we may be very sure that the bluejacket soon became aware of the happening and handled the situation with alacrity and with the usual thoroughness as becomes a seaman of the Royal Navy. For one is happy to relate that we reached the shore in safety and that I arrived home in perfect health within an hour of perhaps the most critical moments of my life. In the circumstances, one might surmise how the infant fared when upon the water? After careful thoughts I consider it very likely that he might well have enjoyed a serenely tranquil experience; for luckily the little fellow was securely strapped to the inside of the perambulator and could not have moved appreciably.

Born at Calbourne, near Freshwater, Isle of Wight on 28th December 1877, my early life was spent in that region till 1881 when my family moved to Atherfield, some 9 miles to the east of Calbourne. This removal was consequent upon my father's appointment to command the Coast Guard Station at Atherfield and as Senior Officer on the coast between The Needles and St. Catherines Point. My parents at that time were well connected with the navy, for my father was the son of a seafarer and entered the Royal Navy as an apprentice on board HMS *Victory* at Portsmouth in 1850, while my mother's brother was serving as an Engineer Officer in the Royal Navy.

Atherfield in 1881, as now, is a fishing village, situated on the South coast of the Isle of Wight. It was then one of the most dreaded spots for shipping in the English Channel. Shipwrecks were numerous there and smuggling was rife. The Coast Guard Station was a large two storied structure built upon an exposed site only twenty yards from a steep cliff. The building, like most Coast Guard Stations in those days, was coated with white paint and presented an imposing sight from ships at sea and overlooked two dangerous reefs jutting into the English Channel. During the south-west gales, these reefs, or the Atherfield ledges as they were called, were lashed by terrific seas and constituted a real danger to sailing ships in the vicinity. Alternatively, in foggy weather, the ledges were of equal peril to both sailing and steam vessels, in that the insetting tide was the cause of many ships coming to grief by grounding on the reefs.

Regarding the smuggling activities these were carried out mainly by the fishermen who were quite numerous along the coast. They were in league with the farmers too, who provided assistance in the way of land transport and storage of the contraband goods. My father therefore, during the course of his duty, was faced with an arduous task. Moreover, his work was made extremely difficult, owing to the fact that while suppressing the activities of the smugglers it was these selfsame men whom he was compelled to call upon to assist in his work relating to the ships and vessels that were wrecked in the vicinity. These fishermen were the only persons who could be found to assist in the operations of the Life Saving Rocket Apparatus, or manning the Coast Guard boat from off a lee shore when a vacant oar was often necessary.

The boat provided for the use of the Coast Guard was a heavily built whaler called the *Lariet* in which my father and his men did sterling rescue work. Although it was recognized by everyone that the most dangerous risk to shipping on the south coast of the Isle of Wight was the Atherfield ledges; curiously enough, the Royal National Lifeboat Institution had omitted to install a lifeboat there. But two fully equipped lifeboats were stationed some distance to the Eastward. One of these was provided at Brighstone and the other at Brooke about four and seven miles respectively from Atherfield. The boats in those days were not fitted with motor engines and propellers, as they are now, their only means of propulsion was by oars or sail. Consequently, the life-boats at Brighstone, much less the one at Brooke were scarcely of any use in the case of shipwrecks at Atherfield. Happily, my father and his crew never failed to launch the old *Lariet* in their endeavours to rescue the lives from ships in distress within that region, whenever it was possible to do so. Indeed, it was known on more than one occasion that he had launched his whaler upon the failure of the Life Saving Rocket Apparatus during heavy gales, when the Brighstone Lifeboat Authority had deemed it too hazardous to send their lifeboat afloat. From these incidents it must not be inferred that the lifeboat men themselves, who were very brave seamen as well as skillful fishermen, would have hesitated to launch their boats if called upon to do so.

Of the numerous wrecks and rescue work in which my father was involved, I would refer to one in particular. The *Atlas*, a Danish barque, was driven on one of the reefs at Atherfield during a fearful gale early in the eighties. Several attempts to reach the vessel by the Life Saving Rocket Line had failed owing to the resisting force of the wind which raged directly on the lee shore. The *Atlas* was a wooden built vessel and in immediate danger of breaking up as the heavy seas pounded her. One mast was broken very soon after she had grounded and had already fallen over the ship's sides; while the boats on board were rendered useless. The position had now become one of extreme urgency and forthwith my father decided to go off in the *Lariet* in an endeavour to save the lives on board the unfortunate vessel. Thereupon he assembled the boats crew and informed them of his intention, and to their lasting honours, all were willing to man the boat despite the advice and warnings against such actions openly given by some experienced fishermen. In this connection however, a goodly number of fishermen were persuaded to assist in the launching. So

Early Life

off they went. After a hard pull on the oars and a gruelling time buffeting against the head wind and tremendous seas, the *Lariet* and her brave crew reached the vicinity of the stricken barque.

The danger here was very real and it required expert handling of the boat to prevent crashing against the ships' side as the heavy seas were breaking over her. With difficulty however, a boat rope was secured to the vessel and my father managed to approach her sufficiently close to enable two or three of the *Atlas*'s crew to clamber into the *Lariet* before the violence of the gale compelled them to drop some distance to leeward again. By closely watching for lulls in the storm, it was possible to repeat such approaches at irregular intervals till all hands were taken off the ship. Splendid achievement as this was, the difficulty was by no means disposed of and a most anxious time was to follow.

The *Lariet* was a comparatively small boat under oars in a mountainous sea and a furious gale, loaded to full capacity with passengers and crew, some hundreds of fathoms off a lee shore lashed by huge breakers. The task therefore was not complete until the men had been landed safely. To do this successfully, it was important first to manoeuvre into position a little to seaward of the breakers upon the beach, while keeping the boat stationary and heading directly towards the shore, or end on to the seas. Then one of the heaviest waves should be selected as it came up astern and when the crest of it was drawing near, the time came for an extra strong pull on the oars while the scend of the wave impelled the boat well up on to the beach. Observance of these details was essential to prevent the boat from prematurely overshooting her waiting positions with the inevitable result of broaching to and capsizing.

Though these difficulties and dangers were encountered, I am happy to record that the Officers and crew of the *Atlas* with their captain were landed in safety midst the joy and admiration of all the spectators who had come from the villages in and around the neighbourhood. Among them, of course, were the fishermen, who had assisted to launch the boat and upon its returns rendered all help possible during the operation of hauling the boat above the high-water mark to safety. Shortly after this rescue was affected the unfortunate *Atlas* broke up and her wreckage was strewn along the shore.

This narrative would most certainly not be complete without special mention of the Coastguard women folk, who rendered such kindly help and comfort to the exhausted survivors from the ship. Soon after their husbands had gone afloat my mother called an improvised meeting to determine the requirements that would be needed upon their return, and to the credit of these practical women, all available comforts were prepared in good time. Their work included the provision of food and dry clothing which surely would be needed, also extra beds and sleeping accommodation for the captain and crew of the stranded ship. Indeed, the later were well cared for in every detail till they departed for their homes in Denmark.

In recognition of this courageous service the Danish Government officially thanked my father and the Coast Guardsmen at Atherfield. In addition, my father was presented with an exquisite Silver Tea and Coffee Service suitably inscribed while his men were awarded a gratuity.

The unlawful landing of contraband goods on the Southern shores of the Isle of Wight was a matter of much concern by the Government Authority at the time of my father's appointment to Atherfield. Its prevention therefore gave rise for immediate consideration and action. It was known that considerable quantities of tobacco, wines, spirits and other articles subject to customs duty, were smuggled ashore within the vicinity of Atherfield; and in due time my father had discovered grounds for suspecting the local fishermen, together with a method employed by them in this nefarious practice. A large number of crab and lobster were taken from the fishing grounds and these were caught in large wicker pots made by the fishermen for this purpose. These pots were grouped by coir rope, baited and sank to the bottom of the sea by large stone sinkers. The outfit was known as a "fishing trot" and many of them were laid by the fishermen who could readily locate them. This marking device presented a simple and very ordinary appearance to the lay person. But on suitable occasion, preferably on dark moonless nights when detection would be almost impossible, small fast sailing craft without navigation lights, would arrive on the fishing ground from France or some other Continental country loaded with contraband cargoes. Shallow water patches would be selected and here the goods would be placed overboard and carefully buoyed similarly to the fishing pots. The little vessels would then depart and as previously arranged leaving local fishermen to take care of their fishing trots till a favourable opportunity for landing the booty presented itself. This operation would be quite safe and comparatively easy on dark nights or during dense fogs when usually only one Coastguardsman could be spared at a time to watch miles of the coastline in the execution of his duty.

The discovery of the smuggler's clever ruse was due to the fact that my father himself was an ardent fisherman; as indeed I was becoming at the time. It was one of my most delightful experiences to accompany him in his private boat on fishing expeditions whenever I was permitted to do so. While the instruction I received both in handling the boat and in the art of catching fish still remains a happy memory.

On a certain occasion my father set out with one of the Coastguardsmen off duty. They had left rather late in the afternoon on this particular day and proceeded well out to sea beyond a number of fishing trots in the hope of catching some large fish, which were often found in that vicinity. As their luck was so promising my father decided continue fishing well after nightfall and after a very successful catch, sufficient for a goodly supply to the neighbours at the Coastguard Station, they called it a day and set sail for home. By this time however, it was late in the evening and darkness had been upon them for some considerable time. With a favourable breeze the boat was making very good progress on the homeward journey when, suddenly they found themselves among an immensely large number of fishing boats. My father's attention was naturally drawn to this and his first observation was the absence of lights, for not a single craft exhibited one. All this, of course, aroused suspicion though my father was discreet enough to continue his homeward trip without apparent concern.

On arrival at the beach, he immediately sent the Coastguardsman who had landed with him to the Chief Boatman with orders to call out and furnish an armed crew for the Service Whaler and to man the boat as soon as possible. This of course caused quite a stir at the Coastguard Station and everyone wondered what was the matter. Shortly afterwards my father had taken charge of the Service Boat himself and was outward bound once more with his men and boat fully equipped for any emergency. Upon reaching the position where so much activity had been going on before, not a single boat or other vessel could be found. After an abortive search however, and feeling that something of importance must surely have been going on in the vicinity, he ordered his men to weigh one of the fishing trots. This solved the problem immediately, for sure enough, no less than six casks of brandy were hauled up in place of crab or lobster pots.

Following the discovery my father returned to Atherfield and posted a number of Coastguardsmen as special watchers from advantageous positions, where a sharp lookout could be kept upon the landing places for some distance along the coast. These efforts were well rewarded a few nights later when some eighty barrels of spirits were seized by my father while the fishermen were in the act of landing them. The culprits were, of course arrested, tried and received

Early Life

due punishment. The result of this was that smuggling of contraband goods at Atherfield came to an end.

As may be supposed the Coastguardsmen in general and the Officer in Command in particular became most unpopular. Any veiled threats of reprisals could be heard from certain quarters in the locality though serious attention was not paid to them till words led to a despicable action in this way. The cliffs overlooking the sea shore for miles along the coast were dangerously steep and erosion in the form of landslips was a common occurrence. In order therefore, to ensure a safe track well inside the edge of the precipice for the coastguardsmen to follow during the course of their duty along the coast at night, or in a dense fog by day, large white washed boulders were placed a few yards inside the edge of the cliff at suitable distances apart. By this arrangement a pedestrian was enabled to proceed safely by keeping the white boulders just a little to seaward and thus avoid the possibility of walking over the cliff. The maintenance of the boulders in their correct positions was obviously an important matter and one can therefore understand the anger of my father- when it was reported to him that this safety device had been tampered with. Upon investigation it was found that some of the boulders had been deliberately removed to the very edge of the cliffs, while others were rolled over the precipice. Obviously, this spiteful work had been perpetrated by some persons who could no longer carry on their lucrative business of smuggling as heretofore.

Though several other incidents were endured, amicable relations were soon restored for the fishermen, who were really a good-hearted lot of fellows, realized that my father, after all, had only carried out his plain duty.

Of the numerous vessels that came to grief and of which I still retain a vivid memory, the wreck of a sailing ship named *Sirenia* was the first. The *Sirenia* was a beautiful British full rigged ship that grounded on the Atherfield Ledge in bad weather in November 1884. The Captain of the ship, whose name was McIntyre, was accompanied by his wife and two daughters and the vessel was homeward bound with a cargo of some 3,000 tons of wheat. It was the *Sirenia*'s maiden voyage home and, up to the time of entering the approaches to the English Channel, she had established a remarkably good voyage. It was therefore extremely bad luck that this magnificent ship, and her valuable cargo were not to reach their destination with less than 200 miles to go. As the weather was so bad at the time the vessel struck, and there were indications that it would become worse, my father decided to use the Life Saving Rocket Apparatus to rescue the lives on board.

The local fishermen were summoned accordingly; and how terribly excited I was to watch the four wheeled contrivance emerge from its storing shed; and to march behind it while it was being hauled by the men with drag ropes to its operational position. At the same time, I could not help noticing how anxious my father was about the stability of the *Sirenia* as she appeared to be straining herself upon the terrible reef as the enormous seas were driving heavily against and over her. As soon as the apparatus had arrived in position the rocket machine was erected and pointed towards the ship while the rocket line had been secured in readiness for discharge. Then one was thrilled to hear my father's voice clearly above the howling wind and lash of the waves, shouting the orders first to "Stand-by" then almost immediately to "Fire". Thereupon, the chief Boatman holding a lighted pull-fire in his hand applied the flare to the fuse and with a splutter and a roar, away went the rocket in the direction of the stricken ship with the rocket line trailing behind it. What an exciting experience it was to watch the missile stand up to its work against the tremendous force of the gale. It was also an anxious moment for my father and the men, for even if its velocity would prove sufficient for the rocket to reach the vessel, there was the chance of an error in the setting of the machine for elevation and or directions with the result that the rocket might fall short, or to the right or left of its objective. However, to the great satisfaction and joy of everyone present it was seen that the rocket and line had passed over the vessel despite the adverse elements.

So far so good, but there were still many technicalities in the drill of the Life Saving Rocket Apparatus crew to be carried out after the Rocket line had been successfully placed on board the ship. I will not weary the reader with all these particulars though I remember them so well after all these years. It is therefore sufficient to mention that when the line had reached the ship, the shore end of it was secured to one end of a stout hempen hawser, which was then, at a given signal, hauled off to the *Sirenia* by her ship's crew and secured to one of the ships's masts several feet above the deck. Following the Captain's signal that all was secure on board, the shore end of the hawser was rove through a block suspended from a tripod and set up taut by a tackle. Then a circular life-saving buoy, to accommodate one person, was suspended from the hawser by means of a runner block, which would enable it to travel between the ship and shore.

All was now ready for the actual operation of rescuing the people on board. Again, I heard my father's words of command to "Man the endless whip" which the crew of the Rocket Apparatus eagerly obeyed. This was followed by his order "Haul out the breeches buoy". Away went the life-buoy trailing below the hawsers towards the ship at a considerable pace. On reaching the *Sirenia* Mrs McIntyre was the first to be placed into it and following a signal "All clear" from the vessel, my father gave implicit orders for hauling in the opposite direction, and so the good lady was brought safely ashore and carefully lifted out of the life-buoy. The rescue of the Captain's wife is one of the most vivid memories of my life, as also was the safe landing of the two Misses McIntyre, immediately followed their mother, who was very anxiously awaiting them. After both girls had been lifted ashore, Mrs McIntrye and the two children were taken to my home where my mother received them and aid everything possible for their comfort.

At this juncture the force of the gale had lessened somewhat while the tide was receding. Consequently, the heavy seas had abated considerably. This improvement in the weather was very pleasing to my father who all the while suffered anxiety as to whether the ship's mast would stand up to the gale or even the vessel herself while the life-saving operation was going on. Since the *Sirenia* was a newly built ship however, her power of endurance was very sound. This fact, together with the better conditions of the weather, led Captain McIntyre to hope and believe that his ship could be refloated. In the circumstances, he decided to remain on board with his first mate and boatswain, while the remainder of the ship's company was taken off by the Rocket Apparatus. When the Second Mate had landed, he informed my father of the Captain's decision, and that he was the last to land for the present.

My father however, feeling most concerned as to the safety of those still on board, dispatched a written message to the Captain by the life-buoy stating that in his opinion the moderation in the weather was only temporary and that the force of the gale would increase as the tide changed to the flood. My father further recommended that the Captain should change his mind, send the two officers ashore and come himself. The unhappy Captain however would not agree and was naturally opposed to the idea of leaving his fine ship while he thought there remained the remotest chance of getting her off those terrible rocks. Accordingly, he replied, stating that, while he appreciated the kindly advice tendered by my father, he felt that he could not leave his ship in the present circumstances. My father therefore adopted the only course left open to him. He divided the crew of the Rocket Apparatus into watches for the night in order to keep the apparatus intact and ready for instant use should it become necessary.

Early Life

As it was feared the force of the wind increased with the next flood tide and a strong gale with tumultuous seas raged for the best part of the night. Still the Captain and his two officers bravely stuck to their stout-hearted ship. Luckily the weather became more favourable during the ebb tide early the next morning when my father was able to go off to the *Sirenia* and persuade the Captain to come on shore. By this time, there seemed little doubt that the beautiful ship would become a total wreck and when poor Captain McIntyre landed with my father, he was a broken-hearted man for he loved his ship. He and his family stayed with us many days before they left for their home.

Although I was only 7 years of age, I remember all the details of how I remained by my father's side on that terrible lee shore while the operation of rescue work was carried out; and how I tried to help in my small way by hauling on ropes and running messages for my father. I remember too, how strenuously and devotedly my mother worked in her earnest endeavour to look after our unfortunate guests. Among these were two men of the ship's crew who became very ill soon after landing; one poor fellow dying early the next morning from the effect of shock and exposure. Some of the crew unluckily fared badly during their transit from the ship to the shore during the fiercest part of the gale; for at intervals the occupant of the life-buoy became completely submerged in the raging seas. This was mainly due to the sagging of the hawser, though no effort was spared to keep it as taut as possible.

Of about twenty vessels that grounded at Atherfield during our 10 years residence there, more than half of them were refloated, especially those that were stranded due to dense fogs in fine weather. It was the greatest concern of my father whenever a ship grounded to refloat her again as soon as possible and to get the ship away without delay. On occasions this was only a matter of some hours, depending upon the position of the vessel and the tide. If a ship could be prevented from turning whilst grounded it might be possible to haul her straight off to sea while little damage was done. On the other hand, if the ship had changed her position whilst aground, this would inevitably seal her fate.

On boarding a stranded ship therefore, it was my father's first care to lay out the ships anchors and cables by boat to prevent her from slewing and to haul the ship off on the flood tide as soon as practicable. This operation of course demanded a sound knowledge of the tides and local currents together with expert seamanship and it was considered that my father's experience in these details were superb. On one occasion only three hours had elapsed between the grounding and refloating of a vessel. A fine performance to be sure.

Among the ships to ground of the dreaded Atherfield Ledge was a large four masted steamer by the name of *Duke of Westminster*. This vessel was ashore for several days but happily she was refloated and continued her seagoing for many years. Later I hope to refer to this ship again in connection with one of the thrilling times of my life.

Apart from the fisherfolk, there were many of the country yokel type living in and around Atherfield and whenever a vessel stranded these fellows would rush to the beach as near to the ship as possible without wetting their hob nailed boots. There all sorts of amusing remarks, recommendations and proposals discussed among them, mostly with a view to giving my father assistance of any kind. In this connection I well remember one old farm labouring fellow by the name of Mornford following my father along the beach and mumbling all sorts of proposals in almost an unintelligible vocabulary. My father apparently did not understand what he was talking about so, said "Yes" when old Mornford wanted a "No" or vice versa. However, before turning away Mornford said: "Baint they be goin' to pull her in any cloaster, 'cos we be waitin' to go out ship."

CHAPTER II

Parents, Early Home Life, Education & Recreation.

---ooOoo---

As the third son and fifth child of a family of four boys and two girls, my early home life was an entirely healthy and happy one. My mother who was ten years younger than my father was born in Cornwall, the daughter of a fairly prosperous farmer and I should imagine that she was more or less a typical mid-Victorian mother. With a family of six, by no means considered a large one in those days, her first care and thoughts were for the welfare of her husband, children and home. Frugality and cleanliness was insisted upon in our home, while extravagance and waste of any kind was taboo. In addition, my mother was a Victorian disciplinarian while being true and just in every respect.

My father was born at Gosport, Hampshire in 1835 and entered the Royal Navy at 13 years of age. His first seagoing ship was HMS *Rapid*, an armed brig of 400 tons. In this vessel he sailed to China around the Cape of Good Hope, arriving at Hong Kong after a long voyage of 9 months duration. Remaining in the Far East for 5 years, the *Rapid* was ordered to the East Indies and 2 years later she returned to England and paid off. Thus, my father as a very young man had completed seven years foreign service. Later he served in the Royal Yacht *Osborne* and was present when the Prince of Wales, afterwards King Edward VII, visited ports in the Mediterranean and toured the cities of the Holy Land.

At the age of 28 my father married and a few years later he obtained a commission in the Naval Coast Guard Service. It was not until he was about 45 years of age that I began to really know him and it gives me much pleasure to record my memories of such a large-hearted, noble and kindly man. Possessing a strong physique rather florid complexion under a flowing beard, and delightfully blue eyes which twinkled above the finest teeth I have ever seen in any man. With cheery voice and dark wavy hair, there was a culture in his manner scarcely seen in seafaring men of his day. He was not over-communicative to his children though adored by us all - a truly ideal father. In family matters my father's opinion was always sought, though important decisions were invariably made by my mother, and she was usually right in her judgments. Though some members of the family seemed not to appreciate her qualities, or to put it in another perspective, they could not see the wood for the trees. At heart my mother was kindly and most lovable.

Educational facilities at Atherfield outside one's home were non-existent. My older brothers and sister were sent to boarding schools at Newport, the capital town of the Isle of Wight, about 10 miles from Atherfield; while the three younger members of the family, including myself, attended the parochial school at Chale, a village three miles from home. Regularly at 8 o'clock each school morning we walked to school over the fields along the edge of the cliff and returned home about 5 p.m. On our way to school we passed a farmhouse where the daily supply of milk for our home was obtained. It was situated about a mile from Chale and as we passed the house my sister Edie or I would hand in the empty milk can and call for the filled can on our way home. The farmer and his wife were a homely couple and with them stayed a little boy Jacky Wilsted. As Jacky was very little younger than I and lived so much closer to Chale than we did, my sister asked him when he too was coming to school. To this the boy replied: "Granfer says, when the cuckoo comes and picks up all the dirt."

On Sunday mornings we attended Sunday school at Chale and afterwards my younger brother and I would sing in the choir of the parish church there; then home for lunch by 1.30 p.m. and set out again in time for the evening church service. Afterwards we would walk another three miles to reach home about 9 p.m. Thus, the strenuous walk of 12 miles ended each perfect Sunday. On occasion, my father and mother would accompany the children to evening church on Sundays. Despite the fullness of our Sunday's occupation, I would invariably be in my place at the parochial school by 9 o'clock on Monday mornings. In this connection it is interesting to recall that for three successive years I was awarded the first prize for school attendance, despite the fact that the pupils for the most part lived in and around the vicinity of the school. I have often thought since, that these long and regular walks to school and church were largely responsible for my sturdy growth especially in view of the inclement weather during the winter seasons.

The little school at Chale accommodated about seventy boys and girls. The Schoolmaster was perhaps a good teacher though his temper was sometimes uncontrollable. He was assisted by a schoolmistress, an elderly lady, very kindly and good. Generally, my school days at Chale were healthy and happy ones though I am bound to admit that the education I received during some four years there was lamentably poor. The teaching of art, grammar, correct speech, address, manners and cleanliness was totally lacking, and the Schoolmaster seemingly thought his duty began with the instruction of the three R's, and ended with his ability to severely thrash the biggest boys in the school. It is true that the majority of his pupils were sons of farm labourers and fishermen, who would leave school as soon as the regulations permitted to follow the calling of their fathers who were mostly illiterate; but there were also a fair proportion of other boys at the school who would soon have to face the world so very different from the back of Isle of Wight. For the latter, the State School Authorities had made no provision whatever. On the contrary they were herded together with boys whose vocabulary was deplorably un-English and naturally harmful to them.

Had it not been for home influence and contact with the Minister of Religion, Reverend Charles Heald and his good sister Miss Rhodes, I believe that my education at the age of 12 years would have been little better than that of natives of similar age in South Africa or India. Indeed, the teaching staff and schools for natives, which I had the opportunity of visiting in South Africa, India and Ceylon in 1920 – 1932, were far superior in every way to that which existed during my 3 years in the parochial school at Chale.

At Atherfield there was no organized sport for children or indeed for men, and if there had been it is very likely that we would have found them irksome. Places of amusement there were entirely unknown. Nevertheless, our Saturdays and holidays were delightfully hilarious whilst playing in the green fields, boating, fishing and romping on the beaches. The dangerous practice of climbing down almost inaccessible ledges and crevices in the cliffs were also indulged in. Our chief attraction being the birds' nests. Jackdaw, starling and sea bird eggs could be taken here, but at what a risk! I shudder to recall these activities in one of the wild spots of England, where one slip of the foot or fingers would have ended one's career by a precipitation of a hundred feet to certain death. Our venturesomeness viewed in the light of the present day was truly incredible and one can only conclude that it was due solely to the entire absence of adult supervision. This however was certainly not the result of indifference on the part of our parents. It was simply due to the fact that during our journeys to and from school and holiday recreations, we seldom, if ever, came into contact with adults. Therefore, our parents were entirely ignorant of the adventures in which we revelled.

Call it bad behaviour or naughtiness if you will, but we seemed to be forever seeking fresh dangers. Even the sheep in their pastures were not immune from our attentions. I remember quite well one of my schoolmates jumping upon the back of a fine merino ewe, which instantly took fright and bolted straight for the edge of the cliff. The boy himself became quite alarmed and barely managed to sidle from his mount before the poor sheep went clean over the precipice. Another time my younger brother almost met his death whilst taking part in a concentrated attack by his fellow schoolboys on an erosive piece of land on the edge of a high cliff. Landslides over the cliffs due to erosion were common occurrences and the portion of earth affected in this instance was indicated by a huge crack extending some forty feet. The whole amount of soil outside the crack had sunk a few inches and from previous experience we knew that it only required a push to send it thundering over the precipice. Here was a chance for some excitement and the boys were not long in trying it out! This was done by a row of youngsters sitting down just inside the fissure at intervals from end to end. Then by kicking together an avalanche was started and many tons of earth and stones were precipitated to the bottom of the cliff with a tremendous roar. At the moment this happened, my younger brother who was an enthusiastic participant in this amusement lost his balance somehow and toppled over the cliff. By some miracle however there happened to be a spur jutting out from the cliff a little more than eighty feet below. On this projection a considerable portion of the debris clung and in turn, the fall of my brother was checked and he remained perched upon the spur until rescued from his perilous position. The boys who witnessed this incident were dumbfounded and could do absolutely nothing in the matter. Happily, one had the presence of mind to bolt home and inform my father, who arrived on the spot with one of his men and a piece of rope in sufficient time to affect the rescue. When my father had descended the cliff he found that my brother was rendered unconscious. This most probably proved a mercy for otherwise he might have aggravated his precarious situation and toppled over the spur on to the rocks some hundred feet below and so to certain death. We were all so terribly excited later to see my brother being carried home by my father. The poor boy was badly lacerated and received a compound fracture of his left leg which laid him low for several months.

Prior to this accident there were no restrictions imposed on any of these activities of the youngsters, except in my home where one was expected to be home before dark; then supper, bathe and early to bed. Henceforth, the route to be taken between Atherfield and Chale by all school boys along the cliffs was taboo and my father directed that we should proceed inland and turn into the Military Road which led to Chale. Incidentally this increased the distance considerably and to those affected the new route was not popular at all.

Living amongst sea-faring people in such a locality inculcated the spirit of adventure. So, it is not surprising that at the early age of 10 years I became involved in an enterprise charged with considerable danger. At this age my younger brother Albert and I, became the joint owners of a dinghy. It was a gift from our parents and going with it we both knew there existed a tacit understanding that we were permitted to use the boat only in fine weather with calm seas. When the boat was not in use it was hauled up, covered and secured well above high water mark at the bottom of the cliff. Whenever we wished to use the boat, some kindly Coastguardsman or fisherman would usually be found to launch it into the sea; or perhaps there would be a couple of playmates available to do the job. Among these was one Rufus Cotton the hardy son of a fisherman whose father had been an inveterate smuggler before our time at Atherfield. After we had left, when a lifeboat was stationed there, Rufus Cotton senior was elected its first coxswain. Rufus junior was about 2 years older than me when one evening at about 5 o'clock we met near the dinghy and very soon afterwards he induced me to try out a trip together in the boat.

It was not an easy job for two youngsters to transfer the boat from her secured position and launch it into the sea, but we contrived to get her afloat somehow. The weather was not too promising but we were not particularly concerned about this, so we pulled out to seaward for some considerable distance. There we lay on our oars while I listened to Rufus who was just in his element and reeling off numerous proposals for our itinerary. The most attractive of his ideas to me was his suggestion to pull out a couple of miles further and haul up a few of his father's lobster pots. So, forgetting the time of the evening away we went. Rufus had often accompanied his father upon a similar operation and knew fairly accurately where the trots were located. It was low water and slack tide when we left the shore and after pulling to seaward for some considerable time, we became tired and rested on our oars once again. Personally, I was relying upon my companion to take the initiative in our effort, for Rufus had a fine reputation among the lads of the village of being an able fisherman and sailor too! Unfortunately, we had not made any observations as to our true position relative to the shore for our minds and eyes were mainly attracted to seawards in order to locate the fishing pots.

We were by now getting very tired after a somewhat strenuous hour and spells on our oars became more frequent. Then suddenly we both became interested to shoreward and on gazing towards the land we discovered that, instead of being off the coast of Atherfield we were now directly south of the high cliffs some two miles eastward while our dinghy was being carried further east by the swift tide. With alarm I looked to Rufus for our next move but his face was inscrutable. Apparently, he had not realised, as I had, that we were in a serious position and from that moment I assumed the initiative and insisted that we should no longer search for his father's fishing trots but pull with all our might for the landing place at Atherfield. This we tried to do but it was too late. Terribly fatigued we struggled on while the strong current steadily forced us astern. We were mercifully ignorant of the serious danger which now beset us, for our little dinghy was only two miles west of the dreaded race off St Catherine's Point. It was getting dark and to make matters worse a choppy sea and fresh westerly breeze had cropped up; furthermore, we had no lantern or means of showing a light.

Had we pulled towards the shore instead of trying to reach Atherfield direct it is probable that we might have beached safely somewhere in Chale Bay westward of St Catherine's Point; but in our anxiety to get home we had not thought of this and anyway, we might have met disaster there. Meanwhile, thanks be to God, my father had already been informed of our predicament by the Coastguardsman on watch, who evidently possessed a true appreciation of our position. The *Lariet* was promptly put to sea and headed in our direction. Fortunately, the tide which prevented our headway accelerated that of the Coastguard whaler and it was not long after they had set out that Rufus and I could see a light approaching and hear a voice calling my name from the distance. This was the welcome call from my father who had arrived in the nick of time to save two venturesome youngsters from almost certain destruction, for our small dinghy could not possibly have stood up to the turbulent race off St Catherine's Point.

During our residence on the Island the younger children of the family seldom visited any place away from home except Chale and its environs. On the occasion of the Queen's Jubilee in 1887 however, I remember my parents taking us to Newport where Queen Victoria had visited; and a few days later to Shorwell where celebrations in the form of sports was held and each child was presented with a Jubilee China Cup suitably inscribed for the occasion. This entertainment was arranged by the Governor of the Isle of Wight who was then Princess Beatrice.

On another occasion my mother and father took us on a visit to Carisbrooke Castle. Here my small mind was centred upon the tragic imprisonment of King Charles I within those stone walls, but soon afterwards one witnessed a more pleasing aspect of the visit where five little donkeys turned a huge wheel to draw water from a well by walking up the boards secured to the inner perimeter of the wheel.

CHAPTER III

I Leave the Beautiful Isle of Wight

---ooOoo---

At the age of 12 years my completely happy and vigorous life in the lovely Isle of Wight came to an end.

My father was appointed to a post at Woolston near Southampton. We were thus about to leave the beauties of these ravines, climes and downs to become acquainted with the 'overners' as the people of the mainland were always called by those born and bred on the Island. In fact this term was used many years later when I was there. In those tranquil days of the Victorian era where strict economy in the National Services prevailed, Cabinet Ministers were for the most part wealthy and an income tax of more than sixpence in the pound would have been regarded as confiscation. Therefore, economy in travel of Government Officials was the order of the day. Consequently, a little sailing cutter named *Spy* was dispatched to Atherfield by the Admiralty for the purpose of transporting my family with household effects to Southampton.

As my mother had experienced a very unpleasant time in this little craft during our previous removal from Freshwater to Atherfield, it was decided that the males of the family only should board the *Spy* and that my mother and sister should proceed direct to Southampton by stagecoach from Chale to Newport, thence by train to Cowes, thence by passenger steamer to Southampton. Accordingly, my father and sons boarded the sailing cutter and we sailed from Atherfield late the same day.

It was very fortunate that my mother and sister were not on board that wretched little vessel during this passage for the wind came up that night with rough seas and heavy swell, which made everything most unpleasant. Our furniture which had been stowed on deck, was swamped by the seas and heavy rain. As for myself, I remember being shut in the deck cabin and tossed from side to side of it and anxiously awaiting the light of day when I would be permitted to go on deck. I believe my father was uneasy about the damage being done to the furniture, indeed it is a wonder that some of it did not go overboard. However, he remained outside the deck cabin with the Officer in Command until we had rounded both St Catherines Point and Bembridge Point and arrived in calmer waters. Unless the wind and weather were favourable, the Revenue Cutter made slow progress on such voyages for they possessed no auxiliary engine as an alternative to sail. However, we arrived at Southampton within twenty four hours after our departure from Atherfield, and this was considered a satisfactory passage.

I found the change to town life very disappointing and quite different to that which I had been led to believe it was. Indeed, for several weeks I was dreadfully sad and longed for the open spaces and quietude of my old home far away from the hustle and bustle of traffic and its attendant noise. At first experience of this I was really scared and pleaded with my mother to return to Atherfield. My mother comforted me so understandingly; she assured me that, with patience, my distraction would soon dissipate. Moreover, that my life would offer better facilities for my education and training for a career; whereas the only occupation that would be open for me if we continued to live in the Isle of Wight would be as a fisherman, or alternatively to follow the plough as a farm labourer! This reasoning inspired some hope in me, and sadly I tried to console my mind in the new environment.

What I missed most was the daily contact with the natural things of life as opposed to the fictitious materialism that now confronted me. Here were human beings herded together in a very limited area, all struggling in a sort of competition for existence. There was the noisy milk boy, the newspaper and butcher's boy, there were also boys about my age who were employed in the shipyard heating and catching rivets, all shaping their careers which seemed unattractive to me. In contrast to this, I longed for just another day on the cliffs, under the clear sunshine with blue seas, the wild birds, trees and flowers; a ramble in the copse and on the green fields among the cattle and sheep. Oh, who would not prefer this real life as I had been so used to?

The school in which I studied at Woolston was quite an improvement on the one at Chale and I did remarkably well during the comparatively short period of my attendance there.

CHAPTER IV

I Enter the Nautical School at Greenwich

---ooOoo---

At the age of 13 years and 3 months, I entered the Royal Nautical School at Greenwich. This school was open to sons of certain officers and men of the Royal Navy and Mariners. Boys were eligible for admission between the ages of eleven and fourteen years, and were required to enter into an agreement, together with their parents, to engage for continuous service in the Royal Navy. I accompanied my father to Greenwich School and according to the terms of entry passed a stringent medical examination by the Doctor; then after a successful educational test of simple subjects I was enrolled as a member of Company Number Six and introduced to a Mr. James Spencer, the Instructor in Charge of this unit. The parting from my mother and home was a grievous one you may be sure, and when my father had bidden me good-bye at the school, I felt sadly depressed.

Greenwich School was a very large establishment accommodating more than a thousand boys. It was equipped with nine dormitories each with one hundred or more beds, a dining hall, gymnasium swimming pool, spacious instructional rooms for seamanship and schoolrooms. Attached to the school was a hospital and a huge parade ground, in the middle of which stood a very large model of a full rigged ship - the *Fame*. This fine vessel constituted the most imposing feature of the school and accommodated a company of sixty boys who slept in hammocks on board. Mast yard and sail drill were carried out by the school boys in the *Fame* similar to that on board the training ships stationed at the Naval Forts in Great Britain in those days. The whole establishment was under the command of a Naval Captain. The Executive Officer who was commissioned from the Warrant Rank assumed command during the absence of the Captain. The other officers included a Surgeon, a Chaplain and Paymaster all Royal Naval Officers. In addition, there was a Headmaster, and six civilian school masters, while ten ex-Chief Petty Officers of the Royal Navy and a Colour Sergeant of the Royal Marines were instructors in the subjects of seamanship, gunnery and physical training. Each of these instructors had charge of a company of some one hundred boys except the company belonging to the ship *Fame* which numbered only sixty boys as previously mentioned. Certain boys were taught various trades such as carpentry, painting, bricklaying, sail-making, tailoring, baking, cooking and laundry work. This of course obviated the necessity of requisitioning services from outside the school and thus effecting economy in the cost of general maintenance of the establishment.

Each boy was responsible for the custody and maintenance of his clothing and severe punishment was meted out to boys who were unfortunate enough to lose any item of his kit. The enforcement of this law was a nightmare for me and to many of my colleagues. The cleaning of dormitories, bathrooms, dining room, including the washing up of the dishes and even the making of beds was performed by the boys under the supervision of the Company Instructor; as also the cleaning of the gymnasium, all instructional rooms and the parade ground. Now all this work might at first, appear to be very useful occupation for the boys, or perhaps good instruction.

As I review the fact now however, I am convinced that these monotonous menial duties during an extravagant portion of each day, was nothing but a time-wasting occupation which monopolised valuable time that should have been devoted to our education in preparation for subsequent service in the Royal Navy. Our work in the classrooms under the able civilian school masters was the only cultural and nautical education which we boys received; but it was precisely this element of our instruction which was cruelly limited. Indeed, given a reasonable amount of time each day for professional instruction under such highly capable Instructional Staff as existed there; it is my considered opinion that Greenwich School would definitely have passed on to the Royal Navy youths equal in ability and of no less potential value to the Service than the boys who were leaving Dartmouth College for entry as midshipmen. Furthermore, if my long since experience in this matter can be taken as a guide, this would have obviated the necessity of loading the Royal Navy with inexperienced Executive Officers from the R.N. Volunteer Reserve in times of war, whose appointments might well and more justly been filled from this source of experienced and continuous service men.

Be that as it may, for my own part I can truly say that after rising very early each morning and completing the various menial tasks to the satisfaction of the authorities there was scarcely sufficient energy remaining in my fatigued body and mind to commence scholastic studies, when attendance at school was due. School hours during the forenoon were between 9.30 and 11.45 a.m. In the afternoon, boys who were being trained for seamen and who had passed a certain standard of education were required to work at a trade selected for them. In this connection the whole of my afternoon on Monday to Friday was spent in the so-called trade of sail-making. A laudable calling no doubt, but in the interest of economy every boy in this trade was exclusively employed in the making of uniform duck suits for the boys of the establishment!

The Captain Superintendent was a strict disciplinarian and was regarded with awe and generally feared by all the boys. Once a day, except on Saturdays, he inspected all the companies drawn up in quarter column formation in the large gymnasium sometimes known as the drill hall. After inspection the battalion would move up to close formation with No. 1 Company facing a large stage. Mounted upon this stage would be the Captain, the Executive Officer, the Doctor and the Chaplain, who conducted a short church service. Corporal punishment would then be executed by the gymnasium instructor. Chastisement would take the form of caning for ordinary or trivial delinquencies and birching for more serious offences. These morning exhibitions had a ghastly effect upon my mind, though luckily, I personally escaped them. It was known by all concerned however, that any boy who attended Captain's defaulters for a misbehaviour, be it ever so trivial, would assuredly be awarded this form of punishment.

This nauseating practice was carried out with an incredible degree of regularity, immediately after Church Service in the presence of one thousand boys and the Staff Officers of the School. In several instances I have seen the Medical Officer intervene during these corporal punishments and certify professionally that the victim could stand no more of such brutality at any rate for that particular morning. It is true that some boys at certain times deserve chastisement on occasion; but this method of performing it was definitely evil. Moreover, it calculated to produce the reverse moral effect of that intended; for it hardened the hearts of some boys. Incredible as this may sound, there was on the part of certain lads even a tendency to regard the habitual delinquents as school heroes!!

Early Life

Recreation at Greenwich School consisted of just what the boys cared to do when they were let loose on the parade grounds but these activities were subject to rigorous taboos. During the course of my two years at the school I do not remember seeing an Officer or Instructor except the gymnasium instructor present at our games, except at the annual competitions when of course, everyone attended. The boys were not encouraged to indulge in inter-company competitions of any kind; therefore, any approach to team spirit in sports was non-existent. Boys were allowed to leave the school for weekend recreation only when parents or guardians called to take them away. Obviously therefore, only a fortunate few could take advantage of this amenity. The establishment was entirely enclosed by iron boundary rails of considerable height and behind this barrier the great majority existed - an indescribably monotonous segregation which would disgrace any reformatory institution nowadays.

Happy release came however twice a year when long leave would be granted and we were then permitted to go home. The long leave periods consisted of fourteen days for Christmastide and five weeks for the mid-summer vacation.

Despite all these restrictions I contrived to maintain an interest in my studies and such games and exercises as were available. Most of my exercises were taken in the gymnasium where I became rather proficient especially upon the horizontal bar. In this activity I was fortunate enough to obtain the kindly aid of our gymnasium instructor. In the second and last year of participating in the Annual Sports competition I was tolerably successful. I won the first prize in my class in swimming; also for diving for discovery of china eggs at the bottom of the swimming pool.

Incidentally this latter competition caused much amusement besides taxing the lung capacity of the competitors. A considerable number of eggs were scattered on the bottom of the pool about seven feet deep and the competitor who recovered the largest number of eggs in the allotted time was adjudged the winner. The two main factors essential for success in this game was quickness in the location and securing the eggs without dropping them and secondly the power of endurance under water to stick out the prescribed time in order to bring up as many eggs as possible to the surface. In addition to my amphibian success, I was the lucky winner of the Senior Long Jump competition held on *terra firma*. The Baroness Burdett Coutts, whose kindly remarks on the occasion were cheery and very encouraging, presented this prize; a handsome cabinet and writing desk, which I still possess today. The Baroness was one of the most popular and interesting ladies of that time. She was also one of the wealthiest persons in Great Britain. I understand that King Edward VII then Prince of Wales said of her: "After mother the most remarkable woman in the Kingdom."

It is an unusual thing to confess that, during the two years spent at Greenwich, I never really overcame homesickness, as my school colleagues appeared to do. Letter writing by the boys had to be done in one of the classrooms set apart in the evenings, and so far as I remember I wrote to my parents incomparably more often than any of my companions. Moreover, I looked forward to my holidays at home as perfectly heaven sent and dreaded the moment when due to return to the school. Before taking these vacations, I would resolve to inform my parents what an unhappy existence it was at school but somehow, I could never muster sufficient courage to do so when opportunity occurred.

These facts have often puzzled me in later life, but I have always dismissed the association of the word "cissy" in this connection; if only because I was the offspring of such an outstandingly brave and fearless father, while my mother was blessed with steadfast courage as well as kindliness. There was perhaps one factor accountable for my idiosyncrasy at the time; namely the entire absence of women or the influence of women in this establishment which housed more than one thousand boys! I will leave it at that as one with very little or no knowledge of psychology.

About 12 months after I had entered the school an epidemic of measles broke out among the boys and I became one of the victims, this was followed by an outbreak of chickenpox from which I also suffered. Hundreds of lads were laid low with these diseases and unfortunately the measles affected me most seriously, while one poor boy who occupied a bed next to mine in the hospital died of it. For several days my temperature was very high and when it rose to 105.4 °F, the School Authority informed my parents of my condition and suggested that my mother should come to see me. In my delirium I was terrified because certain articles of my clothing were missing and that I would be brought up as a defaulter and punished for their loss. I thought my career would therefore be ruined and that I should be sent home in disgrace. However, my mother came up to Greenwich and prior to the day of her visit to my bedside in the large ward I began to recover.

As I review the running of that substantial new establishment as it then was; I cannot but feel that its great potentialities were frustrated by mal-administration, albeit not intentional. From a human aspect it was soulless. This regrettable position was obviously due to the atrocious system of subordinating all cultural learning and the overshadowing of a decent way of life for the boys in the cause of ruthless and stupidly applied discipline.

Part 2

I Join The Royal Navy

HMS Active

CHAPTER V

I Join Her Majesty's Ship St Vincent

--- ooOoo ---

At a little more than 15 years of age on 11th May 1893, I left Greenwich Nautical School and joined Her Majesty's Ship *St Vincent*, the seamen boys training ship at Portsmouth. I had now the pride of enrolling for service in the rating of 2nd Class Boy in Britain's "might, majesty, dominion and power" - the Royal Navy. Though my life in this training ship was to become more or less a resume of that at Greenwich School, it was indeed a much happier one.

The *St Vincent* 's complement, including youths under training, numbered more than one thousand. While the routine and instruction were very much the same as at Greenwich, our recreational amenities were supervised by the officers and instructors and were far more enjoyable. Above all my home was situated only 20 miles distant and I was able to spend my weekends off duty there. Christmas and Midsummer leave were granted also. Progress on board the *St Vincent* was very satisfactory. I studied hard in educational subjects and endeavoured to make myself proficient in Seamanship. My examinations in all subjects were successful and my instructors appeared to be quite satisfied with my performance aloft during masts yard and sail drill. No doubt these successes were mainly due to the experience gained at Greenwich. Moreover, I was now able to receive valuable help from my father during the weekends. I well remember his advice and instruction so kindly given me from time to time and I think the following words of his had impressed me the most, "During your future career in the navy my son – always remember that on all occasions when duty demands your service you must be present personally to carry it out. At times you may be tempted to leave it to the other fellow, especially at night, or when the work is difficult, but this will not do!"

Throughout nearly 50 years' experience in the Royal Navy Service since receiving this advice, I am bound to say that the memory of these words was of inestimable value to me.

The normal period taken to pass through all subject in the *St Vincent* was 2 years. In my case the time thus occupied was only 10 months when I was rated a Boy 1st Class and drafted to Her Majesty's Brig of War *Martin* a trim little sailing vessel of about 400 tons. The *Martin* was commanded by a Senior Lieutenant and the total complement including youths was about one hundred. This brig was commissioned as a tender to the parent ship *St Vincent* for the purpose of affording practical seamanship experience for the senior youths in a sea-going vessel. As may be supposed therefore, naval discipline on board was very strict. For example, boots or socks were not allowed to be worn by any boy whilst on board and walking the decks during drill hours was prohibited. Even on the day of joining the ship, orders were given for everyone to remove their boots and socks before boarding from the boats alongside; and when leaving the vessel, one's feet were bare until one had disembarked into a boat. These taboos applied equally to boys when aloft. All movement was to be carried out at a running pace.

When at sea the *Martin* was confined to the English Channel. Plenty of scope being available there for sailing in all weathers under various directions and forces of the wind and sea, while entering and leaving harbours along the South coast of England. All these conditions of sailing necessitated quick decisions and correct manipulation of the yards and sails. In short - smart sail drill. When we were cruising in the Channel the *Martin* was entirely an independent Command. Upon returning to Portsmouth however, the vessel received all orders from the Commanding Officer of the *St Vincent*.

Though my period of service in the *Martin* was short, I experienced a considerable number of drills and my duties aloft and on deck were therefore strenuous. Here again youths performed all kinds of manual work for long hours each day. Rising very early each morning, hammocks had to be lashed up and stowed in a very limited time, decks would then be scrubbed or holystoned, and guns cleaned before breakfast at 8 a.m. After breakfast and dishing up mess tables, stools and mess deck would be scrubbed and mess gear prepared for inspection. At 9 a.m. all hands would be dressed in the rig of the day and fall in on the upper deck for Division and Prayers. Sail drill would then commence; dinner at noon, clear up decks 1.15 p.m. then work until tea at 4 p.m. and afterwards mast and yard drill aloft until 6 p.m. Hammocks and clothes were usually -washed on Wednesdays instead of drill - clothes lines rigged and clothes hung up. All these tasks are very briefly described but sufficient to show that the physical exertion demanded to discharge them left little energy in the lads at the close of the day and when at 8.30 p.m. hammocks were piped down, we were all glad to be resting in them when the Captain inspected the mess deck for night rounds at 9 p.m. Obviously, there was little time for recreation or even reading. In any case I cannot recall any boy indulging in this except when in harbour on Saturday or Sunday afternoons.

As I write today, in times of human kindness and even courtesy between boys and their masters in well-disciplined schools and institutions of learning; it seems almost incredible that there is any person still living who has been personally subjected to callous, indifferent and brutal methods of teaching of my youth. In this connection I have vivid memories as a member of Her Majesty's Brig *Martin*. Some perhaps might be regarded as amusing if they were not really of serious import. Let me mention only two cases.

Every morning except on Sundays all boys were sent aloft in a race over the topmast head. In the process of the competition there were two flights of riggings to negotiate and the start was given by the officer of the day by the order - "Away Aloft". As the boys would scamper up the rigging of both masts either on the port or starboard side of the deck as directed; each lad would be required to run up the lower mast rigging to the fore or maintop, then, without pause, pass up the topmast rigging to the crosstrees and return to the opposite side of the deck. These exercises were quite laudable and no doubt necessary to ensure that every boy could shape well aloft, but obviously someone must be last in the race on each occasion. Nevertheless, the last boy down on each mast would be "punished" by the award of six to twelve cuts with the cane or with the boatswain's water flagsticks! Being last at any time on board the brig was invariably regarded as an excuse for such chastisement. Here is the second example - The order or pipe "Clear lower deck" meant, as it does now in the Navy, that everyone is required to repair to the upper deck immediately and fall in; and in the *Martin* this order was given very frequently. Now it might occur when almost every boy was in the mess deck and to gain access to the upper deck it would be necessary to pass up the hatchway. The ships Corporal's duty was to report all hands cleared of the lower decks on first hearing the order, station himself at the bottom of the hatchway with a cane in his hand and commence delivering it good and hearty on the backside of the last few boys until they disappeared through the hatch. Of course, the boys had to put up with this senseless and grossly unfair treatment, though again some had to pay for being last on deck!

The popularity of this Corporal (or regulating Petty Officer as this rating is now called) may be gauged by the action of several boys who had received such special attention from him. They contrived one night, to collect all his ready use stock of canes and pass them over the ships side. The matter was of course reported to the Captain who approved of a fresh supply of canes from the boatswain's store. The ships Corporals' anger, however, knew no bounds when he was informed that only one cane was in the reserve stock! Thereafter much amusement was afforded watching the fellow mooching around the ship, glued to his cane and sparing no effort to obtain a case against the culprits while the delinquent storekeeper thought it wise to give him a wide berth!

On completion of my service in the *Martin* I returned to the *St Vincent* and on the 30th July 1894 was drafted to HMS *Victory* the flagship of the Naval Commander-in-Chief at Portsmouth. The *Victory* was Lord Nelson's old flagship at the Battle of Trafalgar and naturally was a great attraction to visitors. The hull of the ship and the original fittings on board had been preserved as far as practicable and the position on the Quarter Deck where Nelson fell in battle was marked with a special plate. The cockpit on the orlop deck where Nelson died was kept in much the same condition as it was some 83 years before. Even the topsails carried by the *Victory* into action against the French and Spanish fleets at Trafalgar were still on board, riddled with bullet holes.

Though my period of service in the old wooden three-decker battleship *Victory* was short I was truly happy there and found the experience very instructive and interesting.

CHAPTER VI

I Join a Sea-going Man of War

--- ooOoo ---

On 6th November 1894, at the age of 16 years and 10 months, I joined the battleship *Inflexible*, the Fort Guard ship at Portsmouth.

Although modern battleships at the time were armed with four 13-inch breech loading guns; the *Inflexible* was still considered the fighting strength of the Navy with an armament of 16-inch muzzle loading guns mounted in turrets. These guns were 80 tons weight and fired a projectile of 1,700 pounds which required a powder charge 270 pounds weight. The loading operations and manipulation of the turrets and guns for sighting on the target were controlled by hydraulic machinery. Her secondary armament consisted of 4-inch breech loading guns.

During my short stay in this battleship, the most interesting and eventful operation executed was a quarterly practice firing carried out from the 16-inch gun armament. These firings took place in the English Channel against moored targets at a range no greater than 4,000 yards. The firing was unconsciously slow and atrociously inaccurate. In fact, gunnery generally in those days and for many years to come was deplorable.

Early in January 1895, I was sent to HMS *Achilles* to take passage to Malta. The *Achilles* was an enormous three masted square rigged army cruiser propelled by steam as well as a large number of square fore and aft sails. She had large muzzle loading broadside guns and belonged to a class of ships all considered obsolescent. She was at the time employed on transport service to carry relief crews for Her Majesty's Ships in the Mediterranean and to bring home ratings due for return to England. There was only a nucleus crew commissioned to take the ship to Malta and return, but a full ships company was made up from the drafts. This method of work your passage transport was, of course, the most economic possible and incidentally the most uncomfortable.

On the day we sailed for the Mediterranean, the ship was packed with an indescribable medley of ratings and a number of Royal Marines. We carried bad weather the whole voyage and used the sails as well as steam power. I was detailed for duty with the fore-topmen and my particular work was in the capacity of top gallant yard man. For one of the loftiest masted ships in the Royal Navy the fore-topmast crosstrees, where I was employed when aloft, was a long way from the deck. Moreover, the comparatively heavy yards and large sails carried by the *Achilles* called for strenuous work aloft on the part of the men handling them especially during the gales and tremendous seas that we encountered.

To add to the general discomfort of this passages the ship was in a terribly dirty condition. Although the usual routine for cleaning ship was punctiliously adhered to, the between decks were as dirty as any collier. There seemed to be coal dust everywhere, especially on the mess deck and the deck below where our kit tacks were stowed. Can one imagine a more stupidly comical order than was given each morning, when the Boatswains Mate piped: "Hands to clean in a white working rig." This necessitated the removal of a thick layer of coal dust from the top of our kit bags before we could remove the articles of clothing required! Nevertheless, spotless white duck trousers with jumpers to match constituted the dress order of the day.

Owing to gales encountered throughout the voyages it took seven days to reach the first port of call - Gibraltar. Here we coaled ship and when the bunkers had been filled, we proceeded to Malta. Strong easterly gales with heavy swells were experienced the whole of this passage taking a further 7 days to complete. The *Achilles* arrived on 21st January 1895 and the ratings who had joined the ship for passage only disembarked the following day.

I was appropriated to HMS *Ramillies* the flagship of the Commander-in-Chief of the Mediterranean Fleet, Sir Michael Culine Seymour. There were a large number of 1st Class Boys in the passage out and much speculation had gone on as to what ships of the fleet we would be drafted to on arrival at Malta. Of course, the Flagship was the favourite, so imagine the thrill and joy I received when I was selected among a few other boys for the *Ramillies*. She was one of five battleships generally known as the "R" class because each of the ships' names was spelt with the initial letter of "R". They were the most modern and formidable battleships then in the world and the *Ramillies* was the leader of this finest fleet.

At that time, there were no less than twelve battleships belonging to the British Fleet in the Mediterranean. In addition, there were cruisers, torpedo boats and other smaller vessels but destroyers were unheard of in those days in the Service. One of the smallest classes of torpedo boat were carried in the battleship and hoisted from their storage positions into the water as required.

The armament of the *Ramillies* comprised four 13.5-inch breech loading guns mounted two in a barbette, which were installed with hydraulic power for working the breech loading mechanism and the training and laying the guns on the target. Each of these guns weighed 67 ton, their length was 36 feet and they fired a 1,250-pound projectile using a powder charge providing a muzzle velocity was 2,016 feet per second. The secondary armament consisted of 6-inch Quick Firing Guns, and a few Q.F. 3-pounders and machine guns used mainly for saluting and arming the various boats belonging to the ship. Many distinguished Naval Officers were serving in the *Ramillies*. Sir William May was the Flag Captain and the Commander was John Jellicoe, of whom we shall hear more of much later.

On boarding the Flagship, I was particularly struck by her extremely smart appearance in sharp contrast to the dowdiness of the *Achilles*. Even the *Ramillies*' side was beautifully coated with black enamel paint and the superstructure was similarly treated in whites while the masts and funnels presented a shade of golden or yellow. The decks were scrupulously clean and the bright work glittered in the sun. Even the large iron shackles on the end of the torpedo net defence booms were burnished like silver. In those so-called good old 'spit and polish' days in the Royal Navy, the battleship *Ramillies* was indeed a shining example. True all this was much overdone and occupied valuable time and energy of the bluejacket which should have been devoted to learning his real job and a better life; but the Commanders promotion, and also that of many other Officers including the Gunnery officers, depended upon the cleanliness in their respective departments rather than the fighting efficiency of them.

I quickly became used to my work and duties in the *Ramillies*. Boys worked as hard as the men, or even more strenuously for naturally they were given menial jobs which were considered infra-dig for men to perform. Unlike later days in the Navy, boys were distributed among the Petty Officers and Seaman's Messes for the sole purpose of performing such work as washing up dishes after meals, cleaning and scrubbing etc. This of course was most unjust especially as the time thus spent was largely part of the official meal times, which in themselves were all too short. Thus, the lads had insufficient time to attend to their personal necessities and suffered in consequence.

The method of training ships companies in fighting efficiency for war differed fundamentally from that which obtains today. All manner of drills and exercises were practiced in the Mediterranean Fleet in the early nineties while the most important function of all was disregarded. I mean the actual registering of hits by gun fire on a target representing an enemy. I have already referred to this subject and it seems almost incredible that this gross inefficiency was going on throughout the whole of the Mediterranean Fleet. Instead "All Hands to" the following exercises were carried out continuously almost every week:

a) "Clear ship for action" - when all obstructions to gun armament on deck were cleared away;

b) "General Quarters" - when all guns and torpedo tubes were cleared away and manned for Action and watertight doors closed;

c) "Get out Torpedo Net Defence" - when the ship was encircled by huge anti-torpedo nets suspended by steel booms;

d) "Man and Arm Boats" - when all boats were hoisted out and QF guns, machine guns and rifles were placed in them.

Afterwards the armed boats were invariably pulled around the fleet, then disarmed and hoisted to inboard stowage again. The above were the major evolutions relating to the Armaments and carried out regularly by ships acting independently or as competitive exercises among the ships of the fleet when in company. There were also other exercises unconnected with the armament of ships; but when dealing with actual practice firings at a target, it was considered that such a matter of vital importance could be dispensed with only once a quarter, and then only at short range, firing at moored (fixed) targets instead of towing (moving) targets as was essential for realistic practice.

One of the reasons for the unpopularity of practice gun firing in those days was in the consequence that the armament equipment and ships fittings and paintwork would become very dirty. Deplorable excuse as this would appear, the ships' officers could certainly not be held responsible for the state of affairs since the cleanliness of their ships was considered infinitely of more importance by officers of superior rank. The immutable rule governing recommendation of officers for promotion was first and foremost a "Clean Ship" and this was enforced by Senior Officers of Squadrons when carrying out their periodical inspections of ships under their command. Happily, though belatedly, all this was changed only just in time to cope with the accurate gun fire of the German warships in the Great War of 1914 – 1918.

While criticism may be offered upon this old method of training the ships companies for war, the system, then adopted was most valuable from the view point of maintaining physical fitness and the encouragement of a spirit of competition among the men of the fleet. Indeed, it was splendid exercise and rare sport for all of us who took part in the drills indicated above. On occasions, there were, perhaps some 10,000 officers and men, all competing for the honour of placing their own ship first; and it was a proud moment for the Captain and ships' company when they saw the Commander-in-Chief's signal indicating the first three ships to complete and receive special mention. No doubt this spirit of competition which has prevailed throughout the Royal Navy for long years has been of incalculable value in the training of the men of the British Fleet. Personally, I was thrilled on such days, though the drills were very strenuous and at times not too pleasant.

I Join The Royal Navy

During some of these exercises the greatest danger and concern for seamen was to steer clear of the Royal Marines who had joined in the fray. I remember particularly on one occasion when shouldering a huge anti-torpedo net between two hefty Marines, that almost at every step taken, I found one of their heavy boots planted firmly upon my bare feet! In later days however, this disability, like many others, has been obviated for sailors and marines alike wear boots on board.

During my time in the flagship of the Mediterranean, the fleet made a cruise to the eastern and western extremities of the Station i.e. Alexandria and Gibraltar. The Red Sea was included in the command but only a couple of sloops patrolled that region. Between the ports of call, fleet manoeuvres were exercised, and during these, special attention was given to the efficacy of the doors closing the various watertight compartments between the bulkheads below the upper deck. This of course was quite normal; but particular attention was given to this subject following the disaster during manoeuvres of the Mediterranean Fleet off Tripoli on June 22nd 1893 when the battleship HMS *Victoria* was rammed and sunk by HMS *Camperdown*.

The *Victoria* was the flagship of Admiral Sir George Tyron who went down with his ship and was lost with a large number of the men. Among the survivors was Commander Jellicoe who was the Executive Officer of the *Victoria*, and was now performing the same duties with us in the *Ramillies*. Incidentally, the *Ramillies* was sent to the Mediterranean to take the place of the *Victoria* only 4 months after that ship went down.

Admiral Hastings Markham flew his flag in *Camperdown* and should have kept the fatal signal at the dip instead of hoisting it right up until a satisfactory explanation as to how the manoeuvre was to be performed had been received from the Commander-in-Chief. But the subsequent Court Martial supported the time-honoured belief in implicit obedience and complete subordination of all brains to that of the man in chief command. At the Court Martial, both Admiral Markham and the Captain of the *Victoria* stated that they knew that the evolution was an impossible one. All thought Sir George was going to do something to avert the collision.

Our cruise in the waters of the Levant was most interesting and the beautiful and spacious harbours afforded all kinds of recreation. Boat racing and fishing expeditions were indulged in. I recall a walk with a couple of other youths from my ship in Argostoli a port in the Grecian Archipelago. On passing through one of the currant vineyards we came across a deep well containing crystal clean and cold water. Around the perimeter of this well was growing an abundance of the finest maiden hair fern I have ever seen. It was a hot day with a scorching sun pressing down upon us, and you may be sure we lingered long at this well with its delectable freshness and beauty.

On our western cruise sometime in March 1895 the *Ramillies* was engaged on a special service relating to the British Royal Family. Queen Victoria's first cousin, His Royal Highness the Duke of Cambridge, was shortly to relinquish his appointment of Commander-in-Chief of the British Army which he had held for 39 years. The Duke was then 76 years of age having become the supreme head of the Army at the age of 37. He was soon to be succeeded by 61-year-old Sir Garnet Wolsley, the noted British soldier who afterwards became Viscount Wolsley.

His Royal Highness had come to inspect the British troops, presumably before his retirement and embarked in the *Ramillies* at Itea. He was so aged and infirm that his movements about the ship were attended with much difficulty. A portion of the Admirals quarters was assigned for his use and to obviate climbing the ladder leading from the deck outside his cabin to the quarter deck, a special chair was provided for him. A sling was fitted to a chair and His Royal Highness would be hoisted in it by a tackle to the deck above. Her Majesty the queen was in the South of France about this time and finally we were ordered to Villafranc where the Duke disembarked to join the queen at Nice.

Discipline on board the *Ramillies* was severe, as in most ships of the fleet. Sight leave was given at Malta and at other British possessions; but afternoon leave only was granted at the foreign ports of call. Personally, I landed from the ship on few occasions, mostly at the foreign places, where I took long walks with colleagues about my own age. There one would be interested in the scenery and for the most part, the customs of the foreign people. This form of recreation suited us very well for we were able to gain a little knowledge in the most inexpensive way. Neither my companions or myself could very well afford any other option on these excursions observing that the pay of a 1st Class Boy amounted to the magnificent sum of 7 pence per day!

Naples was one of the most beautiful foreign ports included in our cruise. The weather during our stay there was ideal and the climate most salubrious. On the cloudless and moonless nights when the volcano of Mt Vesuvius was active it produced a magnificently alarming effect upon the still waters of Naples Bay. Added to this during the evenings were the pretty Italian girls, who came off to the ship in their smart gondolas containing stacks of mandolins and other stringed musical instruments for sale. Some of the girls attended to the purchases, while others played serenades in order to demonstrate the soothing tone of their instruments. The effect was wonderful for I saw quite a large number of mandolins, guitars and so forth acquired in this manner.

One of the reasons for going on afternoon leave was to look about for an appetising meal, owing to the sameness of our limited rations on board. I remember so well going on shore one afternoon at Naples and on entering a restaurant one partook of a most varied and generous feed. There were delicious antipasti genovas, bread rolls and butter, grills, salads and most delicious fruits and red wine. In the serenity of the open air and salubrious surroundings I cannot recall a more enjoyable repast in my career and all for the sum of nine English pennies.

My routine life on board the *Ramillies* was pretty hard and somewhat monotonous, though I never became bored. This was due perhaps to the constant noise and bustle going on amongst nearly one thousand persons in the ship. At sea there was scarcely any quietude throughout the twenty-four hours of the day and this applied also in harbour routine from 5.30 a.m till 9 p.m. A substantial contribution to the clamour of course were bugle calls and pipes from boatswain's mates at regular intervals throughout the day also the hum of electric fans.

On the whole our ship was regarded a comparatively contented ship, though absence without leave and insubordination was not infrequent and punishment was severe. A number of cells for close confinement of defaulters were usually fully occupied, while a lesser punishment, known as 10a, seemed to be going on continuously. A Naval prison was maintained on shore at Malta for the accommodation of men who were found guilty of the more serious offences, such as desertion and certain degrees of insubordination. Offences of a grave nature were usually dealt with by Court martial.

The use of bad language by bluejackets when I was a boy was terribly shocking. This, of course, was a punishable offence, but little was done to suppress it. For youths of my age and to the younger men generally this profanity was most demoralising. In those days the proportion of officers to men was comparatively few compared to those borne in Her Majesty's Ships of today. Nevertheless, I am convinced that this matter could and should have been dealt with more effectively by the Ships Officers. The complement of Officers in all Capital Ships in full commission included a Chaplain of the Church of England and it is my considered opinion that these clergymen could have devoted more of their time on cleansing the language on the lower deck. So far as my memory serves me in this connection, the chief concern of the Chaplains in my younger days, apart from his duties as Instructor of the Midshipmen and officially conducting prayers on board, was to avoid contact with the ratings in their messes and on deck. Moreover, the chaplain was usually among the first officers to land on leave of absence at all ports and even there one could never find them associated with the men of his ship.

I offer no excuse for belabouring this subject because I feel convinced that naval padres of the past, with the support that they would surely have received from their Captains and brother officers missed a golden opportunity of stamping out the deplorable bad language in the Royal Navy had they taken the trouble to organise a crusade against this evil. Moreover, the great social barrier that existed between the officers and the men might at the same time have been bridged, without the slightest detriment to discipline. On the contrary, a happy and efficient ships company entirely depends upon a sympathetic understanding between officers and men. Having said so much about naval chaplains in the old days, it is gratifying to note that their successors of later years, though of inferior equivalent rank, have made some improvements in these matters.

The health of the Naval personnel in the Mediterranean Fleet was far from satisfactory at this period. Intermittent Fever at Malta was endemic and comparatively few escaped its ravages. The sailors called this fever the "Maltese Flux". The Naval Hospital at Malta was often full to capacity with these cases and the number of officers and men invalided home suffering from the disease was a matter of grave concern. For years and years this fever had been rife in Malta, while the only preventative measure that seemed effective was to keep the fleet away cruising or in other ports. However, since Malta was the chief Naval Port and refitting, restoring and repair base this was impracticable; so the fever went on.

It is truly astonishing why the cause of this devastating scourge, which laid thousands of the flower of British manhood low, was not discovered until it had run such a long course. Among the several clues, noted by the sailors themselves, was the fact that total abstainers from alcohol suffered the most, while men who drank beer and spirits heavily were almost immune! A dangerous poser for advocates of teetotalism to be sure, especially as there was an element of truth in it! Further, it was observed that of the numerous surgical cases admitted to the Naval Hospital at Malta, many became infected with the fever during their treatment in the surgical wards. They would then be transferred to the care of the medical branch, and thus prolong their stay in hospital. I understand that a report on the health of the Navy recorded so long ago as 1874 issued by the then Medical Director General, stated that typhoid fever in the Navy was mainly contracted at Malta due to the sanitary arrangements in Malta Harbour. Whether the fever referred to included Intermittent Fever one cannot be sure, but if this surmise be true, it is horrible to contemplate the thousands of Naval men whose health and physique had been broken in the many years involved.

The cause of this disease so peculiar to Malta, which had baffled the medical authorities for so many years was at last found in the early part of this century. A naval surgeon, Basset Smith, after much research, discovered the bacterium causing the disease in the Maltese goats' milk, which was consumed in enormous quantities by men of the fleet on board and by the patients in the Naval Hospital. In fact, it was the only milk obtainable at Malta, except for the privileged few who could afford a limited quantity of cow's milk, was the product from the goat. The result of Dr Basset Smith's happy discovery had, obviously, far reaching effects. The Admiralty took immediate action and prohibited the sale of goats' milk to men of the fleet in Malta. Thus, the health of an incalculable number of men whose bodies, were otherwise sound, was preserved against probably the most devasting disease which had ravaged the men of the Mediterranean Fleet for an incredulous period of years.

Naturally there were repercussions in Malta from the local milk traders and complaints were loud and clamant, for their industry was terribly hit by the Admiralty order. In a measure, perhaps, it was unfortunate, for the milk was purchased by the men very cheaply and had it been pure, would have formed a valuable food for them, that no milk whatever was included in their daily rations, as it was in later days.

Dr Basset Smith was awarded a knighthood upon his retirement from the Service, and became a voluntary pathologist in a London Hospital. It is to be regretted very much however, that when this fine surgeon was performing a post-mortem examination his finger became infected and the poor fellow died of septicaemia.

Unfortunately, it was my luck to fall a victim to Intermittent Fever whilst serving in the *Ramillies* at Malta before the cause of the disease was discovered. I suffered a very bad attack, was sent to the Naval Hospital and thence invalided home on the troop ship *Tyne* which happened to call at Malta on its voyage home from the East. The *Tyne* was packed with humanity; soldiers whose service time had expired and their families, also invalids from both Army and Navy were crowded on board. I was very glad indeed to reach home for it seemed impossible for anyone to recover from an illness in that noisy and uncomfortable ship.

On my arrival in England, I was given leave for a couple of weeks and returned to the *Duke of Wellington* an old Naval Depot ship at Portsmouth and tender to HMS *Victory*; this was on the 11th February 1896.

I JOIN THE ROYAL NAVY

CHAPTER VII

Sailing Ship Days

--- ooOoo ---

Prior to joining the Depot ship at Portsmouth, I had become 18 years of age (28th December 1895) and according to the Admiralty Instructions, all youth of that age were to be advanced to the status of men. So, I was accordingly rated Ordinary Seaman with my pay increased from 7 pence to 1 shilling and 3 pence per day. A few months later I qualified in gunnery subjects for what was known as a "Trained Man" and my pay was again increased by another penny per diem.

Early in May 1896, I was appropriated to HMS *Active*. This very fine full rigged ship was a 6-inch gun corvette and at that time she was wearing the broad pendant of the Commodore commanding the Training Squadron. There were four ships in this squadron including HMS *Volage*, a sister ship to the *Active*, the other two being HMS *Champion* and HMS *Calypso;* all were sailing vessels. The primary function of this squadron was to cruise in the Atlantic and the Arctic Oceans, and so afford valuable instruction to younger men of the navy in discipline and practical seamanship. The ships companies of the Training Squadron were chosen from officers, petty officers and ratings, who had previously served in sailing ships and, in consequence they were generally recognized as among the most efficient and smartest sailor men in the Royal Navy! The above complement, of course did not include ratings below that of Able Seamen. Ordinary Seamen were nominally sent for instruction, but incidentally made up the number of men as required for a full crew to man the yards and ropes necessary for working the ship. The only difference in this arrangement and that in a fully commissioned ship on any other service, was that the proportion of Able Seamen to Ordinary Seamen would be very much greater.

Before joining my ship, I had been well apprised of the above details and also of the fact that Ordinary Seamen were expected to carry out the duties of Able Seamen in every respect. The *Active* was lying at a buoy in the middle of Portsmouth harbour on the day I was sent to her with many others of my rating. As in the brig *Martin*, boots and stockings had to be discarded on the moment of embarking and were not worn on board. After stowing away our kit-bags and hammocks, we were fallen in on the Quarter Deck and detailed for our respective stations. We were first inspected by the 1st Lieutenant whose name was H.P. Ethelstone - with whom I was to serve with again in a ship of the future.

I was detailed for duty as a fore-topman and in this role my special duty was No. 1 of the fore royal yard. To a reader other than a sailor, some explanation is due in order that my particular job in the ship may be clearly understood. In all sailing ships, the organization of seamen was to station everyone so that each mast, yard and sail will be correctly manipulated in all the circumstances required for sailing the vessel. Now a full rigged ship like the *Active*, has three masts to carry the sails. My duties us a fore-topman was to work under the Petty Officer Captain of the Top in all matters, whether on deck or aloft; and as No. 1 of the Fore Royal Yard, I was responsible to him when aloft for the smart and efficient working of the Royal Yard and sail.

After a few days shake down on board, the *Active* slipped from her buoy and we sailed out of Portsmouth harbour for the English Channel to a rendezvous with the other three ships of the squadron. Our ship was fitted with a steam engine and a single screw; but these were used only on very rare occasions, much to the disgust of the stokers who were employed on deck hauling on ropes and so forth when the engines were not required. To goad them to further indignation, the funnel was got down by a hand worked rack pinion which was operated by the stokers themselves. Also, the screw was hauled up clear of the water by a wire pendant with an enormous three-fold purchase, which was manned by seamen and by the stokers. Hauling on that great purchase was accompanied by a tune played by the ships' fiddler, but somehow the stokers pulling on the rope could find no rhythm in his music!

As soon as we had cleared Spithead and were well to the east of the Isle of Wight we hauled to a south-westerly wind and commenced our westerly beat down the English Channel. With the prospect of a head wind for many hours it would of course, been much easier to have shortened sail and steam to the rendezvous; but our Commodore decided to take the hard road and ordered: "Down funnel and up screw!" On one of our tacks, we headed for the land in the vicinity of my dear old home at Atherfield. It gave me quite a thrill as the ship drew closer and closer while my memory went back to the happy days when I lay upon the ground on the top of the cliffs and watched the beautiful ships as they sailed by with their white wings abundantly spread just as my ship was doing at the time. I wondered too, whether some other small boy was watching and waiting for this fine ship of ours to pass on.

Two days later we were joined by the *Volage*, *Champion* and *Calypso* and our Commodore now commanded his complete squadron. After the exchange of the necessary signals the squadron manoeuvred into position led by the *Active* and proceeded together down channel. Being at sea for the first time with four sailing ships in company, all in fairly close formation, produced quite a fascinating effect upon me. The spectacle was most exhilarating and savoured of a yacht race on a grand scale. It was a sight incomparably finer than a squadron of modern battleships in which I had served only a few months before in the Mediterranean. It is true that these great ships produced a spectacle of grandeur and power, as they forged their way through the seas, but the sailing ships presented a delicacy and beauty as they heeled over to their task.

Our Commodore's name was Atkinson, he was a vivid and most impressive personality and seemed to have a complete understanding of a tried and proved seaman. He was a very strict disciplinarian and possessed the inexorable sternness that comes of knowledge, while his temper at times got the better of him.

When we had cleared the English Channel, we sailed for the Arctic circle. This brought the wind on our port quarter and all ships were now running free. This permitted a closer formation being maintained for it was a comparatively easy matter for all ships to keep station by simply taking in the upper sails as the circumstances required. For instance, if one of the ships outstripped her consorts and therefore got out of her proper station her speed would be checked by squaring the royal yards and shortening the royal sails. The ship would then drop astern gradually into her assigned position and the formation of the squadron as a whole would then be preserved. If the ship still persisted in outpacing the others, then it would probably become necessary to shorten one or more of her topgallant sails.

The passage northward was an extremely interesting one. In the days of which I am writing, the officer commanding ship or squadron ruled as absolute monarchs. Once we had left England and out of sight of land all communication with the Admiralty was severed and our cruise to the northern region would not permit mail, and wireless communications were not dreamt of. Infinite trust was therefore placed in our Commodore and it was most intriguing to see him pacing up and down the poop while conducting the manoeuvres of the ship. All orders to the squadron were given by flag signals from our ship and the manoeuvres whilst cruising would include: altering course necessitating the swinging of the yards as the ship helm was moved; putting the ship about (tacking or wearing) shortening and resetting sail; and several others. Many of these exercises would require all-hands-on-deck to man the ropes etc., while the upper yard men including myself would race to the mast head as often as the circumstances required. The practice of reefing sails during gales and setting studding-sails in fine fair winds would also be common practices and notably call for most strenuous activity on the part of all concerned. After each day had thus been spent, we would wash clothes or scrub hammocks in the dog watches and be required for duty in two watches during the night.

After the third day at sea, all ratings would be given salt provisions and ships biscuits. This food was strictly limited and, so far as I can remember, was likely little better than that issued to the men of Her Majesty's Fleet a century before! The following is a description of our meals as issued daily:

Breakfast, 6:30 am: - one pint of cocoa with biscuit;

Dinner, Noon: - pea soup, salt pork with biscuit two days per week; boiled beef and plum pudding three days per week; corned tinned beef or mutton with preserved potatoes for two days per week.

Tea, 4:00 pm: - one pint of tea with biscuits.

A spirit ration comprising ½ gill of rum and 3½ gills of water. Half a pint of grog was issued each day only to each man of 20 years of age and above.

The quality of the food was poor, especially the salt beef and pork which were pickled in wooden casks. The biscuit was very hard and almost tasteless. A small quantity of vinegar and mustard was issued and any salt required must be obtained by crushing the rock salt from casks of pork. Sugar was mixed with the tea but milk was not obtainable. After about ten days, salt provisions a daily ration of lime juice was issued. This was a precaution against scurvy due to lack of fresh vegetables. For men who were required to work rigorously for so many hours each day and then keep watch at night this was a very small ration and would be considered totally inadequate in later days when ships were provided with canteens, refrigerators, milk and sugar rations with plenty of fresh meat and vegetables. The official ration for officers was the same as ours, but additional food carried on board for officers was by no means deficient in vitamins. This included a number of live sheep and poultry kept on deck in pens and a most liberal storage of fresh potatoes and other vegetables. All this and an apparent abundance of wines, spirits and beers would have been ample sufficiency for all officers, from the Commodore to the few midshipmen borne in the ships company.

About the middle of June 1896, the squadron arrived at Reykjavik the capital of Iceland. We had been a considerable time at sea working up the various exercises and one could say that all four ships had reached a high state of efficiency after such consistent sail drill and hard work. The strenuous nature of our work was accentuated by the competitive spirit that had been fostered throughout the squadron. Every exercise carried out would invariably start an inter-mast competition for the first place within the ship and concurrently an inter-ship competition for the first ship to complete her part of the order. Having regard to the large number of mast yards, sails and the innumerable ropes to be handled, it will be appreciated how very often things can go wrong and therefore put a ship last in the competition. Striving to be first was the actual reason for all this strenuous activity. It is true the men who sailed the merchant ships in those days certainly had to perform similar operations to ours in the manipulation of their mast yards and sails, but there was no competition within the ship and little between them and other ships, so logically they took their time about the work. Moreover, they were called upon to do only essential work or drills aloft and on deck and there were insufficient numbers of men in the crew to work in competition with each other.

After such a gruelling time, it may truly be supposed that I was extremely glad to reach port and our first concern was to obtain some bread, fresh meat and vegetables to eat and for the luxury of sleep through the night without being subject to call for night watches. While the ship is at anchor in harbour in moderate weather there is no reason for many seamen to keep watches at night and for the most part it is done by the Quartermaster and Boatswains mates. The squadron stayed at Reykjavik for several days and when the day's work was done, leave to go on shore was given to one watch. This leave expired by 11 p.m. So far as I remember, there was little of importance to see on shore, though I can remember quite a number of women coming into town with their donkeys laden with packs of clothes, which they had taken out to wash at the hot springs some distance away. Evidently, they were quite happy and I suppose were quite satisfied with their days work. Iceland of course is a little south of the Arctic Circle and the climate in the month of June was quite congenial and the hours of darkness were very few.

During our short stay here harbour drills were carried out during the forenoon, except on Saturday, when the decks were holystoned and the ship cleaned throughout, and on Sunday, when Divine Service was conducted by the Commodore. The drills consisted of mast and yard drill for the most part, but on one morning opportunity was taken of moving the ships from one position of the harbour to another by means of the kedge anchors. This was quite a good operation and, of course, the usual competition for first ship to complete the task was keenly contested. The afternoons in harbour were usually spent on repair and refitting work. This would entail replacement of worn ropes, repairs to canvas gear and so forth, in fact between 1:15 and 4:00 p.m. was considered normally a quiet and peaceful time.

After tea at 4.20 p.m. all hands were assembled for evening quarters. This was followed by calling both watches and a drill of short duration which would invariably end with the routine order "Down Top-gallant Mast". Since this meant getting the top gallant and royal yards down before the Mast could follow them, it was my duty as No. 1 of the Fore Royal Yard to run aloft some 120 feet by way of the rope rattlings and a Jacob ladder and endeavour to send my yard down before my competitors could do so. Now there was not much room standing on two iron spurs known as the Jack and perform all the details of this job, nevertheless, it provided grand sport and there was no rapture like the joy of winning even if there was no bitterness like the gall of defeat. With the spars got down, everything would be snugly secured for the night and prepared ready for crossing Royal Yards again the next morning. On certain days the routine would be to send the Royal Yards down only. In which case the operation would be confined to three yards of each ship. Nevertheless, the inter-ship and inter-squadron competition would be equally as keen, if not more so, observing that all the remainder of the Upper Yardmen would be spectators on deck while No.'s 1 and 2 of the Royal Yards were aloft at their work.

I Join The Royal Navy

Obviously, these exercises were fraught with an element of danger, for one slip of the hand or foot would probably be sufficient to cause a man to fall from aloft. Indeed, this occurred on quite a number of occasions during our cruise, and it was a well-known fact that many lives of seamen had been lost by falling from aloft in Royal Navy sailing ships. At the time there was absolutely no chance of observing the present-day slogan of "Safety First". Somehow, one's mast or yard must be the first up or down in the competitive efforts and woe to him who caused the slightest delay in any of them.

Spit and polish were not so dominant in our daily lives as it was in non-sailing ships, though there were certain jobs in this connection which I personally could not regard as pleasant sport. One of these was a routine job I had to perform every morning when in harbour. This was to go aloft and polish the lightning conductor on the fore top-gallant mast. The lightning conductor was a strip of copper about an inch wide, inserted into the after part of the mast throughout its length from heel to truck at the top. Now when the mast was lying on the deck the conductor could be polished easily in about ten minutes, but aloft the job could not be done under about half an hour. The three No. 1's of the royal yards would get the order "Away Aloft" to clean lightning conductor; so the three of us would start from deck with brick and rag and race to the Jack on the Top-gallant mast. From there upwards to the truck was a bare pole, so one had to shin up and hold on with the legs and one hand while polishing away with the other hand. This job over the remaining portion below was fairly easy, because there was the Jacobs ladder and other means of supporting one's body while one could use both hands for manipulating the cleaning gear. When completed one would clear the mast head and return to the deck and report accordingly. The boatswain would usually take the report and inspect the work with his eagle's eye, and if in his opinion there happened to be a suspicion of verdigris remaining, it would inevitably mean that one would be sent aloft again to remove it.

From Reykjavik we sailed for Vadso in Lapland rounding the North Cape, Norway in Latitude 70 degrees North and Longitude 20 degrees East. Gales attendant with heavy seas prevailed practically the whole voyage. Moreover, the climate in the Arctic Circle was extremely cold. Sand was sprinkled on the decks to prevent ice forming and gangways amidships had the length of time in their watches reduced and were issued with special warm clothing. Our work aloft was extremely unpleasant with the freezing wind biting into the very marrow of one's bones while one's bare feet and hands were terribly numbed with the cold weather. During the worst gales little sail would be carried and sometimes we would be reduced to reef the topsails while the Top-gallant Mast was on deck.

As may be expected among the younger seamen in a ship belabouring in heavy weather when everyone was keeping watch on deck for days on end, sleep would come without much inducement wherever one could obtain a sheltered spot on deck. This was a punishable offence and the habit was soon broken in the *Active*. Missing muster in a new watch on deck was another form of delinquency among the younger men who perhaps had slept too soundly and failed to awaken when called to keep the next watch. These offences were regarded as most serious, especially the latter as this might mean that a poor devil who had completed his watch on the lookout in the freezing weather would have to remain at his post until his relief arrived. In the *Active* we had a special method of correction for this offence known as "First Watch" punishment. This would begin at 8 p.m. on the delinquents of the 8 to 12 p.m. watch below. The unfortunate fellow would be ordered to stand to attention on deck under the lee of the mainsail for one hour. This was very a severe punishment, especially when the ship was in the Arctic Region, for it was mercilessly designed for the man to receive the bitterly cold down draught from the huge spread of sail above him for the prescribed time, when otherwise he would be resting for the first watch below in preparation for the ruddle muster at midnight. From a medical point of view alone, this cruelty should have been prohibited.

The Commodore behaved at times in a very terrifying manner and like a hasty martinet was sometimes very unfair in awarding punishment, even to his Petty Officers who were such fine seamen. I well remember on one occasion after he had shaken his fist at the Second Captain of the Main Top and abused him thoroughly for something that had gone wrong aloft calling out "I will disrate you. You are disrated!". This treatment was particularly severe for one of the Senior 2nd Class Petty Officers who was generally regarded by his shipmates as a hardworking and conscientious man and worthy of promotion. Apparently, the Commodore himself thought the same of him later for I am happy to relate that soon after this occurrence the unhappy man was reinstated in his former rating and resumed duty as Second Captain of the Main Top.

In due course we rounded the North Cape and reached Vadso after many days of exercises and drills involving every kind of manoeuvre imaginable. We arrived thoroughly tired and glad of this opportunity for longer hours of sleep. Being Summer time in the Northern Hemisphere, there was of course scarcely any darkness and one could read a book on the upper deck at midnight quite easily without artificial aid. The regularity of darkness following the light of each day is not generally appreciated as the blessing it really is until one is brought into contact with continuous daylight. In those Northern regions one is also fortunate in seeing the Aurora Boreaus often called the Northern Lights. The auroral flashes and display appear as if a number of searchlights were signalling somewhere below the horizon. These are truly wonderful sights.

Vadso situated in Lapland, that very interesting region of the reindeer, which the Lapps use for transport. The Lapps themselves lived in conical shaped wooden huts and are of Northern Mongol origin. I well remember that we arrived there a few days before the 9th August 1896, for it was on that date a total eclipse of the sun occurred in that region. An Eclipse expedition consisting of a large number of observers had come from Greenwich Observatory and elsewhere in the hope of viewing it. Everyone was disappointed however, for the weather was so bad that very little was seen in that particular locality. There was another party which had better luck near Bodo on the west coast of Norway when fine weather permitted a better view. These observers were very fortunate and I believe that the beautiful weather they experienced permitted them to take a goodly number of interesting photographs of the eclipse of the sun in its different phases.

A few days after the eclipse, we left Vadso, and the Squadron commenced another cruise in the Arctic Ocean. The weather behaved very well and as usual there was an abundance of manoeuvres, drills and hard work. The climate, however was extremely cold and, consequently, the drills aloft and on deck were particularly severe to the hands when hauling in the frozen ropes and more especially to the bare feet and toes when working aloft. Then there were the painful sea cuts under the toes. I think, perhaps, that my feet and hands were affected as severely as anyone on board the ship with these. Deep lacerations were made in the palm of the hands and in all joints and under the fingers and toes. These were caused by the comparatively hard rope yarns cutting into the flesh whilst hauling on the ropes and running the rope rattlings of the mast's rigging. Indeed, my hands and toes appeared as if some blunt knife had cut deeply into every joint. No one ever dreamed of reporting such a thing to the ship's surgeon. It simply wasn't done. So, the only relief one could get was from new pieces of rope yarn liberally treated with Stockholm tar with which we bound around each wound and then hoped for the best. If these dressings did nothing else they prevented

I Join The Royal Navy

the introduction of septic poisoning. As may be supposed, these injuries were most severe upon awakening after sleep. They would then become stiff and one would experience excruciating pain when lashing up one's hammock. I found it necessary to use my elbow for the operation of hauling the hammock lashing taut and afterwards the pain would gradually subside as the ordinary work was carried out.

A few days after we had left Vadso, I experienced a very pleasing incident, which I am very happy to record here. I had just come down from aloft, about eleven o'clock one morning after a gruelling time at drills, when I received an order from the Master-at-Arms to attend on the Quarter Deck about half an hour later to parade before the Commodore. Naturally, I was much concerned about this and inquired immediately as to the reason for this procedure. The Master-at-Arms then informed me that it was not as a defaulter that my presence was required; but he could not give me any further information on the subject. Thereupon I approached the Captain of my Top who advised me not to worry about the matter, for he thought I would probably hear something to my future benefit. At the appointed time I went aft to the Quarter Deck where the Master at Arms was busy sorting out the Commodore's requestmen and defaulters. He ordered me to fall in on the right with the requestmen. The Commander and the 1st Lieutenant, A.P. Ethelston were present as also the boatswain of the ship. Presently, the Commodore appeared and in due course I was called before him.

All this time I had wondered what it was all about, but my anxiety was soon dispelled, when the 1st Lieutenant was called, and proceeded to praise my work generally, in particular on the smartness of my drills aloft. He followed these remarks up with a strong recommendation for promotion to Able Seaman. Despite the fact that someone had drawn his attention to my Service Certificate, wherein it was recorded that I was little more than eighteen years of age and rated an Ordinary Seaman only eight months previously, the Commodore called out "Rated" and so I was advanced to Able Seaman at 1 shilling and 8 pence per day.

You may imagine what rapture I was in upon leaving the Quarter Deck. Also, how elevated I felt when the Petty Officer of my mess, who was the 2nd Captain of my Top, greeted me as I went down to dinner with the kindly words: –

"Congratulations Sweetingham, in future you will sit next to me in this mess".

This meant that my position at the mess table was changed from one at the end of the table nearest the amidships gangway to one second from the other end of the table close to the ship's side. Since there were some eight ordinary seamen in the mess all older and therefore senior to me, my status was thus enhanced materially. Moreover, the Petty Officer of the mess had generously arranged to pool the rum rations of all my messmates above 20 years of age, in order that I could join them in their kindly toast on that occasion. Being under twenty years old I was not entitled to the rum ration. That same afternoon the Captain of my Top congratulated me upon my success, and rather set me a higher standard to aim at by adding:

"The fore royal yard has usually been the first to finish in the ship. Now that you are an A.B., it should always be first!!"

Our next port of call was Hammerfest, a town of Norway a little to the Westward of the North Cape. Here the sun does not set from May 13th to July 29th and does not rise from November 18th to January 23rd. Since our stay there was for a few days in August 1895 you may be sure that our share of daylight was very liberal. At that time the fishing industry at Hammerfest seemed very considerable. Huge stacks could be seen along the shore comprising fish which had been cured by drying and salting. Moreover, whales from the fisheries in the vicinity of Spitzbergen and Nova Zembla were brought to Hammerfest. Our time at this port was for the most part taken up with the usual harbour drills and boat exercises, while the limited period available for rest and sleep was much appreciated. During my work aloft I felt that I must put out all my strength and speed in order to justify my recent good fortune. On no account must I let down the First Lieutenant, the Boatswain and my Captain of the Top, to whom I was so much indebted. In all humility, I may here be permitted to mention that on that score the angels were on my side!

After our departure from Hammerfest, we next visited Trondhjem a seaport further down the Norwegian coast, having now crossed to the south of the Arctic Circle. The city lies on the river Nid on the magnificent Trondhjem Fiord and its cathedral is the place of coronation of the Kings of Norway. Our stay here was of short duration and we proceeded still further southward to Bergen. It was on this short passage that I experienced one of the most terrifying moments of my life.

The squadron was running free under full sail at the time and it was clear that the *Active* leading the line had gained speed on the other ships. In consequence, the order "In Royals" was issued to reduce our speed and so allow the *Active* to fall back gradually into proper station. Now unless specially ordered otherwise it was the usual practice to furl the royals when they had been clewed up and the sails thus shortened, so accordingly I returned aloft to furl my sail. In the process of finishing the work and giving the bunt (centre) of the sail a tidy appearance, I passed the bunt lanyard (secured to the sail with a fitted thimble) around the mast then rove it through the thimble and gave one heave with all my might - when the lanyard carried away. Since both of my hands were engaged on the lanyard, the upper and middle portion of my body fell back while a terrifying feeling came over me that my end was near. At the moment the rope parted I was kneeling on the starboard spur of the Jack and in these circumstances, there seemed nothing to stop my momentum backwards and downward head first! Luckily however, I retained my presence of mind; and as I fell, I could see the arm of my yardmate extended in my direction and grabbed it. The whole thing happened in a moment or two and I was in a very precarious predicament. Fortunately, my yardmate was standing in the Jacobs ladder immediately below me and was in a position to see the lanyard carry away. Providently therefore he prevented my fall to some hundred feet below.

Incidentally, this was the fore-runner of two other accidents aloft, one of which alas ended fatally while the other resulted in serious permanent injury to the unfortunate victim. These unforeseen events were followed by the Second Captain of the Forecastle falling into the water from the end of the flying Jiboon and soon after this a man fell overboard from the muzzle end of a 6 inch gun during an exercise of active station. Luckily fine weather prevailed on each occasion and both men were picked up by the lifeboat. By then we were getting too familiar with accidents and the Commodore thought it fitting to address the whole of the ship's company on the matter.

He said, "Accidents in any ship are invariably the result of carelessness. In future, disciplinary action will be taken against anyone who disregards this warning!"

We arrived at Bergen early in the morning, and our squadron presented an imposing picture as we sailed into its very fine harbour. As was the case of most ports of Norway in those days, the fishing industry appeared to be the most important activity going on at this city and the quality of the fish obtainable at the market was excellent. In later years Bergen on the west coast of Norway became an attractive tourist centre. I can quite believe that its quaint buildings and very old cathedral founded in the thirteenth century, together with the bracing midsummer climate, which I well remember there, would afford much pleasure and interest to visitors from other climes. At the time of which I am writing and for about nine years later Norway and Sweden were of course united as one kingdom.

From Bergen we sailed in a north westerly direction and passed many deep-sea fishing vessels of British and other nationalities. At first, we encountered bad weather and for several days heavy seas and rain prevailed. Then the weather moderated and light winds slowed our headway. During one of these afternoons, we passed into a fog bank and soon afterwards the ships got mixed up with several fishing trawlers with their trawls down. As we contrived to manoeuvre clear of one or these vessels, another dimly appeared necessitating again the use of helm and trimming the sails to prevent collision. Increased look-outs were placed on deck and aloft, and all hands were at their stations for emergency while this tiresome business was going on. The nationality of these vessels was in doubt somewhat, for they appeared to be a medley lot and this contributed to the difficulty. The Commodore was not at all happy about this irritating business and stamped his feet on the deck of the poop while yet another trawler loomed up in our way. Then as we passed clear of her he could stand it no longer and bellowed to the skipper, "Will you keep out of my way!!"

Being a still day, the stern demand of the Commodore was heard clearly by almost everyone on board, and we wondered if the skipper was a foreigner and did not understand. Shortly there was no longer any doubt about this however, for out of the mist a stentorian voice burst upon us in truly eloquent English, "You keep out of my bloody way!!"

It is probable that the Commodore thought it best not to pursue the subject further, for no one realised more than he that the obligation lay with us to keep clear of fishing vessels with their trawls or drift nets down.

Several days after this when passing a fishing vessel, the Commodore inquired whether the skipper was in want of anything to which the prompt reply came: tobacco! Thereupon we lowered the sea boat and sent a quantity of tobacco on board. To show that these fishermen were really generous fellows at heart, I must here mention that upon the boats return it was loaded to capacity with very fine halibut, about five feet in length, which the skipper had so kindly sent.

During this longish cruise in the North Atlantic, in which we had plenty of time to work up our knowledge in practical seamanship in all weathers, we had gradually worked across to the Faroes and then came south to Lerwick the capital of the Shetland Islands. There is little I can recall about the Shetlands except for its wild stretch of coastlines teeming with sea birds. But I well remember that right glad the seamen were to obtain some excellent bread, fresh mutton and vegetables after being so long on salt provisions. Many were the longing eyes we cast when inspecting the sheep pens and hen coops on board, from which the daily supply for the Officers had been furnished; while at each port of call, replenishments of such livestock were hoisted on board by the men who knew their diet would be made up from the casks of salt meat only. In harbour sleep too after a strenuous time of toil and watch keeping at sea was truly a real blessing.

Among the personal discomforts one had to suffer on the lower deck of a sailing ship, the restricted supply of fresh water was not the least important. Fresh water in the *Active* was scarce and rationed and the water tanks were well guarded, while every night the quantity of fresh water remaining in the tanks was reported and recorded. Water for cleaning purposes was drawn daily by each mess in the mess tub and after everyone in the mess had washed, the same water was used for scrubbing the tables, stools and mess deck. Some relief from these conditions was afforded during rainfall, when the Boatswain would pipe – 'Up all Mess Tubs '. On some of these occasions, sufficient water would be caught on the upper deck to enable one to bathe or wash one's clothes in water pure and fresh from the heavens. There were no bathrooms for the seamen's use in the

Active while the lavatory arrangements in the ships' head was disgusting. In bad weather I have seen poor young seamen ill from seasickness huddled together on the wooden top of the sail trough while the filthy contents were swishing violently to and fro, with the pitch and roll of the ship.

In the matter of seasickness while being aloft this was unavoidably an unsavoury affair in that seaman were not permitted to come down from aloft, and it was a punishable offence for anyone to vomit indiscriminately. In order therefore to keep within the law, the cap was used under the chin as the receptacle, being suspended from the neck of the unfortunate individual by the chinstay when required. I have mentioned these somewhat revolting conditions purposely in order that the reader may know of some of the hardships endured by the British bluejacket at the time of which I am writing. Incidentally, these men were the worst paid in the kingdom.

We stayed at Lerwick only a little while and it must have occurred to the Commodore that there was yet another harbour exercise for square rigged ships of war that we had not tackled and that we might very well carry out here. This was an operation known as "Porcupine Ship" an arrangement for the protection of the ship in harbour against attack by enemy torpedo, or by steam boat armed with an outrigger gun. Briefly, this protection consisted of a conglomeration of masts and spars some placed on-end over the ships side and others arranged to the best advantage possible. Masts, yards and booms including spares carried were got over the side and every man on board was engaged in turning the ship into a complete shambles. The work involved in this evolution is indescribable while the element of competition contributed to not a few injuries to the crew. However, it was all great fun and personally I enjoyed this interesting innovation in our drills. As soon as the operation was reported complete, all hands were fallen in on the upper deck. Then for our sins, the Commodore ordered: "Cross Royal yards and make plain sail". This meant that everything had to be replaced and more! For not only had the conglomeration of spars and ropes to be replaced, but in addition, all sails had to be loosened and set after the yards had been crossed, ready for leaving harbour. Incredible as it may appear, it is gratifying to record that this was completed and every man was clear of the mast head in an extremely short time. I have never heard of this contrivance actually saving a ship from attack, but for sheer hard labour, and to bring out the qualities, initiative and quickness of action on the part of those concerned, it was certainly most effective.

Whenever we were sailing close hauled to the wind the lee fore brace was a special child of the boatswains', especially after putting the ship about by tacking or wearing. He seemed always afraid that the rope might have stretched or something, since the fore main yard was last braced hard up, and never appeared satisfied that not another inch of the brace could be got down. I have often seen our exacting old Boatswain, Tommy Pipes, when everything seemed to be going along quite satisfactorily, shoot a glance at the lee fore yard arm, then move along the deck to where the brace was belayed and sure enough his boatswain pipe would be heard and the call "Lee Fore Brace!" The men whose duty it was to man the rope would then be greeted with Tommy's gruff voice saying "Get hove to it", meaning get hold of it, and when some half-dozen hauls on the brace had been carried out, he would pipe "Belay", meaning make fast, and be perfectly happy again; even if he had only succeeded in gaining an inch on the rope indeed not a few men would declare, out of the hearing of Tommy Pipes of course, that the nett result of their labours was a loss of a few inches!!

Many years later when staying at a hoarding house in Bombay, I saw a picture hanging above my breakfast table bearing the title "Lee Fore Brace". Nothing I have seen before or since, has reminded me so much of my days in the *Active*. The picture depicted a square-rigged ship, heeling well over, whilst sailing full and by a head wind as I had seen so many times in the *Active*. There stood the boatswain of the ship up to his waist in sea water and piping the heave of a dozen or so men who were putting the whole of their weight on the rope known as the Fore Brace. They too were standing in deep water.

We left Lerwick in a gale which blew for days, and as we were now approaching the end of the cruise and I had become an Able Seaman, I was very anxious to obtain some practical experience of working the helm and steering the ship in the various phases of wind and weather. As a Royal Yardman however, I was precluded from taking my "trick" at the helm when under sail as my services were required aloft at any time or on other special work - e.g. -for shortening and resetting royals as necessary and always during "About ship" (tacking), when the royal yard was required to uncrutch the lee top-gallant backstays and crutch (spread) the weather ones. These repeated duties demanded much of one's energy and the agility of a monkey, to hold on and at the same time to do the work required, amidst swaying yards in a rough sea.

Nevertheless, I somehow contrived to take a sufficient number of tricks at the wheel and thereby gained some very useful knowledge. I cannot recall anything more fascinating and instructive than when I was weather or senior helmsman in the *Active* under plain sail and steering the ship full and by. In a steam ship one is given a compass course to steer by and that is sufficient. In a sailing ship however, this is by no means the case, when one is endeavouring to make a point direct to windward by a series of tacks. Probably the ships head could not be placed within say six points (67°30') from the direction from which the wind is blowing. In order therefore to maintain this course and to prevent the ship from being taken aback, it was one's endeavour to steer so that the weather leech of the main top or topgallant sail is just full and by. These sails can be seen best from the position of the steering wheel. If they begin to shiver it indicates that one must be careful not to allow the ships head to come up into the wind any further and a certain degree of weather helm is necessary to counteract this tendency.

In dark nights with no moon, it is very difficult to be sure of the behaviour of the sails and one found it helpful to steer by a convenient star; by keeping the star in a certain position just clear of the sail. During every minute of my first two hour trick at the wheel, I was conscious of the critical supervision of the Officer of the watch, and the eagle eye of the Commodore scanning the sails as they lifted and filled alternately and when one thought that things were going well, a stern voice from the poop above might be heard - "No Higher" meaning keep her away from the wind or "Nothing Off" indicating that the ships head must not be allowed to wander further away from the close hauled course. All this was splendid training and despite the feeling that, occasional coursing of the ship by my superior officers was thus necessary, I knew that the responsibility for the safe and efficient steering of the ship during every moment of the watch was mine and felt proud of it.

Since the *Active* was the last sailing ship in which I served, I would here like to make a few remarks about an officer of the ship, who, in my opinion, was the most remarkable man on board. He was the Boatswain and admired by the whole ships' company. His knowledge of the ship's masts, yards, rigging and sails with all the paraphernalia relating there to was profound, while his ubiquity was truly marvellous. He was probably about 45 years of age, tall, dark and wore an iron-grey beard. His face was rugged and weather beaten, and doubtless had many tons of sea water forced down the back of his sou-wester and into his oil-skin pockets! During sail drill, his station was on the forecastle looking out for the head sails and all those on the foremast, while professionally he was held personally responsible for the maintenance and efficiency of all standing and running rigging, ship sails, boats, anchors and cables. In harbour, he was responsible for the smartness and tidiness of the ship and her outside appearance. He used to go round the ship in his boat each morning carrying his hand flags, coloured to indicate each mast, yards and ropes that might require attention. The boatswain's mates would be inboard and obey his numerous signals as he made them. Lynx-eyed, the boatswain could foresee danger and whenever there was important work or drill going on, he would be present with his experienced advice. I have known him to tactfully countermand a wrong order given by a superior officer and so prevent a serious accident. Yes, our Boatswain was a truly remarkable man and worth his weight in gold to Her Majesty's Navy. Yet, this grand officer's rank was one subordinate to a Junior Sub Lieutenant!!

Sometime before the cruise was terminated, we carried out practice firings from our 6-inch breach loading guns, and in due course sailed up the English Channel. Here the squadron was dispersed in order that each ship might return independently to their respective home ports. The *Active* continued sailing and reached Spithead in due course, then we proceeded to a buoy at Portsmouth harbour. Later, the Commodore called upon the Naval Commander-in-Chief, and upon his arrival we were informed that the ship would strip to a gantling and prepare for a dockyard refit. We were further told that when this task was completed, leave would be granted for ten days to each watch. Cheered by this news, you may be sure we commenced the work with a will. In a very few days, all masts and rigging above the lower masts and all yards, sails and booms were dismantled together with their running rigging. Only the three lower masts with standing rigging remained with a three-inch hemp rove through a block at the cap of each lower mast. Thus, the *Active* was stripped top gantling.

I fear that if I wrote the details of the work involved in this operation, they would make tiresome reading. Sufficient has already been narrated for the reader to appreciate the strenuous nature of the work, also that the First Watch to proceed on leave had well and truly merited a spell from their labours. I belonged to the Second Watch for leave and till then I was given the job of refitting the running rigging, blocks, tackles and other work belonging to the fore-topmen which the dockyard riggers had decided not to undertake. All kinds of knots, splices, gromets etc. had to be done to prepare the ship for her next cruise. I was exceedingly glad when my turn came to go home on leave and see my family once again.

Home life was like heaven to me, so restful and peaceful, and the 10 days leave passed all too quickly. On my return to the ship, I was informed that, since I was now an Able Seaman, I could not remain in the ship and that I was due to take a seaman gunner's course in HMS *Excellent* at Portsmouth. Although this was inevitable and would be to my future advantage, I cannot say that I was at all happy about leaving the great brotherhood of seamen on the lower deck whose loyalty, cheerfulness and endurance against wind and weather I had come to admire so much. In the athletic field alone, many of these fine men, if they had been fortunate enough to have passed through the public schools and colleges of England, would certainly have achieved athletic distinction; no less than those we hear so much about today, and are regarded as sort of Greek Gods by their fellow scholars. The difference being, that these seamen's achievements and winning of sports events as they did, went unsung to the public and were merely taken in the stride of their ordinary work. Still, there is a divinity that shapes our ends, rough hew them how we will.

CHAPTER VIII

I Join the Gunnery School

--- ooOoo ---

On leaving HMS *Active* I entered the Naval Gunnery School at Portsmouth, situated at Whale Island to the north of the Dockyard. At that time the two establishments were joined by a wooden viaduct, which was dismantled later when a swing bridge was erected between the Island and Northend Portsmouth. Whale Island is referred to in the Navy List as HMS *Excellent*. It was and still is the Royal Navy's Premier Gunnery School and its Motto was displayed in letters of gold under the statue of a magnificent Lion thus:

SSI VIS PACEM PARA BELLUM

(If you wish for peace prepare for war)

This lion can be clearly seen as one passes over the swing bridge at the entrance to Whale Island from the mainland. More than one thousand officers and men were accommodated for instruction on this Island which was regarded as one of the most beautiful spots of the South of England. The Establishment was commanded by a Senior Naval Captain, who had a very large staff of Gunnery Officers, Petty Officer Gunnery Instructors. The lawns and gardens were laid out perfectly and the surroundings were salubrious, while the Gun Batteries, Lecture Rooms and Drill Parade were well appointed.

Our daily routine began by calling the hands at the most respectable time of 7 a.m. Ample facilities for bathing, washing and other amenities were provided. Breakfast at 8 a.m. and the classes commenced gunnery drills at 9 a.m. after being assembled on parade for morning prayers. Dinner at noon and drill in the afternoon would be resumed at 1 p.m. and continue until 3.30 p.m. then tea at 4 p.m. Recreational facilities were splendid; cricket, football, billiards, bowls and all kinds of reading matter were available. In short, Whale Island was indeed a home away from home. The contrast between one's mode of living there, with that one experienced in my last ship was as opposite as poles are apart.

Obviously, the discipline was very strict indeed and, of course, every movement taken by the men under instruction had to be performed at the double. The Gunnery curriculum consisted of Field Training, Musketry, Turret and other gun drills, Hydraulics, Ammunition, Field and Machine Gunnery and Diving. Practice firing from heavy, light and machine guns was also carried out by each seaman. In addition, Officers and Petty Officer Gunnery Instructors were given lectures in Fire Control and Theory Gunnery. Seamen classes comprised from sixteen to twenty in number, while the Officers and higher gunnery ratings, were classed up in numbers varying from six to ten. My age at this period was less than nineteen years, and owing to my early promotion I was one of the youngest able seaman under instruction at the school. I commenced Field Training in a class of eighteen seamen, and being the youngest member of my class, I felt it should be my special endeavour to be a worthy associate. With this in mind I worked hard after instructional hours on the drill books. In this connection I had little difficulty in finding the time for extra studies for one's duty turn only came every fifth night and on other days one was off duty from 3.30 p.m. till 7.00 a.m. the next morning.

The Petty Officer gunnery instructors on the Staff at Whale Island, were specially selected for their particular work. Their knowledge of the subjects to which they were assigned was profound and in consequence, they were regarded with respect by both officers and seamen. It will be agreed therefore, that our instruction in all subjects, was the best that could possibly be given. The examination for seamen gunners was conducted orally by junior staff gunnery officers; while the Officers and higher gunnery ratings under instruction were set examination papers in addition by Senior Staff Officers.

The maintenance and general routine of the establishment was under the direction of the Commander. In this duty, the Commander was assisted by Commissioned Officers from the Warrant rank. One of these officers was in charge of the routine maintenance and cleanliness of the living quarters, another was responsible for all stores, while the other officer supervised the ground staff in their work of beautification of the gardens, lawns and roads. The Commander's room was situated on the first floor of the officer's quarters, with his windows facing the lawn, which he was particularly proud of. He had every cause for this for everyone admired our beautiful five acres of perfectly flat ground bearing the finest and best kept grass imaginable.

I remember an amusing incident relating to the maintenance of this lawn, which incidentally will show the degree of interest taken in it by those concerned. On wet and dewy mornings, the worms would make their appearance on the grass while the crows and seagulls would come at the same time for a succulent breakfast. Since the birds also destroyed the grass right under the very nose of our Commander, he was naturally very indignant about it. Accordingly, he issued orders that a party of seamen was to be detailed each morning from the duty division, for the purpose of chasing the offending birds from his special preserve. All apparently went well for the first two or three mornings, and the sailors you may be sure, made great fun of their job which they regarded as some sort of novelty! But trouble was soon to come, for on one particular morning, some dozen or so seagulls became over persistent and returned to the battle with the worms after the sailors had been engaged with them. The seagulls of course, were spotted whilst in the act by the Commander from his cabin window and this proved beyond his endurance. He therefore sent for the officer of the day and demanded an explanation as to why his orders regarding the birds had not been carried out. The unfortunate junior gunnery lieutenant, with all humility, stated that a party of men had been duly sent out and had completed their work before he had permitted them to leave the lawn. This explanation was not at all acceptable to the Commander who thereupon directed the duty officer to have all the men concerned fallen in on the Quarter Deck. When the men were present, a further investigation produced evidence of crows having been chased from the lawn, but, strangely enough, nobody seemed to remember dealing with seagulls!! Thereupon the Commander dismissed the men and issued an amended order: that in future the men required for this service would be divided into two parties - one to chase the crows, and the other to disperse the seagulls. Furthermore, to obviate confusion between the two functions, the men detailed to deal with the crows were to be dressed in a blue rig, while those associated with the seagulls were to perform this duty in a white working rig!! Truly an exemplar of masterly detail, as befitting this veritable home of discipline.

Of all the subjects of instruction I think that Field Training seemed the most unpopular and we were all very glad to pass through the drill parade to the more interesting work. Turret gun drill

I Join The Royal Navy

appealed to me as perhaps the most fascinating, and I was fortunate enough in obtaining good results in the examination. This drill was carried out in HMS *Hero* a second class battleship attached to the Gunnery School. The *Hero*'s main armament consisted of two 12-inch breach loading (B.L.) guns mounted in a turret on the forecastle. Her secondary armament was made up of 4-inch B.L. guns and in addition, two quick firing 2 pounder Hotchkiss guns, two quick firing 3 pounder Hotchkiss guns, and four 5-inch machine guns mounted in the *Hero*'s top about half way up the mast. This was reminiscent of the days of Nelson, who was killed during the battle of Trafalgar by a rifleman from the top of a French warship.

As muzzle loading (M.L.) guns were still mounted in Her Majesty's ships at the time, the drill for these guns was included in our syllabus. A battery of these huge guns was mounted at Whale Island, together with heavy breech loaders, but owing to some twenty to twenty-five men required to make up a gun crew for the M.L. guns there always existed a certain amount of confusion between the duties of each man. In the course of the drill for these weapons, the replacement of 'supposed casualties' was exercised, also changing numbers at the gun, so that every rating would have an opportunity of performing all duties in turn.

In the matter of casualties, I well remember an excitable, though somewhat amusing drill experience by my class. The instructor was very explicit in his explanation of every detail, while supposed casualties were falling down fast and furious. As each casualty occurred it was the duty of the Captain of the Gun to fill up the vacancy by ordering an appropriate number to take up the vacant positions. On this particular occasion a big Irish sailor was our Captain of the Gun and, at frequent intervals, the instructor indicated that a certain number was to "fall out" thus: "Instructor - Fall out Number 5!" "Captain of Gun - Number 20 take Number 5!" and so on, until so many numbers had become casualties that the drill became somewhat difficult. It must be remembered that the Captain of Gun, not only had to attend to this, but he was responsible for the correct loading, manipulation and firing of the guns; operations that were constantly being checked and corrected by the instructor. In this medley the instructor called out: "Fall out Number 41!", but in his utter confusion and exasperation at the chaotic state of affairs, Pat could stand it no longer and rapped out the stentorian command: "Blast Number 41 - begorra I'll take 41 me bloody self!!".

Rifle practice firing at targets and pistol firing was carried out in those days on rifle and pistol ranges at Whale Island. Although my shooting with both these weapons was tolerably good in later years, it was atrocious then. The rifle used was the old 0.45 inch Martin, and owing to the strong impact of its recoil, the number of rounds to be fired in one day was limited to twenty. Even this number was sufficient to cause an uncomfortable bruise on one's shoulder. At one hundred yards range, firing was carried out from a standing position and unless the butt of the rifle was held firmly into the shoulder one would receive a very severe blow there as the rifle recoiled. At two hundred yards range, the position for firing was kneeling on the right knee while one sat on the right heel, the left knee being bent, so that the left thigh would act as a rest for the left elbow. This was all very well for taking aim, but on firing, especially by a novice as I was, the recoil would cause the butt of the rifle to strike one's shoulder with sufficient force to throw one off one's balance completely. At the longer ranges however, the position of the body was lying down, and this obviated the disabilities I have mentioned, while the energy of recoil could be overcome with comparative ease.

The sea service cutlass, that ancient and traditional weapon of the British navy was still prominently used at this period though later it was used for ceremonial purposes and now it has been regulated to the obsolete armoury. Of all the gunnery drills at Whale Island, I do not think there was a more unpopular one than that with the sea service cutlass. In the preamble given by the instructor he stated that a seaman armed with a cutlass had nothing to fear from any man, no matter how he was armed. The cavalryman on horseback armed with a lance or, the infantryman with his rifle and fixed bayonet would surely succumb to the onslaught of the bluejacket when skilfully using his sea service cutlass!! The drill with this weapon consisted of "Guards", "Cuts", "Points" and "Parries", each movement being accompanied by its appropriate footwork. During the course of my tuition, our instructor was a typical old salt and a mighty man of valour, who wielded this instrument of some 2 pounds 11 ounces in weight as if it was a cane. But to his unfortunate pupils, the weight of the cutlass seemed to increase from the moment we were ordered to stand at the first guard; moreover, in winter time one's hand and fingers, whilst gripping the hilt, would seem to be frost bitten. Our instructor was well aware of all this and would usually search the parade ground for the most exposed spot in which to carry out his drills. His reasoning, was part of the hardening process for us all, and I am sure he was right; for despite the severity and tiresomeness of this drill, the sea service cutlass must have developed the muscles of our arms as no other activity could have possibly achieved. As may be supposed this form of exercise was one of those chosen by the Authorities as an extra drill for delinquents even if they were undergoing other subjects of instruction at the time.

The field guns used in the Navy at that time were seven and nine pounder muzzle loaders. These were then becoming obsolescent and were subsequently replaced by Quick Firing 12 pounder B.L. guns, a vast improvement on their muzzle loading contemporaries. Six of these guns formed a field battery and the drill was one of the most popular among seamen. For drill at heavy guns mounted in turrets, seamen classes were sent from Whale Island to live on board the Battleship *Hero*. This ship was a tender to HMS *Excellent* and was accordingly sent out to sea at frequent intervals to enable the men under instruction to carry out turret gun firings. My term spent in the *Hero* was a very happy and interesting one, while the knowledge gained of her 12-inch B.L. guns mounted in a turret manipulated by hydraulic power was a valuable asset in my future gunnery career.

Any narrative of Britain's Premier Naval Gunnery School at Whale Island, in my opinion, should certainly include a reference to one of its finest amenities - the Fife and Drum Band. We had a brass band, while the artists making up the Fife and Drum Band numbered some sixty persons led by a Chief Petty Officer who was not only a member of the permanent staff. He was really an institution in himself and everyone laughed and joked about the 'The Band Jester'. This company of musicians received its general direction from the Commander, therefore, the band-master was his special protégé and was thereby regarded as an important personage. The members of the band were recruited from seamen under gunnery instruction and there were many privileges afforded them. In fact, apart from their musical practices and actual instruction, they were exempt from all other duties; the band-master therefore, always had a long list of candidates for membership to choose from. His ability to conduct the band on parade with strict discipline and decorum was unquestionable, though it was most unkindly mooted that 'Chiv', as he was called, possessed a strictly limited knowledge of music. Be that as it may, for not being a member of his band I am in no position to form an opinion on the subject.

In this connection however, it seems not entirely out of place to relate the following humorous incident. Old Chiv among many other activities was very keenly interested in the game of football, and a few days before an English Cup Final which was to take place near London, he approached the Commander and requested that long week-end leave of absence in order to purchase certain

I Join The Royal Navy

selections of music in London, which he declared were unobtainable locally. The Commander apparently appreciating the position, readily assented and moreover directed his bandmaster was to be furnished with a service railway pass for the return journey. Early the next week Old Chiv duly repaired to the Commander's office and reported that the result of his mission had been most successful. The Commander, of course, was highly pleased with the news and cheerily asked if he might have a look at some of the pieces of music. Thereupon the band-master produced a huge bundle of music and placed it on the table. After careful scrutiny of the numerous pieces of music before him the Commander looked up and exclaimed, "Why band-master - all this is piano music!"

Nothing daunted Old Chiv who replied, "That's quite alright sir, my band can play any music!!"

Having completed my Gunnery course and passed the examination satisfactorily, I was duly rated a Seaman Gunner 1st Class, which carried an increase of pay by three pence per day. My total pay as an Able Seaman, Seaman Gunner, was thus 1/11d per day, out of which I was required to provide full uniform clothing and, when one could afford it, a little extra food from the canteen.

About this time (April 1897) it became known that HMS *Powerful* a newly built ship, which had arrived at Portsmouth, was about to commission for 3 years service on the China station. We also knew that a large number of ratings similar to mine, would be required to make up the ships' complement and in due course my name was posted, with many others, to be drafted to the *Powerful*. At first, I felt rather disappointed for I had hoped to be transferred to HMS *Vernon* the Torpedo and Mining School of the Royal Navy, for a course of instruction in these subjects and for which my passing out qualifications as a seaman gunner entitled me. But the *Powerful* was a heavily armed ship and required many ratings so one had to console oneself with the inevitable. (I was destined to undergo a very sound course of instruction in the *Vernon* some years later).

In May 1897, we heard of the utter defeat of the Greeks by the Turks on the borders of Thessaly and of the probability that the King of Greece would ask the Great Powers of Europe to mediate on his behalf and his wretched country. The *Powerful* and *Terrible*, her sister ship, were built in reply to the Russian fast cruisers the *Rurik* and the *Rossia*. The *Rossia* was a 20 knot ship with 6-inch steel belt arched deck protection over four-fifths of length of ship with a displacement of 14,200 tons.

The *Powerful* was built by Vickers in 1884-6, with a length of 558 feet over all. This necessitated the building of new docks at Portsmouth as no existing one at the time would take them. She carried no belt of armour, but was given stout arched steel protective decks over her. We felt we could fight the *Rossia* easily on equal terms, even though the *Rossia*'s guns were protected by shields.

CHAPTER IX

We Commission HMS Powerful for Foreign Service

--- ooOoo ---

HMS Powerful

On the seventh June 1897, at the age of 19 years, I joined HMS *Powerful* and on the following day the ship was commissioned for foreign service, with a ships' company of more than eight hundred officers and men.

The *Powerful* was the first ship of a new class of cruisers, and the merits of this ship were much discussed by men in the Navy and in the British and foreign newspapers. A protected cruiser of enormous size in which many innovations had been introduced; the most notable being her water tube boilers and four funnels. The armament consisted of two 9.2-inch MK VIII guns mounted on 6-inch Harvey barbettes one at each end; twelve 6-inch quick firing and sixteen 12-pounder quick firing (Q.F.) guns; also ten 0.45 inch Maxim Machine Guns and one 12-pounder 8 cwt Q.F. Field Gun. She was also armed with four submerged torpedo tubes capable of discharging 18-inch Whitehead Torpedoes.

The *Powerful* was fitted with forty-eight water tube boilers, which generated 25,000 horse power and produced a speed of nearly 23 knots. These boilers were invented by Monsieur Julien Belleville, who had succeeded in perfecting a water tube boiler so long ago as 1855. The water tube boiler fitted in the *Powerful* was more or less in its experimental stage in the Royal Navy, but nevertheless it appeared it had come to stay. From the particulars of the ship given above, it is not surprising

I Join The Royal Navy

that the *Powerful* was considered the crack cruiser in the British Navy. Moreover, she was much longer and heavier than most battleships of her day.

Our Captain, the Honourable Hedworth Lambton, was a brother of the Earl of Durham and one of the Senior Captains in the Royal Navy; a typical Naval Officer of those days, very aristocratic and consistently aloof from all that which made up the life of a humble bluejacket. Nevertheless, he was considered to be a most suitable officer to command a British warship in what were then rather troubled waters of the Far East. The Executive Officer, Commander H.P. Ethelston, was none other than the same splendid gentleman with whom I had already had the pleasure of serving with in HMS *Active* as First Lieutenant and Gunnery Officer. Ethelston was a truly splendid naval officer in every way and none better in the navy could have been chosen to carry out the executive duties of any ship at the time.

It was said that the *Powerful*'s engine room was manned with the cream of the service; and from their conduct and appearance, I am of the opinion that this was very true. The Fleet Engineer, Edwards by name, was most highly respected by all officers and men on board, while his staff of engineers and stokers totalled over four hundred officers and men. This, at first glance would seem a huge number, but as will be seen, was by no means in excess of the personnel required. In this connection, I would mention that there were no less than ninety-six furnaces to be fed with coal under those forty-eight boilers down below, and the consumption of fuel was simply prodigious. The water tube boilers were considered by many engineers at the time to be a very costly innovation, which indeed they were; but like most other equipment classed in this category, it prevailed over all prejudice and stiff opposition, with the result that 50 years later the water tube boiler is installed in every class of fast ship in the navies of the world. Another advantage is that the water tube boiler can be placed lower in the ship and is less vulnerable from enemy gun fire.

Shortly after commissioning at Portsmouth, the whole Empire celebrated the Diamond Jubilee commemoration of the 60th year of Her Majesty Queen Victoria's reign on June 22nd 1897. There was a great gathering of Dominion and Foreign Representatives at London where bluejackets and soldiers lined the streets while the Queen drove in stately array, headed by a naval brigade, from Buckingham Palace through Pall Mall to St Pauls Cathedral. The objectionable words of the National Anthem, I remember eliminated at the time were:

'Confound their politics, frustrate their knavish tricks ...'

and the new verse from now on ran as follows:

'O Lord our God arise, Scatter her enemies,

Make wars to cease;

Keep us from plague and dearth,

Turn thou our woes to mirth;

And over all the earth,

Let there be peace.

Naval ships and vessels were mobilised from all Home Ports, and afterwards carried out manoeuvres and fleet exercises. This afforded an opportunity for the *Powerful* to take part and accordingly, the ship became one of the units of the Home Fleet. This Fleet remained in being for a short cruise only and when it had dispersed, we returned to Portsmouth. There we replenished stocks of coal, provisions and stores before our departure from home waters.

One of the battleships belonging to the Home Fleet to which we had been attached was HMS *Prince George* in which my younger brother Albert was serving as an ordinary seaman. During the cruise we had no opportunity of seeing each other, though our two ships were in company on several occasions. One of such meetings was at Lough Swilly an inlet on the north coast of County Donegal in Northern Ireland. Lough Swilly has a very broad entrance of about four miles and provided a fine anchorage for the ships assembled there at the time. As we were to stay here for a day or two, I had reasonable hopes of paying my brother a call on board his ship. I was most disappointed however, for bad weather prevailed during our stay there, and in consequence there was scarcely any communication between the ships by boat.

About a week after we had left Lough Swilly, I received a telegram from my mother and can you imagine my dismay when I read that telegram saying that she had been officially notified that my poor brother Albert had met with an accident suffering severe injuries to the head and was dangerously ill. Further news stated that my brother had been landed at Lough Swilly and was receiving surgical treatment in a nursing home at Rathmullen. This accident occurred when my brother was being hoisted in a sailing pinnace. As the boat was leaving the water, a large hook secured to the after end of the wire rope sling straightened and struck my brother's face with a heavy blow as the stern of the pinnace fell back into the sea. He was rendered unconscious immediately and received terrible cuts to his face, the marks of which he bears to this day. However, I was very glad to hear before we left England that Albert was receiving excellent attention by kindly people at Rathmullen, and was on the road to recovery.

The *Powerful* having thus completed its shake up during the Home Fleet manoeuvres, left Portsmouth and proceeded to China. The ship was too large to pass through the Suez Canal in those days, so we were ordered to take the route via the Cape of Good Hope. During the passage down the English Channel, preparations were made for a full power steam trial which commenced off the Eddystone Lighthouse and was completed before we arrived at Gibraltar. In an ordinary cruiser, this operation should mainly affect the Engineer's branch, but owing to the new type of boilers, the whole of the ship's company was involved. The fuel consumption was so great that while the stokers were going with all their might to keep the furnaces going at forced draught, a large number of seamen were employed trimming the coal from the bunkers to the stokehold. Moreover, all ashes were got up on deck by the seamen and dumped, over the ships side. (Ejectors were fitted later in ships to discharge the ashes directly through ships side.) This work alone called for the continuous effort of a large party of men. These activities necessitated the organization of the ships' company into two reliefs to carry on throughout the trial. Thus, some six hundred men of a total ships company numbering about 850 were virtually employed under the direction of the Engineer Officer in Charge, while only a comparatively few seamen were available for fighting with the ships' armament. Truly, therefore, the *Powerful* could not possibly fight effectively whilst steaming at utmost speed! The maximum speed obtained at these trials as about 22.8 knots, a wonderful achievement in those days, but at what a cost! The expenditure of coal over a distance of 1,000 miles was well over 2,000 tons!

I Join The Royal Navy

In a newly built ship it is not surprising that mishaps occurred and unforeseen trouble happened during steam trials and the *Powerful* proved no exception to this rule. Among those we experienced were defects to the bearings of the port propeller shaft mainly due to faulty lubrication. This defect gave a considerable amount of trouble during the major portion of our voyage to China. Further trouble was caused by the tremendous heat developed inside the three after funnel casings. These structures were built of steel plates coated with red lead and yellow paint, which caught fire. The top of the ash shoots were situated within these casings, and the work of raising the ash buckets had to be suspended. Consequently, the ashes accumulated on the stokehold plates, which should have been kept clear for the coal loading from the bunkers. Meanwhile, salt water fire hoses were brought to bear upon the fires, which were eventually put out.

While this was going on, I was working with another seaman and a stoker in a middle coal bunker when both the inlet and egress became choked with coal. There we remained imprisoned for an anxious time working and sweating till we were able to enter the bunker adjacent to one of the after furnaces. From there we managed to reach the stokehold only to find the firemen on the furnaces in the act of sending up one of their colleagues in the ash bucket to the upper deck. The poor fellow had collapsed under the strain of work in the stifling heat as the ventilating fans had become defective. The normal way of going on deck by the iron ladders leading up through the funnel casing was impossible owing to the tremendous and asphyxiating fumes; it was therefore necessary for men, on being relieved, to walk to the foremost stokehold and ascend the ladders there.

I have dilated perhaps unduly upon this subject of steam trials in a warship which is ordinarily considered a common event that takes place periodically in every steam ship. I will endeavour to qualify this with the definite statement that after many experiences of steam trials in various classes of ships in the Royal Navy, it is my considered opinion that those carried out in the *Powerful* during her first three years in commission constituted the most hellish infernos imaginable, while the stokers of the ship were loyal and tough in every sense of the word.

On arrival at Gibraltar, not surprisingly, the first thing done was "coal ship". Never before when serving in ships fitted with marine boilers with their modest consumption of coal had anybody dreamed of such excessive expenditure of fuel in such a short time and space. Here we were after little more than two days passage from England, where the coal bunkers were full to capacity of about 5,400 tons, actually short of fuel to the tune of some 2,000 tons! From the point of view of the national economy alone, the use of water tube boilers demanded serious consideration in relation to the construction of future warships, and the maintenance of stocks of fuel at Naval Bases overseas.

After a short stay at Gibraltar, we proceeded to Las Palmas a port in the Canary Islands. As this was also an important coaling station and we embarked coal once again to full capacity. Since our departure from Gibraltar, we steamed at economic speed and consequently the consumption of fuel was very much less. On approaching the equator, the ancient ceremony of entering the Domain of His Majesty King Neptune was commenced. It was estimated that the ship would cross the line about 10 a.m. on a certain day, and during the dog watches of the previous evening Her Britannic Majesty's Ship *Powerful* was hailed by Neptune himself, who appeared over the forecastle head and intimated that it was his intention to come on board at that time. Accordingly, at the prescribed time the ship was hailed again and the Captain stopped the ship while His Majesty accompanied by his Queen and retinue came on board. A large canvas bath filled with salt water, together with a wooden stage and shaving paraphernalia ready for the use of Neptune's Barber and Bears had been provided ready for the fun to commence. The ritual connected with the initiation of all those who had not previously crossed the line commenced with great gusto and continued until every individual, officers or men, including myself, had been through the ordeal. There is no doubt that the Barbers and Bears carried out their duties most rigorously and in the good old-fashioned way. Personally, I felt very fortunate to get away with my eyes filled with soap and my stomach full to capacity with salt water! The ceremony duly over, Neptune and his Queen departed after exchange of greetings with the Captain of the *Powerful* in a most eloquent and breezy manner.

I have crossed the equator many times since and on each occasion it has been interesting to recall the fact that the *Powerful* in 1897 was the first British Warship in which prime English fresh beef originally supplied by the Royal Clarence Victualling Depot, Gosport was issued as a ration for our dinner on that day. The *Powerful* was equipped with an experimental refrigerating plant and the beef issued on this occasion had been kept in cold storage from the day it was embarked at Portsmouth. It must not be supposed however, that we carried a stock of sufficient meat in the refrigerator to issue it daily until we reached the Equator. In all other ships the quantity of fresh meat carried on board, except livestock, seldom held out for more than three or four days at sea. Though the capacity of our refrigerator was adequate only for a very limited number of days meat ration, it is gratifying to know that this was the forerunner of all the cold storages now installed on a larger scale in ships of later years, not only in regard to meat but vegetables and other items of food which, otherwise, would not be carried onboard.

Stealing southward we made short calls at the Islands of Ascension and St Helena and from the latter port we proceeded to Simonstown, the Naval Base at the Cape of Good Hope. Here we anchored in Simons Bay and embarked about 2,500 tons of coal. This would have taken a considerable time to board from a collier, but since none was available, the ships company was required to fill 40 ton lighters from the dump on shore and tow with our boats to out to the ship. This work was carried out entirely by the ships' company, and as the number of lighters was limited, it proved a long and tedious task. Working from 5 a.m. till 8 p.m. throughout the day and in two watches during the night this tiresome business continued for more than three days. Then "Clean Ship" was the order for the next day. Obviously, coal dust was everywhere it not only covered every part of the upper deck and mess deck, but penetrated our kit bags and hammocks, and by the time all clothing and bedding had been washed and the ship tolerably cleaned again, practically a whole week had been occupied in relation to this coaling operation. It was a sharp comparison with ships of modern times, where all that is necessary is for an Oil Fuel ship to come alongside, requiring the attention of a handful of seamen to merely connect up a number of hoses to the oil pipes and attend the valves required while any quantity of oil-fuel may be pumped into the ships oil tanks without even the knowledge of the rest of the ships company! Truly the modern naval man has incomparably less manual work to perform than his forebears!

Our stay in Simonstown was only of short duration, but before leaving I was able to spend a day ashore and visit Cape Town. At that time there were still echoes of the Jameson Raid; that misguided *coup d'etat* attempted by Sir Leander Starr Jameson and his followers less than two years before. On December 29th 1895 Dr Jameson, Prime Minister of Cape Colony, led about six hundred men to attack the Dutch and were defeated on January 1st 1896. This was as it may be, but the German Emperor thought fit to send a telegram of congratulations to the President Kruger of the Transvaal which was rightly considered by the British nation an unfriendly act. President Kruger handed over Jameson and the other prisoners to our Commissioner Sir Hercules Robinson.

I Join The Royal Navy

They were later tried and sentenced to imprisonment. It was said that Cecil Rhodes supported Jameson in this rising against the Transvaal Government, and in consequence, he resigned the position of Premier of the Cape Colony in 1890. Little did we then realise that, before our ship paid off, we were to be seriously implicated in a re-echo of this quarrel between president Kruger and Uitlanders of the Rand, over those rich gold mines in Johannesburg.

Leaving Simonstown, we proceeded to Port Elizabeth and East London in Cape Colony thence to the port of Durban in Natal. The passage around the Cape of Good Hope was not a pleasant one. Tremendous seas were running at the time, which fully tested the sea keeping qualities of the ship. Rolling and pitching heavily we soon became aware of the fact that eight of our twelve 6-inch guns, which were mounted in casemates each side of the messdeck, would be utterly useless when fighting in action against an enemy in bad weather. These guns constituted two thirds of the ships' secondary armament and were normally dismounted and secured on chocks so that the casemate ports could be closed. When the guns were counted for firing the ports were of course opened, but we dared not open them in heavy seas for fear of flooding the ship.

These facts were to become well known from our experience in 1907, yet many warships with similar armament fittings were built some years later including HMS *Good Hope* and HMS *Monmouth*. These two cruisers were sunk in action off Coronel in the Eastern Pacific by the German cruisers *Sharnhorst* and *Gneisenau* on 1st November 1914. Though the displacement of both German ships was less than that of the British cruisers, their guns could be fought in heavy seas because they were mounted on the upper deck.

Owing to bad weather our stay at Port Elizabeth and East London was brief. The heavy seas coming in to the anchorage and prevented communication with the shore by our boats. Tugs were sent to the ship with provisions carried in huge baskets which were hoisted between the tug and the ship. Our next port of call was Durban, the largest port on the East coast of Africa, which owes its importance as the commercial centre of Natal to the coal fields nearby. All was peace in this beautiful place at the time, which was by no means the case when the *Powerful* was to call there on our homeward bound voyage from China some 2 years later.

From Durban we sailed for Ile de France in the Indian Ocean. This island of course was renamed Mauritius when it was made a British crown colony by a treaty with the French early in the nineteenth century. Here we anchored about 4 miles from the port of St Louis and embarked coal one again. As at Simonstown, the method of coaling ship was by means of small lighters, but on this occasion the native Creoles filled the lighters and a large number of them were employed to put it on board, while the ships' company filled and trimmed the coal bunkers. This arrangement was quite satisfactory and somewhat cheering to us until the natives became sea sick whilst tossing about in the heavy swell alongside the ship. There was no alternative but to get them all on board and let them lie down and sleep on the forecastle while the British bluejacket, unhappily, did the work assigned to the less capable Creoles! To be just to these poor puny natives, one must mention that the weather was atrocious with a very heavy swell rendering the filling of baskets and passing the coal up the ships side to the upper deck extremely difficult.

In the circumstances there was little opportunity to go on shore at Mauritius and we were all glad to be on our way to Singapore. After about four days out from Mauritius however, a serious defect occurred to the bearing of the port propeller shaft and we were compelled to steam with the starboard engine only. At the time, the nearest British possession was Ceylon so the ships' course was altered to Columbo where we arrived without the aid of the port engine. Repairs to the defective bearings of the propeller shaft were taken in hand immediately and meanwhile another coal ship was got over and 24 hours leave was given to each watch.

This was my first experience of life 'Out East' and I was much impressed. Incidentally, I was destined to see much more of it when I was to have charge of an important Armament Department in India and Ceylon some thirty years later.

Repairs having been duly made we sailed once more for Singapore. The Fleet Engineer was the most anxious man on board from the moment the Port Engine was again brought into use and for some reason, best known to himself, he had obtained a large quantity of Castor Oil to be specially used for lubrication of the repaired shaft bearings. From observations made by the seaman branch, the ship seemed to be going well and our progress was quite good, but a day or two later it was noted that the Engine Room staff were not so happy about the way things were turning out. The Senior Engineer too, was much perturbed about the frequent requests he was receiving from his men to come up from below for purely personal reasons. Upon investigation it was discovered that the cause of this strange behaviour was the Castor Oil! The handling and inhaling of this lubricant alone was apparently sufficient cause for the distressing effect on the men concerned.

However, we arrived at Singapore in due time, replenished bunkers and proceeded to Hong Kong a couple of days later. We therefore had little opportunity of becoming acquainted with this great British possession with its Malays, Chinese and altogether cosmopolitan inhabitants, though one could appreciate its splendid harbour.

We next entered the South China Sea and made a fine passage to Hong Kong in about four days. On arrival, we embarked more coal of course and replenished the ship with other stores to full capacity. Hong Kong then was the Principal Naval Base on the China Station, which, extended from Singapore to the North West Pacific Ocean, a vast expanse embracing all climates. The *Powerful* moored in the harbour, one of the finest in the world, and as we had become a unit of the British Naval Force in China, under the Admiral Commander-in-Chief, it was up to every officer and man to smarten the ship up to become efficient for any operation that might become necessary. Although the work with these preparations was strenuous, personally I found my duties most interesting. At action stations I was the breech worker of a 6-inch gun and I pulled a bow oar in the starboard sea-boat; a twelve oared cutter. As in the *Active*, I belonged to the fore-topmen's part of the ship. Though sail, except in the boats, was not used. In fact, one could write finished from now on as regards to sailing ships.

Nevertheless, we carried out multifarious drills and ship exercises which provided great fun and fostered the competitive spirit throughout the ship. In all these activities I found once again that the advice and instruction which I had received from my father proved valuable to me. I was imbued with ambition and eagerness to carry out my duties and, at the same time, endeavoured to steer clear of the many pitfalls which beset young seamen of my age. Acting upon my father's advice, it was well to keep a good look-out during important work or drills and contrive to do a little more than one's normal part, and on no account to join the men who fade away from tedious or important duty, leaving someone else to finish. This may appear to touch upon trivial matters of little consequence, but from long years of experience in the Service I have found that this is not so.

I JOIN THE ROYAL NAVY

CHAPTER X

The Powerful Joins the British Naval Force in China

--- ooOoo ---

We stayed a few weeks in Hong Kong and regular leave was given by watches when the day's work was over. Those who did not wish to land could generally find something to do, if only to wash or mend their clothes. Usually on Saturday evenings, when the ship would be all polished up ready for Sunday's inspection by the Captain, the ship's band would come on deck after playing for the Officers at Dinner; and the Boatswains Mate would pipe "Handy to Dance and Skylark". I am of the opinion that this old custom was one of the best recreations available to seamen in ships abroad. The band would play waltzes, polkas, lancers etc., while the sailors danced in pairs. It was grand fun and obviously one of the reasons why the average sailor in those days excelled in this art and required no tuition on shore. It was in the *Powerful* at this time that I became thoroughly acquainted with the various steps also with the sequences of square dances, which were in vogue in those Victorian days. Jazz music was, of course, unheard of and personally I am not very sorry about that! It may here be mentioned that all dancing on board among the seamen was performed with bare feet!

The general canteen service as known today in the Navy, did not exist though during the voyage from England to China a ship's canteen was instituted and from the limited supply available we managed to get along tolerably well. It was the general rule for all ships on the China station to engage the services of Chinese business men, who would undertake to supply certain foods and other necessities not included in official rationing or recognized as a Naval supply.

A Chinese named Attam and another Tom Sing were the two principal canteen proprietors at the time of our arrival in Hong Kong and it was not surprising that these two amiable gentlemen were among the first visitors to the ship. Both Attam and his rival offered their services to manage the ship's canteen and each claimed priority for the job in various ways. From enquiries, it was understood that both these men had good reputations from other ships in the station, so there was some difficulty as to making a final decision in the matter. Consequently, the Captain addressed both Attam and Tom Sing, telling them that both their claims were evidently of equal weight and like the great sportsman he was, produced a brand-new Hong Kong dollar and suggested that they should toss up for it and the winner would be given the canteen contract. With the gambling instinct characteristic of their race both competitors joyfully accepted, and within one minute the coin was tossed and had fallen on the quarter deck! Attam had won! To appreciate the dimensions of this gamble, it should be realized that a huge annual profit was involved. The contract was to provide more than eight hundred men with vegetables, fruit, tinned milk, butter and groceries of various kinds including perhaps, half a million eggs, over a period of well over two years. I have little knowledge as to what this meant in actual profit, but one may be sure that the average Western business man would not have agreed to this method of determining the contract. Truly, it is not far wrong to say that as a people generally the Chinese have no equal in the fascinating game of chance.

In Hong Kong, as in most parts of China, a large portion of the population lived afloat in junks and sampans. To me, it was an interesting question as to how the occupants of some thousands of comparatively small sampans really existed. I had heard when in Malta that the Maltese would somehow earn a living where an Englishman would starve, for in those days, the former survived on a scale very much below our bread line. But when one considered the mode of living displayed by the floating populations of China, one may be fairly correct to assume the same comparison between the Celestials and the Maltese. I have seen no less than a dozen of these unfortunate creatures crammed on board a sampan with scarcely elbow room in which to live.

Their existence appeared to be derived from the offal rescued from the seawater after it had been tipped down the chutes on the side of the ships. Scraps of meat bones, vegetables and any refuse they would scramble for. All was fish that came to their net. The fathers of the family propelled the sampan with oars, and the mothers manipulated the steering oars and directed the salvage operations while the children scrambled for the booty, as a rush of several sanpans was made on each successive splash from the chutes. Tiny babies would be in the scramble too, for the little mites were usually strapped tightly to the backs of the mothers and their elder sisters and assumed a bearing of blissful nonchalance while their little noses were flattened against the backs of their elders at frequent intervals.

In striking contrast to these pitiful scenes, one could see on shore members of the Chinese aristocracy, who wore the nails of their fingers some three inches long to indicate that they were living in the lap of luxury and never stooped to manual work!! The Manchu pigtails were quite the vogue at the time of which I am writing, while the Chinese women commonly bound their feet and subjected their daughters to this form of torture.

By the time we had become familiar with Chinese waters and had worked the ship's company up to a state of efficiency we had come to early 1898, a year of much Naval activity in the far east. Japan had not then become a great Naval Power and although America, Britain, France and Germany maintained their China Squadrons, the naval strength of any of these countries was considerably inferior to that of Britain.

Japan however was a rising power and her aggressive policy regarding China was being closely watched by America and the European countries. Only three years before this time the Sino-Japanese War had been fought (1894-6). Brought about by Japanese ambitions regarding Korea, it ended in amazing defeat of China on the sea as well as on the land. It seemed incredible that a comparatively small nation such as Japan should have so easily destroyed the Chinese fleet and armies, and naturally this was followed by ambitious demands by the victor which was formulated in the Treaty of Shimonosiki in 1895. In this treaty, Japan demanded the independence of Korea, the cession of the Liau-tung Peninsula, Formosa and the Pescadore Islands and in addition, a money indemnity of 200 million taels! By the intervention of Russia, France and Germany however, the cession of the Liau-tung Peninsula was denied Japan and thus she was debarred a foothold on the mainland of China, which was a determined aim. Japan's humiliation was further accentuated by the fact that her demand for the money payment was whittled down to 50 million taels by the machinations of Russia.

Following this a perfect scramble was commenced by the European Powers for concessions in China. Russia, France and Germany - joined by Britain this time - very obligingly helped poor China to pay her war indemnity to Japan and for so doing China repaid them handsomely. Russia

I Join The Royal Navy

obtained valuable rights regarding the railways, mines, ports and territory in Manchuria, also in the Liau-tung Peninsula which Japan had been denied. Russian control in Manchuria was therefore almost complete. Germany secured control in the Shantung Province by the lease of Kiatschow Bay with the right to build a Shantung railway. This incidentally gave the Naval Base of Tsingtao to Germany in 1898. France obtained the right to construct the Yunnan Railway, the lease of Canton Bay, and other material advantages which enhanced her sphere of influence. As a quid pro quo Britain secured her portion of the share out in the form of a lease of Wei-hai-wei, an increase in the area of our colony in Hong Kong and Kowloon, and a valuable agreement regarding the supervision of the Inspectorate-general of maritime customs.

In those days Li Hung-Chang a leading statesman of China wielded considerable influence and in 1896 only a year after the Shimonoseki Treaty, he had made a secret treaty with Russia, in which Russia secured a sphere of influence extending from Manchuria across the Yalu River into Korea. This embraced the important ice-free ports of Port Arthur, and Chemulpo in the Yellow Sea. The position therefore early in 1898, was that China was fast losing her sovereignty, and the life blood of the Chinese was flowing to enrich foreigners, who themselves were suspicious of each other in the rush for extra territorial rights, as these concessions wrung from China were called. Extra-territorially of course gave the foreigners immunity from the jurisdiction of Chinese Laws, and foreign warships, in the harbours concerned remained part of the country whose flag was flown.

Poor China was truly considered legitimate prey by many countries in those days. It may further be noted that the American annexation of Hawaii had only recently been affected and Japan had protested against this in 1897. In these circumstances, it will be agreed that there was sufficient inflammatory material on the China Station to endanger war between any of the European countries mentioned above despite their agreements not to encroach on the sphere of each other.

The British Fleet at the time was not a powerful one and consisted of one second class battleship the *Centurian* (Flagship of Admiral Buller) and the following:

Battleship First Class:
    Immortalate
    Undaunted
    Narcissus

Small Cruiser
    Bonaventure
    Iphegenia

Gun Boat
    Pigmy
    Plover
    Linnet

Sloop
    Algerine
    Phoenix

Torpedo Boat Destroyers
    Handy
    Hardy
    Whiting
    Fame

Admiral's Yacht
    Alacrity.

It is not surprising then that the British Government thought it desirable to strengthen their force by sending out the *Powerful*. Later one of our finest battleships joined us, the *Victorious* whose armament consisted of 12-inch and 6-inch B.L. guns.

It was the custom for all British warships on the China Station to be painted white, but owing to the huge dimensions of the *Powerful* the Admiral Buller approved of the proposal that the *Powerful* should remain painted black. So, we were accepted as the black elephant of the fleet. This of course was mainly in the interest of economy, for the difference in the cost of keeping the ship's sides spotless white as the other ships were, and a respectably looking black, would amount to a considerable sum on the annual expenditure for this service. It was generally thought however, that ships painted white were much the cooler between decks in the tropical climates, and that they presented a less distinct target against enemy gun fire.

Soon after leaving Hong Kong, we visited Chefoo a treaty port in the Shantung Province about one hundred miles west of Wei-hai-wei. Here we anchored some four miles from the settlement, and leave to go on shore was allowed to officers only. The reader of course, will not confuse the Treaty Ports in China with such places as Hong Kong which is a British Colony. There were quite a number of Treaty Ports in China at the time of which I am writing. They have been designated as ports where foreign merchants are permitted to settle and carry on their business by treaties entered into by Britain and other Foreign Powers on the one part and China on the other.

For more than one hundred years this arrangement with China has existed. The first of them was the Nanking Treaty signed at that city in 1842. By this transaction the cities of Amoy, Canton, Foochow, Ningpo and Shanghai became Treaty ports. Nanking itself however, did not become a Treaty Port until May 1899 when we were on the China Station. The institution of these open ports in China was mainly due to so many outrages committed upon subjects of European countries.

It was at Chefoo that we first met a new Russian cruiser named *Rossia*. This vessel was enormous, with four funnels, well armed and equipped, and resembled the *Powerful* in many respects. She had been much discussed in our ship and naturally we were all very interested to learn more about her armament speed and fighting powers generally. It was said that the *Rossia* was designed and built as an offset to the *Powerful* and rumour had it that both ships were under orders to keep within close proximity of each other in case of certain eventualities. This rumour seemed to be confirmed for some considerable period when both snips turned up together in several other ports after we left Chefoo. I recall on one of these meetings at Chemulpo in Korea, when the *Powerful* and *Rossia* were in a state of preparedness for immediate action. Outwardly, of course, no ill will was shown by either ships company, but rather courtesy and pleasantness existed on the part of each other. For instance, Captains would exchange courtesy calls between warships of two friendly countries as usual, and I well remember the *Rossia* manning ship on the occasion of departure to give us hearty cheers, which were vociferously returned by the ship's company of the *Powerful*. It seemed that Russian interests in these waters were so dominant at this juncture as to cause some uneasiness in the so-called balance of power in the Far East, and this was one of the reasons why the British Government negotiated the lease of Wei-hai-Wei.

Although as I have indicated, very friendly relations existed between the personnel of the two most powerful cruisers on the China Station, an element of cockiness was apparent at times on the part of our sporting captain. I remember an instance of this one day when I was a member of the picquet boats' crew. We had come into harbour one night, and found our mutual friend the *Rossia* there, and on the following day the Captain paid a call on board the Russian cruiser. Before

I Join The Royal Navy

embarking in our boat, the Captain instructed the Petty Officer coxswain not to ease speed when going alongside the gangway of the *Rossia*, but to maintain full speed till the bows of the boat was in line with the gangway, and then put the engines full speed astern. This was, of course, nothing but a stunt calculated to alarm the Russians and to impress them of our prowess in the management of a steam boat! If the reader will visualise a fast steam boat 52 feet in length going at utmost speed alongside a ship and then suddenly brought up in this manner, the risk of danger will be realised at once; both to the boat itself and to the engines. However, luck was on our side while the Russian Officers and men stood aghast as we rushed up alongside. I ventured to advance some remark of admiration for his fine work. It was very clear however, that the praise was not appreciated for he immediately spat out the reply: "You are all bloody lunatics on deck!!"

While in Northern waters we crossed Tsu-shima Straits and visited Nagasaki in Japan. Nagasaki was a seaport of considerable importance even in those days, and one was struck with its fine harbour about three miles from the open sea. It is situated on the South West extremity of the islands which make up Japan, and up to 1859, less than forty years before our arrival, it was the only Japanese port open to Europeans.

Our stay here was very pleasant. The Japanese appeared to be little different from the Chinese - save that they were a people of smaller stature without pigtails. Civilian clothes commonly worn today in Japan were almost entirely absent in the streets of Nagasaki. Relations generally between ourselves and the Japanese were quite cordial at this time, and in consequence the ship's company was given leave of absence from the ship for appreciable periods. The men of each watch were permitted to remain on shore for twenty-four hours, subject to recall of course. During my leave here I spent the whole time with a messmate by the name of John Cobby, whose friendship I valued immensely (and of whom I shall again refer to later). For the most part we got around the various interesting places by jinrikishas, and when night came, we returned to the ship by about 10 p.m.

We had not been in Nagasaki for more than a day or two, when to our surprise and keen interest the Russian cruiser *Rossia* entered the harbour. This gave rise to some sensational talk among the ships company and seemed to confirm the rumour about this ship of which I have already mentioned. However, nothing untoward happened and our stay at Nagasaki was most pleasant. As we left Nagasaki one could not but admire the fine natural harbour of this important seaport of Japan, which today lies in ruins from the devastation recently caused by that awful instrument of war - the Atomic Bomb.

From Nagasaki we proceeded to Yokohama, the chief port of Japan situated on the main island of Honshu. A magnificent seaport standing on Tokio Bay less than twenty miles from the capital city of Tokio itself. It will be remembered that later both these principal cities of Japan were almost destroyed by a terrible earthquake on September 1st 1923, but they have since been rebuilt. Here again we enjoyed a considerable amount of leave.

Soon after our arrival at Yokohama, the Japanese seemed to know and understand the primary need of the British Bluejacket when he came in from sea; for several sampans came alongside the ship and began, to cook delicious meals, which they sold to us for very moderate charge. For the sum of 1/4 yen which was then equal to sixpence in British currency, we could buy an appetising plate of piping hot lamb or pork chops with fried potatoes, or a most liberal quantity of fried bacon and eggs. Although Yokohama possessed a fine harbour, buildings in the port itself were not imposing, as the private houses and shops were constructed mainly from the bamboo tree. (No wonder there was so much destruction by fire as a result of the earthquake in March, 1930, however, less than seven years later the city was completely reconstructed on anti-earthquake lines, and celebrations were held there to commemorate the event).

As at Nagasaki I spent my leave on shore in Yokohama with my friend Cobby. Here again we found the Japanese people very amiable and our jinrikisha rides were numerous and pleasant as we visited various places of interest. It was here at Yokohama that I first appreciated the supreme work of that good and Christian organization the Salvation Army, which had extended to some of the foreign ports in the Far East. As a man who has travelled and seen many parts of the world, I have a profound admiration for General William Booth and the great religious and philanthropic organisation founded by him in London in the year I was born (1877). Regardless of race colour or creed, the Salvation Army has done splendid work among the poor and unfortunate at home and abroad. Its activities are widely varied such as: the Mothers House at Clapton, London; relieving the poor at Tokio in Japan; and the establishment of a Leper Colony in Sumatra, one of the Dutch East Indian Islands.

It seemed all very well for Her Majesty's Ships to give extended leave in such ports, which could involve three successive nights ashore, but where were the men with strictly limited means to go for accommodation at night? As a young man of twenty years of age, and landed here in Yokohama with some four hundred of the *Powerful's* ships company, to say nothing of seamen from other ships; there appeared to me to be absolutely nowhere to go for meals and accommodation in decency, except that wonderful institution the Salvation Army Home.

The Home at Yokohama was extremely well kept, the service was excellent, and altogether it was a wholesome place to live in, while the tariff was reasonable and quite within the limited means of an ordinary British bluejacket. However, the sleeping accommodation of this inestimable place was strictly limited, and only a relative few of the men on leave could stay there for the night. True there were rooms in hotels and questionable haunts of sorts, but accommodation in the former was the reserve for the ship's Officers and accordingly banned for the men. If the ships chaplain's showed indifference, and in my opinion, lack of duty in this regard, the commanding officers did at least help in a way, by providing a late boat each night at about 10.30 p.m. to bring off any men to the ship. Though it was well known that all too few availed themselves of it. The difficulty here, of course, was that perhaps a comparatively large number of the men at liberty had imbibed too much by that time, so inclination to voluntarily return to the rigours of naval discipline would not be strong.

During our leave period Cobby and I visited Tokio. The train journey was pleasant through the lovely countryside. Rice plantations and green pastures greatly adding to the beauty all round. This capital of the Japanese Empire occupies both banks of the River Sumida and among the places we visited was the Nyeno Park with its beautiful flowers. In this Park are the Zoological Gardens and the Imperial Museum. Nearby we visited the Buddhist Temple having first to divest ourselves of our boots and put on white galoshes before we were permitted to enter. The Buddhism of Japan, we were told, was really a combination of true Buddhism and Shintoism and the bibles of each religion were used in the Temple. Shintoism, of course, is the National Religion of Japan.

While in Tokio we also saw the manufacture of ornamental tables, chairs and other articles of furniture. After the woodwork had been completed each article was exquisitely decorated with hand paintings of interesting designs and beautifully lacquered. Owing to the ready assistance of my jinrikisha man I was able to purchase an occasional table, which had been finished while we waited, with a lovely golden delineation on a black background. The Japanese from whom I bought the table impressed upon me that the method used by him for coating the articles of furniture was the genuinely famous lacquering of Japan; not the so-called Japanning which was merely an imitation of his process. The table was made to dismantle easily and was packed in a handsomely decorated wooden case, where it remained undisturbed for some two years, then became the property of my mother at home.

My helpful guide the jinrikisha man seemed equally as pleased about my acquisition of the table as I was, and then took us to a place where Japanese chinaware was on sale. Here was veritably the finest collection of moderately priced tea-sets and dinner sets that I have ever seen. The chinaware was of transparent beauty and excellence with lovely shades of coloured artistry on each piece. I possessed no real knowledge of this ware, but was so fascinated with the display that I spent nearly all the money I had at the time in the pockets of my cholera belt, a wide thick belt of flannel, which was included in a bluejackets uniform kit, for the purchase of one of the tea sets consisting of forty-two pieces of chinaware Each piece was exquisitely shaped, and finished and the twelve cups and saucers were similar to beautiful transparent shells of pearl grey hand painted with sprays of cherry blossom and wisteria. This tea set was most efficiently packed and was carefully stored on board the ship, together with the occasional table, and shortly after my arrival home, it was presented to my sister Edith on the occasion of her marriage.

We left Yokohama and again called at Chemulpo, where we met our foreign contemporary the *Rossia* once again. Memories of that beautiful land of Nippon, with as I then thought, the amiable, laughing and kind-hearted Japanese people amidst the wealth of flowers and flowery trees calls to one's mind the following Imperial Rescript, said to be that of the Emperor Jimmu who ascended the throne in the year 660 B.C., "We shall build our capital all over the world and make the whole world our dominion".

In Japan one was told that the people of Japan were divine people and that their Emperor was the divine Emperor, the first of whom Jimmu called Tenshi by Japanese (Son of Heaven) or Tenno (Heavenly King) was the deity. Japanese claim that subsequent Emperor's trace descent from him through an unbroken line, though seven of the Mikados have been women. The present Emperor Hiroshito (born 1901) succeeded to the throne in 1926.

For centuries Japan followed a policy of national isolation. It would appear that the 'Jumper' or Jimrru's Rescript lay dormant for about 2,500 years, when in 1859, Japan sent her Ministers to foreign countries and the country was opened to foreign trade and residence. After 1871, when the feudal system was suppressed, that Japan resolved to model her national life similar to that in Europe. Some Twenty-three years later she cumulatively waged war, beginning with the Sino-Japanese war and steadily annexed foreign territory, by conquest. From that date, Japan has steadily progressed and for many years she has been one of the great powers.

Then the militarists took charge of the Government and Japan invaded China and joined the Rome-Berlin Axis in 1937. By October 1938 all the important cities of China were in Japanese hands. Continuing until 1944, she conquered and occupied an enormous Far Eastern Empire. Then, like a thunderbolt, the Atomic Bomb wrote FINISH to her abominable aggressive designs.

Thus, it seems that though the first 120 rulers of Japan had done nothing to forfeit the confidence of the people in the world's oldest dynasty, maintaining a peaceful and honourable past - the last four Emperors emulated the example of the self-serving monarchs and rulers of Europe, which ultimately confounded them, and brought their country to utter disaster. It will indeed be interesting to see where Japan will go from here. Hiroshito is the 124th of his line.

Not long after we had joined the China Station news came that the United States Ship *Maine* had been blown up in Havana Harbour on February 15th 1898, with the loss of two hundred and fifty officers and men. This incident, it will be remembered, led to war between the U.S.A and Spain. Reverberations of this were already being felt in the Far East. Admiral Dewey in his Flag Ship U.S.S. *Olympia* and four other ships in his Squadron hastened to the Philippine Islands and on May 1st 1898, he destroyed the Spanish Naval Force under Admiral Montojo in Manila Bay. During this action the British cruiser *Imortalite*, commanded by Captain Chichester, was present at Manila but due to leave the China Station so we in the *Powerful* were also sent there to protect British interests in the Philippines. In addition to, the British and U.S. ships of war, a small German squadron came to Manila to represent German interests. Prince Henry of Prussia, a brother of Kaiser Wilhelm, was in command and his flagship was the *Deutchland* and the German cruiser *Kaiserin Augusta* was also in his force.

Our stay in Manila was for several weeks, and when the Spanish Naval Force had been disposed of, and the shore batteries silenced by Admiral Dewey's Squadron, then put out of action by bombardment from the U.S. naval guns; the coast was cleared for landing American troops to occupy the city and surroundings. Trouble commenced between the Americans and the Philippines under their leader Emilio Aguinaldo a native patriot who headed the insurrection, but afterwards swore allegiance to the U.S.A..

Some considerable time was expended by the American troops in their difficult task of defeating these rebels, and assumed control under the first American Commandant Brigadier General MacArthur (the father of the present Supreme Commander of the Allied Pacific Forces). Thus, the Philippine Islands were captured by the U.S.A from Spain, having remained in Spanish possession since their discovery by Magellan in 1521.

We were yet to see much of Manilla for our second visit in the *Powerful* extended over a period of some three months. From observations while we were there, one gathered that reciprocal friendly relations existed between the American and the British Navies. There was no doubt that on occasions where any differences in opinion between the German and American Admirals as to methods of procedures, the British Commanders never failed to be on Admiral Dewey's side of the argument. On one occasion of dissent Prince Henry of Prussia sounded our Captain as to what course he would take in certain eventualities - the Captain of the *Powerful* replied, "Ask Dewey!"

From a recreational aspect during our comparatively long sojourn at Manila we spent rather a lean time. Officers only were given leave there, and the only intercourse with the Americans was an occasional visit from a few of their soldiers, who would come off to our ship in the afternoons. We found these troops very interesting, especially when listening to the description of their engagements against the Philippines. Boat pulling and sailing constituted our main recreations and occasional boat races which afforded a certain amount of fun.

For a few weeks I belonged to a party of divers who were sent from the ship each day to HMS *Plover* one of the two Gunboats which had joined us in Manila. Our job there was to clean the ship's bottom throughout its length. To enable this to be done, two chain lines were rove under the vessel about six feet apart and to these a wooden stage was secured so that the divers could sit on the stage comfortably whilst removing the accumulation of weed and barnacles from the hull. As Manila is well inside the Tropic of Cancer, it is naturally a very warm place in the summer and I well remember heaving round the crank handles of the Diving Pump necessary for the supply of air to both divers during this work, while the perspiration was teaming from my face and body. Naturally then, we did our best to complete the job as soon as possible, but the snag in this endeavour was in the fact that the divers, whilst actually under the cool waters and very comfortably situated only a few feet below the surface were being paid a special diving allowance for every hour so engaged. Therefore, the poor fellows struggling on the pump were entirely dependent upon the divers' pleasure to get on with the job who were subject to somewhat acrimonious criticism as to the speed of their work. Of course there was nothing to do about it but heave round, and for one's sins, obey occasional signals from the divers for More Air!

However, the climax came one day when one of the two divers had inadvertently omitted to secure his scrubbing brush beside him and obviously it floated up to the surface on the end of its small securing line. There it remained like the buoy that watches over an anchor, to the delight of us all in the diving boat while the diver stuck it out for an unconsciously long time. Then the signal to ascend was given to the diver on his breast rope, and up he came to the diving ladder. In due course his helmet was removed and amid the uproarious rapture of all present the diver exclaimed, "My word! That was a hard patch to clean!"

One has often heard it said that 'it is a small world' and I am sure that you will agree when I relate the following coincident. One morning at Manila, I was standing on the forecastle of the *Powerful* talking to a few friends, when someone drew attention to a fine four-masted steamer approaching our anchorage from seaward. Curiously enough I became instinctively interested in this ship and felt that at sometime and at somewhere I had seen her before. The steamer was steadily closing on the *Powerful* and dropped her anchor upon arriving a short distance from us. As she swung to anchor, her stern was so close to the *Powerful*, that it became necessary for her to weigh again and move to a berth so that both hips would be clear of each other as they swung by the wind or tide. Now as her stern swung towards us, I felt a thrill running through my whole body for there standing out as clear as crystal was the name of the ship painted in gold. It was the *Duke of Westminster* on which my brother Benjamin was serving.

My brother and I had very little opportunity of meeting for years prior to this. Indeed, since about ten years prior to this, when he first went to sea as an apprentice in a sailing ship named *Amoy*, I had met him on only a few occasions. The *Duke of Westminster* was on a voyage from Australia to England with a cargo of frozen meat, when her cruise was suddenly diverted to Manila as a food supply ship for the American Navy and Army. You may be sure that I lost no time in paying a call on my brother, who, of course, knew that I was on board the *Powerful* and was expecting me at any moment. Commander Ethelston was extremely kind and pleased to place a boat at my disposal, and accordingly I went on board the *'Duke* and received a most joyful welcome from Ben and his Officer associates. Incidentally, I enjoyed one of the best lunches of my life whilst on board and returned to my ship with much gratification. The *Duke of Westminster* remained in company with our ship till her cargo had been cleared and my brother was able to return my call, but alas, I regret to this day that I was totally unable to return his hospitality on board the *Powerful* being only a Junior Able seaman of a lower deck mess.

The *Duke of Westminster* not only brought me this very pleasant interlude, but by the good grace of Admiral Dewey, the whole ship's company of the *Powerful* enjoyed more than one meal partaken from her valuable cargo. Incidentally, the name given to the food was "Dewey Beef" and "Dewey Mutton"! This kindness of the American Admiral was greatly appreciated, for normally the British and other foreign ships at Manila were officially under Service rations, and no leave whatsoever was given to men of the lower deck, during the war period there.

The Philippine Islands have never been regarded as a health resort owing to its humid atmosphere, and terrific gales and typhoons experienced there; but these adversities were overcome by the European people living on shore in suitable dwellings and supplied with an abundance of vegetables, fruit and other suitable diet. These amenities however, were denied the bluejacket in the *Powerful* on the two occasions we spent at Manila, about five months in all. There we were, cooped up on the lower deck in the intolerable heat, while half the space on the upper deck was commandeered for the use of Chinese laundry men brought down from Hong Kong to wash the Officers clothes!

In such living conditions an epidemic of boils broke out among the men mainly due to a lack of vegetables and fruit, and to the extreme heat. I well remember having an attack of these painful things and suffering from an enormous brute in the calf of my right leg, the scar from which is still with me today. Tempers were ruffled and quarrels occurred between the men who saw so much of one another. Here I pitched in to a mess-mate in defence of my dear friend John Cobby and gave his tormentor a sound thrashing.

Before our final departure from the Philippines, the Officers of the *Powerful*, who were allowed leave daily throughout our stay there, decided to give an "At Home" on board to return the hospitality which they had received from the European Officials and others on shore at Manila. Accordingly, great preparations were made by the men, decorating the ship and in the provision of reserved accommodation for the guests when on the upper deck. The preparations for this social function occupied several days and special food was obtained for the occasion and nicely laid out upon the tables, by the Officer's stewards and servants, under the direction of the Fleet Paymaster.

The arrangements went on smoothly and satisfactorily, and the time had come to bring the guests off to the ship. The Picquet Boat, the Captains barge and the steam pinnacle, all the steam boats were ordered for this service and in perfect weather, with the sea as calm as a lake, the guests streamed up the accommodation ladders, and were received on board by the ships' officers amid the strains of melodies rendered by the full ships' band. The ship was anchored at considerable distance from the landing place on shore, therefore, an appreciable time was taken in the matter of transport.

Then a terrible thing happened! Before the last batch of visitors had arrived on board, the beautiful blue sky became black and threatening clouds appeared, while the wind sprang up almost as quickly as one can write about it. Suddenly a typhoon was upon us; a violent revolving cyclone not uncommon in the Philippines, but apparently centred on the middle of Manila harbour, and heavy seas came up, which rendered it impossible for further communication with the shore by boat. Thunderclaps with lightening and drenching rain followed, and it was feared that it would be necessary to weigh anchor and get the ship under way with the guests on board. As might be expected, everyone who remained on deck was drenched with water and some of the ladies' frocks were spoilt; whilst the ships decorations and the tea tables, so prettily laid out, were ruined by sheets of water which swamped the ship fore and aft. We felt so very sorry for the poor guests, especially the ladies who were so discomforted. Also, for our Pay master, who had worked for long hours over all his preparations, only to find that his efforts were rendered useless in so many minutes.

Happily, the typhoon subsided almost as suddenly as it came on, and the entertainment of the guests proceeded though it was confined to the Captain's quarters, wardroom and gunroom. These Officers Quarters were crowded with hosts and guests, eating and drinking and making merry to the tunes of music while we sailors were busily engaged clearing up the debris and improving the appearance of the upper deck once more. By the look of the guests when they departed from the ship that evening, one imagined that after all, they had really enjoyed their experiences of the day;

I Join The Royal Navy

perhaps a little more than if the original programme of peaceful entertainment had been carried out!

On the first passage from Hong Kong to Manila constituted an easy record in these days, the time taken was well within 48 hours, and the maximum speed attained was 22.8 knots. The coal consumption was of course enormous, but it was a fine achievement for so large a warship. On returning to Hong Kong from the Philippines, one may be sure that we were all very glad to have the opportunity of landing once more, especially to partake in a change of diet. On arrival the ships' company carried out rifle and revolver practice on the ranges at Kowloon and at Stonecutter Island, while the ship was docked for cleaning the vessels bottom. Incidentally, this dock was only just large enough to take a ship of the length of the *Powerful*. The usual night leave was given at Hong Kong by watches with the option of coming off to the ship about 10 p.m. It was customary to land about 4.30 p.m. and for the ordinary bluejacket there seemed little else to do but to take a jinrikisha drive out to Happy Valley, take a walk through the streets of the city whilst daylight lasted, and repair to the Naval Canteen when the men usually drank beer and played skittles until it was time to leave and catch the boat that had been sent from the ship.

Although the health of the ships company was fairly good at the time, it was here at Hong Kong that we had a visitation of that dread disease small-pox. This scourge was more or less prevalent amongst the Chinese of the city at certain times of the year. Naval patients suffering from small pox were accommodated on board a hulk named *Midge* which was moored in the harbour, well clear of the fairway for shipping. Accordingly, the case on board the *Powerful* was sent to the *Midge*. I remember the transport of this case very well for he was taken there in the duty cutter of which I was one of the crew. First, the boats crew were required to carry the man in his cot from the sick bay to the boat, and from the boat when alongside the *Midge* up the gangway to the sick quarters. A ships doctor, was in attendance and when we arrived back to our ship one assumed that the necessary fumigation and/or disinfection of the cot bedclothes and personal clothing of contacts whilst on board would be satisfactorily effected. Be that as it may, I knew for certain that not one of my boats crew comprising twelve able seamen and a petty officer coxswain, was required to do this; and that no facilities were made available for this important precaution against further infection.

I have purposely mentioned this case to indicate the indifference shown in those days as compared with the scrupulous precautions taken against all infectious diseases in British Warships of later days. These matters were left entirely to the ships' surgeon in those days, whereas the Captain and Officers generally have watched and guarded against such occurrences for many years since the time of which I am writing.

Boat pulling and sailing races among ships on the China Station were most favourite recreations, and whenever ships of the Squadron met, there would surely be interesting events to follow. These races of course would be entirely separate from those which made up the events of the Squadron Regatta which was held annually. In sailing ships, the inter-mast and inter-ship mast, sail and yard drills in my opinion afforded incomparably more interest and sport than any other event, though they could not be regarded in the true sense of recreation. In ships without sail however, I think that boat sailing and pulling races offers the greatest sport, as well as providing splendid recreation. Of the two, I put sailing races first. Both in the Mediterranean Fleet and the China Squadron, I have taken part in some magnificent boat races and incidentally, one has seen tremendous sums of money lost and won by the men of the Navy.

Frederick W Sweetingham

The first time we met the *Centurion* we almost immediately received a challenge from her to race our Captain's galley or gig against theirs within a few days. This, of course, was accepted and the event was fixed for about a week later. We knew nothing about the gig belonging to the *Centurion*, but in anticipation of such fixtures we had trained some fine crews in our boats. On the day following the challenge we kept a careful watch on the *Centurion*'s boat when it went for its practice run. Many stop watches were going and the distance over which it ran was carefully pricked off on the chart. Further observations were made during subsequent practice runs by the *Centurion*'s boat and by that means we had come to the conclusion, that the performance of our gig's crew was somewhat better than that of our rival. Despite this however, the crew of the *Centurion*'s gig pulled alongside the *Powerful* and came on board.

The coxswain, a Chief Petty Officer, led them up the gangway, while each of his crew carried a bucket full of Hong Kong or Mexican dollars. The English exchange value of the former was two shillings each, while the latter was standing at one shilling and ten pence per dollar. It might be imagined therefore, that the total amounted to a substantial sum. The Coxswain explained that he had come on board on the eve of the race to wish our ship the best of luck, and although the *Centurion*'s ships' company fully expected our gig to win, they thought a friendly wager in a small way would add a little interest to the race. He had therefore brought or board a few dollars for cover on the basis of an even bet. The presence of the coxswain with his crew and the object of their visit was soon known to everybody in the *Powerful*, and in a remarkably short time every dollar was covered and our visitors had departed.

On the following day, the race was started on a line between the two ships and away went the two gigs on a 4 mile course. At first the boats paced each other fairly evenly until the coxswain of the *Centurion*'s boat turned towards our ship waved his cap in a salute, then to the surprise of us all, our opponents shot ahead like a rocket and increased their lead on our boat so much that its chance of winning the race now seemed hopeless. The result of the contest was a foregone conclusion. The *Centurion*'s gig crossed the finishing line a quarter of a mile ahead of our boat.

The sequel to this trouncing, which came to us in such surprising manner was that our calculation before the race, as I have indicated above, was based upon fairly known data as to the capabilities of our opponents boat and crew; but what we did not know before the race, was that another and far better boat was used by them for the actual race! All Naval Service boats no matter of which class they belong must necessarily be built strongly in order to cope with probable rough usage, the specifications therefore provide for the use of comparatively heavy materials for construction. The *Centurion*'s gig however, was built of lighter construction at the dockyard in Hong Kong and thus it was more suitable for racing than for the ordinary naval service.

When the Battleship *Victorious* joined the China Squadron, her ships company found the *Powerful* painted black with yellow funnels and superstructure above the upper deck, very similar to their own ship. Naturally, they desired to maintain these colours, which for so large a ship, would have been in the interest of economy equally as for the *Powerful*. Accordingly, the Captain submitted to the Commander-in-Chief, who was then Admiral Sir Edward Seymour, that the *Victorious* be exempted from painting his ship the normal colour of ships on the China Station. For some reason however, the C-in-C did not approve of this and directed the *Victorious* to change to white in conformity with the China Station order. Soon after this we parted company with the *Victorious* leaving her when she had completed scraping the starboard side so that the ship was in the piebald state of having black paint on the port side and red lead on the starboard side. About two weeks later the *Victorious* joined us at Chefoo when both of her sides were red leaded.

I Join The Royal Navy

Again, we parted company and the next time we met was several days later at sea. As the *Victorious* approached us she presented her starboard side to view only, and we could see that it was painted white. Apparently therefore, the ship had carried out the C-in-C's order at last, but soon afterwards her helm went over and she turned to the same course as we were steering, when to our astonishment, all we could see was a red battleship out on our starboard beam. No matter how long we remained at sea the colours of this white and red battleship could not very well be changed until she had entered the next port. When we arrived there, however, we found ourselves in the company of the Flag Ship and as a result of this meeting signals began from C-in-C to *Victorious* and things apparently began to hum on board that ship. Within a very short space of time we were much amused to observe the whole of the red side of the *Victorious* swarming with men dressed in a painting rig and sitting on rows of stages rigged from stem to stern. There they were, each armed with a paint or whitewash brush smacking the white paint on to their heart's content. It had taken an unconsumable long time to change this ships complexion, but the job was completed that night. The Admiral had evidently insisted on the moral - "Where there's a will there's a way! "

CHAPTER XI

Wei-hai-wei

--- ooOoo ---

One of the most interesting and pleasant periods of our commission in China was spent at Wei-hai-wei, which afterwards became a British coaling station on the North East coast of China in the Province of Shantung. Wei-ha-wei, it will be remembered, was leased to Britain together with a considerable amount of the neighbouring territory and waters, including the Island of Lin Kung, under a Convention with the Chinese Government on July 1st 1898, for so long a period as Port Arthur should remain in the occupation of Russia. This was one of China's Naval stations before the Japanese captured it in January 1895 and occupied it with troops until it was handed over to Britain.

The British Government at that time acquired the lease in order to restore the balance of power in the Far East. Included in our function there was the landing an occupational guard consisting of seamen and marines, hoist the British Union Flag and assume formal possession until subsequent military arrangements could be made. We found Wei-hai-wei a delightful place, many fertile valleys abound and the climate especially was most salubrious. I was not surprised when I heard some years later that this region was regarded as a health resort for ships' companies and for British Civil Servants stationed in China.

At the time of which I am writing, the Chinese Warship *Chen Huen* was lying sunken in the harbour. This ship was sunk by Japanese warships in a surprise attack during the Sino-Japanese War in 1894. Whenever I recall the pitiful sight of this wreck, I am reminded of a similar attack, which the Japanese made on the Russian battleship *Retvisan* when that ship was lying at anchor in Port Arthur in 1904; also that this treacherous method of declaring war by the Japanese was repeated again at Pearl Harbour some 37 years later. Let us hope, after this thrice repeated act, within the lifetime of a single person, the nations of the whole world will become aware of Japan's inherent perfidy on the part of her rulers.

Though an abundance of fresh vegetables, poultry and eggs could be procured at Wei-hai-wei, pure fresh water for drinking was quite unobtainable. It was therefore necessary to supply the occupational guard with distilled sea water from the ship. Later a distilling plant was installed on shore close to the landing pier, and thus the party on shore became independent of the ships' supply. Some difficulty however, was experienced in the operation of the plant, mainly due to inadequate draught available to keep the fire burning in the boiler. The height of the funnel at the time was about fifteen feet and the Engineer Officer in charge of the apparatus estimated that, at least forty-five feet of funneling would be necessary for the efficient functioning of the boiler.

The existing funnel was similar to a large funnel of a ship. It was made of steel some seven feet in diameter and weighed approximately 2 tons. Three additional lengths had been provided with the plant so the Captain ordered two of them to be superimposed on the original funnel. There were several long scaffold poles available and with the use of these, in conjunction with a goodly supply of slings, shackles, rope tackles and personnel, the operation of erecting and securing the first section was completed in a fairly reasonable time. Then an attempt was made to superimpose the third section which, after about three day's work proved abortive. Nothing had been achieved except that all the scaffold poles, which had been unsuccessfully used as shin legs were broken off, some in the middle and the remainder in various positions of the upper half of the poles.

The Ships' Officer in charge of this work was loath to report the position to the Commander, who subsequently was by no means pleased and recalled all the personnel involved on board. The Commander then reported the failure to the Captain, who I believe was not at all complimentary to the Officer in Charge, when he submitted that it would be futile to proceed with the erection of the third section of the funnel until stronger poles could be obtained. As there were no spars in the ship suitable for the work the provision of new poles would probably have taken a long time, so for the moment, the matter was held in abeyance.

That same day, however, the Captain sent for the Chief Boatswain, who was generally recognized by everyone on board to be an authority on all matters pertaining to rigging and lifting heavy weights. The fine old seaman's name was Maidment and he had many years of experience in Her-Majesty's square rigged sailing ships. Mr Maidment was received cheerily by the Captain who discussed the matter with him and then directed him to go on shore to see what could be done. The Captain then, with the Commander's concurrence, added that if Mr Maidment thought he could undertake the job, the whole of the working party including the officer who had hitherto been employed on the work would be again available if and when required.

Soon afterwards, the Chief Boatswain having inspected the position on shore, reported that with the appliances left and with half the original number of men he would undertake to place the third section of the funnel in one day! The Captain was somewhat sceptical, but with true sporting interest, offered to lay a wager of half a dozen bottles of champagne to $5 that Mr Maidment was over optimistic in the matter. The bet however, was agreed to.

Now I personally was interested in the issue of this pledge, for being one of the new working party and hearing of the wager, I was determined to do my utmost towards success. Early the following morning we landed with Mr Maidment, and sure enough the days operation was successful. By 5 o'clock that evening the third section of the funnel was in position and secured by nuts and bolts to the top of the second section. That night Mr Maidment dined with the Captain but apparently the six bottles of champagne which he had won were not required at the table, for we of the party were afterwards assembled by the Chief Boatswain and disposed of their contents with great satisfaction.

The reader will probably be inquisitive as to how the job was done in view of the previous failure. Briefly, success was due to the difference in the method of using the poles. Instead of erecting them from the ground, two of them were lashed one on each side of the funnel, while a third was used as a cross bar on the top. Thus, a gallows was set up and by means of the purchase the third section was easily placed into position.

At Wei-hai-wei a pantomime was held on board the *Powerful* and the officers and ratings of the ships in company were invited to come and see it. One of the tales from the Arabian Nights was portrayed - Aladin's Lamp - and two of the principal actors in this very amusing play became distinguished Admirals. Lieutenant Halsey (now Sir Lionel Halsey) performed the part of Aladin, while Lieutenant Hodges (afterwards Sir Michael Hodges) represented the Widow Twanky. The play was repeated on two or three occasions so that we were able to extend the invitation to the personnel of all ships present at Wei-hai-wei. The entertainment was a wonderful success, and we of the *Powerful* were very proud to receive many congratulations from our guests.

On a previous page I mentioned about a boat race between the *Centurion*'s and our own ship's gig. Well now, it would not be at all like the *Powerful*'s ship's company to let the matter rest there, so before the cruiser *Bonaventure* left China to pay off in England, we effected an exchange of gigs and became the possessor of what was generally considered one of the fastest boat gigs on the Station and potentially a winner in the return challenge to the *Centurion*.

The change was affected in all secrecy one dark night, and then we got busy in preparing the boat for the race. This operation took some time for every speck of paint was scraped off the outside as well as the inside of the boat, while certain heavy fitting was replaced by one's of lighter materials. The boat was then rubbed smoothly with sand paper throughout and, then a light coat of paint was applied to finish. As a result, the gig had been divested of several pounds weight and offered less resistance when passing through the water.

In due course the challenge was made and accepted. This time, however, the result was the same, though the *Centurion*'s boat only just escaped a dead heat! In the circumstances we of the *Powerful* were perfectly satisfied. Indeed, so long as our ship was taking part in any competitive games we were truly happy, win or lose. In this connection we were fortunate in having a Captain whom everyone regarded as one of the leading sportsmen of the Royal Navy.

When we called at Amoy, Captain Lambton arranged for the *Powerful* to be there at the time of the race meetings. In fact, he entered a horse of his own in one of the races, though I fear with poor results. Apart from the Amoy races however, we found much interest in this old city of China, standing on an island with its walls dating from the Ming dynasty. I believe that the East India Company traded there so long ago as 1670 and it will be remembered that Amoy was among the first treaty ports of China.

On perusal of my Seamans Certificate of Service, which was returned to me by the Admiralty on my promotion to an officer, it is recorded that I passed an examination for Leading Seaman on 16th March 1899. I remember this ordeal very well and included in the subjects were seamanship, signals, boat sailing and practical rigging, wire-rope splicing and so forth. The First Lieutenant, Navigating Officer, Chief Boatswain and the Chief Yeoman of Signals were the examiners in those days.

Examinations in seamanship in the Navy of these days were peculiarly stiff for the younger bluejacket. This was mainly due to the fact that most of the examining officers were elderly men and in consequence, had considerable experience in Sailing Ships. It was therefore natural for them to base the greater number of their questions to the candidates upon the masts, yards, rigging and sails and on the handling of sailing ships generally. Unfortunately, with the advent of non-sailing warships, a large majority of seamen had scarcely any contact with these subjects since they had left the boys training ships. Here again that the experience I gained in HMS *Active* proved so valuable to me.

In this year, the international tension in the Far East eased somewhat, and for the time being it seemed that all the great Powers were satisfied with the working of their respective 'spheres of influence', extra-territoriality, and their uninterrupted spoilation of the heathen Chinese! Like all the other ships on the Station the *Powerful* had been kept on the move in these vast waters, and being the fastest ship, we were called upon, perhaps more than any other ship, for emergency services as the time taken to raise steam in our water-tube boilers was considerably less than that required for the marine boilers in the other ships of the squadron. Moreover, the *Powerful* being commanded by one of the Senior Captains on the station was naturally selected by the C-in-C for the more important services.

Towards the end of the year 1899, while cruising in the vicinity of North China and Japan we received orders to proceed to Hong Kong. On arrival a rather unusual incident involving Naval etiquette, or rather regulations occurred. It so happened that both C-in-C and the Rear Admiral were absent from the port, and in accordance with the regulations of the Service, the Commodore in charge of the Dockyard and other Naval Establishments on shore was in command. Accordingly, his broad pendant was hoisted in the Depot ship to indicate his authority as Commodore-in-Charge, Hong Kong. His rank whilst undertaking this role was that of Commodore Second Class, though his substantive rank was that of a Captain R.N. At the time however, the Captain of the *Powerful* was the Senior Captain, and from the moment we entered the port, our Captain assumed general command at Hong Kong. This meant that the Commodore's broad pendant was hauled down and the Senior Officer's burgee was hoisted in our ship to indicate the transfer of charge. Incidentally the Commodore, thinking perhaps that there was hardly enough room for him and the other person in Hong Kong at the same time, promptly left place on leave which was extended until precisely the day of our departure.

This episode reminds me somewhat of two individuals of not such exalted rank who were serving in the *Powerful* at the same time; the difference being in that both of them were quite happy to share each other's company! They were two ordinary seamen belonging to my mess and often went on shore together in Hong Kong. One's name was Albert and the other George, and about eleven o'clock one night, both these chaps arrived in the mess after imbibing freely on shore. They both kept up an unconsciously long and intimate conversation under the hammocks of their messmates, while they themselves were removing their clothes. At last, they turned into their hammocks, which were slung adjacent to each other in the gangway outside the mess. Then bidding each other good night the following dialogue reached finality to an amusing talk heard by us all.

George: "I say Albert."

Albert: "Yes George."

George: "There are only two good men in this ship."

Albert: "That's a bally fact, George."

George: "You're one, Albert! "

Albert: "You're the other George! "

About this time we had heard that HMS *Terrible*, the one and only sister ship of the *Powerful* was to be commissioned and would relieve our ship on the China Station. Soon afterwards Admiralty orders were received for the *Powerful* to return to England and pay off. This was grand news and we were all delighted with this somewhat premature order to leave China before the *Terrible* had even left home. Accordingly, preparations were made for our departure and we hoisted our paying off pendant at Hong Kong as we steamed out of the harbour for Merry England and Home.

We received rousing cheers from the ships in harbour and the Chinese gave us a brilliant send off. Scores of sampans swarmed around the ship with several Chinese Junks, all letting off fireworks, while the inhabitants of these craft waved us farewell. Incidentally Chinese are an essentially noisy people. In fact, all Orientals are. This is probably due to so much time spent out of doors. Their music too sounds very noisy - symbols, gongs and drums mixed up with tuneless flageolets and badly played flutes together with crackers and other pyrotechnics make up a perfect apotheosis of noise. Chinese too are past masters in the manufacture and use of pyrotechnics. As for their music, however, there is-no doubt that the Chinese has a lot to learn from the Western world about this. In the first place I believe that the scale of Chinese music has only seven notes, and I told Attam once that I did not believe that they used half of them.

Although we were homeward bound and very naturally pleased with the prospect of seeing our loved ones again, I could not but look back upon the wonderful experiences of life in those wonderful countries facing the Western Pacific - Pearls of the Orient with their teeming millions of people. As we were leaving, I personally felt that I had gained only too little knowledge or this vast region, and hoped to return some day to learn more about it.

For a period of time I was fortunate in making a special acquaintance of Attam Junior. A fine educated well spoken Chinese who managed the ship's canteen for his father. Many hours I had spent with him on the upper deck of the *Powerful*, while he would be conducting his business; there we exchanged views of much interest to us both. I must admit however, that Attar Jr had every advantage during our conversations for he spoke the English language fluently and not so carelessly as I. On rare occasions I attempted the middle course language, Pidgin' English, but Attam Jr would have none of it. Politely he would say; "Please speak English"! Pidgin English, as the reader may know, is nothing but mongrel talk. The idiom, it is said, was coined by the Chinese attempt to pronounce the word 'business'. It is of course nothing like Chinese and is really not a middle course for the words used are English. Though modified to suit the Chinese pronunciation e.g.- The letter 'R' is discarded and 'L' substituted. B's, E's and D's are also dropped while P's, K's and L's are used instead. An example of this awful jargon is as follows:

"Too muchee walk - no can stop

He talkey stlong

No sabbee Melican talk

Me talkee Englishee - can do".

Personally, I did not like this gibberish at all, and was surprised to hear from Attam Jr., that even the Chinese from different parts of China preferred to talk Pidgin English, when the dialect used by them made it difficult to converse together.

Attam Jr. told me again and again that his one great wish was to see England, and he had a promise from his father that he should. His ancestors belonged to the Merchant class, but curiously enough he advanced his opinion that the strongest characters among his countrymen were the Chinese farmers. When I inquired as to why his own class of Chinese were not regarded with at least equal esteem, he replied that the Chinese farmer loved his soil and his family who till it. The farmer had simple, frugal habits and prospered for countless generations. On the other hand, the children of Chinese merchants, and Government officials alike, acquired expensive and extravagant habits and seldom prospered for more than two or three generations. He further said that the secret of the farmers prosperity was love of nature combined with his willingness to work throughout the day beginning early in the morning and continuing until well into the night.

I have pondered over these words of Attam Jr. many times, and since those days I have come into contact with many Chinamen, though not of the farmer class, who make up more than 80% of the population. In my opinion no other nationality is so well adapted for getting a living abroad than the Chinese. They are good at almost every occupation more especially as agriculturalists,

I Join The Royal Navy

mechanics, sailors and labourers. Moreover, they possess intelligence and patience, and are self-denying, peace-loving, docile and thrifty. Anyone who has given careful thought to these people, I am sure all will agree that the Chinese are famous for their industry, and though he will not hurry, he will not loiter, and during his labour - rain or shine, snow or heat - is a matter of indifference, for comfort is no enticement for him. His endurance of pain is astounding.

The living race of China constitutes the survival of the fittest, for they endure famine, pestilence and cruel wars internal and external. Yes indeed, China is a vast territory filled with sturdy people, 450 millions of them, and the land is alive with children. With all these characteristics what a people to work in combination with! They would make good anywhere! But why, one may ask, is the Nation as a whole so weak? It can only be due to the corruption of its rulers, the greed of the Chinese War Lords and the battening of the Western Nations on the body politic of China, whose competition they cannot tolerate, for they begin work much too early for us and continue to labour unconscionably too late each day.

But surely China will emerge from this apparent impasse and then the personal qualities of this remarkable nation will find a place high among other great peoples.

Being so very interested in China and the Chinese to this day, I venture to mention a few of my impressions derived from the time of which I am writing and from subsequent contact and study of the wonderful Orientals:

(a) Some Chinese consider that punctuality, ambition and so-called success of Western people are their three greatest vices.

(b) Chinese generally are more philosophic in their conduct of life; serenity dominates rather than efficiency, otherwise insanity, most common in the West, would not be so unusual throughout the ages in China.

(c) The three religions of China: Confucianism, Taoism and Buddhism are all in pursuit of the same goal - viz: a happy life. It would be ungrateful of us not to be happy on such a beautiful earth as ours. Especially those who have lived a long life with time to witness human follies. With the span of life vouchsafed to us, we should be perfectly satisfied. What right have we to expect more?

(d) If in the Spiritual world - there is complete silence, peace and calm - no work, pain or sorrow, it would be a negative idea of heaven. There must be motion and emotion there, or the spirit life would stagnate like a cesspool.

(e) Ch'in Shih-huang, the builder of the Great Wall of China and tyrant, made "libelous thoughts in the belly" punishable by death, destroyed the Confucian books and burned hundreds of Confucian scholars alive. Confucius reduced the great desires of man to two: alimentation and reproduction. Many good men have circumvented the latter, but not even saints have yet circumvented food and drink.

(f) The Chinese, like Europeans, bribe their way into the good will of others by frequent dinners and thus obtain seats of office and promotion. The Medieval Lords of Europe on occasions of weddings or birthdays in their families feasted their tenants lavishly. It was said in China that 'A well filled stomach is in truth a great thing - all else is luxury!' Chinese eat with gusto. As for Western table manners, the child gets his first initiation into sorrows of life, when his mother forbids him to smack his lips! If we do not experience joy when we are eating, we soon cease to feel it and then dyspepsia, melancholia and other ailments follow.

The Chinese may have so-called bad table manners, but obtain great enjoyment at feast. The highest type of life is of Sweet Reasonableness as taught by Confucius' grandson Tsesse.

(g) The problem of Happiness appears to have been neglected entirely by Christian thinkers. Theologists apply their minds not to human happiness but to human salvation. The Chinese consider 'salvation' a tragic word, because they have heard so much about national salvation and the people trying to 'Save China'. Here is a Chinese conception of one of his happiest moments - after travelling the world he returned home and beheld the old city gate and hears women and children talking his own dialect - OH WHAT HAPPINESS!

(h) The typical Chinese will not be hurried, unlike the European who arranges punctual meetings anywhere and at any time of the day or night. An appointment say three weeks hence would not suit a typical Chinese. There was once a great Chinese Ruler and Warlord, who was invited to Europe to meet certain Western statesmen in conference involving Far Eastern affairs. The great man however, was very loath to accept; but after repeated requests he at last consented. Fearing that he might change his mind, arrangements were made for him to take passage in a British warship with all dispatch. Upon reaching his destination, the Naval Officer, who had been in attendance during the voyage, wished him good-bye and said – Your Excellency will be glad to know that the voyage from China to Europe has been completed in record time! We had saved four whole days from the usual time allowed for this journey. To this His Excellency replied – "Well, well, now what am I to do with those four days! "

(i) The Chinese family system provides distinctly for the young and old. Tenderness towards old age is characteristic of the Chinese. If Chinese of old had any chivalry, it was manifested not towards women and children, but towards old people. The reason for this is that the young can get along better without material comfort than old people. A poor child is scarcely aware of hardships and is as happy if not happier than a rich man's child. He may go barefooted but that may be a comfort rather than a hardship, as it is for old people. Sorrows of a child are soon forgotten. In China, people with grey hair would not be seen carrying burdens in the streets. A child above ten years of age is expected to get up before his parents and generally wait on them. The Chinese viewpoint on this is that every child grows old in time, and if he lives long enough, as he desires to do, one might grow old gracefully.

(j) Li Liweng (an old scholar) has pointed out that: Those who are wise seldom know how to talk, and those who talk much are seldom wise!

(k) The Lotus was the flower of the Confucian Doctrinaire. It is a class of flower, by itself a stretch of water lilies, with their perfume pervading the air and their white and red tipped blossom contrasting with their broad green leaves, with water running on them like pearls, and present perhaps the most beautiful effect of all flowers. The Lotus like the gentleman grew out of dirty water, but was not contaminated by it.

(l) It is a beautiful thing to listen to the speech of a cultured Chinese Mandarin. His words core out in perfect cadence, while the Peking accent gives a graceful rise and fall. His laughter is equally regulated and rhythmical.

(m) There is only one form of beauty that is not possible, and that is the beauty of strenuous life, for it does not exist. There are countless other beauties: charm, grace, swiftness, strength, simplicity and so forth.

I Join The Royal Navy

(n) Chinese Emperors were not semi-divine beings like Japanese Rulers. Some Chinese historians however, evolved the theory that the Emperors' ruled by a mandate from heaven, but when he mis-rules, he loses the mandate and his head as well. Too many Emperors of China have been beheaded for Chinese to believe them semi-divine. In support of this contention, I mention the unique case of the Dowager Empress of China, who was born a slave child in 1835, and passing through the Emperor's harem she was promoted his leading wife. On the death of the Emperor, she became Regent until 1889 when the young Emperor terminated his minority. At the time of which I am writing, this same woman in 1898 who had been Dowager Empress dethroned the Emperor and ruled in his stead. Both died suddenly in 1908.

Part 3

The Boer War

Naval Gun at Ladysmith: waiting the word to fire

(Sweetingham as marked)

CHAPTER XII

Homeward Passage Abruptly Halted in South Africa

--- ooOoo ---

A few days after our departure from Hong Kong we arrived at Singapore, filled bunkers with coal and then proceeded to Colombo with little delay. At this time, late in 1899, the Suez Canal had been improved to take larger ships, and it was anticipated that we should go home by that route.

Whilst on this passage, everyone on board talked of little else than what they intended to do on arrival in England. Curios obtained in China and Japan were being meticulously sorted out, packed and labelled ready for presentation to relatives and friends at home. It was most instructive and interesting to watch this performance going on both on the mess decks and the upper deck. Objects of Oriental art collected from various ports by so many men, produced quite an exhibition of articles and workmanship.

Among the Captain's collection were Pekinese dogs and puppies. One of these I believe, was presented to a member of the Royal Family after the ship arrived home, and thus these fine little aristocratic animals set the fashion for dogs in the Homeland for some considerable period of time. Writing about Pekinese dogs, I would like to mention that at the present time I am in daily contact with one of these intelligent little pets owned by my wife's mother, 'Pam Fu' by name. This priceless and exquisite little girl dog, is loved and petted by the whole of my family. It has a pedigree as long as a main top and possesses a handsome appearance, with mostly all the good traits of its race, while scorning the vices peculiar thereto. Why not, then one may ask, should not these little favourites be treated with respect and fondness, observing that their ancestors adorned the Courts of China in a highly cultured state some thousands of years ago, given the civilization of the English ancestral line at that time, was somewhat dubious?

Dwarf trees were also being taken home by the Captain and this was the first occasion on which I had seen the quaint dwarf oaks of Japan. The height of these ornamental trees was about six inches only. To the average European these trees seemed uncommonly rare in those days, but now I believe they are quite easily grown from an acorn in some contrivance where the roots are kept short by cutting off at regular intervals.

At the time we sailed from Hong Kong, diplomatic relations between the British Government and the Government of the Transvaal in South Africa had become very acute and when we arrived at Colombo, the quarrel between President Kruger's Government and the Uitlanders gave cause for much anxiety and it seemed that war was imminent between Britain and the Transvaal Republic. This necessitated the strengthening of the Naval Squadron at the Cape of Good Hope, as it was comparatively weak at the time. The Admiralty, therefore directed that previous orders regarding our return to England were cancelled, and that the *Powerful* was to proceed to South Africa with all dispatch.

Incidentally, the *Terrible* was to further strengthen the Cape Squadron instead of going direct to China to relieve the *Powerful* as originally arranged by the Admiralty. This was our first move in connection with the South African War, which began on October 11th 1899, and which was to prove the greatest conflict in which Britain had been engaged since the Battle of Waterloo.

In order to get an appreciation as to how the South African struggle was brought about, let us trace back a brief history of this remarkable country. To begin, it should be realised, that Cape Town was first occupied by the Dutch East India Company in 1652, and then used as a commercial port en-route to India. Gradually the Dutch increased in numbers and settled further inland with some Huguenots from France, who soon acquired knowledge of the Dutch language. The settlers of both nationalities could not agree with the Dutch East India Company, and at the close of the eighteenth century were in more or less open conflict with them. The settlers mingled with the natives, acquired their lands and used them for labour.

About that time (1795), a British Force arrived in Table Bay and occupied Cape Town and met with no opposition, and. Soon afterwards Britain evacuated the Cape; but in 1806, the British Admiral Sir Home Popham, helped to re-occupy Cape Town and reported that, the settlers were loyal to the British and could be relied on for the defence of The Cape up to a certain extent, and they still dislike the Dutch East India Company. Unfortunately, this amicable relationship of the colonists ended, when Britain abolished slavery in 1834. This and prohibition of official use of the Dutch language, and other irritations led to the Great Trek in 1837, when a large number of settlers, or 'Boers' as they were now called, took their families and all their belongings in bullock wagons into the vast hinterland known later as Orange Free State, Natal and to Southern Transvaal nearly a 1000 miles journey from Cape Town.

Natal became a British Crown Colony in 1843 and the independence of the Transvaal and Orange Free State was recognised in 1852 and 1854 respectively. Henceforth the Orange Free State was consistently friendly towards Britain, while the Transvaal was, for the most part, hostile. By 1877 the Transvaal Government had reached a deplorable state, and to save it from the threatening Bantus and Zulus, Britain annexed it. The power of Cetewayo the Zulu Chief and Secocoeni the chief of the Bantus was subdued, and order again was restored in the Transvaal.

Serious discontent arose among the Boers again in 1830, when they demanded self-government in the Transvaal. Mr Gladstone the Prime Minister of Britain would not agree to grant the Boers Home Rule, and following this, the Transvaal revolted. At the time Britain's military force in South Africa was so small that the Boers defeated them at Majuba in 1881 and afterwards the British Government conceded the insurgents self-government.

Then came the great gold rush at Johannesburg in 1886. Up to this date there existed scarcely a single house on the site of what is now the city of Johannesburg with a population well over a quarter of a million Europeans. This discovery of gold on the Witwatersrand, the gold mining district in the Transvaal, was the sensation of the day and immense wealth has been obtained from its reefs, which extended for miles and miles. In the centre of the reefs stands Johannesburg itself.

Strife was not long coming in this gigantic industry of gold getting; for in addition to the Boer Transvaalers, there was a British population of considerable numbers in their midst who were called 'Uitlanders' (Outlanders). Unfortunately for them, they had no power or even say in the matter, for the Boers held all the control of the Government. Moreover, the Boer Community hated the English people and the Raad or Dutch Parliament under Paul Kruger encouraged them in their hostility towards the Uitlanders.

Then followed the Jameson Raid, which, of course was entirely wrong. This raid was led by Sir Leander Star Jameson, and with the help of his friends Cecil and Frank Rhodes, he organized a fighting force of about five hundred men to invade the Transvaal simultaneously with a rising of

The Boer War

Uitlanders in Johannesburg. The raid started from Bechuanaland on the 28th December 1895, and five days later the force was surrounded by the Boers at Doornkop and was compelled to surrender. The Boers tried the ringleaders and sentenced Colonel Frank Rhodes and Jameson to death, which was afterward commuted. Among them was an Australian Karrie Davies whom with Frank Rhodes I was to meet later. Karrie Davies with one other member of the Reform Committee, had refused to weaken a just cause by asking for pardon of Kruger. The Military Chief Sir John Willoughby and minor officers of the raid were sentenced to terms of imprisonment and the remainder of the force was handed over to the British authorities by the Boer Government.

And so ended a sorry and shameful incident, which brought not only contempt upon its perpetrators, but the world's gaze of astonishment on Britain. Naturally the Jameson Raid did nothing to alleviate the position between Boers and Britain, on the contrary, Kruger's intolerance was intensified, and a petition was forwarded to Queen Victoria praying for redress of their grievances.

Sir Alfred Milner (afterwards Lord Milner) was sent out from England and became High Commissioner at Cape Colony in 1897 and in an endeavour to improve matters he met President Kruger at Bloemfontein. Milner demanded some reform in the franchise of the Transvaal, which would enable the Uitlanders to vote, and suggested an alteration in the parliamentary constituencies in favour of the Uitlanders. Both these demands were rejected by Kruger and the conference ended. Then followed a diplomatic fight between Sir Joseph Chamberlain, Secretary of State for the Colonies, and President Kruger, which culminated on September 3th 1899, when a British note was dispatched to Kruger demanding a franchise for all Uitlanders after they had been in residence for five years, and a readjustment of Parliamentary seats in the Volksread on the lines previously advocated by Milner. In addition, the British demands included equality of the British and Dutch languages for official use. While requesting an early reply to these demands, the British Government ordered 10,000 troops to be sent to South Africa, an equal proportion to be sent from India and from England, bringing the total number of troops in South Africa to about 17,000 men.

Only eight days later (16th September) the Transvaal Government replied with a refusal of the British demands. It was well known at the time, that the Transvaal Government had previously made considerable military preparations, and on October 9th - Kruger sent an ultimatum demanding the withdrawal of British troops which had landed in South Africa since June 1st 1899 and of all troops being sent at the time. Obviously, there could only be one result of this - WAR!

After this digression let me now resume my narrative with HMS *Powerful* going at full speed from Colombo to South Africa. Our first port of call after leaving Colombo was Mauritius. Here, we embarked a half battalion of British Troops for service in South Africa. They belonged to the Yorkshire Light Infantry. About five hundred strong, and a magnificent body of men they were too. So far as I can remember we had no orders from England to take this gallant regiment to South Africa, but Captain Lambton found the way upon his own initiative. The Officers were messed in the Wardroom and the men were distributed among the messes on the lower deck. While this embarkation was going on we procured hundreds of yards of khaki material ashore at Mauritius, ready for making up into sailors uniform suits for issue to the Naval Brigades if and when required.

After a brief stay at Mauritius, we proceeded to Durban at full speed. Here again every available seaman was pressed into the stokeholds and bunkers, and even a few soldiers of the Yorkshire Light Infantry volunteered and were accepted for this work in order that the utmost speed might be maintained. Meanwhile volunteers from the ship's company were called to form a Naval Brigade ready to land if and when required. The calling for volunteers for this service was not really necessary according to the regulations; but among the ship's company were a considerable number of naval ratings whose time had expired in other ships on the China Station and who embarked at Hong Kong for passage home to England. In the circumstances, any of these ratings were given the opportunity to volunteer for land service if they so desired, while leaving a correspondingly large proportion of the *Powerful*'s crew on board for service in the Cape Squadron. The number of bluejackets selected to make up the Naval Brigade was about four hundred all told, including the Royal Marines.

We were at once formed into gun crews, rifle companies and other small parties to complete a self-contained fighting Brigade. Each bluejacket belonging to the Brigade was issued with six yards of the Khaki material purchased at Mauritius and instructions to have it made up into trousers and jumpers of the sailor pattern. In those days most of us could cut out and make up our own clothing, including their best cloth trousers and serge frocks which are not worn by sailors nowadays. Even the cloth caps were cut out and made by many shipmates of mine. It was therefore an easy matter for us to turn out our khaki suits, replete and ready for wear, in the limited time before reaching the next port.

At the time of our arrival at Durban, the Boer ultimatum had not been sent; neither had reinforcements arrived from England or India. The British troops in Natal then was less than 5,000 of all ranks. General Sir W. Peeron Symons who commanded them could not possibly hold northern Natal with such a small force against an enemy force of approximately ten times that number. Pending the arrival of reinforcements therefore, he had decided to give up the extreme northern portion of Natal in the region of Langs Nek and Majuba and take up a defensive position near the town of Dundee some thirty miles on the railway north of Ladysmith.

Here then, with the need of reinforcements was so urgent, was the *Powerful* at the main port of Natal, less than two hundred miles by rail from the British Force, with a contingent of fighting men available to land! Five hundred of the best seasoned troops, together with a Naval Brigade of some four hundred men, including Royal Marines, and one twelve pounder Field gun and two Maxim Machine guns. Surely the Military Authorities in Natal would welcome such a valuable reinforcement. But for some reason, we were not required in this quarter, and orders came for the ship to sail to Cape Town and land the Yorkshire Light Infantry there.

So away we sailed to Cape Town without delay and upon arrival in Table Bay another disappointment was in store, for the port Authorities would not grant the *Powerful* pratique, as we had come from an infectious port (Mauritius) where Yellow Fever existed at the time of our departure. Thus, a further delay in landing the troops was necessary until a clean bill of health could be given by the port Medical Officer.

Naturally the Naval Brigade was disappointed as well as the Yorkshires for in our hearts we hoped to land and go on service with them. The captain too was goaded to exasperation with what he considered an unwarranted delay, for in this regard he had been advised by the ships' medical Officers that the condition of everyone on board was healthy, and this had already been reported to the appropriate authority at Cape Town. But there was nothing we could do at the moment, but to keep the yellow quarantine flag hoisted and hope for the best.

After a considerable period of waiting at anchor in Table Bay with the ship crammed full of men, Captain Lambton could stand the strain no longer. Thereupon he sent a message to the Port Authority saying that, "In view of the imminence of war, this is no time for red tape".

The Boer War

Further he indicated that if arrangements were not made on shore to take off the Yorkshire Light Infantry within a stipulated time, he himself would disembark the gallant regiment by means of the ship's boats. This resolute purpose of our Captain had the desired effect, for soon afterwards the ship was granted pratique, and suitable craft were sent out for the disembarkation of our guests. Technically, it might be thought that the Captain displayed undue impatience; but extenuation must be allowed him when it is realised that, apart from the pressing need of military reinforcements in South Africa, a British Man-of-War is greatly handicapped by having to accommodate such a large number of troops plus many naval ratings embarked for passage home in excess of the ship's complement.

On leaving the ship, the *Powerful*'s crew gave a rousing cheer to the Yorkshires, who upon landing proceeded up country to a place named De-Aar, on the border between Cape Colony and Orange River Colony, which had a railway junction about 70 miles south of the Orange River. Here the Yorkshires took charge of a military base, which was being established there. This was by no means a farewell to these fine troops, for soon afterwards it was to be the privilege for some of the *Powerful*'s bluejackets and Marines to fight side by side with them against the enemy.

We now sailed around to Simonstown, the Naval Base for the Cape Squadron where we met the *Terrible* commanded by Captain Percy Scott of Naval gunnery fame. Both *Powerful* and *Terrible* had now become units of the Cape Squadron under the orders of Naval Commander-in-Chief, Admiral S.R. Harris. Though the Transvaal ultimatum had not yet been delivered (October 9th), it was generally considered that the Boers might have commenced hostilities as far back as the middle of September; for it was well known that they were far better prepared than the British for action in the field, both in men and guns. Indeed, it might have been so, but for some delay on the part of the people of the Orange Free State, who really had no quarrel with England, and were not persuaded to enter the conflict on the side of the Boers before the month of October. Hence the race for time by both military and Naval effort to provide the necessary reinforcements, equipment and supplies to meet the Boer onslaught whenever it might burst upon us.

It was lucky therefore, in so far as the Navy was concerned, that Captain Percy Scott was present during our preparations. A Gunnery expert, second to none in those days, as indeed he proved himself in later years. The Artillery of the Boer Army was particularly strong ranging from mobile 6-inch Creusot guns to 3-inch Quick Firers; also automatic pom pom guns, which were a new creation. On the other hand, the mobile guns possessed by our military forces were nothing better than 18-pounders used in batteries of Horse and Field Artillery, and a few antiquated Howitzers. The effective range of the Boer Creusot (180 pounder) guns, was not less than 8,000 yards while that of the British Field Artillery was only half that distance. Here then was a vital problem to consider and work out and happily Captain Scott, with his gunnery staff on board the *Terrible*, very ably dealt with the matter on the spot. The 12-pounder gun armaments of both *Powerful* and *Terrible* possessed an effective range of 8,000 yards, so a number of these were taken out of their ships mountings and fitted on Field Gun carriages - designed by Captain Scott and Assistant Engineer Rookruge and the Armourers of the *Terrible*. The work was carried out on board the ship and in the Dockyard at Simonstown, and very soon a half dozen of these guns with their specially manufactured carriages were completed and ready for the front. Instead of horse transport, as used in the Army, drag ropes were fitted to the Naval outfits and they were drawn into position by the men forming the gun's crew.

Meanwhile the men of the Cape Squadron generally were making preparations for landing on service if called upon and patrolling around the ships at anchor in Simons Bay. Personally, I remember taking a few turns on patrol in the Picket Boat, when a howling South East gale was blowing, and at certain intervals, we would be due to pass certain ships according to a schedule of time laid down for the hours of darkness.

In the first few days of October rumours were coming to us, that the forces of the Transvaal had been mobilised, and that the Northern position of Natal was seriously threatened. Things were moving fast in South Africa at the time, and we heard that Sir George White, the Commander-in-Chief in India had arrived at Durban, and that about 8,000 of his best troops were pouring into Natal where he had now assumed command of all the Military Forces in that Colony.

Next came the news of actual war, when on October twelfth, a large Boer Force had crossed the border in Northern Natal and had seized Langs Nek. By that time, General White had established his main force at Ladysmith some 30 miles south of Dundee, where General Symons was holding the town. The force in Ladysmith had reached about 8,000 men, while the troops at Dundee were a little more than half that number.

Meanwhile a Naval Brigade was formed under the command of Captain Prothero consisting mainly of Royal Marines from the ships of the Cape Squadron with a few 12 pounder field guns manned by seamen. Included in this force were the Marines from the *Powerful* and one 12 Pound Field Guns Crew. The Naval Officer second in command of this Brigade was our Commander A.P. Ethelston. On one of the gun mountings included in the equipment of this force, the following slogan painted on the trail of the gun carriage read:

'Lay me well and load me tight Boers will soon be out of sight'.

While on another appeared:

'He who sups with me requires a devil of a long spoon'.

Perhaps this doggerel may be considered somewhat boastful?

Captain Prothero's brigade left Simonstown with orders to proceed to De-Aar where they joined forces with our old comrades of the Yorkshire Light Infantry. Shortly after this, on 25th October, Sir George White telegraphed to the Naval Commander-in-Chief indicating that his artillery was deplorably inferior to that of the enemy, and asked for naval long range guns to be landed at Durban, for urgent dispatch to Ladysmith. Accordingly, the *Powerful* was ordered to carry out this service. In great haste, four Q.F. 12-pound guns with mountings adapted for land service by Captain Scott, and two Q.F 4.7-inch guns and mountings were embarked with quantities of ammunition; and away we sailed the next day for Durban at the utmost speed. During the passage to Durban the Captain gave orders for a Naval Brigade to be found from the men who had previously volunteered; and despite the limited time, all was in order before we reached port.

The *Powerful* arrived at Durban on the morning of Sunday 28th, October 1899 and immediate steps were taken to disembark the Naval Brigade under the command of Captain Lambton. The Brigade was composed of 280 officers and two companies of bluejackets armed with rifles and sword bayonets including the following equipment:

two Q.F 4.7-inch guns with crews and ammunition;
four Q.F 12 pounders with crews and ammunition;
two 4.5-inch Maxim Machine guns with crews and ammunition.

The Boer War

Included in the above Force were Pioneers with tools, Medical Officers and their appliances, also a week's provisions for the whole Brigade. Suitable craft from the shore came alongside the ship, and all of the above equipment was disembarked by the ship's company by noon. After landing on the jetty, we were given assistance by the native labour belonging to the Dock and Railway Authority; and on the evening of the same day (Sunday 27th October), the entire Naval Brigade and equipment were embarked on a train ready for departure to Ladysmith.

I am sure it will be appreciated that the effort involved by everyone concerned to complete the lifting and loading of such heavy material was most strenuous indeed. It was, in fact, more than two normal day's work crammed into that one Sunday. Here I would make special mention of the Gunner of the ship, Mr William Sims, who was recognised as the main-spring of the work; for it was he who was personally responsible for the transport of all guns, mountings, ammunitions and spare parts of the Armament Equipment down to the last detail. Moreover, Mr Sim's himself was also required to land for Service with the Naval Brigade.

We appreciated the valuable help given us when loading up the railway trucks with the heavy guns and mountings. Kaffir and Zulu coolies were on this job, and I shall always be impressed by the excellent way in which they worked with us. These great-hearted, fine fellows, all well over six feet in height, with their powerful shoulders and arms, aligned themselves along the length of a 4.7-inch gun which weighed 42 cwt. Disciplined to a man, they intently waited for the first chanty from the headman and while repeating it, all bent down together and gripped that piece of ordnance in their huge fists. Then another chanty was given and repeated, while the 2-ton gun was lifted together as high as the thighs. Following a different chanty, and up went the gun above their heads at arm's length! With the mass of steel in this position, it was thrilling to watch these great souls shuffle along to still another chanty which sounded something like this:

Headman: Can't stop it!
Coolies: Can't stop it!
Headman: Do damn all!
Coolies: Do damn all!
Headman: Work a Coolie!
Coolies: Work a Coolie!

This chanty was repeated until they reached the appointed railway truck, where with masterly strength and precision the gun was placed on wooden chocks and secured by ropes. Both guns were transported in this way for a considerable distance in an astonishing short time. I have seen many hundreds of Kaffirs engaged on transport work since those days, but never have I witnessed the equal of this standard of labour, or anything like it. At most twenty men only could have possibly been ranged along each gun and one might well be astounded at the almost incredible strength and cohesion demanded by the headman from each native to lift and carry more than two cwt over their heads in this manner.

As a humble member of the Naval Brigade, I well remember the tremendous amount of work one had to discharge that day in connection with this landing. The moment I had found my place with my rifle and full war service equipment in the railway cattle truck, before the train moved off, I was well nigh exhausted.

The Officers who landed with the Naval Brigade were the Gunnery and Torpedo Officers, two Watchkeeping Lieutenants, the Gunner, two Engineers (Ellis and Sheen) Medical Officer, Fleet

Paymaster and a few Midshipmen. Those left on board were, the Navigating Commander and the First Lieutenant, who were the only senior Executive Officers of the Military branch, as Commander Ethelston had already landed at Simonstown. Remaining on board also were the Fleet Engineer, Senior Engineer, Medical Officer, Chief Boatswain, Chief Carpenter and a few junior watch keeping officers. For such a large ship as the *Powerful*, a serious reduction in the number of Officers and men in the ship's complement had thus been brought about. In this regard, it was rumoured at the time that Captain Lambton had incurred the displeasure of the Admiral.

It was not known then, how Sir George White became aware of the fact that Naval guns were being specially mounted for land service by Captain Percy Scott before he sent his telegram, and there appeared to be some doubt as to whether it was White's intention that a Naval Brigade of nearly 300 men should be landed with the guns at Durban. Be that as it may, one could not but feel that Captain Lambton took the right course as after events proved. Nothing succeeds like success, and even at the expense of the full fighting efficiency of his ship, it was obviously his right to decide that Naval guns, ammunition and equipment would need naval men to get them into position and to fight against the enemy. Nevertheless, it was indeed his duty, to maintain the full armament equipment of the ships of the Cape Squadron under his command, and to ensure that adequate reserves of ammunition and armament fittings be maintained at the Naval Arsenal Depot at Simonstown.

We left the Railway station at Durban on the Sunday evening of 27th October enroute for Ladysmith. The Captain and Officers were provided with enclosed carriages, while the bluejackets were accommodated in open trucks. I have a vivid memory of that train journey of 200 miles to the North West. All through the night, climbing to a height of more than 3,000 feet, and early the next morning to behold the massive Drakensburg mountains, which seemingly formed an impregnable boundary between the colony of Natal and the Orange Free State. As progress was made, the more bitterly we felt the cold climate of the higher altitude. Strapped to our backs, with the small arms accoutrements, each man had a blanket; but owing to the cramped position in the railway trucks, there was no room to unpack them for use as protection against the cold. Happily, the train stopped at Pietermaritzburg, Escort, Colenso and other places, where very kindly people were waiting to cheer us and to provide everyone with hot coffee, sandwiches and biscuits. We were indeed so very grateful for such kindness, which helped to speed us on our way.

About this time, we were all delighted to receive the first news of our shipmates who had landed a little before the *Powerful* left Simonstown, and went up to De-Aar in Cape Colony. They had not been in contact with the enemy yet, and their message assured us that they were deeply entrenched and very happy.

As the Boers had commenced the first act of war by invading Northern Natal about two weeks before we had landed in Durban, let us now review the position to the northward of Ladysmith, where the British force based upon Dundee had already been engaged with the enemy. When the Transvaal Boers, under the command of General Joubert, had crossed the frontier on the 12th October and occupied Laing's Nek, about 50 miles north of Dundee, their strength was between 15,000 and 20,000 men. But this was not all, for about 10,000 of the enemy raised by the Orange Free State were advancing from the West towards the several passes which cut through the Drakensburg Mountains. If therefore, we bear in mind that the British force available to defend Dundee was less than 5,000 with only three batteries of six guns each, it will be realised that their position was one of great peril.

The Boer War

Seven days later the Boers had moved further south and seized a position at Elands Laagte in a position astride the railway about midway between Dundee and Ladysmith to the south. Here the Boers captured a train laden with supplies from Ladysmith for Dundee, and the same night (19th October) the enemy occupied a position on Talana Hill about two miles North and overlooking the British camp. Early the next morning they opened gun fire upon the British position with great accuracy. This was a complete surprise for General Penn Symons, and he immediately ordered an attack on Talana, which became the first battle of the South African War.

Against devastating enemy shell and rifle fire, the British Infantry and artillery advanced, and about noon on the 20th October, a charge with fixed bayonets was made and amid cheers Talana Hill was captured. This splendid British attack was a lesson to the Boers who skeltered off leaving more than 100 casualties behind them. The victory however, cost the British attacking force 270 casualties in killed and wounded, while 210 men belonging to the flanking cavalry and mounted infantry were missing or taken prisoner. General Penn Symons himself was mortally wounded, and the command was taken over by General Yule.

On the next day General French went out from Ladysmith with a force and won a victory against the Boers at Elands Laagte. Here, as at Talana, the British Infantry stormed their way to the top of a ridge and bayoneted the enemy's guns crews. As the Boers fled from their position they were charged at by the Cavalry and other mounted troops. The British attack involved not more than 3,000 and their losses in killed and wounded amounted to some 250 men. The strength of the enemy force was much greater, and their losses, in killed alone, was not less than 120, together with 200 prisoners. On the morning of the 22nd General French marched his force back to Ladysmith and among the booty that they had captured from the enemy was the British supply train, which had been lost on the 19th October.

Although the victory at Talana was superbly won, and prevented the whole British Force at Dundee from annihilation; still the position there became untenable and General Yule decided to abandon it and retreat towards Ladysmith. Accordingly, he set out from Dundee on 22nd October at a late hour. Since the railway was no longer open to him the force, which had now been reduced to less than 4,000 men, passed through the Biggarsberg Mountain where luckily he was not intercepted by the enemy. Thereafter the going was good and on 25th October, contact was made with the main force at Ladysmith. This retreat was indeed well executed, but the circuitous route taken was fraught with great risk, for it would have required only a small enemy force to annihilate General Yule's column while it was marching the pass of the Biggarsburg.

As the Transvaal Boers under General Joubert were relentlessly closing in on Ladysmith from the North, so too were the Free Staters advancing from the West. By the 27th October, the latter had penetrated the passes through the Drakensburg Mountains and were seen near Pieters, a small dorp only 10 miles on the railway south of Ladysmith. This force had brought guns with them and was obviously attempting to cut the railway between Colenso and Ladysmith, but they were held in check. There was no doubt that the strategy employed by the enemy was most effective; they steadily enveloped our troops bringing up their long range artillery, at the same time entrenching themselves in strong position. The results of each British victory could not stop their general advance, the time had now come for Sir George White to decide whether he should hold Ladysmith or retreat southward.

In this regard, many factors required careful consideration. Firstly, the position of Ladysmith would be most difficult to defend. It was situated on the Klip River at an altitude of some 3,000 feet and almost surrounded by high hills and mountains upon which the enemy guns could dominate the town. Also, it was well known that the strength of the Boer Forces, both in men and guns, was overwhelmingly superior to that of the British. On the other hand, Ladysmith had now become a comparatively large military base centred on railways and roads leading to southern and eastern Natal, which were still open, also to the Transvaal and the Orange Free State. An enormous quantity of ammunition and stores had been accumulated there, and even if this was destroyed before abandoning the town, the moral effect alone upon the enemy and upon the British Nation would have been very great indeed.

Under these circumstances, General White decided to hold Ladysmith with his force of not more than 13,500 effectives including 5,300 horses, 55 guns, of which six naval guns and two army 6.3-inch Howitzers were far and away the most valuable, against an enemy of more than double that strength.

CHAPTER XIII

The Investment of Ladysmith

--- ooOoo ---

The Boers advanced from Nicholson's Nek and occupied Pepworth Hill about 7,000 yards from Ladysmith, bringing long range guns into position there, several quick firing one pounder Automatic Pom Poms and Maxim guns.

On October 27th British reconnaissance parties exchanged shots but nothing serious took place. On the 29th a British reconnaissance balloon was sent up and about 1,200 men belonging to the Dublin Fusiliers and Gloucester Infantry regiments, with a mountain battery, moved out in the night under Colonel Carlton to take possession of Hog's Back, North of Surprise Hill. This position was about two miles from that held by the Boers at Nicholson's Nek. Carlton's force was here to secure the left of a larger force, which followed under Colonel Ian Hamilton, and took up a position within Field Artillery Fire of the Boer positions on Pepworth Hill (about 2,000 yards). To the right of Hamilton was a still stronger force of five battalions of Infantry and three Field Batteries of artillery, under Colonel Greenwood facing the enemy positions at Farquhar's Farm, Lombards Kop and Mabulwaana Mountain; all within range of the British batteries. Meanwhile General French with his cavalry were standing by, under the guns at Bulwana to the right of Greenwoods Brigade.

In the early hours of October 30th practically the whole of Sir George White's combatant force was in the positions indicated above. Very few were left to defend Ladysmith itself. In this plan, the main attack was to be delivered on Pepworth Hill by Hamilton's Brigade. When dawn came the Boers on Pepworth Hill and Farquhar's Farm opened fire on the British Infantry, and later our Field Batteries engaged the enemy and the British positions were held very well. Soon after, it was observed that Carlton's column on the left, was heavily engaged, though the details were not known at the time.

Then, just as the position seemed favourable for an infantry assault against the enemy at Farquhar's Farm, Sir George White received an urgent message from Colonel Knox, who had been left in command at the Base, stating that the Boers were about to make a direct attack upon Ladysmith from the North. Doubtless the advancing Boers from that direction were those expected to have been engaged and held by the force under Carlton. General White however, had no alternative but to withdraw his forces deployed for battle, be it ever so difficult. There was the danger that an order to retreat would not only encourage the enemy, but that the morale of our troops might well be shaken, leaving their positions of advantage behind cover of the kopjes and the prospect of coming under the devastating cross fire of the enemies heavy and light guns and deadly Maxim and Pom Pom machine guns.

Despite these considerations White gave the order for retreat and it was admirably carried out under cover of a masterly screen put up by the British Field Artillery. For a while the gunners stood up well to the gruelling task, but soon their losses compelled them to fall back with the

Infantry, and as the British Artillery retired, so their guns became out-ranged and useless, against the superior range of the Boer guns.

The enemy long range guns now concentrated their fire on the town of Ladysmith itself, and nothing could be done to stop them. It must have been at this juncture (about 9.30 a.m. on 30th October) when we of the *Powerful*'s Naval Brigade was approaching the scene of action. While our train was steaming into the Railway Station at Ladysmith, shells from the Boer long range guns were bursting around us. It was obviously apparent that things were not going well with the British troops, for they could be seen streaming into the town from various directions. However, Captain Lambton very quickly obtained an appreciation of the position, and of the urgent need of long range artillery to silence or check the enemy, who were pouring a galling fire into our retreating army, and into the town.

Accordingly, our twelve pounder guns and limbers were hurriedly got under way and went straight out towards Limit Hill and brought into action against the enemy. The four 12 pound 12 cwt Ship's guns on mountings of special design proved admirably adapted for their work; they were well sighted up to an effective range of more than 8,000 yards, while the range of our 12 pound 8 cwt gun mounted on an ordinary field carriage did remarkably good shooting up to 6,000 yards range. Here then was a fine battery of field guns each capable of firing up to ten rounds a minute if necessary. But accuracy rather than speed of fire was the more important and not a great number of rounds was required to find the range of the enemy guns and to silence them.

Thus ended the first engagement of Royal Naval Men in the Boer War, in what was known as the Battle of Farquhar's Farm. Incidentally, we had arrived just in time to contribute this effort by the last train to enter Ladysmith for many months. The British casualties apart from those belong to Carleton's column to the North West of the town amounted to approximately 60 killed and 240 wounded. Many of the British guns were put out of action including one of the naval guns, an enemy shell having exploded immediately under the gun carriage and wounded most of the gun's crew. Happily, the necessary repairs were quickly affected and the damaged gun carriage was soon ready for action again; and our wounded men recovered their strength within a comparatively short period.

What happened to Carlton's column facing an overwhelming enemy force on Nicholson's Nek is a sad story. On the night of the 29th, they encountered enemy forces in great numbers and owing to lack of shelter they were mown down by the enemy rifle fire. Over two hundred mules drawing their mountain battery of six guns and stores took fright and bolted, while one of our own Infantry regiments fired upon them in mistake, adding to the confusion. They were in a hopeless plight and by ten o'clock the next day, no less than 30 officers and 900 men out of a total of 1,200 all told had surrendered. The Mountain battery, ammunition and stores also fell into enemy hands. More than 50 were killed in battle and only 220, mostly wounded, returned to Ladysmith.

The Naval Brigade was assigned a position on Gordon Hill North West of the railway station where the Naval Camp was established. Earth works thrown up for protection from enemy fire, and about 800 yards to the East and West of the Naval Camp, positions were selected for mounting our two 4.7-inch guns. The work on these operations was carried out in great haste during a truce that had been arranged between General Joubert and General White to bury the dead and collect the wounded. Before the bombardment began again both Naval guns of heavy calibre were in position and prepared ready for action.

All this of course took time, but by working unceasingly day and night, the engineers assisted by the gun's crew had completed the work in a very satisfactory time. The completion of earthworks and sandbag parapet with embrasure, of course, was a job which took longer time. The 4.7-inch gun position to the east of the Naval Camp was on Junction Hill, while the one to which I belonged was on Cove Redoubt. The Gunnery Officer of the *Powerful*, Lieutenant Egerton, was in charge of the former gun, while Lieutenant Lionel Halsey was in charge of Cove Redoubt.

As we were taking advantage of the armistice, to set up our own defences ready for the next fray, so too the Boers were making great progress in bringing up reinforcements and guns and strengthening the earthworks behind them, taking care to conceal themselves as much as possible among the ridges and hollows of Kopjes and the trees on the mountain slopes. It is helpful to appreciate that the town of Ladysmith was situated in a basin surrounded by high hills and mountains, all held by the Boers except Wagon Hill and Caesars Camp about 3 miles southward. Whatever may be said of the general strategy, and decisions taken by both British and Boer Commanders, it was now certain that Ladysmith was virtually in a position of siege, and every effort was being made for the departure of civilian residents and others who did not belong to the combatant forces. Soon there would be no further opportunity to leave, for the enemy would be astride the railway line leading southward.

On November 2nd the Boers bombarded Ladysmith from their long-range positions, and all Naval guns entered into an artillery duel for well over an hour. Since the Boer guns were mounted on heights that dominated almost every camp inside Ladysmith, they were able to enfilade them with ease and nothing but the Naval guns could stop them. This day however was a sad one for we of the *Powerful*, for about 6.30 a.m. our beloved Gunnery Officer Lieutenant Frederick G. Egerton was seriously wounded by one of the Long Tom's shells. He had both legs shattered by a Boer 6-inch shell, and as the bluejackets who formed our gun crew were lifting him on to a stretcher, he cheerfully remarked, "No more cricket for me".

After amputations were made on both legs he rallied in the afternoon and became quite cheery. But the poor fellow died the same night.

In memory of this officer, The Commander Egerton Prize was founded in 1901, and the dividends arising from a sum of £500 given by relatives and invested in Government securities is employed by the Admiralty in awarding the prize to the Officer who, when qualifying for Gunnery Lieutenant, passes the best practical examination. Egerton was promoted to the rank of Commander R.N. posthumously.

In the afternoon of the 2nd the last train from Ladysmith left for Pietermaritzburg with General French on board, who had left his Cavalry in Ladysmith. When the train had arrived at Pieters, a small railway station about ten miles on the journey, the Boers attacked the train with rifle fire and a Maxim 1 pound Machine Gun (Pom Pom). The train was riddled with shells, and had it not been for the great skill and presence of mind on the part of the engine-driver, this train would doubtless have been wrecked, and General French captured by the enemy. This lucky escape marked the severing of railway and telegraph communications between Ladysmith and the outside world.

There is no doubt that the British position not only in Natal, but in the whole of South Africa had now become grave. A small British force under Colonel R.S.S. Baden Powell made up of irregular troops were already besieged in Mafeking, and by October 24th, the Boers under Commandant Cronje began to shell the town with heavy guns. Kimberley too, in Griqualand West, was cut off from the outer world about the middle of October and by the end of the month it was closely invested. Here Lieutenant Colonel R.G. Kekewich commanded a small force of about 600 Regulars and 2,000 Volunteers was shut up. So too was Cecil John Rhodes, a former Premier of Cape Colony, who had a great interest in the De Beers diamond mines there.

Incidentally, other South African celebrities in the persons of Colonel Frank Rhodes, Dr Jameson and Sir John Willoughby of Jameson Raid fame were with us in Ladysmith; and during the bombardment on the 2nd November a shell crashed into the Royal Hotel where they were staying. It was thought at the time that the enemy had especially aimed at this hotel in the hopes of bagging these men who were hated by the Boers, and regarded as the arch-demons who were mainly responsible for the war.

On Saturday 4th November, Sir George White sent a message to General Joubert requesting that all sick and wounded, women and children and non-combatants might be permitted to leave Ladysmith without being molested. His intention was, of course, that they should be given a clear passage by rail preferably to the South of Natal, and thus obviate the exposure of these helpless persons to further enemy action. Furthermore, it would greatly relieve General White of the responsibility of feeding and caring for a large number of persons, and so strengthen his defence position.

This was a tall order for General Joubert to consider, and had he been say a German or Japanese Commander the request would have been given a peremptory refusal. However, the Boer General with the graciousness of a great and kindly man that he was, went a good half way and consented to the formation of a neutral camp for sick, wounded and all non-combatants at Intombi Spruit, about three and a half miles on the railway South of the town. Food, water, medical supplies and attendance were to be supplied from Ladysmith and a railway train could be used daily for this purpose. Since Intombi Camp would be situated very close to the enemy lines, the Boers of course were in a position to inspect the train, which was to operate under a white flag. A condition of this concession was that those sent to the neutral camp were to be regarded as on parole and were thenceforth not to take part in the war. Many of the so-called leading personalities in Ladysmith considered that General Joubert's terms were arbitrary and dictatorial and would show a pusillanimous spirit if accepted. However, it was a matter in which the sole responsibility lay with Sir George White and it is my considered opinion, that in accepting the offer he was quite right.

Accordingly, on the next day, Sunday 5th November, several train loads of our sick and wounded, women and children and other non-combatants could be seen leaving the Ladysmith railway station for the neutral camp at Intombe; where they remained for the duration of the siege. Throughout this Sunday, the Boers refrained from shelling the town as indeed most of the Sabbath days to follow were more or less observed without active hostilities.

As in all wars, and long before Quisling was born, wild rumours were spreading amongst us that spies were in our camp and were in contact with the enemy either directly or using Kaffir runners between the lines. Their job of course was to locate and report all defensive positions held by us, and details of the military and naval personnel who occupied them; also the location of the ordnance stores, supply depots, and the situation of General White's Headquarters. Last but not least, it may be added, the haunts of their bitter personal enemies, those celebrities of the Jameson Raid. All these details would be most useful to General Joubert in the estimation of the direction and range for his guns, and in his paramount objective: to capture the town of Ladysmith as he had sworn to do.

This talk of espionage continued for a considerable time, so all of us were on the lookout for strangers within the camp, though, personally, I do not remember observing any roving around the positions occupied by the Naval Brigade. The matter was got over very soon by the introduction of Official Permits to bona fide civilians and arresting the undesirables.

The Boer War

The bombardment of the town and the exchange of fire from our Naval Guns had now become a daily occurrence, and in the hope that the Boers would soon make a general attack from any direction, we were busily engaged in strengthening our positions. Earthworks were thrown with large boulders and bags filled with sand, while the gun fire continued generally, the enemy rifle fire concentrated on our outer defences. The most vulnerable of these being held by the Devonshire and Manchester Regiments. The Imperial Light Horse dug well into the river bank and formed caves into which they could go for shelter during bombardment.

It seemed however, in the early days of the siege, that the sick and wounded were cared for in far more exposed positions than those of the combatant forces. The Town Hall upon which the Red Cross was flown and the Convent Hospital which was built on a high ridge presented a most conspicuous target. Both these hospitals had been hit by enemy shells. They were directly in line of fire of our naval guns; the shells falling short of our targets might well have accidentally hit these hospitals. The risk of exposing the hospitals with patients and the splendid nursing sisters was most unfortunate, though unavoidable at the time. It might be asked why these patients were not sent direct to the Neutral Camp at Intombi; but this was impracticable for once a man was sent there it was forbidden that he should return to take part as a combatant again. It is therefore only the worst cases of sick and wounded combatants that were sent out of the town.

The first enemy attack of any importance, other than by general bombardment, came on the 8th November, which began with heavy gun firing between the Naval and Boer long-range artillery. Incidentally, the hospital on Convent Hill was hit on this day. Later Boer riflemen had a sharp attack on Caesars Camp, Wagon Hill and Maiden Castle about three miles South of the town, which were held by the Manchester Regiment. As the attack developed so the enemy guns concentrated their fire on their targets, while our soldiers put up a grand defence.

Both Naval 4.7-inch guns were engaged in this fight, and our gun on Cove Redoubt paid particular attention the enemy guns on Bulwana. We first drew the fire of their heavy Creusot firing a 96-pound shell putting it out of action for a considerable time. After frequent engagement between our Infantry and the Boer Riflemen, from fairly good cover on both sides, the attack ended with seemingly few casualties on either side. During the firing we were soon to discover that the Boers heaviest Creusot guns, 'Long Toms' as they were called, fired shells of 6-inch calibre weighing about 100 pounds, with a propelent charge which emitted an enormous cloud of white smoke each time the guns were discharged. In contrast to this our guns fired a projectile of only 45 pounds weight filled with lyddite bursting charges as well as with gun powder and shrapnel. The propelent charge of our 4.7-inch guns consisted of 5 pounds 7 ounces of cordite, which when fired was almost smokeless. We observed also that the muzzle velocity of our gun, and therefore its penetrating power, was much superior to that of the Boer guns.

Our calculations of the relative velocities were proved over and over again in this way: just before the enemy fired at us from any of their long-range gun positions, we could plainly see the great long chase of their gun pointing towards us at considerably greater elevation than it was necessary to lay our gun to fire at them. Then a huge cloud of smoke would envelope their gun, which indicated that it had been fired. We in our turn would have the gun loaded, sighted and laid for elevation and direction on the enemy positions and the breech firing arrangement brought to the ready. As soon as their puff of smoke appeared our gun would be fired too, and the time of flight of our shell would be so much less than that of our enemy's, that it enabled us to spot the result of our fall of shot before their projectile arrived. The difference in times of flight, of course would vary according to the range, for instance, the enemy's gun on Pepworth Hill was about

6,700 yards distant, while the gun on Bulwana Mountain exceeded that by some 1,700 yards. Even when firing at the gun position on Pepworth Hill the difference in time of flight was appreciable, but when firing at the gun position on Bulwana the difference in time of flight of the two shells allowed us a very comfortable time in which to spot our fall of shot before it was necessary to bother about the enemy's shell coming to us.

Another advantage we had in the matter of relative concealment of fire between the two types of gun. The cordite propellant which we used was almost smokeless, and the flash could not usually be seen by the enemy while they were enveloped in the smoke of their own guns. Here I would mention that Captain Lambton christened the Q.F 4.7-inch gun on Junction Hill 'Lady Anne' and the one mounted upon Cove Redoubt 'Princess Victoria'. The former was so named as a compliment to the Captain's sister. For some unknown reason the latter gun possessed another name – 'Bloody Mary'. This was not a mark of courtesy to anyone and personally I did not like it.

On November 9th a really serious attack was made by the Boers on our positions. Early in the morning their guns again began bombardment from Bulwana and Pepworth Hill to which we replied with alacrity. The first assault was made against Observation Hill about 1,500 yards North of our gun in Cove Redoubt, which at the moment was held by only a few men belonging to the 5th Lancers. A cavalryman's carbine rifle is not much good against the expert marksmanship of the Boer's Manser Rifles, but fortunately the Rifle Brigade moved to their support and stopped the enemy's advance. There was plenty of cover for both sides, and the engagement developed into a long-ranged rifle duel behind kopjes and boulders. Characteristically the Boers did not show themselves in any numbers though their fire was severe enough to keep our men behind the physical features of the ground, which are admirably adapted for this kind of warfare.

When the attack on Observation Hill had been beaten off the Military field batteries obtained their chance of firing 15-pound shrapnel amongst them from positions North of Range Post. Meanwhile two machine guns operated from Kings Post causing considerable losses, while our casualties were only few. During this engagement, our gun on Cove Redoubt engaged Long Toms on Pepworth Hill and Lombards Kop which were shelling the Liverpool Regiment holding Tunnel Hill. One shell from Pepworth burst very close to General White's Head Quarters behind Convent Hill. Afterwards our attention was called to the Long Tom on Bulwana while it was shelling the Devonshire Regiment holding Helpmaker Hill and the Manchesters on Caesars Camp and Maiden Castle.

While these operations were going on all around the eastern semi-circle of Ladysmith, the naval Brigade had not forgotten that this day, the 9th November, was the birthday of the Prince of Wales. Captain Lambton therefore, ordered that a Royal Salute of twenty-one guns at Noon in celebration of the occasion; just as a Salute would have been fired had we been in the *Powerful* at the time. Accordingly, we of the Q.F. 4.7-inch guns crew in Cove Redoubt fired our quota of rounds at the enemy gun position on the top of Bulwana, and a Boer force assembled on the slope of Bulwana preparing for a rifle attack against Maidens Castle and Caesars Camp. At a given time, through the telephone communications between the guns, three cheers for His Royal Highness the Prince of Wales was heartily given by the lusty bluejackets who represented the Senior Service at Ladysmith.

So far as I know, this salute constituted a most unusual record in the annals of Naval History. A Royal Salute fired from guns in ships of the Royal Navy is carried out with blank powder charges only, and this event was unique in that full charges of cordite with shotted rounds were fired. The intervals of the gun fire in this Salute were so accurately timed that even the soldiers of the Rifle

Brigade stationed not far from the guns were most curious to know more about it. Doubtless the enemy thought it wise not to press home their attack, which lasted for the best part of the 9th. At any rate the attempted assault on our position was a failure. Their losses, seemingly, were many more than ours, which amounted to no more than thirty men killed and wounded.

Things had moved so fast for everyone belonging to the Naval Brigade that, till well into November, one had little time to collect one's thoughts, or give any serious study as to the real position we were in. It was evident however, that there was little hope of fighting our way out of Ladysmith against such a large number of Boers from the Transvaal and the Orange Free State who now surrounded us. Every day the Naval guns were keeping the enemy at bay, while shells from his Long Toms, and other long-range guns of smaller calibre, kept up a continuous bombardment of the town.

Captain Lambton had, of course telegraphed for more ammunition to be sent for every gun, but this was now impossible. Therefore, it was therefore necessary to conserve the original outfit of cartridges and shells that we had brought with us. To we of the 4.7-inch guns, this was particularly galling. For we had to put up with the exasperating fact that while the enemy possessed an inexhaustible supply of ammunition from which they bombarded us incessantly. All we could do was to pick out the enemy gun which was reported to be causing the most devastation at any given moment, and with much care in countervailing the elements affecting the ballistics and accuracy of our fire, engage that particular gun with our precious rounds until we could check his fire or put him out of action.

Bad as things were in this respect, the position became worse from about the middle of November. The Boers had brought down a 4.7-inch gun overnight and mounted it on Surprise Hill about 4,000 yards North West, and in a commanding position overlooking our gun on Cove Redoubt and the ridges held by the Kings Royal Rifles. The enemy opened fire upon us the next morning and we could see, upon examination of the copper driving bands on portions of exploded shells, that we were up against a brand new gun. At the moment it began to fire we were actually engaging a Long Tom on Bulwana bearing South West or actually in the opposite direction to our new friend. So, we swung our gun around on Surprise Hill, and it cost us only a few rounds of ammunition to find the accurate range and to put our new acquaintance out of action by a direct hit at this comparatively short range. Immediately afterwards we swung back to the Bulwana again and after firing a few rounds at what we had now come to regard as an old acquaintance, she too was perforced to cease fire. The Boers of course possessed the necessary facilities for the repairs or replacement of these guns and accordingly we were again in action against them a few days later.

Hurrah for a pleasant change, for we had heard amidst this unceasing killing and maiming that a very brave lady of Ladysmith had given birth to a fine baby. The mother was Mrs Moore, the wife of a local farmer. She had refused to go to Intombe Camp or to a dug-out for protection and preferred to risk the danger of the enemy's shells by remaining in her homestead until the baby was born.

In order to conserve food for our horses and cattle it had become necessary to send some trek-oxen out to graze in No-Mans-Land, between the Boer position and our defensive lines. These herds were under the charge of Kaffir boys and on one morning towards the end of November, they had strayed dangerously close to the enemy in search of better pastures. Every endeavour was made by our mounted men to divert the cattle back, but under cover of the enemy shell and rifle fire, a party of Boers suddenly appeared on the spot and rounded up the whole lot of about 250 oxen. This was truly a humiliating incident as well as a serious one.

A few days later the Boers mounted one 6-inch Creusot gun and a 4.7-inch gun on Middle Hill, westward and behind Waggon Hill about 8,500 yards south-west of Cove Redoubt. These guns became conspicuously unpleasant and claimed the attention of the Naval batteries. In addition, the Royal Artillerymen moved two very old howitzers to positions on Waggon Hill but well screened from the view on Middle Hill. These twin weapons lobbed shells of 60 pounds weight and I believe they were manufactured in the year 1878. Despite their age, they worried the two newcomers on Middle Hill so much, that the Boers shifted them to positions of Telegraph Ridge; only to be assailed again by the ancient twin Howitzers from new positions about 1,500 yards to the westward of our Naval gun on Cove Redoubt.

A considerable number of heavy guns were being added to new enemy positions and about this time two more appeared on Lornback Kop. The fire from these also claimed the Naval gunners attention. As one of these Boer guns had been directing its fire upon General Headquarters and other buildings in the vicinity, General Sir Archibald Hunter, the Chief of Staff, originated the idea and successfully carried out a night attack on the enemy's big gun positions on Lombard Kop (or Gun Hill). On the night of the 7th December, General Hunter went out with detachments of British South African Volunteers belonging to the Imperial Light Horse and Natal Carbancers. They passed successfully through the Boer's pickets and then ascended Lombards Kop. Although they created considerable noise in the advance over the kopjes and up the hill, it was surprising that no resistance was offered until they had almost reached their objective. Then came the Boer challenge "Wie gat daar?" and immediately our splendid fellows rushed towards the guns against enemy cross rifle fire. Several of our men fell, but by means of a clever ruse which gave the Boers the impression that a bayonet charge was coming, they dispersed and the attacking party entered the gun positions and carried out the demolition work. They mutilated the breeches of a 6 inch Creusot gun and a 4.7 inch howitzer found in sand bagged parapets about 100 yards apart. They removed the gun sights and breech blocks which they carried away with one automatic Maxim gun. Further, the chases of both guns were damaged beyond repair by the detonation of Gun Cotton Charges.

> *It was very dark on the night of this daring exploit and the small force returned to Ladysmith at daybreak the next morning with their trophies. Previously, the devastating fire from these Boer guns had forced several regiments, including the Imperial Light Horse, out of their camps and to pitch their tents in other positions. So it was gratifying to see them get their own back somewhat, especially as their losses were only one killed and four wounded. An item of some interest in this capture was a letter written by a Boer to his sister which contained the following extract, "We see the Rooincks (English) moving in the town every day and bombard it with our cannon. It would be dangerous to attack. Two of their Naval guns give us a very warm time - often unbearable on account of their excellence. A good deal of blood will have to be shed before their surrender as Mr Englishman fights hard and well and our burghers are a bit shaky."*

It must not be supposed that General Hunter selected the colonial Troops for this exploit because they were regarded to be more reliable than the Regular troops. Rather it was because the British Regiments were needed for the more important duties of defending Ladysmith as a whole. Each had their sector in the defensive organisation, and this responsibility called for diligent watchfulness throughout the hours of darkness, while remaining on the alert for numerous and instant call to arms. Time and time again, however, these British Tommies had requested that such service might be allotted to them. At last, Colonel Metcalf of the Rifle Brigade obtained permission from Sir George White to deliver a night attack upon Surprise Hill. The objective, to destroy the 4.7 inch gun which had given his men holding the post near Cove Redoubt so much annoyance and trouble for so long.

Accordingly on December 10th about 450 men of the Rifle Brigade left their camp at 10 p.m. and in due course an advance party reached the crest of Surprise Hill, through wire entanglements, and charged the gun position with fixed bayonets. The gun was mutilated by a gun cotton charge, but unfortunately there was delay caused by a misfire of the safety fuse. This gave the enemy time to intercept some of our men during their retreat from the gun position. Confusion followed in the darkness and a sharp engagement with rifle fire at the foot of the hill ended with the enemy being driven back. When the Rifle Brigade had reached Ladysmith, it was found that their losses were far greater than those which had occurred as a result of the sortie on Lombard Kop three days before. Colonel Metcalf's total losses amounted to fifteen men killed or mortally wounded, thirty-nine wounded while eight prisoners were taken by the Boers. The enemy losses were of course not then known, but they afterwards admitted to one hundred men killed and wounded.

It must be admitted that sixty-two British casualties was a large price to pay for the loss of one gun which was replaced by a new one within a few days. After the sortie at Lombard Kop, it was apparent that the Boers were much better prepared for such attacks, by the fact that their guards and pickets had been enormously strengthened on Surprise Hill, while a complicated defence of wire entanglements had been erected around their positions. Consequently, these raids were not repeated again during the siege.

One must here mention the splendid work of the irregular troops, who formed General White's Scouts and guides. It seemed that they were always on the move and must have been a valuable asset to the Intelligence Service within Ladysmith. Among these were several Basutos. From our gun position we often watched these fine fellows on their Basuto ponies going across No-Mans-Land between the British and Boer lines, and on many occasions, they would become a target for the enemy riflemen. I remember well one of these men coming into our lines under Mauser fire at the utmost speed taking cover at one side of his mount. Unless one looked very closely one would imagine that a galloping pony only could be seen so perfect was the body of the man streaked beside it.

CHAPTER XIV

Events Elsewhere in South Africa

--- ooOoo ---

After forty-one days of the siege, let me now set down some of the activities which had meanwhile been going on elsewhere in South Africa.

As in the case of most wars in which Britain has been involved, the usual dilatory method of mobilisation of the Military Forces for service in South Africa involved the Cabinet Committee of National Defence and was subject of much criticism both at home and abroad. The Committee included the Right Honourable E.J. Gochen, the Duke of Devonshire, the Marquis of Lansdowne, the Right Honourable A.J. Balfour and the Prime Minister the Marquis of Salisbury.

Actually, mobilisation was not ordered by the Committee, until October 7th, and did not begin until two days later. The total force then decided upon was about 50,000 men, to which must be added small contingents of troops amounting in all some 2,000 men raised in the Colonies of Canada, New South Wales, Victoria, South Australia, Queensland, Western Australia, Tasmania and New Zealand.

At this time, Field Marshal Viscount Wolseley was the Commander-in-Chief of the British Army, and embarkation of the troops commenced at Southampton on October 20th. Thus began the transport of the greatest expeditionary force 6,000 miles overseas in previous military history. The sea transport of British Troops for the Crimean War was considered an enormous operation, but, the number of troops and the distance involved was little more than half that in this case. The sea transport was arranged by the Admiralty and the troop ships were escorted over the route to Cape Town by battleships and cruisers of the Channel Squadron.

On October 31st General Sir Redvers Buller, arrived at Cape Town and assumed command of the Army Corps, as Commander-in-Chief of the British Forces in South Africa. Soon afterwards, November 9th, the first troop transport, *Roslin Castle*, arrived from Southampton. Sir Redvers Buller decided to move half his force to Natal for the purpose of relieving Ladysmith, and send a division under Lord Methuen in a campaign to relieve the diamond city of Kimberley, which was hard pressed by the Boer Commandoes at that time. The Military Officer in Command of Kimberley was Lieutenant Colonel R.E. Kekewick. His troubles were accentuated by the behaviour of Mr Cecil John Rhodes, who did not agree with the manner in which the Military Commander was conducting the defence of the city. Moreover, the fall of Kimberley would have been a great financial gain for the enemy. The base from which General Methuen's Relief Force was organized at De-Aar about 70 miles south of the Orange River which formed the boundary between the Orange River Colony and Cape Colony. This had been established before the arrival of Lord Methuen, and as the reader may recall, was the place where the first Naval Brigade to land under Captain Prothero was sent with our old friends the Yorkshire Light Infantry.

The first serious engagement between General Methuen's force and the Boers was at the battle of Belmont some 15 miles North of the Orange River, near the railway 45 miles south of

THE BOER WAR

Kimberley. Here the British Force numbered nearly 10,000 including the first Naval Brigade composed of bluejackets, marines and a battery of 12 pound guns, which landed at Simonstown under Captain Prothero. Early in the morning of November 23rd this force set out to deliver an attack on strongly entrenched positions held by the Boers. A savage encounter ensued while our men advanced in the open under deadly rifle fire from the enemy. With bayonets fixed the British troops reached their objective and charged the Boers who retreated. A halt was made on the top of the hill while our artillery fire was poured into another enemy position. Then at 8.15 a.m. the Infantry resumed the advance. It was at the storming of this second position that the Naval Brigade did fine work by shelling the Boer position with their 12-pound guns. Under cover of this fire, and that of the Field Artillery, the gallant Infantry Regiment went forward against a withering rifle fire but with considerable losses. Soon the position was taken and the enemy had scampered away to establish a third position. By 6 a.m. the following morning, that third position was captured and thus the Battle of Belmont was won. The Australian, New South Wales Lancers were engaged in this battle and performed some good fighting here by protecting the Ninth Lancers with rifle fire, when the latter had got into difficulties. The N.S.W. Lancers, I believe, happened to be in England when the War broke out and embarked in one of the first troop ships leaving for South Africa. The British losses at Belmont were relatively heavy, 300 Officers and men were either killed or wounded.

On the 25th November, a further advance was made by General Methuen's column and at 6 a.m. the Field Artillery and Naval 12-pound battery opened fire on the enemy position at Enslin about 10 miles north of Belmont, at 7 a.m. the Infantry again commenced the attack which was led by Naval bluejackets armed with rifle and sword bayonets and the Royal Marines. The Yorkshire Light Infantry was also present in this assault. The advance was made in extended order, each man being six paces apart. It has been said that the straightness of this line of seamen and marines was simply perfect; one might imagine it was an advance in drill order, rather than against the rifle fire of determined marksmen as the Boers most certainly were.

Early in this attack Captain Prothero was wounded, and our beloved Commander A.P. Ethelston, with whom I had served in HMS *Active* and for nearly 3 years in the *Powerful*, was killed by a rifle shot through his heart. Major Plumbe commanding the Marines was also killed about the same time. Nevertheless, the relentless advance up the hill by the Naval Brigade continued while the losses mounted. Then just before our men reached the top of the ridge, the Naval guns poured its fire upon the enemy position, and our old shipmates of the Yorkshire Light Infantry went up the slopes to support and cheer on our Naval bluejackets and marines in their last final rush. Thus the Boer entrenchments at the top of the ridge were captured and the battle of Enslin (Graspan) was won, and the enemy fled northward.

Soon after this battle had been fought, we of the *Powerful* in Ladysmith heard of it together with the news that, of a total of 365 men of the Naval Brigade, no less than 101 Officers and men were killed or wounded, including the death of Commander Ethelston. We felt sad in the thought that our brave Commander and his fallen comrades would not return to the *Powerful*, still we were extremely proud in the knowledge that they rendered such valuable service in Lord Methuen's advance to the Modder River preparatory to the relief of Kimberley. It was also very gratifying to read a copy of a message from Queen Victoria which ran:

> *The Queen desires that you will convey to the Naval Brigade, who were present at the action of Graspan Her congratulations on their gallant conduct, and at the same time express the Queen's regret at the losses sustained by the Brigade.*

After the Boers had taken siege of Ladysmith, one might have thought that General Joubert would have promptly followed up his successes by a rapid advance to the South of Natal. But apparently, he decided that his main force would be sufficiently occupied outside Ladysmith, and only small commando forces could be spared for operations in the region of Colenso. This town, situated on the Tugela River, was evacuated by the British on the 2nd November and the small garrison there withdrew to Escort nearly 30 miles further south. The Boers then occupied the strongest positions north of the Tugela, where they entrenched themselves behind heavy guns, which commanded the railway and road between Colenso and Ladysmith.

The capital of Natal, Pietermaritzburg, about 50 miles South of Escort was placed in a defensive position by Volunteers raised in the Colony. Meanwhile, Captain Percy Scott landed from HMS *Terrible* with bluejackets and Naval guns at Durban where, as Commandant, he organised the defences of that port. Each day an armoured train was sent out from Escort to reconnoitre towards Colenso. On the 15th November this train was wrecked near Frere and five men of the reconnaissance party were killed and 80 were captured by the Boers, whilst 35 got away on the engine or escaped through the bush. Mr Winston Churchill who was then nearly 25 years of age was captured with the 80 men and taken to Pretoria. Mr Churchill was actually acting as a war correspondent for home newspapers in England, but since he was armed when captured, the Boers regarded him as an enemy combatant and made him a prisoner of war with the British Officers. Two months later however, (January 14th) he escaped from the State Model School, where he was imprisoned at Pretoria and afterwards reached the neutral port of Delagoo Bay. This ever intrepid and wonderfully fearless man, as everyone knows to this day, was not content with this and a few weeks later joined the Natal Army again under General Buller.

On November 21st, the Boers reached the furthest point south during the war. This was in the vicinity of Mooi River about 35 miles north of Pietermaritzburg. The place was held by a British force some 4,000 strong and after robbing some farms of cattle and looting generally, the Commandoes were engaged in sorties with the British troops before a withdrawal to Colenso.

Then, on November 27th, General Buller arrived in Natal and took over the command. Here he collected a force south of the Tugela River composed of : - four Infantry Brigades five Field Batteries - one Mounted Brigade - two mobile 4.7-inch Naval guns - fourteen mobile 12-pound Naval Guns manned by bluejackets.

The Naval guns had been landed from HMS *Terrible* by Captain Percy Scott for the defence of Durban. These 4.7-inch guns proved a most valuable addition to the 30 guns comprising the Army Field Battery, on account of their greater range and muzzle velocity and heavier projectiles. Captain Jones of HMS *Forte* commanded the Naval Brigade, while Mr Gunner was his very able assistant.

By 11th December, the whole of the above force of some 21,000 men was ready to advance to the relief of Ladysmith, and on the 13th, General Buller gave orders for the Brigades to move out and for the Naval guns to open fire on the Boer entrenchments at long range. The enemy force awaiting his attack was estimated to be about 30,000 men while the positions occupied by them on the Tugela heights were almost impregnable. I do not propose to go into further detail of General Buller's three unsuccessful and the fourth and final successful attempt to drive the Boers from their tremendously fortified positions on the Tugela River and around Colenso. But I trust that the reader will appreciate the hard and gruelling task he had undertaken in order to force the passage of the river in face of accurate and deadly fire from the enemy long-range guns, machine guns and rifles.

The Boer War

The Battle of Colenso, General Buller's first attempt to relieve us had been fought with disastrous results. Early the next morning the Boers outside Ladysmith celebrated Dingaan's Day by firing every long-ranged gun into the town. Several casualties occurred and, as usual, the Naval guns were very active, firing our shells at the big gun on Bulwana and elsewhere. Dingaan Day is a festival day of the Boers which celebrated the dreadful battle of the Blood River about 100 years ago. At that time, Andreas Pieterius slaughtered the Zulus and thus took revenge for the massacre of the Boers by the Zulus at Weeneu (or Lamentation).

Then followed the most depressing news for us all, for General White received a heliograph message from General Buller informing us that he had failed in his effort to relieve Ladysmith. The text of No. 88 Cipher, 16th December read:

I tried Colenso yesterday, but failed; the enemy is too strong for my force, except with siege operations, and those will take one full month to prepare. Can you last so long? If not, how many days can you give me in which to take up defensive positions? After which I suggest you firing away as much ammunition as you can. I can remain here if you have alternative suggestion, but, unaided, I cannot break in. I find my infantry cannot fight more than ten miles from camp and then only if water can be got, and it is scarce here. Buller.

In a later message (No 92 Cipher, 16th December) Buller requested to add to end of message No 88 Cipher the following words:

Whatever happens recollect to burn you cipher and decipher and code books and any deciphered messages.

General White, of course, viewed this message very gravely and replied:

I will not think of making terms till I am forced to. You may have hit him harder than you think. Things may look brighter. The loss of 12,000 men here would be a heavy blow to England.

During the battle of Colenso Victoria Crosses were won by Captain Congreve and Lieutenant H.S. Roberts, who was killed in an attempt to retrieve guns which had been captured by the Boers. The fathers of both these Officers had been awarded the Victoria Cross. They were Lord Roberts of Kandahar, who incidentally succeeded Sir Redvers Buller as C-in-C South Africa in December 19th, and the other was Captain W. Congreve of the British Rifle Brigade. I believe this was a first in relation to the award of this great honour.[1]

---

[1] Correction. The father of Lt Roberts was indeed Lord Roberts of Kandahar who had won the VC for his actions on 2nd January 1858 at Khudaganj, near Lucknow during the Indian Mutiny. However, Captain Congreve's father hadn't won the VC, but the Captain's son would. Captain (later General Sir Walter Norris Congreve, VC, KCB, MVO, KStJ, DL), was the father of Major William La Touche Congreve, VC, DSO, MC, who won the VC posthumously during the Battle of Delville Wood on 20 July 1916. The Roberts and Congreve families are two of the three instances of fathers and sons having won the VC.

CHAPTER XV

The Ongoing Defence of Ladysmith

--- ooOoo ---

The weather now had for some time been very hot and incidentally, on this most gloomy morning, it had reached a temperature of 107 degrees Fahrenheit in the shade. I well remember discarding the khaki military uniform with which we had been issued before landing from the *Powerful*, and donning my cool sailors' suit which I had made from the six yards of khaki obtained at Mauritius. This material was very much finer and lighter than that used for the Army uniform and consequently our regimental comrades became quite envious in this regard.

South Africa is indeed noted for its capricious climate, for in a matter of 24 hours the range of temperature would commonly extend from about 30° F. at night to well over 100° F. in the afternoon. Sanitary conditions were now becoming very bad and flies were simply terrible. Just below Cove Redoubt, horses in the Cavalry lines were staked out and perhaps this increased the number of flies in our vicinity. These pests were everywhere around us, and before any food was put into one's mouth it was always necessary to brush off a layer of black flies from it. Even a dry Army biscuit would be completely covered with flies as soon as it was exposed for eating.

A few days before Christmas, we were startled with the news that Sir George White had been hit with a shell splinter fired from Long Tom on Bulwana. Happily, it was not so bad, for although several shells had hit one of the rooms at Head Quarters and completely shattered the furniture, Sir George was ill in bed in another room where he was suffering from an attack of fever. Following this, the members of his Staff, successfully persuaded him to transfer Headquarters to a safer position. Exceptionally enough, the enemy guns shelled the C-in-C's new quarters on the very day that the change was affected.

On Christmas Eve our isolated little party forming the gun crews on Cove Redoubt were scrounging around in the hope of something extra to the service rations for Christmas dinner, when a kindly message was received to "Come and get it." This communication came from one of the Naval gun crews stationed about half a mile eastward. At first, we thought it was a hoax, for on the day previous the matter had been mentioned in the hearing of a member of the other gun crew. However, I intimated that there might be something in it and volunteered to go and find out. This was immediately agreed to and I set out on the mission of hope. Imagine my surprise when I entered the gun emplacement to be greeted by a half dozen cheery souls who, with compliments of the season, presented me with the ham of a wild boar. Naturally I was very curious as to who killed the pig, for I made it clear that no one at our gun had ever seen a wild boar or any other wild animal in or around Ladysmith. However, these good Samaritans offered no explanation and I felt it prudent not to pursue the question, so the origin of this valuable gift remained a mystery. After an exchange of views on the general situation and the prospects of being relieved, I departed with profuse thanks on behalf of my mess mates in Cove Redoubt.

The Boer War

Now the open veldt in this area was well within the range of enemy 37-millimetre pom-pom guns mounted on Thornhill Kopke. It was also in sniping range of the Boer rifleman who frequently came down the slope of the same hill for a practise shoot at anybody who happened to be about. I of course, was well aware of this before I set out on this mission, and was rather gratified that nothing untoward happened on my outward journey. But I was not so fortunate upon returning; for on covering a distance of about 500 yards, with the boar's ham on my shoulder, I found myself the centre of attraction from our friend the enemy from Thornhill. I do not know which was the most unpleasant sound, the thud, thud, thud of the pompoms as they embedded themselves into the earth around me, or the whistle of the Mauser bullets in my ear. Instinctively however, I dropped flat upon the ground and lay there and the enemy fire ceased immediately. After a short while, I proceeded on my way without further incident.

Many times, I have wondered why the Boers did not open fire again as I resumed my journey, and can only conclude that it was my luck rather than good will on the part of the enemy. In all land wars, one hears of sniping at individual foes, but personally, I could never find any patience with subtle warfare of this nature. Certainly, such behaviour is utterly opposed to the noble tradition of our forebears: the Knights of old!

But after this digression, let us see what happened to our Christmas fare. Upon returning to my gun-mates, it was a joy to watch their faces, as they beheld the magnificent gift. Our next question was, who should cook the joint on Christmas Day ? Ordinarily, our daily rations were drawn from the Main Naval Camp, but prudence suggested it wiser not to advertise our luck in that direction, so permission was obtained to use an oven for roasting the pork in one of the private dwellings adjacent to the Cavalry Camp of the 19th Hussars. Accordingly at 8.30 a.m. Christmas morning, the joint was deposited in the oven and a Kaffir boy was given a couple of shillings to guard it during the absence of our man who undertook to do the cooking. In due course, about 12.30 p.m. all were assembled with great expectations of a sumptuous dinner, when suddenly our amateur cook burst in upon us with the cry that the pork was missing!! An agonised moan came from us immediately and the blood of the Kaffir boy was demanded!

Meanwhile, there was no alternative to bully beef as usual. Later the wretched Kaffir boy was produced and with tears streaming from his large black eyes he admitted that he had fallen asleep on his job. Well, what could be done about it? Disappointing as it was for us all, the only course remaining was to forgive that black boy, though one could never forget!

Here I am bound to remark upon the difficult problem of food supply, not only to the fighting personnel, but also to the large numbers of sick and wounded and civilians who were accommodated at Intombe Camp. As Military Governor of Ladysmith, Colonel Ward possessed the power of requisitioning all articles of food and drink from the various proprietors of shops and provision stores in the town. But before this was done, black marketing had begun of all commodities, particularly fresh meat, vegetables and dairy produce. To give the reader some idea as to the fabulous cost of these items, I will mention just a few prices that were asked for, and readily obtained, before Christmas Day:

- fowls and ducks, 9 shillings to 11 shillings each.
- eggs, 9 to 10 shilling per dozen, according to size.
- Butter, 9 shillings a pound.
- preserved fruit 7 shillings, six per bottle
- condensed milk 5 shillings a tin.
- new potatoes were sold for 1 shilling each and even more!

Of course, these luxuries were far beyond the means of the British soldier or the Bluejacket, and therefore we were little interested in these prices at the time. However, there were extremely wealthy men in Ladysmith, including many in the ranks of the Colonial regiments and especially the troopers of the Imperial Light Horse. So far as I can remember, all spirituous liquor was commandeered mainly for consumption in the hospitals; though we were informed on Cove Redoubt that a bottle of brandy could be obtained for about 3 pounds sterling!

Except for a few novel greetings to remind us of the festive season, the Boer guns were quiet on Christmas Day. A few shells fired into Ladysmith were found to be duds, in that plum puddings were substituted for the explosive charges, and on the body of the shells were engraved the words "with the compliments of the season". This demonstrated the fact to all of us that, unlike ourselves, the enemy had no thought for economy of expensive ammunition. Had he known it, these shells were regarded as most valuable trophies to the finders. Alas however, they proved an indirect cause of the death of two of our beloved shipmates, who were members of the Rifle companies in the Naval Brigade. One was Able Seaman Payne and the other, Ordinary Seaman Dudley Wheeler. a countryman of mine who hailed from Ventnor, Isle of Wight. He was older than I, though still an Ordinary Seaman, because, as he insisted, that his rating of senior Ordinary Seaman in the ship, was very much preferable to that of junior Able Seaman! Hearing that high prices were given for these inscribed Boer shells, they commenced a search for them and discovered a large unexploded live shell instead, the fuse of which had failed. Thereupon, both men foolishly attempted to remove the fuse with fatal results. The shell exploded and the unfortunate fellows were killed. The complimentary shells fired by the enemy were, of course, plugged and did not contain fuses or any explosive whatever. The danger of these projectiles lay in the event of directly hitting some body or some habitable structure.

On the early morning of December 28th, incidentally my 22nd birthday, we could see through our large telescope, a fairly large number of Boers moving about on the slope of Bulwana Mountain immediately below the Long Tom gun. As this gun was silent at the time, we thought perhaps that the activity on the side of the mountain was the fore-runner of an attack by riflemen. Accordingly, we planted a few rounds of lyddite and shrapnel in their midst which caused them to scatter out of sight behind the boulders. Later, stretcher parties were seen at work apparently removing the wounded. Personally, I did not like this apparent wantonness and would have much preferred to wait and see if this comparatively small party of Boers were really bent on some mischief before effecting their massacre.

New Year's Day of 1900 was celebrated as just another day of artillery duel between the Naval Guns and the enemy artillery, which continued as usual on the following days. About this time, we had several distinguished visitors to our gun position including Colonel Frank Rhodes and two war correspondents, Mr G.W. Stevens of the Daily Mail and Mr Maud of the Graphic. They were keenly interested in our firing at Long Tom on Bulwana and when the engagement had ceased, they sat beside us inside the gun enclosure and exchanged views with us upon the prospect of relief, the conditions of life in Ladysmith generally, and at our gun in particular. We enjoyed their company enormously and found their visit a very instructive and interesting one. We hoped they would come again and give us further encouragement in our work for generally we were much isolated from the people of Ladysmith, and the only other visitors to call occasionally was Captain Lambton and General Sir Archibald Hunter the Chief of the General Staff.

Another war correspondent of note, who was present throughout the siege, was Mr H.H.S. Pearse of the Daily News. I remember seeing him on a few occasions though I had not the pleasure of speaking to him. Talking of journalists, I must here mention that, owing to the lack of world news, two small newspapers were published, which afforded much amusement to anybody who could obtain copies. One of these publications was called the "Ladysmith Lyre" and the other "The Ladysmith Bomb Shell". Both papers lived well up to their titles and exhibited topical cartoons with screamingly funny sketches of enemy and other personalities. Mr Stevens, I believe was responsible for the Ladysmith Lyre which comprised one sheet only; but alas this kindly friend of the bluejackets died only 6 weeks before Ladysmith was relieved.

The greatest assault by the Boers on our position in Ladysmith was made on January 6th 1900. It put the previous serious attempt on November 9th in the shade, and came as a complete surprise. The enemy was in an easy position to observe that General Buller's Army was making great preparations for his second attempt to relieve us, and accordingly was determined to strike an all-out blow against us before the relieving force could begin its next attack.

Until now, most of us had gained the impression that the Boers would not storm defensive positions held by us and push home an attack by their riflemen. This would be playing our game. Theirs was to defend advantageous positions, which by their mobility, they could seize with less loss to themselves. However, this time General Joubert was apparently determined to capture Ladysmith at all costs and was confident that by surprise and audacity he would succeed. Strong enemy reinforcements were collected including about 7,000 Boers from Colenso, combined with the greatest number of Transvaalers and Free Staters that had yet been concentrated in one assault. Only the day before the 'Lady Anne' Naval gun was removed from Junction Hill to Wagon Hill, but unfortunately the 4.7 inch gun and mounting was still loaded on transport bullock wagons at the time the assault began and was therefore out of action the whole time.

General Joubert's plan of attack was to assault and capture the vital southern bulwark of the defence of Ladysmith viz. that great ridge 14 miles long known as Caesars Camp with its extension to the westward another ¾ mile called Wagon Hill. The plateau being from ¼ mile to ½ mile wide. Simultaneously an attack on Observation Hill, the opposite side of our defensive position to the North was to be made, while Boer demonstrations were to be carried out in other quarters in order to prevent our defending forces from being transferred to reinforce our troops defending our southern defences which was the main object of the enemy attack. The gun on Bulwana and Telegraph Hill and other guns brought up from the South were to assist their riflemen by enfilading fire along the plateau as required. There is no doubt that had this plan succeeded, as well it might for our defence to the South was deplorably weak, Ladysmith would have eventually fallen into the enemy's hands. Only 80 men of the Light Horse held the western end of Wagon Hill, together with the Manchester Regiment on Cura Cap, no more than 1,000 men all told were stationed to defend this enormous southern defence.

The enemy began the attack about 2.30 a.m. (6th January) and passed our pickets on the south western slope of Wagon Hill. By 3.15 a.m. they had gained the crest of the hill and poured a murderous fire against our men as dawn was approaching. At the same time, the Boer guns around Ladysmith commenced a fierce bombardment of our defence positions, while the searchlight mounted on Bulwana was used to aid the enemy's movements at the foot of the ridge and up the slope covered with brushwood and boulders. Brigadier General Ian Hamilton, in general command of the southern defences, quickly ordered reinforcements and by 5.30 a.m. the Gordons and Devons reached Wagon Hill and checked the Boer advance on the plateau.

Soon after this attack on the extreme west, the enemy moved along the whole southward ridge of Wagon Hill and Caesars Camp and engaged the Manchester Regiment with accurate rifle fire.

Meanwhile, another force of Boers passed the pickets of the Manchester Regiment, through the Mimosa Grove and ascended to the crest of the eastern extremity of Caesars Camp , arriving at about 4.15 a.m. Here they met effective resistance from the Manchester's and the Boers had to fight very hard, winning the crest of the ridge by daylight. By 6 a.m. the 53rd Battery of Field Artillery was able to come into action at the close range of 2,000 yards, considerably helping the Manchester's by shelling the Boers as they were streaming up the south-eastern slope of Caesars Camp. As soon as the 53rd Battery had moved into action, Long Tom and the howitzer on Bulwana stopped shelling Caesars Camp, and poured in a tremendous fire amongst the artillerymen.

Meanwhile, Sir George White had ordered the Rifle Brigade to reinforce the Manchester's, where they arrived and stabilised the position. Back on the other end of the plateau on Wagon Hill, the Boers had substantially increased their gains and when dawn came, they were pouring in a deadly rifle fire into the comparatively few men holding the plateau. The situation therefore was most serious. For it must be remembered that the physical condition of our men was very poor, owing to limited food and restricted medical attention, while the Boers were strong and healthy. As the men of the Light Horse fell back with the Naval guns crews, the Boers advanced and captured the Naval gun position. But our Gunner, Mr Sims, led his bluejackets and succeeded in retaking the guns again for a while. As the reinforcements arrived the struggle became fiercer and fiercer and the casualties increased on both sides. Hand to hand fighting occurred while Mr Sims and his bluejackets and engineers were sent out to mount the 4.7-inch gun, lost it and regained it more than once. While all this was going, on more reinforcements were being sent for our men. Even the dismounted men of the Cavalry went up the ridge and performed good work. As more reinforcements arrived so the position improved, and by 10 a.m. the severity of the fighting had eased from sheer exhaustion on both sides.

By noon the position had apparently improved on both Wagon Hill and Caesars Camp, but an hour later the Boers made another determined attack on the western extremity of Wagon Hill, driving our men back. Here Mr Sims rallied his men again, and the enemy advance was repulsed. It was indeed an anxious time for Sir George White, who by now had informed General Buller by signal that he was hard pressed in Ladysmith.

Then after a blistering hot day, a thunder storm broke over the whole scene; drenching rain poured down upon Briton and Boer alike. By 4 p.m. overshadowing black cloud had replaced a clear blue sky and the Boers fearing a counter attack increased their rate of fire to an intensity not reached before from one end of the long ridge to the other. Then the Manchester's advanced and forced the enemy over the edge of Caesars Camp as the rain ceased, and reinforced by the Rifle Brigade and the Gordons, they were able to break the Boer's stubborn resistance and drive them down the slopes of the hill by about 5.30 p.m.

But the Boers were still in strength at the other end of the ridge at Wagon Hill. But Ian Hamilton was making preparations to recapture their position. About 5 p.m. therefore, he had brought up three companies of the Devons and when everything was ready, their objective was pointed out, and the order "Advance" was given about 6 p.m. Away went these gallant men, with fixed bayonets and a cheer, right across that open space of about 150 yards in the face of deadly rifle fire. On they went against the Boers, who were crouched behind boulders firing for all they were worth, until the Devons were upon them. Then they turned and ran for the next cover, while they further depleted the ranks of our men by intense fire. Then darkness fell and the Boers retired down the hillside, but still with stubborn coolness and extreme courage. So after more than 15 hours of desperate fighting, the greatest attack of the defences of Ladysmith ended in failure.

The attack on Observation Hill, though determined and supported by enemy artillery, also failed and the enemy finally withdrew during the great thunderstorm. Our losses were 168 killed and 249 wounded, while the Boer losses were reported to be 64 killed and 119 wounded. I am happy to relate that Mr Sims was specially mentioned for his bravery and untiring service he gave with the bluejackets and few Engineers together with the Imperial Light Horse. After all, this small party took the first shock of the enemy attack and stood their ground manfully on Wagon Hill till the Gordons and other reinforcements arrived, and continued the fight thereafter. In recognition of this fine work Mr Sims was promoted to the rank of Lieutenant.

The following day (7th January) a Thanksgiving Service was held in the Church of England, where a Te Deum was sung and Sir George White was present. Afterwards Sir Redvers Buller signalled his congratulations to Sir George White on the gallant defence of Ladysmith.

From now onwards the daily bombardments continued, but the enemy made no further determined attacks by Boer riflemen on our defences. Scarcity of food, enteric, malaria, dysentery and the abominable flies became a most serious problem to combat, as the mortality and number of men on the sick list increased each day. Some of the *Powerful*'s strongest men, who hitherto had been regarded as the healthiest, began to waste away with disease and starvation; then the inevitable removal to Intombe Camp and death would follow. As I think of these dark days now, I cannot help believing that had it not been that providence found relief for us through the kindliness of the Chief Commandant of the Boer forces, hardly a man would have been left strong enough to hold out. It was that brave and honourable old man, General Piet Joubert of Huguenot descent, who most chivalrously granted Sir George White the use of the neutral camp at Intombe, where the defenders of Ladysmith could send all incumbrances. Fighting men who were down with disease or wounded, all civilian men, women and children, were cared for 4 miles away from the town. If we consider this for a moment, it will be readily seen that, apart from the frightful congestion in the town, which would have been subject to every attack by shell fire, it enabled the medical authority to materially reduce the infection and daily additions to the sick lists. By this wonderful act of goodness on the part of our Christian foeman, though clearly opposed to his military demand, thousands of lives were spared us, and the strength of our defence was so immeasurably increased as to enable us to hold out until relieved.

In the light of subsequent wars against Germany and Japan, it leaves no doubt whatever, that refusal of permission to install such a neutral camp at Intombe, as it certainly would have been, Ladysmith would surely have fallen to the Boers.

On January 11th, a message from Queen Victoria thanking the defenders of Ladysmith for their gallant defence on the 6th January was received with much appreciation by everyone. A few days later we could hear the Naval 4.7-inch guns belonging to General Buller's force firing a large number of rounds, and our hopes again were aroused that this was the beginning of another advance for our relief. Then came the gladdening news that the relieving army had crossed the Tugela both at Pitgieter's Drift to the eastward and Trichart's Drift about 5 miles further to the West. Afterwards we were told that a mounted force had reached Acton Homes 22 miles westward, where a good road led straight into Ladysmith. The thundering of General Buller's guns far away to the South was like music in our ears, and watching the bursting 4.7 in lyddite shells on the heights of Spion Kop was verily balm to the eyes.

By the last week in January there was great expectation of sensational news from General Buller and there were persistent rumours coming to us that the Boers had been driven off Spion Kop and that we might soon expect a successful issue from this battle. But it was not to be. General Buller had met another setback in the battle of Spion Kop and evacuated his positions there. On the 27th January, practically his whole army was withdrawn to the south of Tugela once more. Naturally Sir George White, was seriously perturbed about the position and urged Buller to obtain another division of troops (from Lord Roberts who was now in Supreme command in South Africa) to make sure of success; as Ladysmith was doomed if he tried and failed again. To this Sir Redvers Buller replied saying that it was his intention of having another "fair and square" try to get through to us, but expressed the fear that his force was not strong enough.

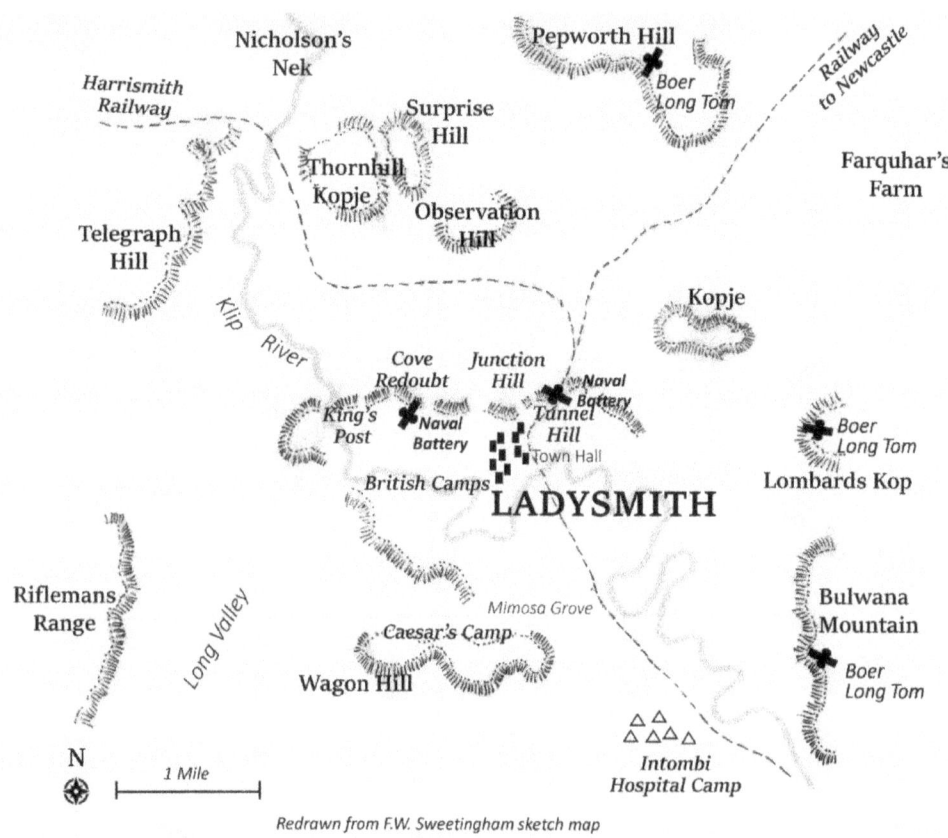

Sketch map of Ladysmith siege from author's pencil sketch

CHAPTER XVI

The Siege Lingers As We Await Buller's Troops.

--- ooOoo ---

Towards the end of January 1900, I met the Gunner Mr Sims, who asked me if I had seen the notice board in the Naval Camp. To my reply in the negative, he informed me that I might have a look at it for the announcement of my promotion to a Leading Seaman. My friend John Cobby was present at the moment, and after receiving kindly congratulations from Mr Sims, we left him and proceeded to the Notice Board. There it was, nailed to a tree and exhibiting the following words:

Frederick W. Sweetingham - Able Seaman promoted to the Rating of Leading Seaman as from date 11th January 1900.

Naturally I was delighted and more especially with the congratulations from my comrades, including the Captain of both 4.7-inch guns and Petty Officers Fisk and Lee. I could do no more than be grateful for their kind remarks for it was impossible to celebrate the occasion in the usual way amongst bluejackets on board ships of the Royal Navy.

From now onwards the question of food in Ladysmith became increasingly acute. The meat and biscuit ration was reduced and the meat ration was made up from horseflesh. Cavalry horses were now slain instead of being allowed to die from starvation or rinderpest. In addition, Colonel Ward had established a plant for conversion of horseflesh into a sort of Bovril, though it went by the name of chervil, mainly for use in the hospitals. The horseflesh was issued to us minced, flavoured with some spice, which we cooked in a water pan as no fats were available. The mixture thus cooked however, was quite palatable. Vegetables of course, had long been unprocurable, while tea went the same way. Coffee however, held out in a remarkable manner by adding ground maize to it until, we were told, the rate of coffee to the other constituents was only about ten per cent.

Our water supply was taken from the Klip River which was invariably muddy. A plant was therefore, installed to purify it, but this did not materially change the colour. Both of our Naval Engineers were enthusiastic workers at a water condensing plant, which was made from Railway materials. Mr C.C. Sheen R.N. (afterwards Admiral C.C. Sheen) and his opposite number Mr Ellis turned out considerable quantities of drinking water in this way.

For sailors suffering from internal disorders a mixture which tasted very much like carbonic acid was kept in a stone jar outside the Sick Base Tent, and one could help one's self to it as required; the vessel known as the fuelopeners bottle. Tobacco was very scarce and though this did not personally affect me, I could not help sympathising with my comrades who felt the need of it so very intensely. It was really pathetic to see them scrounging around in their endeavour to obtain minute particles of the weed and when these were exhausted any dried leaves were used as a substitute.

As if the suffering of the unfortunate people down at Intombe Hospital was not already enough we heard that scurvy had broken out there, mainly due to the want of fresh vegetables.

Early in February, General Buller informed us by heliogram that the Boers had commenced building a dam across the Klip River south of the Bulwana Mountain. The intention of the Boers was to build a dam 30 feet high and it was estimated that this would have flooded Ladysmith and incidentally isolate Intombe Camp. Consequently, we began shelling the Boer operations from positions on Caesars Camp with a 12-pound naval gun and smashed them up before the work could be completed. Meanwhile the 4.7-inch Princess Victoria gun was heavily engaged with the enemy's Long Toms as they attempted to interfere with the good work of our 12 pounders. During these artillery duels Lady Anne's twin sister on Cove Redoubt obtained a direct hit inside the gun emplacement of Long Tom on Bulwana. They evidently had put our most dominant opponent out of action for several days, during which we could see much activity going on at this gun, presumably in their endeavour to effect repairs so the gun could be fired again.

Sir Redvers Buller tried to break through the Boer defences again on the 5th February. This time he placed several pontoons and crossed the Tugela with a large force of Artillery, some 4 miles south-east of Spion Kop. Early on the 6th February, Buller directed his main attack across the Tugela at Vaal Krantz further to the right and only 500 yards to the north of the river. Here the Boer leader Louis Botha was in command of the defenders of this important height. Under cover of a heavy bombardment, Vaal Krantz was captured on the 6th only to be abandoned the next day. After this failure General Buller signalled to General White saying that he was going to "slip back" to Chieveley and would soon drive the Boers off Hlangwane and afterwards take Bulwana Mountain from the South. We were invariably reminded of these reverses by a searchlight display given by the Boers on the top of Bulwana, while a severe bombardment from Long Toms was fired into Ladysmith. These night shellings, however, proved of little value to the enemy and caused little damage.

Though the repeated reverses of Buller's Army was the cause of much depression and disappointment among us, in truth it must be said that everyone in the beleaguered town felt confident that Sir Redvers and his gallant troops would ultimately succeed. As the sand of time were ominously running to a climax, so the popularity of this fine 60 year old General increased. We of the Naval Brigade, together with our soldier comrades would not hear a word spoken against him even in the darkest hour. We had passed through those terrible heights immediately North of Tugela and knew how incomparably difficult it must be for the much revered General to bring up his men, against perhaps the finest riflemen in the world, without enormous losses; a factor which this humane man had ever in mind. We knew that Sir Redvers had previous experience in this kind of mountainous warfare in the Zulu War of 1878-9; and when it was rumoured that Lord Roberts was considering relieving Buller of his command, I well remember the words of our military comrades, who remarked, "If Roberts does that, then inevitably the position will become worse".

Field Marshal Lord Roberts had arrived at Cape Town in the *Dunottar Castle* with his Chief of Staff Major General Lord Kitchener on January 4th, and succeeded General Buller as Commander-in-Chief in South Africa. On taking over command, we heard that Roberts wished General Buller to continue his personal command of all operations in Natal, and that it was his intention to assume personal command of operations elsewhere.

Early in February we received the news that Lord Roberts had left Cape Town for the front, and now we heard by heliograph that he had arrived in the Orange Free State in order to personally direct operations there. His immediate objective was the Relief of Kimberley, and an advance on

Bloemfontein, while the strength of his Field Force was some 40,000 troops. It was therefore hoped that the Free Staters around Ladysmith would be attracted home in the defence of their capital city and so relieve the pressure.

The health of everybody seemed to be affected in some way. Many of our fellows who had landed with a liberal amount of avoirdupois had been reduced to mere skeletons. News from Intombe Camp was particularly depressing. The death rate there had been steadily rising and by the middle of February was no less than fifteen a day, while the total record of patients who had died at Intombe during the one hundred days of siege had amounted to five hundred.

Stories about the black-marketeers added somewhat to the gloom, though personally I was not in the least affected about it. An egg at 4 shillings and twopence each would have cost me two day's pay, while other commodities outside the service ration were being sold at extortionate prices to the few who could afford to pay for them. Meanwhile I managed to appease my hunger with the bare Service ration of an Army biscuit and one quarter, a little horse mince and an ounce or so of mealie meal each day.

CHAPTER XVII

The Battle of the Tugela Heights and the Relief of Ladysmith

--- ooOoo ---

Splendid news had now reached us from the West. Kimberley had been relieved on 15th February, and a force of Cavalrymen under General French had ridden into the town. Simultaneously we heard that General Buller had commenced operations in his fourth and last endeavour to relieve us. For days past we could hear the thundering of his heavy guns and watch the bursting of lyddite and cannon shells as they crashed upon the heights held by the Boers.

It was now that Buller's artillery had been reinforced with a 6-inch naval gun capable of firing 100-pound shells. Thus, three distinct types of naval long-range guns were bombarding the enemy positions on the Tugela Heights at a distance ranging from 4 to 6 miles, while each gun was capable of firing lyddite or shrapnel shells as necessary. One can imagine therefore, that Sir Redvers set a high value on the help that was given by the bluejackets under the command of Captain Jones R.N.

Only a few days later we heard that the British troops had driven the Boers from their commanding positions South of the Tugela River and had captured Cingolo Nek, Monte Cristo, and Green Hill on the 18th. The key position of Hlangwane Mountain was taken on the 19th and the advance across the river was well under way by the 22nd. The indomitable valour of Buller's Infantry regiments was again proved by the frontal attack under terrible enemy fire and capture of Hedge Hill. Then on the 26th we heard that Buller was going strong and that the Boer Commandant Cronje had surrendered to Lord Roberts with over 6,000 Boers. We had no time for small talk now, all of us were on tiptoe with expectation for further news from Buller. We felt that the tide was now at last to turn.

Success after success was reported. Seventy guns ranged along the northern slopes of Hlangwane and Monte Cristo were pounding the Boer positions on Inniskilling Hill, Railway Hill and Pieters Hill, which were taken by the 27th. This was the Anniversary of Majuba Day and it brought us new confidence, with the message from General Buller -"Doing Well". Pieters Hill was less than 8 miles from Ladysmith and marked the extreme left of the Boer defence line; with this key position seized from the enemy, a way was opened to Ladysmith past Intombe Camp. By now the Boers must have known with their profound insight that further defence was hopeless. Though they had put up a gallant and stubborn fight, we now knew that a grand victory of British arms was near.

But there still remained the chance that the Boers would make a final stand on Bulwana. This apprehension was soon disposed of, when we plainly saw the sheer legs rigged above the Long Tom gun on Bulwana, and behind it, Boer wagons by the score trekking to the northward. There was no more doubt Commandant General Joubert had given the order for general retreat. There was no further need for conserving our ammunition and our Cove Redoubt 4.7 gun expended its ammunition upon the enemy, wrecking the sheer legs and stopping the work. The Boer Army was

The Boer War

defeated and in full retreat, while huge convoys of enemy wagons could be seen moving northward in the region of Spion Kop. The next day, 28th February, no reply came from Long Tom on Bulwana and it was presumed that it had been dismounted during the night in order to join the northward trek.

During the last week, rations had been increased or decreased according to General White's hopes or fears of the success of General Buller. On the afternoon of the 28th a heliograph message was received from Sir Redvers saying, *"I beat the enemy thoroughly yesterday and am sending my cavalry on as fast as very bad roads will admit. I believe the enemy to be in full retreat."*

It was very true. Thank God this fine soldier and his heroic army had come through at last. At twilight on the evening of the 28th February, a composite mounted regiment including units of the Imperial Light Horse and the Natal Carboneers, which formed a small advance guard of Lord Dundonald's Cavalrymen, rode past Intombe Camp into Ladysmith. This advance party was under the command of Major Gough, and as they arrived at the main street of the town, Sir George White with his staff met them, and after greetings of a dramatic nature, three cheers were called for our grand old General whose leadership was a subject of admiration throughout the siege of 118 days. During a pause in this spontaneous applause Sir George whose voice was full of emotion said, "I thank you men, one and all, from the bottom of my heart, for the help and support you have given me, and I shall always acknowledge it to the end of my life. It grieved me to have to cut your rations, but I promise you that I will not do it again. I thank God we have kept the flag flying."

Then three cheers were given for Sir Redvers Buller, and afterwards the gathering sang 'God Save the Queen'. The defence of Ladysmith was an ordeal that I endured during a very impressionable stage of my life, and I shall cherish the memory of it as a glorious episode of my career.

On March 1st Sir Redvers Buller himself rode into Ladysmith where he met Sir George White and after a short interview, he returned to his Head Quarters which had been established close to Ladysmith. Meanwhile, the divisions of his army were being brought up and pitched their camps on the plains to the southwest of the town. On March 3rd General Buller rode at the head of his victorious army into Ladysmith. It was indeed a grand sight to watch those strong robust fellow's stride into the town, though it was somewhat marred by the presence of the fever stricken emaciated figures who had lined the streets to welcome them. Their thin pale faces and faint cheers contrasted so much with the bronzed and healthy appearance of Buller's men, as they swung by with vigour and buoyancy. A special feature of this march was that the place of honour at the head of the Army was given to the Dublin Fusiliers, whose losses in battle had been so severe. These fine troops were wearing sprigs of green in their helmets in memory of the Emerald Isle. Other Irish Regiments had fought with exceptional valour during the storming of the Tugela Heights and in recognition of the valour of the Irishmen on this occasion, Her Majesty the Queen expressed her wish that the "Wearing of the Green" on St Patrick's Day was to be observed in the future; also that a Regiment of Irish Guards be instituted.

On Sunday March 4th, a great Church Parade assembled for a Thanksgiving Service to God. Generals Buller and White were present. After Divine Service, General Buller addressed the great assembly of troops thanking both relieving and relieved forces for their strenuous exertions and congratulating them upon the result. Of all the public ceremonies which I have attended, and they have been many, this was truly the most impressive one of my life. I can picture Sir Redvers even to this day standing by the Army Chaplain, and when I remember the relentless criticism of that great soldier and gentleman in association with the earlier failed attempts to relieve Ladysmith it makes my blood boil. He had been cruelly slandered in the press and by calumnious critics in the clubs of England and abroad. In fact, General Buller tackled the most difficult military task that British Arms had to that time encountered, and he himself did not fail. For those se backs at Colenso, Spion Kop and Vaal Krantz were due to the British Military System rather than to any man of that time.

Let us examine the case more closely. Buller's campaign was not an expedition against the frontiersmen of India, or the savages of Africa, which hitherto, had been regarded as war. It was real warfare, necessitating frontal attacks against fearless and stubborn fighters occupying almost impregnable positions. The enemy, defending themselves with up-to-date instruments of war, were expert marksmen, mounted and possessing a special aptitude for mobility and taking cover. Compare this with the British Military System, which General Buller had thrust upon him. Where ever he moved his large army of men, it was hampered with a cumbersome commissariat, other paraphernalia, supplies of all kinds, which had to be moved in hundreds of slow-moving wagons driven by oxen negotiating difficult and tortuous roads and passes. The mention of these factors alone will suffice to show that the responsibility of deploying masses of exposed men and material to attack was enormous, and one which called for encouragement and concern in the event of reverses rather than vituperation and calumny. We may consider ourselves fortunate in having the lessons drawn from General Buller's achievement of the Relief of Ladysmith as a guide to the British War Office in conducting the two World Wars that have followed.

Sir Redvers Buller commanded at Aldershot before he was appointed to the Command of the Army Corps in South Africa in 1899, and upon his return to England from the Boer War he was again appointed to the Command at Aldershot. In a speech delivered in October 10th 1901, he referred to his critical dispatches to Sir George White and his irritation by the relentless persecution which was still being directed against him at the time. Buller perhaps, outreached himself in his self-defence and was consequently relieved of his command.

Soon after the dispersal of the Church Parade I joined a small party of bluejackets and went out to a nearby camp of one of the regiments of the relieving force. It was an Irish Regiment in which one of our comrades expected to meet a relative. On arrival we were received with sincere greetings and almost before we could enter into conversation or exchange views, a liberal supply of bully beef and biscuit was placed before us. Since the rations of the Naval Brigade had not then been increased materially, one may be sure that this kindly act was in response to the hungry appearance that the sailors had presented!

The following day we were able to make the acquaintance of members of Buller's Naval Brigade. We learnt that the losses in General Buller's Force during the battles fought from February 13th to 28th were heavy. But it is safe to say that after the relief of Ladysmith, Buller's Army, with brilliant strategy, cleared the Boers from their strong positions at Masuba in Northern Natal with comparatively few casualties. From there he rapidly advanced in the Transvaal to Volkrust, clearing the Boers from Northern Natal. By the 4th July, Buller's Army had made a junction with Lord Roberts Force which had relieved Kimberley, occupied Bloemfontein and captured Pretoria from General Louis Botha on June 4th, 1900. Pretoria.. At that time, Lord Roberts himself was in Pretoria and had set up his Headquarters there.

Following these rapid military achievements, it was hoped that the South African War would have ended. Indeed, negotiations had already been opened with the influential Boer Leader General Botha, and had it not been for that formidable man General Christian De Wet, who was disrupting the communications in the Orange River Colony with considerable success at the time, that long and tiresome third stage of the war would not have happened. The strength of General Buller's Army during the operations for the relief of Ladysmith was 30,000 men and the total losses exceeded 5,000 men as indicated below:

	Killed, wounded and missing
Battle of Colenso	1,125
Spion Kop	1,733
Battle of Vaal Krantz	374
Battle of Tugela Heights	1,926
TOTAL	5,158

The total number of British Troops in Ladysmith when the town was isolated and surrounded by the Boers on October 30th 1899, were 570 Officers and 12,900 men. This number included the Irregular Troops, Natal Volunteers as well as the Regular Army under General White. To these must be added 2,000 civilians, 3,200 Kaffirs and Cape Boys and 2,500 Indians. The above figures totaled more than 21,000 persons, who had to be fed, whereas the fighting strength of General Sir George White's Army was no more than 10,000 combatants, including the Naval Brigade. Details of our casualties during the siege are as follows:

	Killed	Wounded	Missing	TOTAL
Through enemy action	244	841	14	1099
Through disease	541			541
TOTAL	785	841	14	1640

It was never intended that Ladysmith should form anything beyond a stationary hospital. It was therefore, only equipped with appliances with which the Army took the field. To give some idea of the enormous work carried out by the medical staff in Ladysmith and the terrible suffering due to steady increase of disease, the following details are also appended:

Total admitted to Hospital	10,690 men
Patients in hospital on 15th Nov	370
Patients in hospital on 1st Dec	469
Patients in hospital on 1st Jan	1,600
Patients in hospital on 1st Feb	2,472
Patients in hospital on 1st March	2,000

Of the nominal strength of fighting men on the day of the relief, very few if any officers or men were fit for action in the field.

Of all the regiments in Ladysmith during the siege, the most to be pitied in my opinion were those included in the Cavalry Brigade. Sir John French probably anticipated this before he left by the last train as previously mentioned. A cavalryman without his horse is in much the same position as a sailing ship without sails. These fine fellows of the 5th Lancers, 18 and 19th Hussars and 5th Dragoon Guards were terribly sad in the loss of their horses. Death from disease increased at an alarming rate and owing to scarcity of fodder many were slaughtered for human consumption. Only horses used by Sir George White's Staff and for Field Artillery could be maintained. The men of the dismounted Cavalry therefore, were detailed for outpost duty in the trenches similar to the Infantrymen. It was a curious sight to see them striding out at night, with carbines and their lancers, which to the bluejacket appeared very much like the Naval Boarding Pikes, which we were trained to use on board in those days.

The third stage of the war commenced in July 1900. It was entirely different from the others, in that, comparatively small numbers of opposing combatants faced each other in the British endeavour to complete the conquest of enemy territory and subdue the Boers by mopping up operations. This necessitated the employment of nothing more than brigades or battalions, whereas it had required strong divisions and Army Corps to fight the Boers in the early stages of the War. Nevertheless, this warfare did not cease until the Treaty of Vereeniging was signed between Great Britain and the two Republics of the Transvaal and the Orange Free State, whereby they were annexed on May 31st 1902.

During the South African War much had been said of the British Volunteer Regiments, who came out to fight for their country. This of course, was before the days of the grand Territorial Army initiated by Lord Haldane; though the Militia Force was in being and many thousands of this force volunteered and went to South Africa. Of the volunteers who came out, it seemed that the Imperial Yeomanry (mounted troops) and the City Imperial Volunteers attracted the most attention. In December 1899, the C.I.V's were raised by the Lord Mayor of London, who undertook to raise, equip and transport to South Africa, a corps from men of the various Volunteer Regiments in the London area; all at the expense of the citizens of London, and all specially selected men and the best marksmen. Incidentally, it was decided to present the Freedom of the City to all members of this force. This corps included Artillery, Mounted Infantry and Infantry Regiments, while care was taken to select men of a higher social standing than that of the common soldier. It was natural therefore, that though its individual members merited every praise these comparatively small forces of special volunteers were much overrated by the masses in England.

THE BOER WAR

By contrast however, one cannot help remarking that too little was said of those fine men from the Colonies who volunteered and went to the aid of the Mother Country.

The Boer War proved a crucial test of the relations between the Colonies and the British Government; and in those dark days of October to December 1900, the result was shown as clearly and quickly as the action of acid on litmus test paper. Apart from Cape Colony and Natal, who were most directly affected by the issue of the war; Canada, Australia and New Zealand were solidly behind the Mother country and sent substantial forces to our aid. It was true that the Colonies of Australia were directly interested in the South African situation in that the safety of the Cape Route for shipping was involved. This question affecting their vast overseas trade is still of the greatest importance today.

By early November 1899, Australia alone had sent to South Africa 1,200 Volunteers from New South Wales, Victoria, Queensland, South Australia, West Australia and Tasmania; including a Squadron of New South Wales Lancers who were training in England; and no less than 80 Infantrymen from Tasmania. In all, Australian Colonies sent 6,328 Officers and men to South Africa by the middle of May 1900 and 16,632 throughout the war.

	By May 1900	TOTAL
New South Wales	2,694	6,945
Victoria	1,423	3,757
Queensland	864	2,370
South Australia	571	1,432
West Australia	475	1,129
Tasmania	301	749
TOTAL	6,328	16,382

The Volunteers raised and sent from the Colonies of Canada, Australia and New Zealand during the earliest days of the war amounted to nearly 11,500 men and later a total of about 30,000 Colonial Volunteers had reinforced the South African Field Force. If this figure seems rather small for an aggregate population of more than 10 million in the British Colonies, it was certainly not through lack of loyalty or zeal, but rather through want of forethought and organization.

Of the above figures it must be mentioned that more than one half were sent from Australia, including the famous Australian Bushmen, mounted men of whom about 1,400 left Australia before March 1900. This force were all accustomed to the rough and tumble life of the 'back blocks' of Australia, and would easily find themselves at home on the Veldt and prove a match for the Boer at his own tactics.

Canada had no direct interest in the War, as in the case of Australia and New Zealand, but it is interesting to note that in March 1900 Lord Strathcona the High Commissioner for Canada in England (and Governor of the Hudson Bay Company) transported, at his own expense, about 600 rough riders known as Strathcona's Horse. It is said that this cost him nearly a quarter of a million sterling. To these must be added the Canadian Mounted Rifles made up mainly from that splendid body of men the North West Mounted Police in Canada.

The loyalty of the Crown Colonies was demonstrated in a similar manner to that of the above self-governing colonies. The Federated Malay States, Ceylon, Burma, Trinidad all contributed men and materials. Last but not least India sent her Army under Sir George White, the 16th Lancers which joined Buller's forces in Natal. Also under the patronage of the Indian Princes, a Corps of Mounted Infantry - Colonel Lavisden's Assam Valley Light Horse early in March 1900. Though the loyalty of one native of India has since been questioned, I would like to mention the valuable service that he rendered to the British Army throughout the campaign in Natal. I refer to that saintly Indian statesman Mohandas Karamchand Gandhi, who had then been in the legal profession in Natal for some 6 years. Gandhi organized an Ambulance Corps of Indians, over a 1,000 strong, which tended to the wounded on the battlefields at Colenso, Spion Kop and elsewhere, to the admiration of the British troops advancing to our relief at Ladysmith. I shall have more to say about this wonderful man and his activities in Bombay, when I was there many years later.

All this splendid proof of loyalty and good will on the part of the countries making up the British Empire most certainly had a considerable bearing upon the attitude of foreign countries towards the British Government. Since the average foreigner had no knowledge of the circumstances which led to the Boer War, he was naturally in sympathy with the Boers, especially as gold had recently been found in great quantities in the Transvaal. Germany in particular was especially interested in the quarrel, as previously indicated in the Kaiser's telegram to Kruger after the Jameson Raid. The Foreign Press did not attempt to conceal its vituperation and calumny directed against Britain. The malicious caricatures indicating contempt of our Army during the early days of defeat, and the oft repeated reports of the annihilation of General Buller's army, and the fall of Ladysmith, all tended to show their hatred for England and thirst to show that the British Empire did not really merit the great world position that it claimed to occupy.

There was some allowance to be made for the feelings of the people of the Netherlands. After all the Boers had the same ancestry, and moreover the Transvaal Government had made a policy of giving the best professional positions to men of Dutch nationality to the detriment of the British Uitlanders. As for the leading European countries, especially Germany, France and Spain, whose jealousy of Britain was notoriously apparent at the time, there was one definite reason which prevented their hatred from developing into open hostility; that was in their consideration of the sure shield of England - the British Navy!

In the matter of the feelings of the United States of America during the Boer War, doubtless there were numbers who sympathised with both Briton and Boer. Only two years previously, the United States herself had experienced a war against Spain; and in their policy relating to Cuba and the Philippine Islands, the attitude towards the British people and Government was most cordial. This aspect was seen in a previous chapter in which the visit of the British China Squadron to the Philippines was referred to. In the circumstances, it might be said that the attitude of the Government of the United States of America was in the main both friendly and sympathetic, and many Americans were found among the volunteers in the fighting forces of Britain in South Africa. What more can be said, when it is remembered that the American public generously subscribed to a fund for the provision of the fully equipped Hospital Ship *Maine* which rendered such splendid service during the South African War. This valuable ship was afterwards presented to the British nation and was again in service as a fine Hospital Ship during the subsequent Great Wars.

Before relating our departure from Ladysmith, I feel that it is a fitting place to say a few words about two important personalities from whom we took our parting. I refer to the Civil Head of the town and to the Military Commander throughout the siege. The Mayor of Ladysmith, Mr Farquhar, was a Scotsman whose sense of responsibility regarding the safety of the civil population of the town was to be very much admired. During the negotiations between Sir George White and General Joubert on the effect of shell fire into the town; it was the Mayor who strongly deprecated the suggestion of certain ultra-patriotic citizens of Ladysmith to belittle the generous offer of General Joubert and refuse the enemy's terms; an offer which happily, Sir George accepted. Also, much admired was our beloved Commander George Stewart White, an Irishman in his 65th year, with considerable military experience in India, and had won the Victoria Cross in the Afghan War of 1878-80. His health during the siege was not good and like many others had suffered from the fever. His Head Quarters accommodation was no better than that of other Officers, and was exposed to the daily bombardment. He inspired us all with the determination to hold Ladysmith at all costs, even if relief failed. Thus, the British flag was kept hoisted in the beleaguered town under the leadership of Sir George, whose name has found an honoured place in the annals of British history. On his return to England, White was appointed Governor and Commander-in-Chief of Gibraltar with rank of General.

Not that long after the relief of Ladysmith, the *Powerful*'s Naval Brigade had orders to return to the ship, which was at Simonstown. This meant that we would have to first go to Durban and embark for passage to the Cape Peninsular by sea transport. Accordingly, we bid farewell to our comrades and friends and departed early one morning. As we marched out of the town, I well remember, taking a last look at the Ladysmith Town Hall with its clock tower, which had been destroyed by Boer shells. Mule wagons accompanied us with a certain amount of our baggage on this march of about 7 miles to the railway station at Nelthorpe. Mr Sims was very ill at the time, but we arranged to take him with us on a stretcher fitted to a light conveyance on wheels. It was thought by many that he should have remained in Ladysmith with others of the Naval Brigade who were too ill to move; but it was his express wish to come, and we were all very glad about it. The Boers had broken up the railway lines in numerous places, but the Royal Engineers had contrived to get an engine and a few railway carriages as far North as Nelthorpe so we boarded the train there.

During the first part of the march most were so highly elated that we did not realise what a tedious journey it would prove to be. Personally, I was able to stick it out the whole distance. But several of our poor fellows were so weak and emaciated that they were compelled to give in and complete the remainder of the journey by a few portable railway trolleys, which had been brought into use. Our journey by train to the South was completed with few interruptions and we arrived at Colenso about 6 p.m. There we changed into ordinary railway carriages and after partaking of some food continued the journey southward. During the night we passed through Escort and Pietermaritzburg, where the people of these towns were very kind and gave us refreshing drinks and food.

The following forenoon we arrived at Durban where Captain Percy Scott (who was then Commandant) and men of HMS *Terrible* received us with great joy and hospitality. A luncheon had been kindly arranged for us in the Goods Shed at the Railway Station and this was the first really good meal that we had even seen for several months. I'm afraid that most of us paid the penalty for overeating all the good things so liberally set before us. After luncheon we embarked in a British transport and sailed for Simonstown the same evening. A fine reception awaited us there, by the ships of the Cape Squadron, and by the Mayor and citizens of Simonstown. It was a grand feeling to return to the dear old *Powerful* and to mingle once again with old shipmates whom we had left behind to keep the flag flying in the Squadron. Amidst all the rejoicing however, there was a streak of sadness in our thoughts of messmates who had lost their lives on African soil.

A bumper mail from England awaited our return to the ship, which afforded a pleasant occupation for most of us, as we read our letters from home, which had accumulated for months. Her Majesty, Queen Victoria had kindly sent to each one of us for a New Year's gift, an elegantly designed red, blue and gold tin box containing chocolate. The box was embossed with the insignia and portrait of the Queen and the words: 'South Africa 1900'. I still possess my treasured gift and hope it will become an heirloom. I must also mention the kindly thought of that great friend of the bluejacket Miss Agnes E. Weston, who instituted the Sailors Rests at the principal naval ports in England. Miss Weston had sent each one of us a Christmas pudding hermetically sealed in a tin. It was the good lady's intention that the gift should reach us before Christmas 1900, but when I opened my package, three months later, I found the contents in a most delectable condition. Better late than never!

Since the *Terrible* was present at Simonstown and ready to take our place in the China Squadron, orders were received for the *Powerful* to return to England.

Part 4

Growing Experience In The Royal Navy

CHAPTER XVIII

Return to Portsmouth.

--- ooOoo ---

Before the *Powerful* sailed for England, the good people of the Cape Peninsula sent on board gifts of fruit, vegetables and port wine, which were truly appreciated. I would mention here that, presumably due to over-eating after so long on a starvation diet, the majority of the Naval Brigade contracted that morbid disease of the bile - jaundice. This was marked by a yellowness of the skin and the whites of the eyes; and now unfortunately, whilst there was plenty of food, many of us suffered from loss of appetite. Very hard luck after nearly four months on short rations. I was a victim of this disorder which, of course, became the subject of much merriment on the mess deck. The sailors of course, soon coined a suitable phrase to indicate the sufferers - we were known as the "Canary Party". The restrictions placed upon our diet added to the discomfort for we were not allowed our ration of rum, nor to imbibe in the daily allowance of gift port wine. The latter was issued in the dog watch when the Boatswain's Mate would pipe, "Do you hear there - Naval Brigade lay aft for issue of port wine. Canary Party muster for'ard outside the Sick Bay!"

This was always followed by roars of cheering and some groans!

We called at St Helena and Ascension Island on the homeward voyage and from the latter the ship embarked about twenty very fine turtles. These were perfect monsters, the largest being nearly five feet long and about 300 pounds in weight. The ships marine butcher had charge of the turtles and a few were killed by him and the parts distributed for making soup and other food delicacies. The killing of these enormous creatures however, was beyond the capacity of the butcher singlehanded, so a little seamanship was introduced in the murderous method adopted. They were laid out on the Fore-topmen's deck so the Captain of the Top and a couple of hands made the necessary preparations so the butcher could then perform the execution speedily and let us hope painlessly as circumstances permitted. A large number of eggs in various stages of development were recovered from the female turtles, while the carapace was preserved as trophies. Two of these were afterwards sent to the Naval School at Portsmouth where they were polished and adorned the walls of an Officers Mess, presenting an appearance of shield shaped trophies.

Everyone had by now shaken down in their jobs though many changes were made in our duties. Being now a Leading Seaman I had left my former colleagues in the Fore-top for duty as bowman of the Captain's Galley. This was the six oared gig and it was reserved for the exclusive use of the Captain. When the boat was not required for use, the crew were employed mainly on the maintenance of the boat, or work in connection with the Captain's cabins, for which the Petty Officer, Captain's Coxswain was responsible.

Towards the end of this voyage homewards, one witnessed an almost unbelievable incident regarding the disposal of certain naval stores. In those days, and incredible though it may appear, a surplus of consumable stores was regarded in a manner almost as serious as a deficiency. In consequence, the Store Keeping Officer took good care to expend such items so that they would not be shown in the store Ledger on paying off. This was usually done by transfer to another ship if practicable, or by dumping them overboard at sea! I have seen both these methods employed. This pernicious practice, involving criminal waste was entirely due to the stupid regulations governing the maintenance of stores and keeping of stores accounts. Each ship was furnished with an established proportion of consumable stores which was considered sufficient to last for a given period of time; and it was the duty of the store keeping officer to maintain this proportion and to periodically obtain replenishments from the Dockyards. In theory this appears to be a very sound arrangement; but when ships were on foreign stations and often at sea for long periods in foul weather, there must be occasions when, owing to extraordinary wear and tear the allowance would not be sufficient. For example, there was an enormous quantity of hempen rope, comprising the running rigging, boat falls and so forth; which must be replaced for safety reasons as soon as undue wear is apparent. In order therefore, to provide for such a contingency, the Store Keeping Officer demanded to replenish in full, on each periodical occasion, whether the remains of his stock warranted it or not. Imagine this system going on for a number of years, and one can easily realise how common the accumulation of surplus rope was in ships when due to pay off. But this would not matter very much if it were permitted to be returned to the Dockyard store as surplus to requirements. But such an elementary course was not allowed, without inquiry as to breach of regulations forbidding the accumulation of surplus stores.

On our arrival home an enthusiastic welcome was awaiting the *Powerful*. As we steamed into Portsmouth Harbour thousands of people had lined the shores of Portsmouth and Gosport and were waving flags in kindly greeting while cheers came from the men who manned the ships, that were dressed over-all with flags in honour of the occasion. HMS *Victory*, Nelson's Flag Ship at Trafalgar, was moored in the centre of the Harbour and flying the flag of the Admiral Commander-in-Chief at Portsmouth; while the crew of this grand old ship cheered us lustily as we steamed past her. Our huge paying off pendant, which we had hoisted when leaving Hong Kong, was again streaming some hundreds of feet astern and with pride and thankfulness we arrived alongside the Jetty. Standing with the Naval Commander-in-Chief were many prominent persons of the land, who were waiting to come on board to greet the Captain and his ship. Among them being his brother, the Earl of Durham.

The greatest notability for whom I was looking however, was my mother, father and sister Edith, who had come from Woolston, near Southampton by train and were among the relatives and friends on the wharf awaiting the ships arrival. This was truly a happy meeting and to add to our joy, all members of the Naval Brigade were granted 10 days special leave commencing from that very day. So, to be sure, when I journeyed home by railway with my family, this afforded one of the highlights of my life.

It was on this occasion of landing that another rare privilege was granted us, in that the Custom's Authority at Portsmouth had kindly given us what is known as a 'Free Gangway'. This meant that the unprecedented permission was given us to take on shore contraband goods such as tobacco, cigars, scents etc., free of duty, upon declaration of the nature and quantity of such articles. Though I shall feel very grateful for this during my lifetime, I have never heard of a similar privilege being granted; neither can I imagine any Authority of modern times ever dreaming of such relaxation on the part of the present vigorous collection of Customs revenue.

Life amid the congeniality of relatives and friends at home, soon enabled one to regain health and to assume a robust appearance. At least I presume it was so in my case for at that time several recruiting sergeants were doing good work for the Army, and I particularly remember that on one

Growing Experience In The Royal Navy

day no less than three of the gentlemen in different parts of Southampton, were of the opinion that my immediate future would be much improved if I enlisted for service in South Africa.

On returning to the ship after this delectable leave, we joined in the task of preparing the ship for paying off. Meanwhile, Her Majesty the Queen most graciously entertained the men of the *Powerful*, who had fought at Ladysmith and at Enslin, to a luncheon at Windsor Castle. The beloved Queen, who had then reached the age of 81 years, received us most kindly, and afterwards came down the line of tables in her wheeled chair, accompanied by General Sir George White, who had arrived home in the 'Dunvegan Castle' on April 14th 1900. Her Majesty chattered with Sir George as she moved along and stopped occasionally to speak some kindly words to her guests. I remember very well that Her Majesty halted quite close to where I was sitting, and Sir George White by her side cheerfully remarked - how very sorry he was that he was unable to provide us with a meal this delicious when in Ladysmith. To others he kindly referred to the Naval Brigade as his 'Band of Hope' that arrived at Ladysmith in the nick of time. This entertainment was indeed a happy and memorable one; and the Port Wine served at the close of the luncheon was the most exquisite I have ever tasted. It was said that a special vintage of the 18th century had been served and well it might have been!

A few days later the Lord Mayor and citizens of London entertained the *Powerful*'s Naval Brigade to luncheon at the Mansion House. This too was most enjoyable, while many kind remarks were made about us. On that same afternoon we were entertained at Lloyds, by the famous London Corporation of Marine Underwriters. The representatives of this great institution (founded in a Coffee House by Edward Lloyd in the 17th Century) gave us a wonderfully kind reception; and before leaving, each man was presented with a handsome silver tobacco box bearing the Lloyds crest and the date of the function - 7th May, 1900. I prized this gift very much indeed coming from the renowned Lloyds of London.

Another most generously kind entertainment to the Naval Brigade of the *Powerful* was a banquet at Portsmouth. On this occasion the Mayor and citizens gave us a great ovation at the Town Hall. Here each member of the Naval Brigade was presented with a souvenir from the Lord Mayor. This was a beautifully inscribed silver hunter watch made by the well-known firm of Smith and Son, the Strand London. A splendid gift and a remarkably good time-keeper to this day, and I valued it very much indeed. Still another donor, was that great lady Miss Agnes E. Weston known as the Sailors Friend, who kindly gave each man of the *Powerful*'s Naval Brigade a case containing a wooden pipe, tobacco pouch and a silver match box. This gracious act was typical of the good lady of whom I have referred to in a previous chapter.

On the 8th June 1900, the ship's Company of the *Powerful* paid off and after foreign service leave, I returned to HMS *Duke of Wellington*, the hulk of an old battleship which was then used as the Depot Ship for seamen of the Portsmouth Division. Some 1,100 men were accommodated in this ship during my short stay. There my mind was occupied mainly as to how soon I could be drafted to a sea going ship. Messing accommodation in the *Duke of Wellington* was extremely stringent as each mess was crammed with about double normal capacity; consequently, a large number of one's messmates were compelled to take their meals amidships and perch on the cables or bitts whilst having dinner. As the messdeck was so crowded, so too was the sleeping accommodation. Hammocks were slung over the mess tables and gangways, all packed liked sardines in a box. Discipline however, was strictly enforced and the army of Ships' Corporals (Regulating Petty Officers as they are now called) seemed to be competing each day among themselves in their endeavour to bring up defaulters.

Frederick W Sweetingham

In previous pages I have referred to the bluejacket's uniform, and how sailors made their own clothes; but now I must mention that here, in the Naval Depot Ship, ready-mades were stocked and woe betide any seaman who had turned out his own uniform clothing, unless the garments were cut strictly to service pattern. Unfortunately, I numbered among these. During the previous 3 years abroad, I had, like many others, purchased the raw material from the slop room and made my own garments measured to fit. If one had any desire to be dressed smartly this would mean that a departure from the service design and measurements was necessary in almost every particular. Bell bottom trousers for instance were cut to about 30 inches in circumference, whereas the regulation purser's dimensions was in the region of 20 inches; the cut for jumpers, collars, necks for flannels, caps etc. were similarly affected. Now one of the most important functions performed in a Naval Depot Ship, even to this day, is to ensure that all bluejackets possess a full kit and wear nothing but the regulation uniform. Inspection was therefore necessary and this was carried out by Ships' Corporals under the direction of an executive officer.

In due course the whole of my kit was laid out for inspection and the measuring tape was freely used upon every garment of my own manufacture, which I was informed would have to be altered where practicable or new items would be supplied on payment in lieu. This applied to my cloth trousers and best serge frock (the main sailors suit of those days), all other serge, drill or duck suits. The only practical remedy was the purchase of a new regulation outfit. Unlike the soldier, the bluejackets had to purchase every item of his clothes, and thus one was made to pay for his time and labour spent mainly when his messmates were enjoying themselves on shore or asleep in their hammocks. My pay at that time was 2/1d per diem and the cost of replacements for my clothes ran up to more than £7. Nevertheless, I was permitted to retain my bell-bottomed trousers and other naval trimmings, which I wore again after leaving the Depot Ship.

About this time, I recall an amusing incident when on shore leave at Portsmouth one evening. There I met an old shipmate an Irishman - Jim Flanagan by name who had just left a boxing booth at a street corner after putting up a fight against a professional boxer. Incidentally his opponent had laid odds of four to one against any competitor who might enter in combat. After his fight, Jim emerged from the booth with his face bleeding and so horribly disfigured that one could scarcely recognise him. Accordingly, I questioned him as to his awful appearance. Jim solemnly told the story and then added, "Begorra I'm quite satisfied - for my 5 bob was returned for putting up a good fight!"

On the 31st of July 1900, I left the *Duke of Wellington* and joined HMS *Australia*, a belted cruiser of the Home Fleet. The ship was normally stationed in the Southampton waters, but while Her Majesty the Queen was in residence at Cowes, Isle of Wight, the *Australia* was detailed for service as Port Guard ship there. As a young Leading Seaman of some ambition, my aim was to work hard in the performance of my duties and to obtain further promotion. In this I was very fortunate, for a vacancy occurred in the rating of Second Class Petty Officers borne in the complement of the ship, and this was awarded to me on the 19th September 1900. On promotion, the duties of Captain of the forecastle were assigned to me. Here again I was fortunate in that the Captain of the forecastle of the starboard, or opposite watch to which I belonged, was a very senior Petty Officer named Tim Francis; a very fine seaman with long experience in square rigged ships. Tim was also a gentleman in every respect and it was my great privilege to enjoy his friendship as well as his kindly help and guidance in our combined duties. There were some 30 seamen in each watch of our part of the ship, and when Francis was on leave, I was nominally responsible for the work of some 60 forecastle men. Petty Officers of the present day are not encouraged to lead their men

Growing Experience In The Royal Navy

by giving a hand themselves in the matter of important work, but in those days, this was the usual practice; in continuation of the custom in square rigged ships where the Captains of the Tops were compelled to handle jobs during difficult and dangerous operations, where the lives of men were involved.

Now Tim Francis belonged definitely to this old school of Petty Officers and naturally I felt it incumbent on my part to emulate his example and thus a sort of friendly rivalry went on during general drills and in ordinary work. We, of course did not perform the menial tasks of cleaning, scrubbing etc., but when leading our topmen, say at scrubbing or holystoning the decks, both Tim and I would be found on deck in our bare feet with trousers turned up working the salt water hose while urging our topmen to put more weight on their utensils so that the forecastle deck would appear like a hounds tooth and outshine the decks in the after parts of the ship. Petty Officers of modern times might regard it as infra dig to paddle around the decks with bare feet every morning as we did no matter whether there was ice or snow lying about. However, I am still convinced that it was necessary in the interest of true discipline not to expect or insist upon the men being so exposed while their leaders wore sea boots and stockings! Moreover, the old way certainly led to cheerfulness in work exhibited in those days which has not been excelled since.

In the matter of drills, I well remember one incident in the *Australia* which nearly cost me my life. This happened whilst getting under way; when weighing anchor, it came up to the cat-head 'a cock-bill' (vertical) instead of horizontally as it should have done in order to secure correctly upon the anchor bed. The trouble was that, before the anchor had been dropped, a number of strands of rope had been used to stop the ground chain neatly along the cable for sake of a tidy appearance, and these hempen strands were expected to carry away in turn as the ground chain took the weight of the anchor when hoisting it to the cathead as had always happened before. It so happened on this occasion that a strand which had been used for securing the ground chain to the anchor shackle came from a new piece of 4-inch rope, and that an inexperienced young sailor had taken a couple of turns through the anchor shackle before securing it up. In consequence it was strong enough to hold fast instead of automatically carrying away as its turn came to take the weight of the anchor. Now the situation was that the ship was under, way while the anchor swaying from the cathead could not be secured until the offending strand was cleared, allowing the anchor to change from vertical to horizontal position. Quickly perceiving this, I leapt from the forecastle on to the anchor and with a sharp knife and a clear conscience severed the strand of rope. Immediately of course, the 4-ton anchor toppled and I toppled too, and as I clutched the rope's end more tightly in one hand, I came bang into the ship side and almost simultaneously the stock of the anchor swayed violently and dented the side plate of the ship about two inches above my shoulder. Luckily Tim Francis was attending the ropes end to which I was hanging and I was hauled on board perfectly unscathed. Later in the day the Captain George Neville who had seen the incident from the navigating bridge sent for me, and in a kindly manner, asked me whether I suffered any ill effects of it. He seemed very pleased with my reply which was truthfully in the negative.

Life on board the *Australia* was a particularly happy one for me. With the exception of Gunnery Firings and occasional drills, we had little to do but to keep up the ships smart appearance and to stand by for calls as required in the service of Queen's Guard Ship. While the ship was in Southampton waters, we were stationed in the stream off the famous Military Hospital there. This afforded me opportunity of spending an evening or two in my home at Woolston about 3 miles distant.

Frederick W Sweetingham

On Christmas Eve 1900, good fortune again favoured me with promotion to Petty Officer First Class. This came as a most pleasant surprise and I felt quite embarrassed when Captain Neville congratulated me on the performance of my work as Captain of the Forecastle and, in the presence of Commander Lumsden and the First Lieutenant Bush, formally announced my promotion. As I walked off the Quarter Deck, there was dear old Tim Francis, who had evidently known about it; he greeted me with hearty congratulations on what he considered a record at the extremely youthful age of less than 23 years. Although promotion on the lower deck in those days might have been more accelerated than that of later years, still the average age for advancement to Petty Officer First Class would not be less than 28 years. I spent Christmas Day with my old messmates, but on Boxing Day, Tim insisted upon introducing me to his messmates - all First Class Petty Officers, whose mess I was now to join.

At Cowes much yachting activity could be seen and it was a grand sight to watch those beautiful vessels trying to get to windward of each other after the preparatory gun was fired before the races were commenced. The Royal Yacht Squadron at Cowes was and is to this day, the premier and most exclusive yacht club in the British Empire. At that time, The Prince of Wales, later King Edward VI, was its Commodore. The German Emperor Kaiser Wilhelm II, was a member while the membership included a large proportion of the British aristocracy. There was a special jetty in front of Cowes Castle, (the headquarters of the Squadron) where no one but Naval Officers or members of the club may land. At Cowes Regatta, thousands of people crowd upon the sea-front to watch what is doubtless the greatest yachting carnival in the Empire. Yachts are not only sailed and raced here, but in White's Yard at Cowes some of the finest of these vessels in the world have been built.

On landing here, I took the opportunity of visiting the western half of Wight to see the environs of my birthplace. This beautiful little Island comprises a total area of only 155 square miles, length 23 miles, broadest width of 13 miles and circumference of 60 miles. I cannot imagine so many and diverse beauty spots encompassed in so small a space. I think it was Sir Walter Scott who described this island, home of Alfred Lord Tennyson, as follows: "That beautiful island which he who once sees never forgets through whatever part of the world his future path may lead him".

If and when I return to England, I shall certainly spend a time in that peaceful and lovely isle once again. When I was there last, the old stage coach had survived the advent of railways in the eastern half of the Wight, while the present railroad from Newport to Freshwater in the west did not exist. To my mind, galloping along by stage coach is the jolliest mode of travel, which also includes the stoppages at the pubs for meals and exchange of horses. Down that way too, is the Needles; these three tall slender chalk pinnacles off the extreme western end of the island where the lighthouse is situated. In later years, many were the nights of howling gales that I have welcomed the sight of this lighthouse from the bridge of a destroyer as we nosed our way into the calm waters of the Solent from the turbulent seas of the English Channel. Passing inside the Needles by day one sees the imposing cliffs of Alum Bay presenting a panorama of unexcelled beauty. The colours of these cliffs appear to change like a chameleon, with the brightness or dullness of the sky; the tints of colours ranging through white, yellow, grey, purple, red, blue and black.

The Isle of Wight, though always sparsely populated, has ever produced a hardy race of people though for three centuries after the Norman Conquest it was one of the most tranquil spots in Britain. Doubtless the Solent Waters had saved the Island from the quarrels that were going on between the Kings and Barons during that period on the Mainland, and consequently they took no part in the strife of Civil Wars. But in the early 14th century, after rumours of an attack upon England by the French, preparations for war were made and the landowners were required to provide trained armed men for the defence of the Island. Then in the year 1340, during the reign of Edward III, the first test came as to their fighting qualities and those hardy men of the Wight were not found wanting. In the summer of that year a French fleet arrived off St Helens followed by the landing of an enemy force. Vigilance was the watch word of the courageous Islanders in the eastern region of Bembridge and Brading who met the invaders in battle array between St Helens and Nunwell. The Frenchmen were slaughtered in great numbers and driven off their Island homeland. The leader of these gallant horsemen was one Sir Theobald Russell who died of wounds received in this battle and was buried at Yaverland. Sir Theobald was a prominent land owner of Yaverland and a kinsman of the legendary Island family of Nunwell founded by d'Orglandes (afterwards known as Orglander). d'Orglandes came uninvited at the time of the Norman Conquest, and established a Manor House and squirearchy of landed proprietors in the Eastern part of the Isle of Wight; that has perpetuated for more than 800 years. His line of male descendants was not broken until the death of Sir Henry Orglander the 7th Baronet of Nunwell in 1874.

Thus, from their earliest history my countrymen had proved their worth in the defence of their beloved Island; as in later generations, repeated attempts to invade the Island by the French followed and ended in failure. Nor were these tough Islanders always content to wait the coming of the enemy; for in 1488, whether with the approval of his brother-in-law Henry VII or not, the Captain of the Wight, Sir Edward Woodville, with 400 gallant men-at-arms sailed from St Helens on a summers day to fight for the independence of Brittany. There they joined four times their number of Bretons and fought the French in the Battle of St Aubin. Alas, however, these 2,000 English and Breton men were severely defeated; Sir Edward Woodville was killed, and according to the story, only one of the Islanders returned home. It is not surprising that the Islanders have always been a hardy race for, their employment has mainly been in agriculture and fishing. All kinds of products from these two industries have been exported to the mainland including sheep's wool, which is particularly noted for its fine quality.

During my time in the *Australia*, Her Majesty Queen Victoria died, on 22nd January 1901, in her stately marine palace at Osborne, East Cowes, after nearly 64 years of wise and beneficent rule. Later Osborne House and grounds were handed over by King Edward VII to the nation as a memorial to her late Majesty the Queen. There are some 2,000 acres in this estate; in 1902 a portion was appropriated as a convalescent home for a small number of Naval and Army Officers; and in 1903 the Royal Naval College was stationed there.

January 22nd was a great day of mourning for the nation. Though the German Emperor had displeased the British public of late, on this occasion he behaved very well, and with great difficulty he travelled to England to be present with the Prince of Wales at Osborne House before the great life of Queen Victoria came to an end. The following day the Prince of Wales took the oath as King Edward VII at a Privy Council Meeting at St James' Palace London. This was followed by a most beautiful and impressive service in Westminster Abbey on Saturday 26th January.

The Queen's funeral took place a week later, at which the King and Queen Alexandra and the Kaiser were present. The Queen's coffin was placed upon a gun carriage drawn by horses and riding in the procession were Kings, Princes and celebrities from many countries. The Navy was well represented by a Brigade of bluejackets. The funeral service was held in St George's Chapel Windsor, and while the procession was approaching the Castle, one of the horses took fright and became unmanageable. The men of the Navy came to the rescue and protected the coffin, which was in danger of being forced off the gun carriage. The horses were taken out and their harness was replaced by drag ropes from the Naval Field Gun Battery which were manned by the bluejackets who drew the gun carriage nearly a mile through the town to the Castle grounds. There the Queen's coffin was taken to the Albert Memorial Chapel, where it remained until Monday 4th February. On that day the Queen was buried at Frogmore by the side of her beloved husband the Prince Consort who had died in December 1861. The burial service being attended by members of the Royal Family only.

In March 1901, a Petty Officer Gunnery Instructor left the ship and as there was no one available at the time to relieve him. The Captain was directed to select a suitable Petty Officer already in the ship and to promote him to the Acting rating. The Gunnery Officer, who was also the First Lieutenant, recommended that I should be given the position, and accordingly I was promoted by the Captain to the non-substantive rating of Acting Gunnery Instructor. In reality it was not so surprising, for after paying off the *Powerful* I knew that I was due to requalify for Seaman Gunner at the Gunnery School and, with this in mind, I had kept myself up-to-date in the subject. At certain times I had voluntarily assisted the Gunnery Instructor in the training of his classes and had sometimes taken classes for him myself during his absence from the ship. Though I remained in the same Petty Officers Mess, the acceptance of these full-time gunnery duties, necessitated the handing over of my part of the ship to another Petty Officer, who thus became Captain of the Forecastle of the Port Watch. The rating of Petty Officer and Acting Gunnery Instructor carried with it an increase of pay of course, and this brought my daily rate to 3/3d. It was now up to me to work harder than ever and in the dog watches and week-ends I waded through many of the Gunnery Text Books in order to improve my instructional ability.

In due course my very happy and interesting period of service in *Australia* came to an end when I was relieved by a fully qualified Gunnery Instructor sent from HMS *Excellent*. I was drafted to the Gunnery School, my second appearance at Whale Island and early in 1902 after going through a long series of instruction and examinations I qualified successfully and was recommended for the Instructional staff of HMS *Excellent*. Whilst undergoing the qualifying course for Gunnery Instructor a grant of £8/10/- was paid to me in respect of my war service in South Africa. I never knew how this sum was calculated, but was given to understand that this was the amount due to Leading Seamen who landed from the Royal Navy.

CHAPTER XIX

Life as a Staff Gunnery Instructor.

--- ooOoo ---

In a previous chapter I have remarked upon the staff personnel and the routine carried out in the Gunnery School, but the conduct of my life under training was necessarily different to what it had become as an Instructor. The instruction to which I was assigned was in the Heavy Gun Battery, while the classes consisted of Long Course Officers qualifying for Gunnery Officers, Short Course Lieutenants, Sub-Lieutenants, Seaman Petty Officers and men.

Here everything was taught about all guns and mountings in the Service. This included Gun drills, shooting, shipping and assembling of breech mechanisms and all parts of the mountings, sights etc. Later, the instruction in Light Quick Firing Guns, Field and Machine Guns, which had hitherto been regarded as a separate entity, was included in our syllabus. The Staff Instructors Mess was a perfectly delightful institution. Every conceivable consideration was given to enhance the status of these comparatively few Petty Officers, by the Captain, the Commander and other Staff Officers of the Establishment; and the esprit-de-corps of every single member of the mess was superb. There were about 34 Petty Officer Instructors on the staff and, of these, many were very senior and wore three badges which indicated that they had served as seamen for not less than 13 years and were over 30 years of age. Observing that I had more than a year and a half yet to serve before becoming entitled to a second badge on my 26th birthday, one can imagine that I had to go all out in my job to keep in step with this thoroughly efficient and loyal lot of fellows. At first, I suffered somewhat from an inferiority complex, though despite my juniority, I met with the greatest courtesy and kindness from my messmates, many of whom were about 40 years of age, married and fathers of children.

While our instructional duties were strenuous and exacting, the hours never seemed too long and the subjects were so interesting that one felt there was always something more one could impart when the bugle for ceasing was sounded each day. Our duties at night were essential for the good working of the establishment, while the amenities in the beautiful surroundings of Whale Island were most beneficial to one's health. On the playing fields we played cricket, football, tennis and sometimes that mighty strenuous game of push ball. The last time I took part in that game my job was not to push the ball, but to haul off the opponents who were pushing it against our team. This was during an inter-mess competition and when it was over I suffered from sheer exhaustion!

Throughout the summer months, evening practice at Tipnor Rifle Range and revolver shooting was indulged in, while our indoor recreations included billiards and American bowls which were within the precinct of a fine reading room and library. I have already referred to the special interest for the welfare of the instructors shown by the Captain and Gunnery Officers of the *Excellent*, and in this connection I would mention one matter which, in my opinion, was regarded by my colleagues as one of the most valued assets relating to our status. I refer to the uniform dress approved to be worn by all Staff Instructors during drill hours and also in silent hours. The dress for all other ratings dressed as seamen, except on Sundays and on special occasions, was serge jumpers, serge trousers and gaiters. But as a distinctive uniform for Staff Instructors serge frocks buttoned at the wrists and blue cloth trousers with gaiters were worn. This was in line with the distinctive dress of Staff Officers and Officers undergoing instruction; the former wore blue cloth suits with black gaiters, while the latter wore blue cloth coats, with white flannel trousers and brown gaiters of the same pattern and colour worn by the seamen. Although this distinction in dress may appear trivial and unnecessary, there is no doubt that it enhanced the position and prestige of both Staff Gunnery Officers and Petty Officer Instructors alike. Moreover, when each day a thousand Officers and men were on parade or at instruction, it obviated any confusion in the personnel that might otherwise have occurred. In later years this dress distinction was abolished for Petty Officers and I well remember discussing the matter with my colleagues, and all agreed that the detrimental effect upon the Staff Instructors was most marked. Indeed, it is my considered opinion that a bluejacket in the Navy may possess decorations and medals galore for any kind of service or ability, but it is to be regretted that to the detriment of the Service they are of little real value when compared to some distinctive dress.

At the beginning of June 1902, everyone at the Gunnery School celebrated the Peace which had been proclaimed between Britain and South Africa, when the Treaty was signed in Vereeniging with the Boers. This was a happy prelude to the coronation of King Edward VI for which elaborate preparations had been going on for some time. Decorations and illuminations were being prepared in the naval port of Portsmouth as in all other towns and cities in the land. The Navy was particularly active at this time commissioning a large number of every class of ship in the Service for the enormous fleet which assembled for the Naval Review at Spithead, which was to take place on June 28th. The Army too was making grand preparations for a Review and Tattoo at Aldershot, where some 30,000 troops including the Colonial Regiments were assembling.

At Whale Island, a battalion of blue jackets under arms were being specially trained to represent the Navy at Trafalgar Square where they were to be stationed during the Royal procession through the streets of the City of London from Buckingham Palace to Westminster Abbey. I was attached to a company of this battalion and well remember the training for the great event which involved long hours kept standing to attention, accompanied with strict prohibition of nature's call. It being impressed upon everyone that we should be marched to Trafalgar Square early in the morning and occupy the position assigned to the Naval Battalion and thenceforth not a single man would be permitted to leave the ranks for any purpose whatever. It was estimated that the coronation procession would not be past Trafalgar Square until well into the afternoon so the necessity for this personal restraint was apparent in the unusual circumstances.

It was intended that the Naval Battalion should go to London on the day before Coronation Day and accommodation for the night had therefore to be arranged. In relation to this, I was sent to London in charge of a party of men to prepare a school in Pulteney Street for the accommodation of my company. Only a few days were allowed for this, and though we worked hard and accomplished the job, time afforded the opportunity of seeing some of the decorations in England's Capital City and to mix with the London throng. The Royal Palaces, Whitehall, Kensington, Parliament Houses and the great Squares of Belgrade, St James and Grosvenor, all presented views of festoons, triumphal arches or some other such structural grandeur; likewise, the streets leading to them like Bond Street, Piccadilly and Park Lane. The decoration of Westminster Bridge designed by students of the Royal College of Art, was particularly fine.

London, indeed was working at full pressure on these costly arrangements for Coronation Day on the 26th June.

Envoys of the Royal Families of Europe had arrived in England. Monarchs sent their kinsmen including heirs to their thrones. Russian and Austrian Grand Dukes, Indian Princes, relatives of the Shah of Persia, the King of Ethiopia, and even an Imperial Prince from Japan were among the celebrities who had come to London. Also invited were the British Colonial Ministers, a precedent which happily marked the progress of the overseas territories and the importance in which they were regarded by the British Government, which had not hitherto been shown. The Right Honourable Joseph Chamberlain was Secretary for the Colonies at the time, and the Colonial Premiers were: Sir Wilfred Laurier (Canada), Sir Edmund Barton (Australia), Sir Gordon Spring (Cape Colony), Sir Albert Hime (Natal), The Right Hon. Richard Leddon (New Zealand), and Sir Robert Bond (Newfoundland). This assembly of Prime Ministers together with representatives of the Governments of the Crown Colonies met for the first time in history and were able to deliberate and exchange views in committees presided over by the Colonial Secretary. This indeed marked a tremendous stride in the advance of our Empire overseas and the shaping of its destiny.

Amidst all this, came unpleasant rumours like a bolt from the blue, that His Majesty was most seriously ill. Following this, Official Notices were posted in London on Tuesday 24th June, stating that the King was suffering from peritonitis, but it was hoped that His Majesty would be able to go through the Coronation Ceremony. Later in the day it was announced that the King had passed through a serious operation and that his life was in danger. These bulletins were published over the names of Britain's greatest physicians and surgeons including Lord Lister, Sir Francis Laking, Sir Thomas Smith and Sir Frederick Treves. Happily, after a period of deep anxiety, it was announced on 5th July that His Majesty was out of danger. Meanwhile the Coronation Ceremony had been postponed.

Having disposed of our extempore arrangements for billeting and replaced the desks and other fitting at the school, I left London and returned with my party of seamen to the gunnery school at Portsmouth.

The Naval Review at Spithead had been arranged to take place on June 28th or two days after the original date for the Coronation in Westminster Abbey. There had been great expectations in regard to this event and thousands of sightseers from all parts of the country had come to Portsmouth, Southampton and the Isle of Wight to witness Britain's Majesty, Dominion and Power represented by the great assembly of Warships. There have, of course, been many reviews of the Fleet before and since, but on this occasion about 20 battleships, and 25 cruisers were present and some 80 smaller vessels including Torpedo Boats and Destroyers. In addition, there were foreign Warships representing the navies of no less than 16 nations of Europe, America and Japan. One might imagine the feeling that pervaded the personnel of this grand assembly of ships when the signal was made announcing the postponement of the Coronation!

After so much effort, there was nothing more to do but to disperse all those ships and vessels which had been so carefully moored in their respective positions. On July 15th the King accompanied by Queen Alexandra, to whom so much sympathy was due, came to Portsmouth and was taken on board the Royal yacht *Victoria and Albert* which proceeded to Cowes. There the small Royal Yacht *Osborne* joined the Royal Party and about a week later the two vessels steamed round the Isle of Wight and returned to their moorings at Cowes. This trip was arranged on the advice of the King's medical men, who wished him to take the sea air during his convalescence. Doubtless, the health of His Majesty had benefited most satisfactorily on board, for it was in the

Victoria and Albert that the King appointed August 9th for the Coronation Ceremony. Accordingly, the King and Queen left the Royal Yacht early in August and were back at Buckingham Palace again on the eve of the Coronation.

During the first week of August, the Naval battalions at Whale Island to be stationed at Trafalgar Square were again preparing to go up to London; but this time no arrangements were made for billeting overnight. We therefore boarded a train very early on the morning of Coronation Day and on arrival in London proceeded to Lambeth Palace Gardens where breakfast was provided. Immediately afterwards we marched to Trafalgar Square and took up our appointed positions. This was about 7 a.m. and even at that early time crowds of sightseers had already taken up their positions at the sides of the streets, or upon the huge stands that had been erected for the purpose. At 11 a.m. the King and Queen left Buckingham Palace in the State Coach escorted by the Royal Horse Guards and a cavalcade of Aides-de-camp and others. The procession passed along the route to Westminster Abbey where Their Majesties alighted and entered. Here awaiting in their gorgeous robes were members of the Royal Family, the Duke of Norfolk (Earl Marshal) and other Lords and their peeresses, Knights of the Realm- Archbishops of Canterbury and York, the Prime Minister of England and a host of the Empire's highest dignitaries, to pay homage and perform their respective roles in the Coronation of the King and Queen. Of this great function I knew nothing, but while all this was going on, we of the Naval battalion were patiently waiting at our post under the shadow of Nelsons Column. With the great ceremony over about 2.30 p.m. the return from the Abbey to Buckingham Palace was made by Their Majesties and as the procession passed by, one could obtain a glimpse of the King and Queen wearing their crowns. Riding on horseback were some notable sailors under whom I had served. Admiral Sir Michael Culine Seymour, Admiral Sir Edward Seymour and several others. There were also the conspicuous military figures of Lord Roberts and of Lord Kitchener, who had arrived in England only a month before making peace with the Boers in South Africa. The Beefeaters too were marching immediately behind Field Marshall Lord Roberts.

After the King and Queen had returned to Buckingham Palace and the great Coronation Day was over, we of the Naval battalion marched to the Railway Station and entrained for Portsmouth arriving at Whale Island that same evening. On Saturday 16th August, a great fleet of ships had again been assembled at Spithead, and the King and Queen reviewed them from the Royal Yacht as they passed down the four lines of ships. The fleet comprised mainly of ships that had assembled there in June, though the number had been somewhat reduced. That night all ships were magnificently illuminated while search light exercises were carried out on a grand scale. Two days later the Fleet dispersed and so ended the last of the Coronation celebrations in honour of King Edward VII.

Although I felt that my career in the Service had, so far, been a successful one, I was by no means satisfied with my position as a Lower Deck Rating, for my ambition was to become a Commissioned Officer in the Royal Navy. There were definitely no short cuts to this, as was the case many years later, the only course open to Petty Officers being the Warrant Rank as the next step. At the time only five branches of these officers were appointed to sea-going ships; they were - The Gunners and Boatswains promoted from Seamen and the Signal Boatswain, Carpenter and Warrant Engineer. Today there are more than three times that number of Warrant Officer branches in the Royal Navy. Many of the Gunners and Boatswains were in command of Torpedo Boats, Gun Boats and other vessels of the Royal Navy, and scores of such vessels were commanded by them during the two Great Wars. A board of Officers was appointed periodically

Growing Experience In The Royal Navy

for the examination of Petty Officer Candidates for the rank of Gunners and Boatswain. This board was presided over by a Naval Captain, and included a Navigating Commander, and usually three Chief or Senior Warrant Officers of the military Branch.

In April 1903, I presented myself for examination in seamanship before such a board, which was held on board HMS *Victory*. As this was a somewhat transitory period between the passing of square-rigged ships of war and the iron clad ships propelled by steam only, it was a matter of chance whether the questions would be mainly connected with one kind of service or the other. In my case, I was confronted by a board of Officers who had served most of their days in corvettes and other sailing ships and in consequence my examination, apart from navigational subjects, was mainly related to seamanship in ships under sail eg. mast and yard drill, tacking and wearing ship, anchor work and so forth, to which I have referred in previous pages of this chronicle. My examination commenced at 9.30 a.m. and except for a break for lunch at mid-day, continued well into the afternoon. I well remember the ordeal and how glad I was when the President said, "That is all Sweetingham!"

Happily, I passed successfully and felt very proud when I was informed of the result. One point that I am certain of, is that I was fortunate in having previously served in HMS *Active*. For without the knowledge and experience gained in that Corvette, I am sure that I would have failed to pass the examination of that particular Board. In the matter of examinations, it is open to comment as to whether oral methods, such as this, or paper tests are the more satisfactory. Personally, I am inclined to favour the latter, though, it is nice to feel that one did survive such a mental gruelling before a body of hard-baked and weather-beaten Naval Officers as was my experience at 25 years of age.

After obtaining an Official Certificate stating that I had passed in Seamanship for the rank of Gunner R.N., I commenced a long course of instruction at the Gunnery School in applied mathematics and various subjects of Gunnery, practical and in theory. This included a course in diving. By the end of April 1904, I had passed successfully in all the above subjects which included paper and oral examinations and obtained 94% of marks in the grand total of all subjects. This left further courses and examinations in the subjects of Torpedo, Mining and Electricity to be completed; and accordingly, I was sent to HMS *Vernon*, the Torpedo School at Portsmouth, for the necessary courses of instruction.

My disappointment of about 8 years prior to this, and to which I have already mentioned, was now to be effaced by a much longer and more thorough course than the one I had hoped to receive at that time. The atmosphere in the *Vernon* was entirely different from that which prevailed in the Gunnery School, but one found the subjects taught were perhaps more interesting. Instead of a spick and span shore establishment, such as at Whale Island, where orderliness and discipline in every detail were rigorously maintained, here was an old hulk, known the *Vernon*, which accommodated several hundred men. We were huddled together in a crowded mess deck for meals with little observance for cleanliness, and there was an entire lack of discipline, scarcely any recreation, and no privacy whatever. Owing to the absence of a clockwork routine and disciplinary restraints, one often heard the praises of the *Vernon* sung as opposed to the so-called awful life of gas and gaiters in the *Excellent*. But for my part, I would prefer life in the latter establishment at any time.

The *Vernon* was moored, head and stern well up the Portsmouth Harbour and filled out with every conceivable appliance for the instructions relating to Torpedoes and Naval Electrical

Equipment. Another hulk known as HMS *Acteon* lay at her moorings about a cable distant affording instruction in Mining, counter-mining and demolition work.

The Instructional Staff of Officers and Petty Officer Torpedo Instructors, like that of the Gunnery School were very sound and efficient. All members having specialized in the subject to which they were assigned. During my time, lectures and practical instruction was of the highest order and the whole staff were equally as keen as their contemporaries in Gunnery at Whale Island.

Running Torpedoes from above water tubes was carried out in a Torpedo Gun Boat commanded by a Chief Torpedo Gunner, while submerged Torpedo Drill and firing was performed in HMS *Devastation* a 2nd class battle ship of about 9,000 tons. This ship, I believe, was the first battleship commissioned without sails in the British Navy. The largest torpedoes in the Service in those days were the 18 inch, but a 14 inch torpedo existed for arming small craft including steam boats carried by large ships. The steam boats were not fitted with torpedo tubes, but with a dropping apparatus that looked like a pair of tongs hung over the side of the boat to which the torpedo was suspended. Thus, it was necessary to steer straight for the target before the torpedo was dropped.

Instruction in the use of search lights was also given in the *Vernon*, also the internal electric lighting of ships, which was the entire responsibility of the Torpedo Officer. Depth charges filled with T.N.T explosive as we know them today, were not then in service, neither were submarines. But an offensive weapon was fitted to fast steam boats carried in ships for action against enemy vessels. This was known as the "Outrigger Charge", which consisted of two 164-pound canisters of wet gun cotton filled with primer and detonator. The outrigger charge was secured to the forward end of a long spar, which was carried longitudinally about 5 feet above the centre line of the boat. To permit this arrangement the funnel of the boat was lowered on its hinge and the charge was exploded by firing the detonator electrically. This apparatus was for use preferably on dark nights when the boat armed with the charge was supposed to creep up, bows on to an enemy ship, tilt the spar until the charge was well below the water line of the target and then fire. After firing we were instructed to go full speed astern and get away as best we could! The chances were however, that the boat would be so damaged herself, that escape would be problematical.

The fitting and laying out of mechanical and electrical mines, and running lines of counter-mines, were also subjects taught in the *Vernon*. After fitting, the mines would be placed with launches or pinnaces and towed to the mining areas. This of course was heavy work and required much caution and thoroughness, especially when the operations were carried out in bad weather. Demolition operations were carried out on a small islet in Portsmouth Harbour and these were most varied and interesting. Before proceeding to carry out the practices we were given a course of instruction in the fitting and preparation of charges on board the *Acteon*. On one of these occasions, I well remember an exciting incident caused by some young Sub-Lieutenants, who were also under instruction in this work. It was during the dinner hour, when the instructors had gone to the *Vernon* for their meal, while we of the classes had remained on board to partake of ours, which we had brought with us. There was no special place assigned to us for eating, so we just sat about on deck in an impromptu manner. All went well until the meal was over when suddenly a terrific explosion was heard and quite a commotion going on amongst the Sub-Lieutenants. Naturally we were all attracted to the scene of the explosion and there we found that a large and heavy grating belonging to the after part of the upper deck was shattered, while a gaping hole had been blown in the ship's stern! Luckily however, no one was seriously injured. The loud report of the detonator quickly aroused everyone on board the *Vernon* which was only a short distance away.

Steam boats and pulling boats from her came alongside with Officers who immediately proceeded to investigate matters.

What had happened was that, after locking up the explosive store prior to going to the *Vernon* for his dinner, the Sub-Lieutenant Instructor had unfortunately left the key in such a manner that one of his pupils was able to appropriate it and together with one or two colleagues had fitted a live demolition charge and placed it in the position indicated. Then, by means of an electric battery and circuit they fired the charge, taking precaution to keep clear of it themselves. Of course, there was trouble brewing for the Senior Officer of the Sub-Lieutenants, and also the few members who were actually implicated in this madness. As part of the punishment, their leave was stopped for a considerable period while they were confined to spare cabins on board one of the ships in Portsmouth Harbour!

In July 1904, I completed the course and examinations in the *Vernon* and after a most interesting and, on the whole, enjoyable period, I returned to HMS *Excellent* and resumed my job on the Instructional Staff of the Gunnery School, pending promotion. Soon after, a certificate was handed to me, showing that I had passed all subjects in the Torpedo School with 88% of full passing marks. My name was then duly recorded on the waiting list for promotion to Gunner R.N. 1st Class. Since I had now been home from Foreign Service about 4 years, my turn should have come again, but it was thought probable that my promotion would occur in the near future, so I was appropriated for further duty at Whale Island. However, I was disappointed in this, for owing to retrenchment and other unforeseen reasons, only one vacancy in four created by the retirement of Gunners were being filled at that time. Luckily in my case, I could very well afford to wait, for my age was much below the average of Petty Officers whose names were on the roster for promotion.

Captain Percy Scott had now taken over the command of the Gunnery School and many changes were being made in the methods and syllabus of instruction. The time spent at Field Training, Gun Drill and so forth was drastically curtailed, while that devoted to Gun shooting was rightly increased twofold. The Captain's striking personality began to tell very soon. A brand new heavy gun battery, built on the northern side of the Island for the sole purpose of Gun Drill, was completely transformed into one applicable for shooting only. Dismounting gear was swept away from the gun positions, while all kinds of devices for teaching the art of good shooting were installed. This indeed was all to the good, and many of us who had seen his good work in South Africa, could often be found defending him against Naval men of the old school who looked upon his inventions and innovations as time wasting gadgets which interfered with Naval discipline and spit and polish. As I look back on all this, it seems incredible that though we possessed fleets of fine battleships and cruisers, armed with great guns at enormous expense to the Nation, not one unit of these fleets, with their renowned Admirals, Commanders-in-Chiefs, could effectively engage an enemy fighting ship at a range of 3 miles. Happily, Captain Scott, supported by that great Admiral and Naval Administrator Sir John Fisher (afterwards Lord Fisher of Kilverstone) who was then a First Sea Lord of the Admiralty were now implementing drastic changes and wonderful improvements were being made in the accuracy and rapidity of Heavy Gun Firing in the British Navy.

Strangely enough very few Naval men seemed to realise the value, or to care much, for gunnery progress, and the science of long-range gun firing was afforded little attention. In keeping with strict discipline, drills at guns were insisted upon, but this entailed for the most part, loading of guns, the exercise of ammunition supply and the manipulating of the gun mountings. True, there was a limited amount of firing practices carried out with small ammunition at short range. This was usually done when the ship was at anchor while the target was towed around; good aiming practise for the gun layers only. This was not followed up by realistic firing conditions at full calibre practices, but was invariably carried out by ships under way at ridiculously short ranges rarely exceeding 4,000 yards against moored targets. Even so, very few direct hits were obtained and providing the fall of shot was correct for line and over the target, everyone felt happy about it. An occasional correction would be made to the adjustment of the sights and this would generally cause delay in the firing. Everyone in the ship would appear glad to get this tiresome business over and no arrangements were made to spot and record the actual fall of shots. It therefore follows, that in effect these test firings were practically useless; in that nobody knew whether the gun layer fired each shot when his sights were on the target but himself, while the Officer conducting the practice was ignorant as to where the shots were actually falling. Moreover, the necessity for frequent adjustment of the sights for change of range and deflection due to the speed of the ship was usually ignored.

To the names of Fisher and Scott one must add that of Captain John Rushworth Jellicoe (afterwards Earl Jellicoe of Scapa) who did much towards the improvement of gunnery in the Navy. Soon after the time of which I am writing, Captain Jellicoe became Director of Naval Ordnance and as a young man he served as Staff Officer in HMS *Excellent* Gunnery School when Lord Fisher was Captain-in-Command. It must be realized that without the whole hearted support of higher Officers with influence, Captain Scott could not possibly have brought about the improvement in Naval Gunnery in such a remarkably short time; especially as this matter involved extra cost on the approved Naval Estimates. During his appointment in Command of HMS *Excellent* the gun layers tests were carried out from HMS *Narcissus*, a cruiser armed with 6-inch and 4.7-inch guns. The target consisted of a piece of canvas about 8-feet square mounted on a wooden raft, which was towed by a destroyer. The gun crews were specially trained for rapid loading which reached the respectable standard of about ten rounds per minute, and each gun layer was required to pass a special eyesight test before taking the qualifying course.

Many days instruction was given in the new converted battery at Whale Island, where several types of aiming and gun laying apparatus were installed. After this, firing tests were carried out at sea in gun boats, using aiming rifles and small-arm ammunition. Then the candidates for gun layers were sent out in the *Narcissus* for final tests with full calibre ammunition. The test at that time was that each man was required to fire ten rounds from a 6-inch gun in a limited time. The fall of each shot was spotted by the layer who was required to order any adjustment to his sight as he considered necessary. Meanwhile, independent spotters recorded each fall of shot for line and the shots over or short of the target were ascertained by a graduated rake on board the towing vessel and duly recorded. Thus, a complete record of each test was kept. Long-range firing under proper control was the duty of the Fire Control Officer, who could be pretty sure that all salvoes fired from his qualified gun layers were correctly aimed. I will not weary the reader with details of long-range firing, which involved accurate estimation of the range, relative velocity of the firing ship and the target, direction and velocity of wind, wear of guns, temperature of cordite propellent and so forth. But this matter was taken up by Captain Scott, who introduced a Fire Control installation at the Gunnery School.

From that year until this day, Fire Control of Armaments of all ships in the Service, have been the subject of scientific research and improvement. At that time the *Revenge*, a sister to the *Ramillies* in which I had served, was employed as "Gunnery Firing Ship" for heavier guns worked by hydraulic power. The ratings who fired these guns were usually Petty Officers and were called

"Captain of the Turrets". Many of these were also Gunnery Instructors and they were responsible to the Gunnery Officer for the maintenance of everything within the revolving structure of their turrets as well as the magazines and shell rooms at the bottom of the ship. From now, their guns were placed under the new fire control system. Accordingly, the *Revenge* was equipped with an improved range finder, a Fire Control Tap and Transmitting Station with improved rangefinders, instruments for calculating the rate of change in range and deflection due to speed of both our and enemy ship, range keeping clocks, improved sights for guns, special voice pipes and electrical transmitters and telephones to communicate with each gun turret. The transmitting station was situated in a compartment behind armour and below the waterline, so that personnel and instruments were well protected. The firing trials carried out with this control system were so encouraging that other ships were selected for equipment in a similar manner. Accordingly, large orders were given to armament firms for the manufacture of the necessary appliances.

With the advent of long-range firing the necessity for a perfect combination of quick loading, accurate firing and sound spotting and control of fire was absolutely essential and to achieve this Captain Scott worked prodigiously. In all my experience in the Service, I know of no other Captain in the Navy who had personally attended to such small details in furtherance of his great project. I have been present when he had spoken to ratings and given them advice on the working of various fire control appliances and even to very junior men during the setting of sights and the loading of guns. This was something quite new at Whale Island, and much appreciated by the men and their Instructors. In silent hours these incidents would be discussed by the bluejackets in their messes, and I am sure that their gunnery efficiency was advanced thereby.

Soon the rate of fire in the *Narcissus* had increased astonishingly while 80% of misses on the canvas target was soon to be transformed into 80% of hits! One day during this steady progress, Captain Scott ordered a full parade of every Officer and seaman under instruction at the Gunnery School. Some 800 Officers and men were present and in the centre of the parade ground stood a huge specially rigged up dais. The stairs and floor of the structure were covered with red carpet, while decorative flags fluttered around it in the breeze. Standing conspicuously alone by the dais was Able Seaman Hollinghurst. When Captain Scott appeared on the scene which I remember so vividly, Hollinghurst was directed to ascend the dais, then Captain Scott ordered everyone on parade to attention, and he exclaimed, "There stands before you - the only pebble on the Beach!!"

A few days before this Hollinghurst had achieved, what was considered a wonderful record on board the *Narcissus*. Firing ten rounds from a 6-inch B.L. gun in 2 minutes, obtaining eight hits on a moving canvas target. The Captain then joined Hollinghurst on the dais and delivered an interesting speech regarding the average low standard of gunnery in the Navy and the shocking waste of ammunition which it entailed. He then added a few encouraging witticisms, so characteristic of this truly great man, and encouraged every one present to aim for still higher proficiency. I am bound to say that this episode aroused an incalculable stimulus in the effort for further improvement by all concerned. Indeed, it was not long afterwards that 100% of hits on the target could not be regarded as uncommon in gun layers tests.

In 1905 Captain Scott relinquished the Command of HMS *Excellent* and became Rear Admiral. Sir John Fisher was still the First Sea Lord and, doubtless, recognising the value of Scott's work, created an appointment for him known as "Inspector of Target Practice". This appointment, together with his superior rank enabled Admiral Scott to continue his good work in the cause of Naval Gunnery in large numbers of ships in the Home and Mediterranean Fleets. Several months later when Admiral Scott had returned from a tour of inspection of long range firing by ships belonging to the Mediterranean Fleet, I was present at a Gunnery Lecture given by him. During the course of his address, the Admiral specially mentioned certain firings that had taken place under his personal supervision and then went on to remark upon the firing of a certain ship sometime before he had commenced his inspectorate. Instead of using a long range battle practice towing target, which had been recently introduced, this particular ship for some reason or other had selected an islet to shoot at; and by the independent records of the shooting which had been taken, it appeared that the result of the firings were most unsatisfactory. The target face of the little island was several times greater in area than the standard target which, of course, would have been a moving one. Now before mentioning these particulars of the firing, Admiral Scott indicated the name of the ship and asked if there was anyone present who was on board at the time of the practice. Without hesitation one Officer stood up looking quite happy and seemed only too pleased to say that he was. Like a flash the Admiral retorted, "Well - How did you miss that island!"

I feel in honour bound to make these digressions because I know definitely that common sense and genuine interest had at last been inculcated into the teaching of gunnery science rather than blustering so called discipline the very anathema of learning.

Inevitably, this most vigorous change in the Gunnery activities of the Navy, which had also been extended to night firing with search light control, revolutionised the life of ships companies in H. M. Ships. The routine was largely governed by the requirements of the Gunnery Departments, practice allowances of ammunition was substantially increased while cleaning wood and brightwork, so beloved by all Commanders of ships, had become quite a secondary consideration. Previously the Commander or Executive Officer of a ship employed the seamen entirely as he thought fit and since his promotion had depended upon a scrupulously clean ship, it was only human that the men for the most part were engaged with the scrubber or brass rags. Now it became law that Gunnery Officers were to have first call upon every man, including non-seamen for daily or nightly duty within the fighting organization of the ship. Gun firing, loading drills, aiming practices, spotting and fire control thus became the subjects of intensive training in all sea going ships and at the three Naval Gunnery School at Portsmouth, Devonport, and Chatham. The analysis of results which followed all gunnery firings would keep the Gunnery Officer and Staff going long after the operations, while the promotion of this Officer depended considerably upon the fighting efficiency of his ship and the position it held in the gunnery record of the Squadron or Fleet in which he served.

At that time there was a most energetic young Gunnery Officer who had devoted special attention to Long Range Fire Control. He was Lieutenant F.C. Dreyer and after many experiments of trials and errors he invented a very ingenious apparatus known as the Dreyer's Plotting Table. This proved an important appliance in the Fire Control System of most ships was is still in use in the Navy in World War 2. Typically, guns of all calibres were laid and fired by the Captain of the Turret. In certain circumstances however, smoke created by the firing guns, or from the funnels of your own ship or ships in company, would cause much trouble and delay in sighting the target. Also spotting of the fall of shot by the gun-layer who fired it, was usually very difficult, especially in bad weather when great movement was on the ship. These impediments to accurate fire soon became a special subject of consideration of Admiral Scott with a view to rectification. This led to an entirely new device for firing, which was known as the 'Gun Director'. This wonderful contrivance enabled all heavy guns in a ship to be sighted laid and fired by one Officer or Petty Officer stationed well aloft with a comparatively clear view of the target. Thus, individual firing by each gun layer was relegated to a secondary system. This was made possible by the erection of a revolving tower at the top of the foremast, equipped with a complete gun sight similar to those at the guns. A specially trained Director Layer with his trainer and sight-setter would manipulate the apparatus in exactly the same way as a gun. The sight of the director was of course graduated, similarly to the sights of all the guns it controlled, and by means of electrical transmitters, each gun could be laid for elevation and direction in harmony with the director. Certain adjustments were necessary at the receivers to correct errors due to 'dip' - height of director sight above the guns and for 'conveyance' - the lateral distance between the guns and the director. When the guns were thus laid on the target, they were fired electrically by the Director Layer from his master firing pistol. It will therefore be seen that this system of firing has overwhelming advantages over the old method, in that the guns are fired simultaneously by an observer admirably situated and free from obstruction, noise or other disturbances experienced by the gun layers at the guns. Moreover, the Gunnery Control Officers position is in close proximity to that of the Director Layer and in consequence the control of fire is more easily maintained. One must not suppose that Admiral Scott and his hardworking staffs of Gunnery Officers produced all these improvements so vital to the Navy with the whole-hearted sympathy and help. Many obstacles and frustrations resulted from the traditional prejudices of those of whom it was duly expected. This was particularly noticeable in the initial stages of this great project, when the appliances were mechanically and electrically crude and unreliable. Defects in the technical performance of the various instruments came very nearly to defeating the system altogether, while the slightest failures were unduly dilated upon by persons who included even the gun-layers themselves. However, sheer hard work and perseverance prevailed.

Shortly before the Great War of 1914-18, Admiral Scott initiated grand contest in order to prove the merits of Director Firing over the system of individual firing of guns. Two battleships of the Super Dreadnought class, each armed with ten 13.5-inch guns were selected to carry out competitive Battle Practice Firings; the *Orion* to fire under the control of individual gun layers, while the *Thunderer* used the Director Firing Apparatus. It was arranged that both ships should fire at targets under precisely the same conditions regarding ranges and the weather. The first test was carried out in fine weather and that the results were about equal. This naturally gave those opposed to change to suggest that we should let well alone and that Admiral Scott might pack up his contraption and remove it. But Scott was far from being disheartened and initiated another trial in bad weather, when the old method had shown its weakness more definitely. This time the result was overwhelmingly in favour of Director Firing and a win for the *Thunderer*, with the shooting from the *Orion* both for speed and accuracy was completely outclassed. Director Firing was accordingly adapted in all modern battleships and battle cruisers in the British Navy and afterwards smaller ships were equipped with directors. Large orders for the manufacture of components were given to armament firms for the equipment of the new Queen Elizabeth class of battleships which were barely completed before the declaration of war in 1914.

I have reflected on this subject on many occasions and cannot but conclude that the combined efforts of those two great sailors, Admiral of the Fleet Lord Fisher and Admiral Sir Percy Scott, came into force only in the nick of time and one shudders to contemplate what would have happened to the British Fleet and indeed the British Nation during the first Great War, had it not been for this fact.

Whilst it was usual for the instructors at the Gunnery School to be assigned to one particular subject, but there were a few exceptions. I remember having to instruct the Officers of the Royal Naval Volunteer Reserve belonging to the London Division in all subjects relating to the Gunnery syllabus. In civil life many of them occupied important positions in the metropolis and the Officers of No 1 Company were members of the London Stock Exchange. All excellent fellows, willing and eager to work and perform the drills, be they arduous, in their desire to become efficient in Naval Gunnery. Sometime later I had the honour and pleasure of accepting a personal invitation from them to go up to London and referee a field gun competition between the various companies of the London R.N.V.R.'s. It was a most sporting and friendly event and although the performance of all the gun crews was good, No 1 Company won the contest.

Towards the end of the year 1905, I became interested in motoring which was gradually becoming the new form of travel. As I look at the beautiful streamlined cars of today, I sometimes think of the 45 horse power De Dion contraption which was the first motor vehicle that I had ever driven. The engine had one cylinder only and an enormous fly wheel, and I was told that the starting handle of this engine had the bad record of injuring the wrists of several fellows and breaking the arms and fingers of an unfortunate few! There was a sort of syphon pipe fitted to the petrol feed system, to which one was required to apply one's mouth. The act of sucking this pipe gave the first impulse to the petrol from the storage tank to the carburettor. I well remember driving this vehicle over the bridge from Whale Island to Portsmouth and rattling its bones on solid wheel tyres along the Commercial Road while backlash in the steering gear forced one to charge wildly from one side of the road to the other! All was well however, for it was the only four-wheeled vehicle in the streets without a horse, and so long as one continued to blare rapid toots on the huge bulbous horn everybody within fifty yards of the De Dion would give one a wide berth in which to manoeuvre. It may be of some interest to note, in this connection, that only 8 years prior to the time of which I am writing the law would have required me to employ a man carrying a red flag to precede the car in order to give warning of my approach and I am not quite sure whether this order had not been rescinded 8 years too soon!!

Early in the year 1906 a Technical Institute was founded in HMS *Excellent* by Lieutenant Oliver Backhouse R.N. (afterwards Admiral Oliver Backhouse C.B.) who was then a Staff Officer at the Gunnery School. The object of this was mainly to provide vocational training in the driving and maintenance of motor cars for Petty Officers who were within one year from completing their service time for pension. Since the use of private motor cars was coming increasingly into vogue, it was thought that after training, these Petty Officers with their thorough knowledge of discipline and so forth would make admirable motor drivers in private life and this proved very true. However, my particular interest in this very excellent project was to first take the course and acquire a certificate of competency and then assist in the instruction of future candidates. Lieutenant Backhouse possessed a new Beeston Humber Car which he very kindly used while personally instructing the first class, of which I was a member. All instruction was carried out during silent hours, that is after Gunnery Instructional hours, so that this purely voluntary Institute caused no inconvenience to other activities on Whale Island.

The syllabus covered a course of teaching for several weeks and the subjects came under the heading of theory and practical. They comprised lectures on the Internal Combustion Engine, general construction of motor vehicles, stripping and assembling of all working components of the car, and driving and general maintenance. On completion of the course a theory paper examination was set followed by practical driving and maintenance tests. A certificate of competence was awarded after successful examination, and I have always been proud of the one awarded to me. Lieutenant Backhouse was most ably assisted by his younger brother Lieutenant Roger Roland C. Backhouse R.N. (afterwards Sir Roger Backhouse E.C.V.0. K.C.B. C.M.G.), who often lent his Coventry Humber car to the Institute for driving instruction. Yet another Gunnery Staff Officer rendered tangible assistance - Lieutenant Henry Crosby Halahan also lent his car and personally instructed members of the class in driving and maintenance. Truly a grand gesture on the part of these splendid Naval Officers as they devoted their personal efforts in the welfare of the Petty Officers concerned. Nor was this all, for quite a few candidates were found jobs through their kindly agency and influence. I am writing these facts with considerable feeling for the like of which was very rare 40 years ago in the British Navy, when officers of considerable means were prone to aloofness rather than such kind helpfulness towards the men of the lower deck.

Since the gunnery duties assigned to me at this period were mainly connected with heavy guns, one often found oneself out in the *Narcissus* with classes of Officers and seamen doing their qualifying examination in firing. I have many reasons for remembering my work in this ship, and not the least was an injury to my hearing which was disabled almost permanently by the blast of gun fire. Even to this day I still suffer from its effect. Owing to heavy demands in the fleets for personnel qualified in this subject, there was much pressure of work going on in the *Narcissus* to cope with these requirements. This meant that some hundreds of rounds of gun firing had to be completed each day and it was necessary to put some ginger into the drill and loading of these guns in order to complete the heavy programme each week. To obviate this, it was customary for the Staff Instructor supervising at each gun, to be as close to the gun as possible in order to ensure that no delay occurred in the operations. During the week I have in mind, I was in charge of the aft 6-inch B.L. gun on each broadside, and owing to inclemency of the weather on the first two days we fell considerably in arrears in our programme. Thereupon, the third days firing was commenced soon after daybreak and continued well on in the afternoon. The port and starboard gun was fired alternatively as we steamed up and down the firing ground with the destroyer towing the target. As usual, I experienced singing noises in the ears at first, which increased with the number of rounds fired. By the time we had completed the firing, my head was aching terribly and I had become completely deaf. No less than 500 rounds had been expended between the two guns which were so hot that one could have baked a pie in their chambers! With both guns trained forward, and their breech blocks open I had left them to cool off when I was informed that an instructor who had been stationed at a 12-pounder had injured his hand and, in consequence the class formed up around this gun were waiting to continue the fire. Thereupon, I went forward, assumed charge and commenced firing and continued the firing until each man of the class had expended his prescribed number of rounds.

This brought the days shooting to a close and feeling very tired I went down to the mess for a cup of tea. On many occasions before this one, I had experienced much the same symptoms immediately after a normal day's firing and the deafness with head ache would disappear a few days later. This time, however, it was very different. The ringing in my ears continued and I remained alarmingly deaf for a long period. Never before or since, have I been actually present at heavy and light Q.F. guns which had discharged nearly so many rounds successively in one day. Cotton wool stuffed into the ears has a shielding effect against such injury, but for some inexplicable reason I had omitted to use this precaution, in the metaphor of locking the stable door after the horse had bolted. I have always since done this when present at gun firing.

In the spring of 1906, I extended my activities to rifle and revolver shooting. The Gunnery School at Portsmouth was furnished with excellent ranges, where seamen were given courses in musketry, and during the evenings and weekends I put in a considerable amount of practise in this health giving and competitive sport. Each year the Navy sent representative teams to Bisley in order to take part in competitions for the United Service Challenge Cup with Service Rifle, the Whitehead Challenge Cup with Revolver and other events under the rules of the National Rifle Association.

The Bisley Meeting was held during July 1906, when about 130 separate Rifle and Revolver competitions were open to members of the Royal Navy, the Regular Army, the Royal Marines, the Militia, the Yeomanry, the Volunteers and All Comers including Ladies. The most important competition at this meeting of course was "His Majesty the King's Prize", open only to Volunteers with the Service Rifle. There were three stages in this great event and 100 shots were fired by each competitor over ranges from 200 to 1,000 yards. The highest possible score being 355 marks. The winner of the King's Prize in 1906 was Captain R.F. Davies of the 1st Middlesex V.R.C who attained 324 marks. His prize included a Gold Medal, Gold Badge and £250. Of the huge number of Volunteers who entered the competitions, five-hundred received money prizes mounting in all to £2,320. Another important event at the Bisley Meeting was for the Ashburton Challenge Shield open to eight pupils from the Public Schools having an enrolled Volunteer Corps. This was won by Dover in 1906 with Winchester second and Harrow third.

The United Service Challenge Cup competition was opened to the Regular Forces of the Army and Navy as well as the Volunteers, and our team was known as the Navy Eight. The qualifying stages for the selection of this team commenced simultaneously with an inter-ship competition at the three Naval Ports of Portsmouth, Devonport and Chatham. At the Portsmouth rifle range, there assembled some 200 Officers and men from the various ships belonging to the Portsmouth Division. Each qualifying shoot consisted of seven rounds plus a sighting shot with a Service Rifle at 200, 500 and 600 yards. This was repeated on five consecutive days and the fifteen competitors who had attained the highest aggregate score were chosen for the Inter-Port competition. In this competition I was fortunate enough to gain the second place.

Following this, the Inter Port meeting was held at the Naval Establishment at Devonport. Here the shooting occupied a period of 2 weeks on the Treval Rifle Range where five qualifying shoots were carried out each week making ten in all under the Bisley rules for the United Service Cup. Of the total of forty-five competitors who had thus met from the three Naval Ports, twelve men were selected to go to the Bisley meeting where further qualifying competition was conducted for selection of the Navy Eight.

My stay at Devonport was a very pleasant one and during the evenings and the week-end I was able to visit my relatives and the old farm area which formerly belonged to my mother's family. I found there the beautiful sunshine and salubrious surroundings of England's West Country, which provided all the attributes required for good health so very necessary for accurate shooting.

A very keen contest took place on the Rifle Ranges and I am naturally proud to record that I found the fourth place thus making the Navy Twelve. Having completed this contest, the competitors from Portsmouth and Chatham returned to their own ports and in due course I went on to the Bisley Meeting. Here the Naval representatives were given accommodation under canvas in the Bisley Camp, which was quite close to the Rifle Ranges and on ground hired from the War Office, by the National Rifle Association. The surroundings of this pretty little village in the Home County of Surrey were most charming and life among the hundreds of people who had gathered for the annual event was most congenial. We of the Navy lost no time in making the acquaintance of our rivals from the Army. They were accommodated in a huge marquee tent, and when I asked one of them why they occupied such palatial quarters while the Navy Twelve had just a bell tent, he said, "We bring up sixty men from whom we select our Army Eight! "

Growing Experience In The Royal Navy

However, they were grand fellows, most of them Sergeant Majors and Sergeants and sporting competitors.

Since the United Service Cup competition was one of the last events of the Bisley meeting we had several days in which to resume our qualifying competition for the selection of the actual Naval Team. Accordingly, we lined out on the appropriate ranges each morning preceding the date of the contest and completed our final tests. In these competitions I was again successful and was therefore included in the "Navy Eight".

During these days we were able to work up our shooting for other competitions in which the two permanent services were allowed to enter, such as that for the Brinsmead Shield which the Navy was often successful in winning. This competition was for teams of six with Service Rifle. This event was a particularly interesting one - each team was required to advance on a Mullens (disappearing) target in the figure of a man, and fire one shot when it appeared at irregular times, between the ranges of 600 yards and about 250 yards. It is a remarkable fact that the Navy had won this shield for several years running about the time of which I am writing. In addition to this, the principal event for revolver shooting - "The Whitehead Cup Competition" was invariably won by the Navy. Of course, we took advantage of entering several of the private sweepstakes competitions each day. In these, one purchased unlimited entry tickets for 2/6 at the rifle and pistol ranges. In these I was fairly successful at the share out at the close of each day, though obviously the marksman with the longest purse possessed a decided advantage.

Bisley of course, is the greatest shooting centre in Britain. Even in those days some two hundred targets were exhibited over distances ranging up to 1,200 yards. This included the famous Century Butts where no less than 100 targets could be used at one time at various ranges. Till this visit I had seldom fired at ranges beyond 800 yards, and to my astonishment, I found them much easier for competitive shooting than those at the shorter ranges. The private competitions I remember included very interesting prizes given by the newspapers, Daily Graphic, Graphic and the Daily Telegraph, for shooting over the ranges of 200, 500 and 600 yards respectively, while the aggregate of these firings comprised a competition given by the London Stock Exchange. On the whole I was very fortunate in these events, and won a few substantial prizes. The weather conditions on the whole were good, though the wind usually became changeable and therefore tricky during the afternoons. It was grand to watch the Veterans shooting however and to see how they overcame their disabilities. On several occasions I had the good fortune to shoot beside these grand shots, who were only too pleased to put me up to a wrinkle or two regarding the peculiarities of the force and direction of the wind on the ranges at Bisley.

We Naval men of course used the Service Rifle and sights in all competitions. Though in certain events and all the daily sweepstakes, specially manufactured rifles and sights were permitted to be used, together with accessories such as sight verifiers, coloured paints and orthoptics. In this connection I well remember an amusing incident when competing in the daily sweepstakes at 600 yards range. This was open to All Comers while the entries were unlimited at 2/6 for each sweepstake. On approaching the firing point, I noticed a well-dressed fellow in civilian clothes shooting alone while the Official scorer was recording the value of his shots on the blackboard mounted on its easel. It was customary for two or three to fire on one target at a time, so after watching the competitor for a while I purchased a ticket and commenced shooting beside him. My shooting companion seemed very irritable and in the few minutes that I had observed his firing he had discarded two tickets after scoring a magpie and an outer and commenced all over again after I had fired my first shot. We both were shooting bullseyes alternatively until he had fired his third round which scored an inner to the left of the bullseye. The Official Scorer called his name and then shouted, "Inner four".

This error was plainly due to a sudden change in the velocity of the wind, which neither of us had noticed at the moment, but profiting by his misfortune, I quickly readjusted my sight, fired and scored another bullseye. After confirming the cause of his error, my fellow competitor proceeded to rub out a painted line on his back sight, apply a verivier, scribe a new sight line and after re-adjusting his orthoptic he took aim and fired. By this time the wind had reverted to its former state and produced an inner to the right. This sort of thing went on until the last round was fired when he exclaimed, "To hell with this damnable paraphernalia. I have black and white paint, verivier telescope and everything except bullseyes!"

Had my friend applied another axiom to the old proverb and added 'wind to time and tide waits for no man'; it would have taken him only a fraction of the delays between his rounds and, we may be sure, better results!

Several Naval Officers and men came to Bisley to witness the United Service Cup Competition, which was the most important event for the Permanent Services of course. This took place a day or two before the close of the Bisley Meeting and although the wind was tricky, the light remained fairly good. I must admit that I opened my shoot with a certain trepidation, fearing that I might let my team down. One must always bear in mind that the best of marksmen have their off days, and as an example of this, one of our most consistent shots was dropped out of our team for cracking up only a couple of days previously. However, I soon settled down to work and held my own in all three ranges finishing with the second highest score in the Naval Team. I consider that an experience at a Bisley Meeting is well worthwhile for anyone, especially for those who are as interested in shooting as I was. It is certainly a grand assembly over a considerable number of days in July, a most glorious month in England. Competitors from the Dominions and Colonies and quite a number of shooting celebrities with whom one was able to exchange views on the highlights of the shooting world - among them were the following all excellent shots with both Rifle and Revolver:

Mr Maurice Blood - Irish R.A.

Sgt. Major J. Wallingford - School of Musketry.

Chief Gunner A. Raven - Royal Navy.

Captain J. Rankin - 6th V.B. Royal Scots.

Sgt. H. Ormmundsen (G.M, S.M) - Queens Edin.

Arm Sgt. G.E. Fulton (G.M.) - 13th Middlesex V.R.C.

C.P.O.R. Figg. - Royal Navy.

P.O. R. Evans - Royal Navy.

Major S.E. Rodway - Royal Marine Artillery.

One should also mention Lieutenant H.C. Halahan who captained the Royal Navy Team that won the Whitehead Challenge Cup (Revolver) and whom I regarded as a personal friend.

Encouraged by these successes, I entered again in the Inter-Port competitions in the following year. My shooting was even better and I won a place in the Navy Eight once again, but, alas, I was unable to accompany the team to Bisley, though the cause of this was quite another matter. Perhaps my experiences relative to the use of small arms have been somewhat dilated, but I feel that it has some bearing on the lessons of the Boer War and perhaps to the two great wars that followed. If fighting men are still to be armed with a rifle they should be encouraged to be experts in shooting with it as the Boers were. There is far too much time occupied in ceremonial drills with the Rifle than actual shooting on the ranges. During the Boer War, and I have no doubt in later wars, thousands upon thousands of young men were called up and pressed into war service who had never before handled a rifle. They were then taught the ceremonial drills fairly soundly, but little about the judgment of distances, sighting and wind effect, before being sent to action against past masters at this game as the Boers certainly were.

It was also in the year 1906, that I made the acquaintance of the American born aviator and inventor Mr Samuel Franklin Cody. Prior to this he had come from America in pursuance of experiments relating to kite flying for naval observation purposes. Cody had come to Whale Island to discuss this matter and to try out his kites. He was then in his middle forties, born in 1861, a stockily built man sporting a typical American goatee beard after the style of his namesake William Frederick Cody of Buffalo Bill fame. His kite flying experiments with man-lifting kites were carried out from the lawn at Whale Island and a couple of seamen were detailed to assist in his operations. On many occasions when passing across the lawn to the Heavy Gun Battery, I would stop and engage in conversation with this remarkably indomitable man, and on several occasions, when I saw that he was in trouble with his kites owing to the violent winds, I was truly glad to send over a few seamen to help him out of difficulties.

Even at an earlier time, Cody had been a firm believer in the coming of heavier than air flying machines, and for his efforts was the subject of much ridicule regarding his prematurely airy ideas. These critics were proven wrong when the American brothers Orville and Wilbur Wright were to practically solve most of the problems and make flights in their glider driven by a petrol engine in 1903. He assured me, at Whale Island in 1906, that air flight would soon be used for normal transport.

Cody persevered in the pioneering work of aeronautics and constructed the first practical British flying machine in 1909. It was a biplane similar in appearance to his man-lifting kites though of course driven by motor power. It was in August 1912 during flying trials conducted on Salisbury Plains that he won the first prize for British aeroplanes in this biplane. It was a fine achievement for a man who had started life as a cowboy and a wonderful advance on his man-lifting kites, which I had assisted him with.

Poor Cody, alas lost his life in a flying accident on August 17th 1913 at the age of 52 years. It was sad to hear of his death though gratifying to know that I was privileged to help him with his early experiments on the man lifting kites.

Early in 1907, General Louis Botha, who had defended the passage of the Tugela Heights against Sir Redvers Buller, and afterwards succeeded General Joubert until the end of the Boer War, came to England. In this year he became Premier of the Transvaal and had come to attend an Imperial Conference in London. During his sojourn, General Botha came to Portsmouth and visited the Naval Establishments including the Gunnery School at Whale Island. Thanks to this great soldier and statesman, much bitterness was avoided during the peace negotiations between Briton and Boer on the conclusion of the South African War; and it was a happy augury for the future relationship between the two countries to witness the great welcome that General Botha received throughout Britain.

On the day of his visit to Whale Island, he was accompanied by many notabilities, including Cabinet ministers and the Naval Commander-in-Chief at Portsmouth. After a formal inspection of the establishment, he was conducted to a seat on a special stand that had been erected and from which he was able to witness a Naval display which had been prepared for his entertainment. This consisted of mock landing operations of a Naval Brigade in an attempt to attack and occupy Whale Island against a small Naval defending force. The Invading force had commandeered all the steam and pulling boats belonging to the establishment, about a dozen in all, and at a given signal several hundred Officers and men swiftly landed on the North side of the Island and made a surprise attack. Field Guns and limbers, with ammunition complete were run ashore on wooden gangways inclined from the bows of service launches as they were beached, while machine guns and Rifle Companies were landed from sailing pinnaces and cutters. The alarm was given to the defenders who quickly brought up their field artillery machine guns and riflemen. A devastating fire commenced from both sides with blank cartridges. It was all very imposing and great fun for the whole personnel engaged in it, and we were told that General Botha was most interested and pleased with the operation. Whilst it was just a sham fight, quite a few lessons were taught and it may be that some of the seeds of experience sown at that time matured even in the landing of invading forces during the two great wars.

The 11th June 1907, was a red-letter day for me as I was promoted to the rank of an Officer in the Royal Navy. Warrant Officer, it is true, but as Gunner 1st class, and, according to the King's Regulations and Admiralty Instructions, this promotion carried with it the status of an Officer. As mentioned earlier, this was the only course open to a seaman for advancement to the commissioned rank at that time, and I felt satisfied that I had attained this position at the comparatively early age of 29 years, despite an unusually long time of waiting on the roster. The week-end following my promotion was a very happy one indeed, I had already been congratulated by the Captain and Staff Officers with whom I had ties of friendship, and now I proceeded home on a long weekend leave to celebrate my promotion. My father overwhelmed me with congratulations and I felt truly glad to assure him that my successful progress in the Service was mainly due to his kindly advice and guidance ever since I had entered it.

During the resumption of rife practise for the selection of Naval Representative Team for the Bisley Meeting in 1907, I think it is truthful to say that I met with the greatest misfortune of my life. Whilst loading the rifle I somehow jabbed the index finger of my right hand on to a sharp corner of the bolt. This caused a certain amount of pain and bleeding, but I took little notice of it at the time and continued my shooting for the day. The following day I continued my practice with the rifle with just a small bandage upon my finger, but during the afternoon the wound became infected and painful. That night, I was somewhat restless, while the throbbing of my injured hand was disturbing. Nevertheless, with a new dressing on my finger, I went over to the Rifle Range for the usual shoot. I commenced at 200 yards, and went back to 500 hundred yards range, but by now I was not feeling at all well. Thereupon, I proceeded to the Sick Bay and after my temperature had been taken, I was ordered to bed. Fleet Surgeon Hume then examined the wound and after making an incision and applying a dressing he placed me on the sick list. I was terribly disappointed about this, for I keenly wanted to keep up my practices in the Rifle and Revolver teams. That night, however I felt really ill, my temperature was rising and the throbbing pain from my finger kept me awake. The Fleet Surgeon was very kind and tried another incision above the knuckle, but the germ persisted and I realized that I was suffering from septicaemia. In almost as many days, no less than eight incisions had been made extending from my finger to well up my arm. My temperature was still high, but still I had hopes of an early recovery and begged the Doctor not to send me to hospital as he had suggested. Meanwhile, my comrades in arms, on the ranges, came to the sick bay and kindly assured me that my place in the team would be only temporarily filled and thus encouraged my hopefulness.

I began to get better and my temperature improved, while the doctor displayed great kindness and consideration by day and by night. I had lost considerable weight, but aided by a special diet, I was soon walking about again. It was bad luck however, for the Bisley meeting was now on and I had thus missed it. My health was improving daily and there was very prospect of my return to duty within a few days. But worse fortune was yet to come when, to the doctor's dismay, I reported that trouble had commenced in my right thigh. I felt a perfect culprit after all that Dr Hume had done when he said that I must at last, go to the Naval Hospital. My disappointment was terribly severe at the time, for about a week earlier, I had news from my mother saying that my poor father was seriously ill and that I should not now be able to obtain leave to see him as I had planned to do.

When I arrived at the Hospital my health generally was pretty good, though my thigh was very painful and swollen. Dr Todd, the Senior Surgeon of the hospital examined it and ordered me to bed. I remained there for about 2 weeks when the swelling of my thigh had gone down and I was again able to walk about without pain. Then I walked about a lot, and after a few days of this treatment, I persuaded the doctor to release me for duty. Several Naval Surgeons had examined my thigh, though none of them was able to diagnose the trouble. Accordingly, I returned to HMS *Excellent* and obtained a weeks leave and enjoyed it all the more happily when I found my father's health had considerably improved.

In November 1907, I was appointed to HMS *Prince George* for Quarter Deck duties and joined the ship on the 23rd. The *Prince George* was a battleship having a primary armament of four 12-inch guns mounted two in a turret, and the secondary armament consisted of 6-inch Q.F. guns. The ship was also armed with Q.F. 12 pounder guns for auto torpedo attack and also two submerged torpedo tubes. At that time the *Prince George* was Flag Ship of the Admiral commanding the Reserve Fleet in Home Waters and hoisted the Flag of Rear Admiral Farquar. Captain A.L. Cay was his flag Captain, a very fine seaman with a promising career which unfortunately was cut short later in the prime of life during the Battle of Jutland.

The Commander was Francis Martin Leake one of the most interesting Naval Officers I have ever met. I like him immensely and got on very well with him. He was totally unlike the average conservative type of Officer of the day and introduced many innovations and ideas, which I consider were helpful in relation to the gunnery training of seamen; although he was not a qualified Gunnery Officer himself. I had made his acquaintance before in the *Narcissus*. During the gun firing there, I had seen him impose his so-called idiosyncrasies upon the Gunnery Officers, who had come from Whale Island to the consternation of those worthy fellows. As Commander of the *Narcissus*, he was really the busiest Officer on board but somehow found time to take a most active part during the instruction of gun layers. I saw him, on not a few occasions, standing on the deck watching intently every shot fired from a certain gun, then suddenly go straight to the gun and personally superintend the firing himself. To behave in such an unconventional manner, no doubt was regarded as bad form, but Commander Leake would have his say in everything going on in his ship; and in my opinion, he was usually right.

Soon after I joined the *Prince George* we carried out a long period of working up the ships company in gunnery and torpedo firings and, as in the *Narcissus*, everyone was astonished to see our non-gunnery Commander take so much interest in the fighting efficiency of the ship. Being the Flagship, frequent boat service was going on between the *Prince George* and other vessels of the fleet, and on one occasion I remember there were three boats lying off our ship waiting to come alongside in their proper turn. Seeing this, Commander Leake appeared at the top of the gangway and directed the Officer of the Watch, who happened to be myself at the moment, to beckon the boats alongside and summon the coxswains to fall in on our quarter-deck. When this had been done, I reported that One Petty Officer and two leading seamen were fallen in and awaiting instructions. Thereupon I accompanied the Commander who, upon taking up his stand in front of the seamen, began addressing the Petty Officer after scrutinizing the badges worn by all three seamen:

Commander: "You are a Gunlayer and I observe that the other two coxswains are Seaman Gunners?"

Petty Officer: "That is so Sir! "

Commander: "Well now, Gunlayer, tell me. What does a shot over look like ?

Petty Officer: (rather taken a back) "It looks like a shot over Sir! "

Commander (pointing to the Leading Seamen) - "What is your answer to that?"

One of the Leading Seaman, squinting at the Commander, then gazing with astonishment at me replied, "It looks alright Sir!"

The Second Leading Seaman added, "Yes Sir! It looks all right! "

Though rather ambiguous, the answers from the two Leading Seamen did not satisfy the Commander who had not started a round of laughter. Thereupon the Commander looking again serious sent a message asking the ships' Cook to appear on the Quarter Deck.

Presently, the Cook, dressed in white suit and cap, saluted and uttered loudly, "Yes Sir."

Commander to Cook, "I say Cook, will you please inform these gunnery ratings what a shot over looks like?"

Cook without hesitation replied, "A hit"!

Commander to the three Coxswains, "There now! The Cook is quite right. When you go back to your ships tell your messmates what my cook has said."

The Cook's answer was quite correct of course, and one may be sure that the gunnery ratings of the whole Fleet soon got to hear of this jovial incident with doubtless some good effect.

Although I assisted Lieutenant Dewar in the gunnery work of the ship as much as possible my appointment for Quarter Deck duties included watch-keeping at sea and in harbour in turns with Lieutenants employed on these duties. Unfortunately, the Boatswain of the ship was unwell for a very long time, and in consequence the Commander wished me to help in his work, which I was very glad to do. General work around the ship came to me as a most agreeable change from the hard slog of gunnery, that I had previously experienced. I always loved a turn of seamanship reminiscent of my early days in sailing ships and a chance for this came my way in the *Prince George*, when the Commander informed me that we were going up to Rosyth and that our topmast would have to be lowered and housed to provide sufficient clearance for the ship to pass under the Forth Bridge. In modern battleships, it was most unusual to disturb the masts and yards, and in the *Prince George* this had never been necessary heretofore; and consequently the paint and rust had done its work only too well. However, once again my experience in the Corvette *Active* had helped me and the task was completed quite satisfactorily before we reached the bridge. Target work as a change from gun firing was another one of the jobs assigned to me by the Commander during Gunlayers Tests. In bad weather this was a job of great difficulty. However, on all occasions when I had returned to the ship after missing a meal because of these operations, I would be greeted with a kindly smile from Commander Leake who would see that a tasty repast awaited me. It was a case of willing horse with me, I would gladly take on any task for Commander Francis Martin Leake who was such a loveable gentlemanly fellow. Years afterwards, I met him when he was a Commodore-in-Command of a Squadron during the Great War and I was delighted to resume an all too short acquaintance with him again.

During my time in the *Prince George* a serious accident occurred though happily without loss of life. The ship was moored to a buoy in the middle of Portsmouth when a south-westerly gale had got up. It was on a dark night about eight o'clock and a strong tide was running out of the harbour. I was on duty at the time and happened to be standing on the forecastle when suddenly one felt a shudder under one's feet. I quickly looked around but saw nothing, though I was convinced that something unusual had happened. Immediately afterwards I heard a peculiar noise coming from forward while the lights on the shore seemed to be changing their bearings. Thereupon I rushed to the forecastle head and had a look at the ship's cables, and as they were secured properly to the buoy, one assumed that all was well and that the apparent of bearing of the lights was due to the ships slewing around the buoy. Another look however, convinced me that despite the condition of the cables and buoy the ship must be adrift. By this time another Officer and some men had come on the scene to find out what was the matter and then we let go the sheet anchor. Meanwhile, the ship had been carried by the ebb tide and before she could be brought up by her sheet anchor, a tremendous bump was felt followed by a crash on the starboard side. We had collided with HMS *Shannon* a brand new armoured cruiser which had arrived. only the day before.

There we sat pat across the *Shannon*'s ram with an enormous hole in the starboard side of our ship. Happily, the enormous strain that had then been added to the *Shannon*'s moorings was reduced somewhat as our sheet anchor took a hold in the muddy bottom. Nevertheless, the strong outgoing tide threatened to carry away the *Shannon* from her moorings. Nothing further could be done than to close all our watertight doors and signal for tugs to tow the *Prince George* clear. The Captain, Commander and most of the other Officers of the ship were on shore at the time and were coming off to rejoin the ship as the emergency Dockyard tug was taking us in tow. When we had been towed clear, our searchlight was played upon the *Shannon* and, so far as one could see, that fine Cruiser had not been damaged at all.

Owing to the hole in the side of the *Prince George* we were placed alongside the jetty for the night and entered the dry dock for repairs the following day. In a few days however, the necessary repairs had been completed and the ship was again ready for sea. At the Court of Inquiry which immediately followed the mishap, it was definitely concluded that no blame was attributable to the Ship's Officers for the ship's cables were well secured to the buoy all the time, but the chain moorings had parted below so it was clear that the responsibility for the unfortunate occurrence rested with the Dockyard authority.

I shall never forget the anxiety of Captain Cay as he came on board that night and how immensely relieved he was to learn all the facts, which later had exonerated his ship's Officers at the Court of Inquiry. It was also gratifying to feel that I was on the spot at the critical moment and thus able to contribute my effort towards relieving the terrific strain on the *Shannon*'s moorings.

The general opinion of the Boatswain and various other officers of the ship, was that the *Prince George*'s anchor was dropped just in time to save the *Shannon* from breaking away from her moorings with grievous consequences to both ships.

Before a Warrant Officer could be confirmed in the rank, it was necessary for him to obtain a special certificate of competency in Naval Signals. The knowledge required was sufficient to prepare the candidate for command of a vessel, and comprised All Flag Signals including the International Code, Semaphore and Morse Code and the ability to send and receive signals by night flashing lamp. A knowledge of Service and International Code Books was also necessary. During my study of the above in the *Prince George*, I was helped materially by the Flag Lieutenant, Poe by name, and thanks to him I had no difficulty in obtaining my Signals Certificate. Following this, I received my Warrant from the Admiralty; a document drawn up on parchment. As it is worded rather quaintly, I present a copy of it here as a matter of interest:

By the Commission for executing the Office of Lord High Admiral of the United Kingdom of Great Britain and Ireland.

To: Mr. Frederick William Sweetingham.

We do by Virtue of the Power and in His Majesty's Fleet authority to us given hereby constitute and appoint you Gunner in His Majesty's Fleet authorizing and requiring you from time to time to repair on board and take charge as Gunner in any Ship or Vessel which you may hereafter at any time be duly appointed and you are properly to officiate in all things relative to the Duty of your Station observing and executing the Instructions for the Gunners of his Majesty's Navy and being obedient to such Commands as you shall from time to time receive from your Captain or other your superior Officers. And for your so doing this shall be your Warrant.

Given unto our hands this fifteenth day of August 1908.

By Command of their Lordships With Seniority.

W. Graham-Greene; W.H. May; S. Winsloe.

11th June 1907

In these democratic days, one might consider that this Warrant is expressed rather sternly, especially as such obedience was demanded for a rate of pay of 5/6 per diem, out of which one was required to purchase and maintain an expensive uniform and settle considerable mess bills.

On April 5th 1908, I received a telegram from home informing me of the death of my dear father. This was the greatest personal blow I had received in a lifetime of 30 years. It was with some difficulty that I obtained leave to attend my father's funeral; and it seemed a very long time before I could fully sustain this sad bereavement. My work in the ship about this time was particularly arduous; perhaps providentially so, for the oft recurring memories of my beloved father and perfect guide would invariably accentuate my sorrow.

CHAPTER XX

Life in Destroyers and Torpedo Boats

--- ooOoo ---

On the 21st August 1908, I was appointed to HMS *Peterel* a Torpedo Boat Destroyer of the 30-knot class attached to the Second Destroyer Flotilla. There were only two large flotillas significantly called 'Running Flotillas' in those days, the other being the First Destroyer Flotilla. Both were under the Command of Post Captains known as Captains 'D'. The First Flotilla was based at Harwich in the North Sea and commanded by Captain Lewis Bayly, while Portland in the English Channel was used as a Base for the Second Flotilla.

I joined the *Peterel* at Portland and the Lieutenant in Command greeted me very kindly as I went on board. Beside him, was the Engineer Officer one Griffiths W. Jones, a jovial Welshman, who was certainly very popular and well-liked by everyone on board. There was also a Sub-Lieutenant belonging to the ship who had arrived a few days before and with whom I was to take turns in the duties of Officer of the Watch at Sea and Officer of the Day in Harbour. The Lieutenant in Command was an Officer of private means, married and spent most of his time on shore at Weymouth whenever the Flotilla was at the Base. At this time, both the 1st and 2nd Destroyer Flotillas were working strenuously and the 30-knot class was getting worn out. But under the driving power of Admiral Fisher, who was still the First Sea Lord, Britain was building bigger and better Destroyers just as the size and efficiency of her Battleships and Cruisers was improving. Our Navy was by no means alone in the race of Naval armaments for the German Navy was in the competition under the direction of Admiral Von Tirpitz and the German Destroyer Flotillas were working equally as hard as we were.

A few days after I had joined the *Peterel*, the Second Destroyer Flotilla sailed for tactical and other exercises, and I became fully occupied making myself acquainted with the armament equipment, the efficiency of which was my personal responsibility. This was done between regular watches I kept with the Sub-Lieutenant on the Navigating Bridge. The Flotilla consisted of 16 destroyers made up of 30 knotters and the River Class, under the command of Captain Walter H Cowan (afterwards Admiral Sir Walter Cowan K.C.B. D.S.O. M.V.O.). With the official title then of 'D' Captain he was accommodated in HMS *Sapphire*, a scout class of vessel much larger than a destroyer, but with sufficient speed to enable him to lead the flotilla. After a good shake up in manoeuvres and tactical exercises in the English Channel, the flotilla returned to harbour, refilled the coal bunkers, embarked provisions, water etc., and remained at short notice for sea again. The flotilla was formed into four divisions each led by the Senior Officer of the vessel in their respective divisions. During the manoeuvres, precise station keeping at different cables apart between units and divisions was practised. Here the cohesion of the engine room was most essential in order to respond promptly to the revolution indicator operated from the bridge. This was not always an easy matter in our little vessel when in bad weather, but our cheery sporting Engineer Officer was always on the top of his job, and thus we were able to cope with the ever-changing speeds as required.

This first experience of handling a destroyer as Officer of the Watch impressed me very much, and I must say that it came as a pleasant change from my previous duties in a battleship. I was thrilled and filled with admiration when standing on the navigating bridge whilst manoeuvring with fifteen other vessels at varying speeds up to about 20 knots, and to watch the whole flotilla conforming their movements together as successive signals from Captain 'D' were hauled down in the *Sapphire*. On the Navigating Bridge of the *Peterel* there was very little room to move with the steering wheel, engine room telegraph and revolution indicator, and to cope with the movements of signalman whilst hoisting and hauling down his flags. But I enjoyed every moment of it and compared this with my previous duties in the *Prince George* where one was too busily employed to look around and see such a splendid panorama of what other ships were doing.

Before going on the next cruise, the flotilla was engaged for several days carrying out practise gun firings by day and night followed by torpedo practices. The day firings and torpedo running were performed in Weymouth Bay and the night firing operations were conducted further to seaward. The weather conditions were not at all unfavourable, though I thought at the time that the standard of gun firing left much room for improvement. I also gained the impression that too much stress was laid upon manoeuvres at the expense of the fighting efficiency of the armaments. There seemed at that time to be an unlimited quantity of coal for expenditure, while the amount of ammunition for gun firing was strictly limited.

During the torpedo running, everything appeared to be going along satisfactorily until two destroyers lost torpedoes. Captain 'D' then took a stern hand and many signals passed between him and the unfortunate vessels who were ordered to search and sweep for them until found. It was long after the firing was over when both torpedoes were recovered, and by that time the destroyers concerned were glad to return to harbour.

Soon after these exercises, the flotilla put to sea for another cruise with the intention of making a reconnaissance sweep towards the approach to the English Channel. The barometer was falling and a strong south-west wind and moderate to rough seas had got up as we cleared the race off Portland Hill. Later in the day we were steaming against really heavy weather. The *Peterel*'s turtleback forecastle drove deeply into the waves as green seas came right over and swamped the Navigating Bridge. I was on watch at the time and could see how the other 30 knot destroyers were behaving and knew that we were cutting the same capers. They were all lurching about, pitching and wallowing as they buried the fore part of their hulls into the seas. The oilskin and sea boots that I wore became drenched with sea water, and after another quick and lively motion a heavy sea drove on the little bridge, bent the bridge rails and dislocated the chart table. Still, we plugged on at the same pace while I could see the cheery face of our Engineer bobbing up and down during the lulls, in expectancy of orders to ease speed. The hatches were battened down, of course, and the galley fire was put out by sea water entering the funnel.

Though the River Class Vessels appeared to be labouring in the heavy seas and generally bad conditions, it was a striking contrast to observe the manner in which their high forecastles lifted to the head seas and compare this with the low forecastle of the 30 knotters as they shovelled green seas directly onto their navigating bridges.

Before going to the wardroom upon relief, I went down to the seaman's mess deck to see how the men were getting on. Most of them were young fellows with little experience of the Navy and were prostrate with sea sickness, and the deck itself was awash with sea water. There they were, in stifling foul air, noxious enough to overcome the stomach of the strongest seaman. Nothing however, could be done for them so I proceeded to the Wardroom for a rest and to remove my sea boots and oilskins. There I found Jones beaming with smiles and waiting with a can of hot tea to warm the cockles of one's heart. Knowing that the galley fire had been out for some time and that a cooked mid-day meal would be out of the question, I asked him how he had come by this hot drink, but upon this point he was both deaf and dumb. A little later our dauntless Mess Steward, Thomas by name, came along with a grilled chop and a hunk of bread from I know not where. The Lieutenant in Command then joined us and propping ourselves against the mess table enjoyed this delectable repast together. Although the air in the Wardroom was pretty fetid and sea water had found its way down there too, still it was an incomparably better habitation than the bluejackets mess.

Later I learned that the resourceful Thomas had contrived somehow, with the Engineer to boil the water for making tea and grilled the chops actually inside the furnace door of the ship's boiler room! Thomas was equally an expert in other matters relating to the provision of food for the Wardroom. I have known him repeatedly to go ashore in some outlandish spot, with other stewards of the flotilla, and Thomas alone would come back with a fowl, or some fish and vegetables for dinner, while his comrades would return to their respective vessels and report: No Luck!

It is usually thought that service in torpedo boats or destroyers is a sure cure for sea-sickness, but this is by no means true. I have known many men in the navy and officers too with experience in destroyers who were invariably sea sick in rough weather. When a destroyer is on voyage in bad weather and steaming against heavy seas, the Commanding Officer will regulate the speed of the vessel to avoid damage to the structure, as far as possible, and similarly, when cruising in a Flotilla, the Captain 'D' or Senior Officer may order the speed to suit all vessels of his command. But when destroyers are engaged on Active War Service such as forming a screen for a Battle Fleet every unit must maintain its station and advance at the speed of the fleet at all costs. Each destroyer therefore must stick it out whether sustaining damage or not, with the hope perhaps that the Admiral commanding the fleet might signal that the ordered speed may be reduced if it cannot be maintained without undue damage.

Upon our return to Portland, the *Peterel* was due for Captain 'D''s inspection, and although general efficiency of a destroyer in those days certainly counted towards promotion of its Commanding Officer, the cleanliness and smart appearance of the vessel was regarded as even more important. Accordingly, we buckled to, and the *Peterel* was thoroughly cleaned both inside and out for this important event. The armament was all bright and shiny while the woodwork on the seaman's mess deck was as clean as a hound's tooth. The mast and funnels were painted, rigging renewed where necessary and the ships side was scrupulously cleaned and repainted a dull black colour. The Engine Room Branch under our ever cheery old Engineer co-operated enthusiastically. When Captain 'D' came on board a few days later we received him with much pride and confidence as to the result of his official inspection! We hoped that in accordance with the custom of the Service he would walk around the Upper Deck while questioning the Officers on certain matters, then be so pleased with everything that just a cursory inspection of the Engine Room and lesser decks would satisfy him.

In this however we were quite wrong! To our surprise he went straight forward to the seaman's mess deck, and rooted out the clothes, towels and all the personal belongings of the men and inspected a considerable number of these articles. From there he went to the fore-bridge had a look round and thence to the Wardroom where the Ships Log, Registers, Stores Accounts and Wine Book were laid on the table for inspection. Being a short dapper man, the Captain moved about with alacrity and then went on deck again to inspect the seamen and stokers who had been fallen in there since his arrival on board. Passing smartly down the ranks, he suddenly stopped and raised the collar of one of the men, then asked him his name. He then went to the gangway called his boat alongside and departed. This was the most extraordinary Captain's inspection that I have ever experienced throughout my naval career and I felt so sorry for our Lieutenant in Command. Not a single word was mentioned about the armament equipment, the engines or anything except the clothes belonging to the men; and unfortunately, there was nothing complimentary to say about that. There were no bouquets thrown to us, but emphasis was made on the discovery that a man was wearing a blue collar belonging to another man!

Life on board the *Peterel*, though strenuous, was on the whole quite invigorating and of boundless interest. When the flotilla went into Portland Harbour about half of the vessels would anchor in the stream, while the other half berthed alongside the jetties known as the pens. The Officers of the latter would then assemble ashore to exchange views on the various incidents which might have happened during the cruise. But long before we could land, every dog that belonged to the flotilla - and there were many would leap ashore and provide amusing entertainment in combat. I have seen some really first class dog fights on these occasions. Almost every vessel owned a dog and vied with each other in keeping the most fearsome animal in the flotilla. Some Officers and men would go off to Weymouth, and our evenings in harbour were never dull. Officers of a number of vessels would take it in turn to visit their opposite numbers and have dinner, play cards and pass convivial hours together. Very crowded in the wardroom on such small vessels, but nevertheless truly interesting and happy for all.

Our Captain 'D' was regarded by the personnel of the flotilla, as a martinet. Doubtless there was reason for this for he certainly was a strict disciplinarian and generally feared by his subordinates. Gunnery Officers, by nature of their training and duties, were usually accepted as necessarily strict disciplinarians. But with all my experience of this branch, I was astonished to find that the brand of discipline displayed in the Second Destroyer Flotilla outclassed any that I had seen before. But there was a marked difference the discipline carried on in big ships as compared with that in our destroyers. The former was designed and indeed did help to instil into Naval personnel the art of gunnery efficiency, and was therefore good for the Service. While the latter constituted a terrifying exactitude in the minor matters, concerning spit and polish, dress and so forth, which obviously had nothing to do with fighting efficiency. Perhaps that was due to the fact that commanding officers of destroyers in those days were not regarded in the Navy as "Specialists in the sense that Gunnery, Torpedo or Navigating Officers were. They were selected from the ranks of Lieutenants and Commanders, commonly known as Salt Horse Officers, who hated gunnery, and true enough were the first to ridicule the gunnery discipline in large ships.

Before the Running flotillas were formed, when all destroyers were based on the Principal Naval Ports at home and abroad, the appointments of their Officers were of a sinecure nature. In harbour for weeks on end, their work for the most part consisted of detached coastal duties requiring limited time at sea and plenty of shore leave. This lax condition of service afforded then plenty of time and leisure in which to enhance their status, and instead of being known as mere Lieutenants like their comperes in large ships, Lieutenant-in-Command assumed to title of Captain when on board. Even Sub-Lieutenants on certain occasions were given command of torpedo boats, though everyone knew that their qualifications by no means warranted these high-flown names. I have mentioned this point because I believe that Destroyer Service in the earlier days suffered through lack of driving power on the part of the Senior Officers of the ports in which they were based, and who must have been aware of this. Some 10 years before the date of which I am writing, there were flotillas of destroyers and torpedo boats in commission attached to Portsmouth, Devonport and Sheerness; yet in the system prevailing at the time, not only the troops and forts were under the Military Authorities, but submarines and mines, which was really navy work, were also under the Royal Engineers, while the torpedo defence was under the Admiral. Most incredible of all was that Naval ordinance guns and ammunition were supplied and inspected for maintenance by War Office Officers and not by Admiralty Gunnery Officers. This mixing of Naval and Military duties could not possibly lead to all round efficiency. But this was all put right years later and our dependence on the Army Ordnance Department ceased.

During my service in the Second Destroyer Flotilla, I experienced some hard times and sleepless nights during those notorious south-west gales that prevail in the English Channel. But for all that, I was ever conscious of the fact that it was not the officers who really suffered so much. Especially the Executive Officers who, in fair or foul weather, would be on deck most of the day and so enjoy the fresh air, which was denied the stokers and Engine Room personnel generally. While the wardroom was fairly comfortable in normal weather, it was usually tolerable in bad weather and at all times it was incomparably more comfortable than the seamen and stokers mess deck. Here they were confined in a small dark noxious space with little chance of a decent meal until the vessel returned to harbour. One was deeply impressed too with the lot of the stokers on watch in the stokehold in bad weather, when their strength and ability would be taxed to the utmost in their endeavour to keep adequate steam in the coal burning boilers. There would certainly be no smiling steward like Thomas to greet them as they came off watch and provide them with a tasty meal. Still all on board appeared happy in their own way, and personally I found it a most interesting experience.

Happily, the life on board modern destroyers has improved immensely since the days of the old 30 knotters. Vessels of later times were about three times the size of the *Peterel*, while the accommodation for the ships company and provision of sanitary arrangements and other amenities are vastly superior. Last, but not least, the boilers of all modern destroyers are oil burning instead of coal, which was the cause of so much labour and grimy work in past days.

In fact, some pleasantness came our way in the *Peterel* and one of them in particular was most unusual. This began with the receipt of a letter addressed to the Ward Room Mess from a Wine merchant firm asking whether we would be good enough to test a few cases of port wine of different vintages, with a view to future supply to HM Torpedo Boats and Destroyers. The reason stated was, that owing to the quick motion of these vessels, difficulty had been experienced in the preservation of the clearness and taste of wine after some time of storage on board. Naturally we were unanimous that something should be done to help the firm in this important matter, and a prompt reply was forwarded to that effect adding that the Flotilla would be going to sea for a lengthy cruise in a few days and it would be appreciated if the wine was delivered on board before we sailed.

Sure enough, a half dozen cases turned up the day before we commenced the cruise with the request that two bottles from each case might be returned after the trials and if the wine was found to be quite palatable, we might retain the remainder of the consignment for consumption on board. Following this generous offer Jones and I began to collect the necessary data for a report upon our return from the cruise. In this connection a somewhat elaborate chart was compiled indicating the number of days on which the wine was stored, the weather report, and the roll, yaw and pitch of the vessel covering the whole period at sea. The result of our labours I am happy to relate proved entirely successful, for upon sampling a bottle of wine from each case at the end of the cruise, we of the *Peterel*'s wardroom were bound to agree that the beverage was most delectable and exhilarating, while no sign of discolouration or lack of flavour could be detected. In due course, therefore, a very favourable Wardroom report was submitted to the firm, well amplified by our very attractive chart! Accompanying this report and in accordance with previous instructions one bottle of wine from each vintage was returned to the proper authority.

Another amusing episode was in relation to the wind vanes carried at the top of the foremast of the destroyers. Since these vanes were not official fittings, they were acquired privately and the design was usually associated with the name of the vessel to which it belonged. The *Peterel*'s wind vane was in the form of a sea bird, while the vane carried by HMS *Flying Fish*, our sister destroyer in the Flotilla, was prettily designed to represent that animal. The *Liffey* however exhibited a shiny pig for her wind vane which had been privately acquired by the Lieutenant in Command. This vessel, one of the River Class destroyers, was manned by a goodly number of Irishmen and it was soon apparent that they were not at all pleased with the wind vane of their ship, and took the necessary steps to acquaint the Lieutenant-in-Command of their outraged feelings. Thereupon the latter assembled his ships company and addressed them saying, "As a Scotsman I purchased the wind vane in Edinburgh, and therefore the pig is not an Irish one at all!"

To their credit the cheery Irishmen broke into roars of laughter and so far as I know the matter ended there.

It was about the time I was serving in the 2nd Destroyer Flotilla (1908-09) that the growth of the German Navy began in earnest. Admiral Von Tripetz was then at the zenith of his career and power. Rumours were spreading that the Kaiser was backing him in his endeavour to create a Navy equal in strength and efficiency to that of the British. We possessed the big gun Dreadnought battleship which had been in commission some 18 months and three more ships of this class were being built. In addition, three fast Battle Cruisers of the Dreadnought type had already been laid down. The Germans however, had now gathered considerable information regarding the construction of these ships which was destined to revolutionize the navies of all great powers. The fighting power of pre-Dreadnought ships was definitely inferior and our great fleet of these ships was obsolescent and no match for the Dreadnoughts.

The main advantage of the Dreadnoughts was that they carried ten 12-inch B.L. guns in five turrets, whereas the pre-dreadnoughts were armed with only four guns in two turrets, one at each end of the ship. The striking power which the Dreadnought could deliver at its opponent was therefore overwhelming. Moreover, the accuracy of fire was improved as the increased number of rounds fired in each 12-inch gun salvo made it easier to spot the fall of shots on the target and thus, obtain a straddle and maintain the hitting range more readily.

Admiral Tripetz was soon to appreciate this and Germany commenced building Dreadnoughts accordingly. Our Navy at the time possessed an overwhelming preponderance of pre-dreadnoughts over that of German Navy and for this reason it gave rise to considered opinion of many naval men that Sir John Fisher's introduction of the Dreadnought class, which rendered all these fine British ships obsolescent, was a mistake. Be that as it may, the die was cast and the race of building dreadnoughts between Britain and Germany began in earnest. However, it must be admitted that with all the thought, study and labour in the previous construction of the British ships, Germany was given a head start so to speak.

Growing Experience In The Royal Navy

In the construction of battleships and other large fighting vessels generally there are four desiderata - speed, armament, defensive armour and fuel carrying capacity. If it is necessary to secure all these objects, ships of a certain size must be built. But if the size is decreased it must first be decided which of the four wants may be sacrificed. Now the choice of course will be according to the circumstance of the nation or Empire. If a nation is satisfied with defensive naval strategy the fuel carrying capacity may be reduced, but a nation believing in an offensive policy as Britain has always done, must certainly not surrender fuel carrying capacity. The basis of this calculation together with the number of ships to be maintained will depend upon the comparison between the Naval force of Britain and foreign Powers. The standard set by the Admiralty for some years before the time of which I am writing, was that the strength of our Navy should be equal to the two fleets of the greatest Foreign Powers, which were then France and Russia; and that our ships should be constructed for offensive naval strategy. That is for our fighting ships to be able to concentrate quickly to any point where she is to fight and to possess the ability to fight with equality of power when they get there. The first function is a matter of strategy, while the second is of tactics.

Since warships represent in their design not only the Naval opinion but necessarily the industrial ideas at any particular age, there were few changes made in their design and armament between the days of the Spanish Armada in the year 1588 and for years after the Battle of Trafalgar. Throughout this period of about 250 years the materials for constructing ships were wood and the propulsion was by sail which necessitated masts riggings and yards, while muzzle loading guns were mounted on the broadsides firing round shot. The only progress made during this long period was by increasing the size of the ships, their seaworthiness, speed under sail and the number of guns mounted. As there were no torpedoes, mines, depth charges, submarines or hostile aircraft to worry about, fighting ships could only be defeated by superior gun power. Consequently, when designing ships with their attendant frigates, corvettes or sloops, there was very little fear providing our ships were more strongly built for defence, faster in speed, and able to stand up to the stresses and strain of strong winds, heavy seas and fire from heavier guns. Superior offensive and defensive power and speed constituted the main necessities and the best warship was the one that possessed them all, for by these means she is able to seek out and destroy the enemy.

With the advent of the Industrial Age, it became possible to construct the iron clad warship with steam propulsion and rifled guns capable of firing long explosive projectiles instead of the spherical shot as used in guns before. This permitted a definite increase of range with greater accuracy of gun fire. Moreover, such vessels were perfected with defensive belts of armour. This was a well-marked epoch which brought a great revolution in the construction of warships, and from that time until the present day of super-dreadnoughts the advance has not been halted.

About this time an unfortunate incident occurred between Admiral Lord Charles Beresford, Commander-in-Chief of the newly constructed Channel Fleet (known then as the Home Fleet) whose flag was flying in the Battleship *King Edward VII*, and Rear Admiral Percy Scott, commanding the 1st Cruiser Squadron, to which the Armoured Cruiser *Roxburg* belonged. It caused much concern, more particularly among officers in the Service who were especially interested in gunnery. The opposition to Admiral Scott by certain senior officers to which I have already referred, was still considerable and the feeling against him had become aggravated by the fact that he was constantly bringing forward new devices to improve the shooting in the Navy. These changes which often interfered with the routine of ships and Fleets were regarded as innovations by the conservative element and were disliked intensely.

Admiral Scott however, usually retaliated by strong criticism of the existing system of instruction in gunnery. On this particular occasion, Admiral Scott's Cruiser Squadron belonging to the Home Fleet was carrying out gunnery firings in the English Channel off Portland; when the C-in-C signalled to Scott to bring his squadron into harbour and prepare the ships for an important visit a few days later. It so happened that all ships of the 1st Cruiser Squadron, except the *Roxburg*, had completed their firings and upon receipt of the C-in-C's signal the *Roxburg* requested permission to stay out until finished. Admiral Scott was in sympathy with the idea, but could not approve of the *Roxburg*'s request and sent the following characteristic reply, "Paintwork appears to be more important than gunnery, so you had better come in, in time to make yourself look pretty!"

Unfortunately, a copy of this signal was shown to Lord Charles Beresford, who obviously became furious, and shortly afterwards he made the following general signal to the whole fleet, "It has come to my knowledge that a recent signal was made by Rear Admiral 1st Cruiser Squadron to *Roxburg* - (the wording of the signal was actually repeated)".

"I consider this signal to be contemptuous in tone and insubordinate in character. It is accordingly to be expunged from the signal logs of all ships concerned."

How this signal came to the official notice of the C-in-C, despite the fact that it was only intended for the commanding Officer of the *Roxburg*, was the subject of much discussion and rightly condemned by many persons in the fleet; though, admittedly it was improper.

Nevertheless, it was a demonstration of the friction that existed between Admiral Scott and Lord Charles, who belonged to opposite camps in the Navy. It also displayed the eagerness of Beresford to publicly reprimand one of his subordinate Admirals, rather than frown upon the informer. Evidently the Admiralty did not regard the matter too seriously for Admiral Scott continued in his command, despite the strained relations existing between the two Admirals. It was a matter for regret however, that Admiral Scott was not given a command of Vice Admiral, though a grateful country awarded him a baronetcy K.B.E. and a money grant in recognition of his great service to the all-important subject of heavy gun shooting in the Navy. When his Admiral's Flag was struck for the last time, he still devoted himself to the cause of gunnery, more particularly in perfecting the apparatus for Director Firing, which revolutionised the accuracy in shooting and was barely completed in time for the outbreak of war in 1914.

In June 1909 I left the *Peterel* and was appointed to HMS *Diamond* for service in the Reserve Destroyer Flotilla based at the Naval Port of Chatham. The *Diamond* was a vessel of the Scout Class and was commanded by Captain Godfrey Paine the Captain 'D' of the Chatham Destroyer Flotilla. When the Royal Flying Corps was established by Royal Warrant in May 1912, Captain Paine was given command of the Central Flying School, while Commander Sampson became Officer-in-Charge of the Naval Wing. Captain Paine became afterwards Air Vice Marshall Sir Godfrey Paine.

There were a considerable number of destroyers and oil fuel burning torpedo boats in this Flotilla, but they were invariably kept in harbour with a reduced crew, which included the Commanding Officer and Engineer Officer only. Whenever they were required to go on a cruise for gunnery and torpedo exercises, Officers and men were sent to them to complete their complements and that was the reason why I was appointed for duties in the Flotilla. On arrival at Chatham, I received orders to join HMS *Locust*, a destroyer of the 30 knot class but somewhat older than the *Peterel*. The vessel was moored in the stream at Sheerness and a few hours after embarking we prepared for sea, and early the next morning the *Diamond* led the flotilla out into the North Sea.

The *Locust* was then commanded by a most lovable Officer, who greeted me on board in a very kindly manner. He was Lieutenant-Commander Berwick Curtis (later Vice-Admiral Berwick Curtis C.B. C.M.G. D.S.O.). As soon as we cleared the approaches to the Thames, we altered course to the northward, and running before a strong south-east gale we made an excellent passage to Scapa Flow. No Sub-Lieutenant had joined the ship, so during the trip I kept even watches with Curtis, who had received me so kindly and acted rather like a friendly host, than the usual aloof commanding officer of those days. Of course I had recently experienced hard service as a Destroyer Officer, and was quite prepared and eager to carry out the necessary Gunnery and Torpedo duties, as well as to assist in every way I could as second in command of my new vessel. All I can hope is that this desire was adequately fulfilled under such a perfect Officer and gentleman.

In due course we arrived in the Pentland Firth and the flotilla entered the enormous harbour of Scapa Flow in the Orkney Islands, which was becoming quite a rendezvous for ships and squadrons when carrying out battle practice and other exercises; and was later to become an anchorage and shelter for the Grand Fleet at War some five years later. Having completed our Gunnery and Torpedo firing and the usual flotilla manoeuvres, we left Scapa Flow for passage back to Chatham. A south-east gale with a heavy sea prevailed throughout this trip, which limited the speed of the flotilla considerably and caused much damage to the bridge structure and other gear on deck. The *Diamond* led the Flotilla and the *Locust* was stationed next astern.

During the daylight on this run, Curtis and I used the Flotilla Leader as a perfect breakwater by merely keeping station off her starboard quarter as close up as possible, thus all on board were able to take their meals in comparative comfort. This however could not be practised safely by night, so we took up station further astern. It is remarkable the amount of still waters and shelter a destroyer can obtain from a larger vessel in this manner and Curtis and I were very much amused to watch the heavy seas crashing over the *Diamond*'s port bow, while the *Locust* was speeding along under the Scouts lee quarters, in comparative smooth water to the comfort of all on board our little vessel. The manoeuvre however was not without anxiety for us on the navigating bridge, for one had to be very careful with the helm and the revolutions of the engines in order to preserve a safe distance from the ship next ahead the whole time.

I well remember this particular run for I suffered excruciating pain from my right thigh, probably due to over exposure to the severe weather. It was inflamed and enormously swollen and as there was no doctor on board to alleviate the pain. There was nothing to do but stick it out. This I was able to do by stretching my sore leg full length along the signal locker upon which I sat during my hours of watch keeping on the bridge. The locker being placed in position so that I could reach the engine room telegraph and be closer to the helmsman at the same time. After arrival at Chatham the swelling and pain subsided though the root of the trouble was still there.

A day or two later a telegram was received with orders for me to proceed to the Battleship HMS *King Edward VI* at Portsmouth, and take up an appointment for Gunnery Instructional Duties. Curtis, however, was very anxious about the condition of my leg and suggested that I should remain at Chatham for a while for medical treatment, and he would telegraph to the ship to that effect. I felt however, that I should follow my instructions and accordingly took leave from him. I had, of course, informed him of how the trouble started, as I have related to the reader earlier, and before saying good-bye, Curtis very kindly handed me a letter of introduction to Sir

Watson Cheyne, and advised me to call upon that eminent surgeon at Harley Street as I passed through London on my way to Portsmouth. The following morning, I called on Sir Watson who examined my thigh and stated that he would perform a surgical operation upon it if I could obtain the necessary leave to come to London again. This I promised to do if possible and continued my journey to Portsmouth. Despite my haste to join my ship, I found that the *King Edward VII* was not in port when I arrived in Portsmouth. So, I proceeded to HMS *Excellent* the gunnery school and presented my application to return to London. But alas, the medical authority would not approve of my returning to London, and I was sent to the Haslar Naval Hospital at Gosport for treatment instead. Since this consisted of a few days in bed after an abortive X-ray test, I was not at all pleased about it, for the Senior Surgical Officer claimed (though quite wrongly as it proved later) that a surgical operation was definitely not necessary. Incidentally, in my written application to return to London, I specially remarked that an operation there would be entirely at my own expense.

My journey down from Chatham to Portsmouth had its compensations for I experienced quite an amusing, if difficult, episode when leaving Kings Cross Station after my interview at Harley Street. My luggage included an Admiralty pattern sea chest, which formerly belonged to my father. It was a strongly constructed wooden box furnished with metal strips and handles and fitted with separate compartments including a zinc lined stand for a wash basin. The chest was closed with a heavy metal bound hinged lid, on the inside of which, a looking glass was fitted together with hinged candlesticks on either side. It was all replete with the bulk of my uniform clothing and also contained my private Colts' Revolver in a wooden case. Rather a formidable item of baggage which could not have weighed less than two hundred weight!

Upon leaving the *Locust* at Chatham the chest was taken to the railway station by a conveyance provided by the Navy, but upon my departure from Kings Cross to Waterloo the fun began. In the first instance two railway porters struggled with it and then suggested that I should leave it to be forwarded by goods train sometime later. I had half a mind to adopt this reasonable advice, but thought perhaps that my new ship might sail from Portsmouth before the chest turned up; so I decided to go through with the encumbrance, cost what it may. Accordingly, the porters wheeled the offending article outside the station and called a taxi. As usual there were plenty of taxis about and one was readily selected, but as soon as he became aware of the ownership of the chest he bawled out with a choice Cockney accent, "Gaw Blimey Sir! I can't take that Bleeding Out-House Sir!"

Thereupon I burst into laughter and exclaimed, "Well porter I shall be glad if you will get me a conveyance that will take it"!

Just at that moment a disreputable looking individual in a well-worn bowler hat and standing beside what appeared to be the most ancient horse I had ever seen called out, "Hoy Sir! What's the matter?"

By this time, I had quite realized that the position, though very humorous, was somewhat serious in that the time remaining to catch my train at Waterloo had become strictly limited. I therefore approached the man in the bowler and with utmost caution and tact I induced him to allow my 'bleeding out-house' to be placed upon his ancient four wheeled vehicle, commonly known as a growler. Fearing that even now he might change his mind, I climbed aboard and away went my whiskered John mounted on his box with the entire contraption.

Of course, there was some strife in the off-loading operation at Waterloo Railway Station; but I found the railway porters very kind and no real difficulty was further experienced. Realising however the risk I had taken and what might have happened if the creaking roof of that growler had crashed over my head during that drive through the streets of London; I considered myself most fortunate. Moreover, I shall always feel grateful to that genuine old public servant and his ancient horse and contraption as long as I live.

On leaving Haslar hospital about a week later, I was informed that the *King Edward VII* was not coming to Portsmouth and that I was to join the ship at Cromarty in Scotland. This meant a long train journey, and in due course I arrived on board and took up my appointment.

The ship was one of the finest battleships of the pre-Dreadnought type and was the Flag Ship of the 2nd Division of the Home Fleet, flying the flag of Admiral Sir Berkely Milne, and commanded by Captain Osmond de B. Brock (afterwards Admiral of the Fleet Sir Osmond de Beauvoir Brock G.C.B. K.C.M.G. D.C.L., OXON). This ship was a very happy and efficient one and my messmates, mostly all of whom I already knew, were quite a band of brothers. All ships of the Division based on Cromarty were carrying out Fleet Exercises, battle practice firings and so forth, and I quickly settled down and found my job most interesting. On completion of this work, we proceeded on manoeuvres and arrived at Portland, our normal base towards the end of year 1909.

We were all looking forward then to a spot of Christmas leave but alas, it was not my luck for the many activities, including much ladder work and climbing aloft found the weakness in my thigh once more and I entered the hospital at Portland the day after our arrival there. This hospital was then under Fleet Surgeon Parker who received me very kindly and was not long in discovering by X Ray the cause of my trouble. A few days later I underwent an operation and Dr Parker removed a piece of bone about an inch long and half an inch in circumference. The bone was perforated and had a cord like appearance and had obviously broken away from the thigh bone some two and a half years before. I now had reasonable hope of a permanent cure and was looking forward to rejoining my ship, but the wound became stubborn and simply would not heal up.

Dr Parker however, was very kind and seemed to have much more patience than I. Then by probing very deeply, he removed yet another piece of bone about the size of a pea. This of course, had prevented the wound from healing, but now it healed quite satisfactorily and I was fit for duty in a few days. Meanwhile however, another Officer had been appointed to carry on my work in the *King Edward VII* and, to my joy, I was appointed for Gunnery Instructional Duties in the Dreadnought Battleship *Bellerophon* one of the ships of the First Division of the Home Fleet.

I lost no time in joining this fine ship of improved Dreadnought type, newly built and completed at Portsmouth about the middle of 1909. She, with her two sisters the *Temerani* and *Superb* all of 18,600 tons displacement and armed with ten 12 inch turret guns were the most powerful ships in the Home Fleet. Their predecessor, the *Dreadnought* herself, was the Flagship of the Home Fleet flying the flag of Admiral Sir William May, who had taken over the post of Commander-in-Chief from Lord Charles Beresford who hauled his flag down for the last time and soon afterwards entered Parliament as a member for Portsmouth. Vice Admiral Sir Berkeley Milne was the Second in Command of the Home Fleet and flew his flag in the *King Edward VII*.

The Captain of the *Bellerophon* was Hugh Evan Thomas, with whom I had already served as a boy in the *Ramillies* when he was a lieutenant. I felt it an honour to be selected as an Instructional Officer in gunnery in the very latest type of Dreadnought Battleship afloat and commenced my duties full of interest and energy. Moreover, it gave me much pleasure to assist the Gunnery Officer of the ship who was considered one of the ablest experts in the profession at the time. He was

Lieutenant C.V. Usborne (afterwards - Vice Admiral C.V. Usborne C.B. C.M.G) and the pleasant association with him has remained in my memory ever since.

Although I had seen and handled most of the gunnery fire control instruments before, I was now able to study the Fire Control equipment as a whole and soon became thoroughly acquainted with the entire system throughout the ship including that of local control in the event of the primary installation being damaged by enemy fire. Gun Drills and Fire Control exercises were carried out five days in every week whether at sea or in harbour and this included range taking exercises from numerous Barr and Stroud range finders fitted in the fire control tap aloft, in the gun control armoured tower, and in each turret. These instruments were concentrated upon battle practice targets or supposed enemy ships while the resultant ranges were rapidly transmitted by electrical receivers to a room behind armour protection and below the waterline known as the Fire Control Transmitting Station. There they would be plotted on a table upon which a graph paper roll would be electrically driven and thus the mean geometrical range of the target was obtained. By applying corrections due to direction and velocity of wind, and barometer readings the mean gun ranges were obtained and then applied to a range keeping clock, which in its turn, was set according to the relative speeds and courses of the ship and its target. The resultant ranges shown by the hand of the clock were then passed to the turrets. Further corrections were also applied to the gun sights to counteract the loss of muzzle velocity due to erosion of a particular gun and also the temperatures of the various cordite magazines. The whole of this system of communication was under the direct control of the Gunnery Spotting Officer whose position in the ship was aloft, or in the armoured Gunnery Control Tower. Voice pipe communication, where practicable, duplicated the electrical transmitting and receiving instruments.

A large increase in the allowance of ammunition for practice firings was approved about this time and target practice at increased ranges up to 10,000 yards were frequently carried out by all ships of the Home Fleet. The Admiralty doubtless having due regard to the growing German Fleet and their intensive training in battle practice firings and other warlike activities.

It was part of my duty to instruct the midshipmen as well as the seamen in all methods of fire control and gun drills. Some of these young fellows were very keen to learn all they could and afterwards qualified and became Gunnery Officers. Many differences of opinion and acrimonious arguments occurred between the Officers of the Gunnery Branch and the Commander or Executive Officer who had many matters outside Gunnery to deal with. The Commander of the *Bellerophon* had himself been a Gunnery Lieutenant in another ship, and knowing the ropes was able to frustrate the Gunnery Lieutenant and myself on many occasions in our endeavour to keep the gunnery training up to the mark.

Unlike the immediate past days of spit and polish it was now realized that fighting efficiency was really what mattered, and so long as this was attained together with a reasonable standard of cleanliness and hygienic conditions in a ship this would be sufficient. Despite this however, the old order died very hard, and even at this time some of the Senior Naval Officers commanding fleets and squadrons were still inclined to recommend Commanders of ships for promotion on the strength of the so-called smart and clean appearance of his ship rather than its fighting efficiency.

For this reason, it was our task in the *Bellerophon* to approach the Commander with utmost tact on numerous occasions in order to overcome the grudging manner in which he would allow the Officers and men to leave other work to attend to their battle stations. Curiously enough, I found the non-specialist Executive Officer would continue to get his multifarious jobs done with as little disturbance to us as possible, but the ex-Gunnery Officers were most uncompromising. Many were the times that I had requested, on paper or verbally, the release of a certain number of Officers and ratings for gunnery duties and watched the Commander appropriate scores of men needed for jobs outside my department. Then with only a handful left he would turn to me with a grin and exclaim, "There now Sweetingham, you may have *all these* for gunnery!!"

However, one endeavoured to see the humorous side of these encounters and happy to feel that, in the main, the Gunnery efficiency of the *Bellerophon* was not below that of any other unit of our Battle Fleet.

A few months after I had joined the ship a very amusing incident occurred. At the time, the fleet was at Portland and the C-in-C had received a telegram from Whitehall, informing him that some Abyssinian Chiefs were on their way to Weymouth and requesting that a visit be arranged for them to ships of the Fleet upon their arrival. Admiral May the Commander-in-Chief of course acquiesced, and accordingly passed the information to all ships by signal ordering that a salute was to be fired on the occasion. Also certain ships, including the *Bellerophon*, was to receive the Chiefs on board, during their itinerary. In due course the Chiefs arrived in regal splendour and were ceremoniously received on board the flagship *Dreadnought* by the C-in-C. The ships of the fleet then fired a gun salute and the dusky potentates were royally entertained and escorted by the Admiral's staff to the *Bellerophon* and one or two other ships of Britain's might, majesty, dominion and power. All seemed to go very well and our guests returned to the flagship where they took their departure from the C-in-C after an enjoyable visit. A special boat was arranged to take the Abyssinian party back to Weymouth where they entrained for London.

Later it was discovered that the whole thing was an audacious hoax. Neither the Admiralty nor the Foreign Office officials knew anything about the affair and naturally the C-in-C was furious. Most searching enquiries followed, and it was revealed that this huge joke was instigated and perfectly carried out by a few disguised students, whose family connections were influential in Government affairs in London. The success of their adventure was due, in a large measure, to the fact that the original telegram sent to the fleet bore the name of a high Government Official of the British Foreign Office – Hardinge, the Permanent Under Secretary for Foreign Affairs.

One can imagine how Admiral Sir William May felt about it and the very mention of Abyssinia was in future taboo on board his ship. Unfortunately for him, or rather one of the ships under his command, there soon followed a sequel to this story, which might be interesting to relate.

During the visit of the Pseudo Chiefs, it was noted that not one of them could speak a word of English and conversation was strictly carried on through a so-called interpreter who had accompanied them from London. Whenever they were especially pleased or interested with anything they saw on board, joyous demonstrations would indicate their feelings followed by repeated ejaculations of the words 'Bunga-Bunga'. Little was known about Abyssinia by men of the Navy in those days or of its native language, so the Officers present in their blissful ignorance joined in the merriment by repeating 'Bunga-Bunga!'

Now it so happened that the Home Fleet Regatta took place soon after this hoax, and on such occasions it was the custom for a couple of ships boats to be rigged decoratively and manned by a funny party who would pull the boats from ship to ship bringing music, song and revelry with them. Significantly on the morning of this Regatta, the C-in-C signalled an order that ships of the fleet were not to rig boats with funny parties. This of course was observed by all ships present. When the signal was made however, one of the cruisers was absent at sea and did not arrive until the Regatta had started. In blissful ignorance of any order to the contrary, the new arrivals promptly rigged out and manned a funny party boat with a band and several men dressed as Abyssinian Chiefs. Then with a hearty cheer from their ship, they pulled with boisterous gusto straight for the Flag Ship *Dreadnought* with intermittent shouts of 'Bunga Bunga'!

But as they drew near the gangway of the ship, they could see that obviously there was something amiss. No cheery greeting of welcome came from the *Dreadnought*, but rather a dull sinister silence prevailed as the boat came up alongside. The solitary figure of the C-in-C awaited them with exemplary coolness and self-control. Though extremely angry at the moment, he soon forgave and forthwith gave instructions that the offending boat and her motley crew were to return to their ship immediately.

In August 1910 our Captain (Hugh Evan-Thomas) exchanged commands with Captain T.D. Napier who was then commanding the Royal Navy College at Dartmouth. Our new Captain was an extremely lovable Officer and a perfect gentleman. He possessed many attributes which endeared him to the whole ship's company of the *Bellerophon* and it was my privilege and great pleasure to serve again under his command in the Grand Fleet during the War 1914-18.

I had not served more than a few weeks in the *Bellerophon* before I realised the great advantage of the disposition of all her big guns, but also in the time taken to ready the ship for action against the enemy. Normally, in the pre-dreadnought type, there were boats, davits, stanchions, ventilators and other top hamper obstructing the movement of certain guns and the line of sight and fire of many others. All this at the cost of considerable time and labour, had to be cleared away before the guns could be brought into action. This however was obviated when at sea by the modern structural arrangements of the Dreadnought type.

In the construction of the earlier Dreadnoughts, including the *Bellerophon*, an important innovation was introduced, in that the Wardroom and officers cabins were situated in the fore part of the ship. This arrangement was by no means appreciated or favoured by the Officers themselves, especially in heavy seas and bad weather when everything would be battened down. The extreme pitching of the ship, attended by the unpleasant smells coming from the muddy cable lockers, were not at all appetising during meal times in the Wardroom, or periods spent in cabins. Owing to the adverse reports from Officers serving in such ships, the later design for accommodation of officers was altered to the centre and aft part of the ship as usual. In this connection, I am of the opinion, that while the above experiment lasted, it definitely favoured the seamen of the messdecks. Moreover, it gave the Officers a taste of what the bluejacket has had to contend with throughout the ages, forced attention to the matter which resulted in several improvements in ventilation and hygiene, which had been long overdue. Truly its and ill wind - etc.!

One very interesting and pleasant episode that occurred in my time in the *Bellerophon* was when we were in Northern Waters. It was in September 1910 or thereabout that we had come down from Scapa Flow to Invergordon, and were invited to take part in the Northern Athletic Meeting which was to be held in the Highland Capital Inverness. The Mackintosh of Mackintosh had extended the invitation to the men of the Home Fleet, and to be sure we were delighted to join in the sports of this Highland gathering. Many of our fellows entered in the racing events and a few ships entered a tug-of-war team including the *Dreadnought* and ourselves.

The result of this competition however was a lesson to me, as indeed it was to most of the men of the Fleet present. In the selection of the ships' teams, weight seemed to be the predominant factor in the choice of men, and the result was that the naval teams were made up of an average of 14 stone men. The *Bellerophon*'s team, to which I belonged, was beaten by the *Dreadnought*'s in the semi-finals, leaving the latter to face a team from the Seaforth Highlander Regiment (I think it was) in the final stage. The lining up of these two teams presented a remarkable contrast in avoirdupois; for the total weight of the men of the Scottish Regiment averaged little more than 10 stone. But they were men of fibre and trained to pull on the rope with wonderful strength and cohesion. Our calculations upon the appearance of the contestants suggested that the hefty *Dreadnought* team would simply walk away with their opponents, but we were soon undeceived. To our amazement the *Dreadnought* team was defeated quite early by these sturdy Scots.

There were of course, certain events in which we of the Navy did not take part. These included the fine old Highland sport of Tossing the Caber and Sword Dancing to the skirl of the bagpipes. The airs of the Scottish homeland, played by the fully trained and expert members of the pipe bands were particularly melodious. While the pipers and drummers clad in their traditional highland dress and colourful tartans, as approved by the Chieftain of their respective clans, were of special interest. We spent the whole day at this fine Highland Gathering and experienced full enjoyment of such a great novelty; especially to those of us who had come from the home counties of England. Moreover, it was a pleasant break in our strenuous grind of Naval work of those days.

During the Autumn of 1910, Britain was favoured with a visit by an American squadron of four battleships. On meeting this squadron, we exchanged the usual courtesies which were followed by a series of entertainments. One British ship was assigned to specially look after the welfare of the contemporary American ship and under this arrangement, we of the *Bellerophon* assumed the happy duties of hosts to the ship's company of the U.S. Dreadnought Battleship *Delaware*. Luncheon and dinner parties on board were arranged and altogether we and our American cousins shared enjoyment to the full.

During these festivities I particularly remember being present at a luncheon in the Commissioned and Warrant Officer's Mess in the *Delaware*. We began with the usual cocktails then sat down to eat about one o'clock. After wading through a full course of most delectable food amid the flow of wines, spirits or beers, a huge punch bowl was placed on the table and thus the merry function of about two hours duration was closed. It must be remembered that this was before the days of the American prohibition laws, and the official rationing of food in England was unheard of! When we returned to the *Bellerophon* that afternoon, it was approaching the time to dress for dinner, but this was necessarily a frugal affair after our experience of 'some lunch' as it was called in the U.S.S. *Delaware*.

Since my pleasurable acquaintance with American sailors in Hong Kong, many years before, I have often thought that men of these two English speaking navies should be given the opportunity of mingling in harmony more often. Not only for such hilarious entertainment of each other, but for the more important purpose of normal conversation when exchange of views on world affairs and other interesting matters would cement the bonds of friendship between the naval personnel of the two great nations.

Personally, I have always enjoyed the company of the U.S. Naval Officers and men, and was very happy indeed to renew the acquaintance of so many of these fine fellows during the course of my duties in World War II.

CHAPTER XXI

Back to the Mediterranean on HMS Aboukir

--- ooOoo ---

Having completed a very impressionable period as Gunnery Instructional Officer in the *Bellerophon*, I was appointed to HMS *Aboukir*, for the same duties. The *Aboukir* was a fast Cruiser of 12,000 tons, 250 feet long by 113 feet wide, armed with two 9.2-inch, twelve 6-inch and twelve 12-pounder guns. She was also equipped with two 18-inch submerged torpedo tubes and belt of 6-inch Krupp armour amidships. Her boilers were of the coal burning type developing 21,000 horse power which gave her a speed of 21 knots. An innovation introduced in the *Aboukir* was the fitting of non-flammable wood, which sometime later was objected to on the grounds that it deteriorated the gold lace of Officers uniforms stored in Chests of Drawers made of this material. The *Aboukir* belonged to the Cressy Class cruisers which were laid down in 1898, and at the time of which I am writing, she had just returned from service in the Mediterranean to recommission again for a further period with the Mediterranean Fleet.

Sweetingham in Argostoli, Malta (1911)

A few days after I had joined the ship, we sailed for Malta where the *Aboukir* became a unit of a Cruiser Squadron commanded by Rear Admiral Gamble who was flying his flag in HMS *Bacchante*. Our ship was commanded by Captain Cuthbert Hunter who was fairly senior on the Captain's list and well-liked by his officers and men. Soon after we arrived on the station, Hunter grew a beard and to emulate his example all officers of the *Aboukir* followed suit! I remember this very well, also the comical appearance of some of my brother officers. The Captain's beard and a few others were quite respectable, but I'm afraid that many of his imitators could produce only a half-hearted grizzly assortment and was the cause of much ridicule! Happily, this dishevelment was of short duration for the Captain appeared one morning with his face again clean shaven and his officers followed the example. Personally, I was glad for I never felt clean during my attempt to grow whiskers. Though I tried all one could to cultivate an orthodox outfit known as a 'Torpedo Set' - a moustache kept fairly short with the whiskers closely cropped and leaving a thickset pointed beard.

GROWING EXPERIENCE IN THE ROYAL NAVY

The Mediterranean Fleet at this period was far below the strength of the Home Fleet. On the previous occasion in which I served there, the biggest and most powerful battleship that the Navy could produce were stationed there; but now all the Dreadnoughts and most other modern ships were attached to the Home Fleet, while the Atlantic Fleet, under the Command of Vice Admiral Sir John Jellicoe, absorbed the next best pre-Dreadnoughts which included six battleships and four armoured cruisers. Personally, I felt it rather sadly to serve in this second-rate fleet after leaving the magnificent Home Fleet. But the changes and chances of the Naval Service seemed to bring their compensations and I soon found that my work in the beautiful surroundings of the Mediterranean was much more pleasant than that in Home Waters. Instead of the cold bleak weather and grey mists of the North Sea and English Channel, here was the salubrious climate and sea under a radiant sunny sky. True it was gunnery and still more gunnery as in the *Bellerophon*, but under far more pleasant conditions by day and by night. Furthermore, unlike the period of my former service, the Mediterranean had now become one of the healthiest Naval Stations in the world. The dreaded intermittent fever, which had laid low the flower of our seamen, was entirely eradicated.

Our stay at Malta was of short duration for the new ship's company of the *Aboukir* was due for a gruelling series of drills and gunnery practices before the ship could be regarded as an efficient fighting unit of the Fleet. Accordingly, we left the still waters of Malta Harbour and the pretty dgarsaks with their high Venetian prows skimming over them, and proceeded to Argostoli on the Greek island of Cephalonia of the Ionian Group. The magnificent harbour of Argostoli formed a base on which we carried out our gunnery and torpedo firings. Here our work continued by day and by night until it was considered that we had reached a standard of efficiency to qualify our ship to join the fleet as a fighting unit.

During the afternoons of Sundays or of days when our exercises were over, I found it wonderfully relaxing to land at Argostoli and take long walks in the beautiful surroundings of these fertile lands. It had the effect of an exhilarating tonic to get so near God's earth and to watch the peasants cultivating those acres of soil which for the moment prompted a desire to give up one's continuous grind in Naval gunnery and seek a tranquil life in some beautiful environment such as this. During one of these walks, I well remember coming to a well, and peering down, I beheld the lovely bowers of maidenhair fern growing around its perimeter. The long fine hair-like stalks suspended their green and delicate fronds which formed shadows of exquisite beauty on the cool waters beneath.

We spent several weeks at Argostoli and having completed our drills and firings, the *Aboukir* joined the flag ship and took part in fleet manoeuvres. My life on board the ship generally was a very happy one. All officers from the Captain down to the midshipmen were a fine lot, while I should say that the Petty Officers and men were above average and made up a cheerful ship's company. Moreover, the *Aboukir* shaped well in all our competitive firings and sports within the Mediterranean Fleet. However, many of our Officers, curiously enough, were the victims of Army red tape which I had not previously seen encroach upon the daily lives of Naval officers at sea. So I feel that it might be of some interest to make a brief record of the facts in these memoirs.

It so happened that during the *Aboukir*'s previous commission, His Royal Highness the Duke of Connaught with Princess Patricia and their entourage were accommodated aboard during an official inspection of the Military Forces in the Mediterranean. Since this tour of inspection was to have occupied a considerable time and necessitated calling at several ports, special accommodation was arranged for the Royal Party by the Dockyard Authorities at Malta. This was done by modifying the existing Captain's and Officer's quarters in the ship, and of necessity, several officers were compelled to use less cabin space, while others were required to give up their cabins entirely. The ships Officers however, gladly put up with personal inconveniences while the Duke and his party were made as comfortable as the circumstances permitted. Soon after the completion of this Royal Tour, the *Aboukir* was sent home to pay off and recommission for service again as I have already mentioned.

Now one of the chief concerns of Naval Officers when first joining their ship is to locate and occupy his cabin and the importance of this will be appreciated when one feels that this small space is to be his living and bedroom for the duration of his appointment. Our astonishment can be imagined when several of the *Aboukir*'s Officers, including myself, were informed that although the number of cabins on board were more than enough to accommodate us all, it was regretted that the quarters, which had previously been occupied by the Military entourage, could not be made available! The reason given for this extraordinary statement was that the forbidden cabins contained certain articles of furniture and fittings within them that were the property of the War Office; and that until such articles were disposed of, the cabins affected were to be kept locked and their military contents guarded. The utter absurdity of this order, which remained in force for a long time after His Royal Highness had given up the accommodation constituted, to my mind, a Masterpiece of Red Tape.

While cruising in the Levant during the summer of 1911 we called at Jaffa in Palestine and a party of Officers from the ship, including myself, obtained leave to visit the Holy Land. There were eight of us, including the ships chaplain, who had kindly arranged for accommodation on shore and for a guide. The Captain was very interested in our pilgrimage and extended our leave to allow our stay at Jerusalem over three days. We left Jaffa by train early one morning and after an uncomfortable journey in the heat of an oppressive sun arrived at Jerusalem and stayed at the Hotel Olivet. At that time the country was under Turkish rule and had been for some 400 years, but after World War I of course, Jerusalem became the seat of Government of Palestine under a mandate granted to Great Britain in 1922.

Our tour of the city was extremely interesting. It is situated on a plateau about 3,000 feet above the level of the Mediterranean Sea, and its population included quite a medley of Arabs, Armenians, Turks, Jews and Europeans. The Eastern people one saw in the streets were comprised mainly of poor clad pedlars and countless beggars. Indeed, for a city of such great and glorious memories for all Christian peoples, it appeared most dowdy and disappointing. Some of the buildings however were very fine especially the Mosque of Omar and the Great Synagogue. Our guide was very able and eloquent and conducted our party to most places of interest. One of these was the Temple which, we were told, stood upon the original site of that erected by King Solomon. Inside this temple our attention was drawn to two large pillars enclosed within a circular iron fence having spiked bars and standing nearby on guard was a Turkish soldier. We were told that the reason for this curious arrangement dated a long way back to the reign of one of the Kings of Israel. It was the belief in those days that unless one could pass through the narrow space between the two pillars the Kingdom of Heaven would be denied him. But when this particular King attempted to pass between the pillars he was too rotund to do so. Becoming so angry and troubled at his failure the King thereupon instituted the erection of the fence and posted the guard with orders that passage by anyone between the pillars in the future was forbidden.

One of the most impressive events during our itinerary in Jerusalem began with our assembly at the place which is reported to be the site of the Judgment Hall where Pontius Pilate delivered

Christ to the Jews on the day of the Crucifixion. I well remember setting out from here enroute to Mount Calvary, or Golgotha as it was called. We halted at the supposed spot where Cyrene Simon was compelled to bear the Holy Cross and at places along the route where other incidents occurred as recorded since that memorable day. This truly impressive march called to my mind those wonderful paintings of Italian art which depict these incidents while an extraordinary feeling of depression came over me as I passed along the road towards Mount Calvary. Indeed, what could be more inspiring to the genius of those great masters of art than this? And we might well ask, who has done more for the cause of Christianity than those painters of those beautiful pictures associated with this sacred story. Upon the actual site of the Crucifixion stood the Church of the Holy Sepulchre, the traditional position of the Cross being marked by a star within the chapel. All this was so very interesting, and I am thankful to have had the privilege to have followed this memorable course in biblical history.

We found the Mount of Olives, east of Jerusalem and after which our hotel was named (Olivet). The flower beds there were well kept, though the pleasantness of the scenery here was sadly marred by the presence of lepers who were allowed at the time to beg in the vicinity. Doubtless, since 1922, under British Mandated Rule, some hospital or other suitable place has been allocated for the care of these poor unfortunates. From the summit of the Mount where Christ ascended into heaven, can be seen a fine view of the city across the Valley of the Kidron, while on the slope of the Mount nearer Jerusalem is the pretty garden of Gethsemane where Judas is said to have betrayed Christ and where excavations have revealed the remains of an ancient church of the fourth century.

Among other impressive features of interest during our visit to the Holy City was the Jewish Wailing Place - a recess built up of stone where Jews could be seen making their lamentations. As one gazed into this place one could not help thinking that more privacy was necessary for these wailful proceedings going on before the prying eyes of visitors and others not belonging to the Jewish religion.

On the second morning of our visit, we procured donkeys and rode out of Jerusalem to Bethlehem about 5 miles distant to the south-west. It was a sweltering hot day and the journey along the dusty road was responsible for progress of some languidness. On the way we came to Rachel's Tomb, a squarish building which covers the supposed site of the original grave. Here we halted awhile and rested the donkeys before continuing the journey. In the Old Testament it is mentioned that Rachel, the favourite wife of Jacob and mother of Joseph and Benjamin, was buried on the borderline of Israel and Judea. One noticed that a little beyond the tomb the road divides leading in one direction to Hebron, the sacred city and abode of Abraham and the first capital of King David, while the other road leads to Bethlehem.

The approach to Bethlehem is at the bottom of a hillock, so we dismounted and led our mounts unto the township of sacred memories. Despite the cobble stones and narrow streets so familiar in the towns of Palestine, Bethlehem impressed me as being an unusually clean and orderly place. There were no garbage heaps or offensive odours as experienced in Jerusalem, while the inhabitants appeared to be generally of a better type. Every one of them seemed to be employed in some useful manner and consequently we were not accosted by beggars and the like. Furthermore, I gathered that, unlike most Middle Eastern communities, the people of Bethlehem practised a particularly high standard of morality.

We entered the Church of the Nativity situated on the immortal site of the humble stable in which a child was born nineteen hundred and ten years before the time of which I write. Here, according to St Luke: "Mary brought forth her first-born son and wrapped him in swaddling clothes and laid him in a manger, because there was no room for them in the inn". Later the famous grotto of the Nativity was built on this spot by the Empress Helena, wife of Constantine. The Church of the Nativity built over the crypt, is probably the oldest Church in the world. The sacred ground upon which it stands belonged to several religions including Roman Catholics, Greeks, Copts, Syrians and Armenians. No less than fifteen lamps were kept burning there by night and day, and the rays of light from them illuminate the symbolic words: *His de Virgine Maria Jessus Christus natur est* (Here from the Virgin Mary, Jesus Christ was born). The church building was divided by rows of classical pillars into three main portions - so far as I remember, the centre belonged to the Roman Catholic Church and contained the Crypt, while the two adjacent portions formed the Greek and the Coptic (or early native Christians) churches.

We were told that on Christmas Day, all the churches held their commemorative services and at times quarrels arose as to the priority of the ceremonies. Each denomination advancing different reasons for holding their particular service first. According to what I could ascertain at the time, it appeared that ordinarily, the denominations would take regular turns, but when this arrangement became unsuccessful and priority was insisted upon and taken by any particular sect, the congregations of other churches affected would assemble outside the church and noisily protest. While this unseemly behaviour was in progress the Mohammedan Turkish soldier posted nearby, would endeavour to keep peace on earth and good will among these Christian peoples!!

While at Bethlehem we went to a certain distance outside to a point overlooking the Dead Sea. In reality this is a lake some 1,300 feet below the level of the Mediterranean Sea. The source of the River Jordan which enters into the Dead Sea is about 1,100 feet above sea level, while the water of the Dead Sea contains more than seven times the per centage of salt as that of ordinary sea water. Ordinary fish, of course, cannot live in the Dead Sea though I understand that a kind of shrimp is found there. Truly remarkable waters and perhaps admirably suitable for teaching timid bathers to swim; for here the water is so dense that the human body cannot sink below its surface, while the shark or other dangerous fish do not abound. The Fields of Boaz were also seen from our point of vantage outside Bethlehem. According to the biblical story it was there that the husband of Ruth met her while she was gleaning in the fields. Of further interest too we could see in this magnificent view of the Holy Land, the distant village of Beit Sahour where we are told the Shepherds watched their flocks by night at the time of the birth of the Holy Child.

Before returning from Bethlehem, we visited the shops displaying the locally made articles. One of the industries there was the manufacture of useful items such as picture frames, paper knives and so forth, also ornaments. The materials used being wood from the Cedars of Lebanon sent from the Syrian mountains some 100 miles distant, and from the mother of pearl. The finished articles were exquisitely made and sold at reasonable prices. I bought quite a number of them to add to my stock of souvenirs and for gifts to my family. We returned to Jerusalem on the evening of the day of our visit and on our way witnessed one of the most glorious sunsets I have ever seen. It seemed all so beautiful and resplendent, and so fitting to the close of this memorable day.

The Hotel Olivet in Jerusalem was considered to offer the best accommodation for European visitors in the city, but in truth, I was not very impressed with the sleeping arrangements in the stifling atmosphere and a plague of flies and other pests that existed at the time. Without proper thought, I had removed the mosquito net from over my bed before turning in, but was soon awakened by mosquitoes of an extraordinary large kind that stung me viciously. The following day we returned to Jaffa by train, but before embarking in the ships boat which awaited our arrival, I had an unlucky experience in regard to the many souvenirs which I had brought during the tour. Before leaving Jerusalem, I packed them carefully as I thought, into my suit case which I handed to an Arab porter for conveyance from the Railway Station at Jaffa. To my dismay, when I arrived on board the *Aboukir*, I discovered that all the articles which were made from mother of pearl except a small picture frame had been smashed to pieces! Since I had handled my suit case so very carefully whilst it was in my possession, I could only conclude that the damage must have been done by the carelessness of the porter. My disappointment was further accentuated because I knew my chances of ever making such purchases again in the Holy Land were very remote. There is however, some consolation in having the unscathed picture frame; still in my possession.

Before the completion of our stay in the Eastern Mediterranean, one of my ardent wishes was fulfilled in a visit to the seat of early European civilization the famous city of Athens the capital of Greece. From the day of the ships' arrival at the Piraeus till our departure the weather was perfect and I availed myself of every hour possible during a stay of several days to see and learn as much as I could of this city, which under Pericles, in the fifth century B.C., lived a people endowed beyond all others with the love of beauty and art.

Athens itself is situated upon and around a group of hills four or five miles from Piraeus its seaport. Of the many ruins of wonderful architecture that one sees in Athens is the Acropolis- the remains of the great citadel which still dominated the city. From the site of this imposing mass of structure a splendid view is presented and many fine modern buildings of the city can be seen. The mass of rock upon which the Acropolis stands is more than 500 feet high. The remains of the glorious Parthenon with its mighty columns, said to be the loveliest building of antiquity, was still a monument of superb design though much of it had crumbled. Another place of interest was its Stadium comprising an enormous arena of enormous length which as this Greek name implies measures one stade (606 and 2/3rd English feet). Surrounding the centre portion of the arena is the racing track which can easily be seen from the gallery of seats sloping upwards from its perimeter wall. The seating accommodation here must have been sufficient for many thousands of people to witness wrestling and other forms of athletic exercises. The stadium appeared to be of modern construction, and though one had seen the contemporary stadiums at Wembley and other centres of sport, one could not but recall the stories of the Gladiators who had appeared in this arena to fight unto the death, with others or with wild beasts, for the amusement of those in the gallery. I saw as much of this interesting place as I could, but my visit was much too short.

In the Autumn of 1911 we returned to Malta, where the ships' company carried out an annual course of musketry on the Rifle Ranges. One of our Senior Lieutenants whose name was Colin E.M. Law, was nominally in charge of these operations, but it fell to my lot to conduct the rifle and revolver practices, and to march with the Small Arm Companies to the ranges at Corrodina; while Law proudly rode at the head of the force on a white charger! Curiously enough sometime later, this same Officer performed precisely the same function when we were serving together in HMS *Drake* on the Australian station - when we carried out the Musketry Instructions of that ships company. Law and I were great friends and we were to be shipmates yet again in HMA.S. *Encounter*. His father, whom I also knew, was the Naval Chaplain of Greenwich Nautical School during my term there.

Soon after we had completed our Musketry Course, the Mediterranean Fleet held its Annual Pulling Regatta in the harbour of Malta followed by the periodical sports held on the parade ground at Corridena. In both these fine competitions I am happy to record, that the ships company of the *Aboukir* shaped remarkably well. When all the excitement of these events had passed and the

Mediterranean Fleet was preparing for further manoeuvres, the Flag Ship of our Cruiser Squadron, the *Bacchante*, was ordered home to pay off. It was thought then that as the *Aboukir* was a sister ship, we might become the flagship and have to accommodate Rear Admiral Gamble and his Staff. There were other changes impending in the fleet about this time, and I well remember Captain Hunter's opinion expressed on board at this juncture, that he firmly believed war with Germany was fast approaching and that we should therefore be prepared for any news regarding the movements of ships.

When the *Bacchante* steamed away from us on her homeward passage she flew an enormous paying off pendant while her band played the well known tunes, "Rolling home to merry England" and "Fall in and follow me". The ships companies present gave her a rousing cheer as the *Bacchante* steamed passed them and soon that fine cruiser disappeared from view. There was an early sequel to this incident however, which proved terribly disappointing to the men of our sister ship. For soon afterwards, the *Bacchante* was recalled and the *Aboukir* received orders to proceed home in lieu of her! The reason for this was unknown at the time, though many of the *Bacchante*'s men swore that it was because their Admiral preferred to remain in their ship rather than transfer his flag to the *Aboukir*! Be that as it may, in due course we left the Fleet amid cheers while our band played the same melodious airs that the *Bacchante* had chosen only a couple of weeks before. Of course we felt very sorry for the *Bacchante*'s Ships Company in their disappointment, for they had been on the Station much longer than we had.

After passing through the Straits of Gibraltar, homeward bound, news came to us of the grounding of the P & O Steamer *Delhi* near Cape Spartel (on the Atlantic side of the Straits) with the Duke of Fife and the Princess Royal and their family on board. Fortunately, the Atlantic Fleet was at Gibraltar at the time, and with the aid of their ships the Royal Party was landed safely. All the passengers on board were saved, but sadly the *Delhi* became a total wreck.

Our homeward passage was completed in November 1911, when we arrived at Portsmouth. Important changes were now taking place at the Admiralty. Mr Winston Churchill had become First Lord in place of Mr Reginald McKenna who went to the Home Office. It was also announced that Admiral Sir Francis Bridgeman was relieving Admiral Sir Arthur Kingvet Wilson as First Sea Lord, while Vice Admiral Jellicoe was appointed Second in Command of the Home Fleet, in succession to Prince Louis of Battenberg, who was to become Second Sea Lord.

As the *Aboukir* steamed into Portsmouth Harbour, we noticed that HMS *Drake* was lying at the farewell Jetty there, and upon enquiry, it transpired that the ship was commissioning for service as Flag Ship on the Australian Station. Little did I suspect as we passed the fine ship that I would be joining her within a few days.

Immediately after securing to our moorings however, a signal was placed into my hands stating that I had been appointed to HMS *Drake* and was to join the ship as soon as possible. Amongst my mail was a letter from my old friend William H. Rhind who was then Chief Gunner on the Staff of HMS *Excellent*, conveying his hearty congratulations upon my new appointment. Rhind had previously served a number of years on the Australian Station and we had had many talks about the great island continent and the small isles of the South Pacific.

Of my many Scottish shipmates and friends in the Service, Rhind was the wittiest. Himself happily married, I often think of the reminder he gave me in that letter of the fact that I was still a bachelor; adding significantly that the girls of Australia were handsome, carefree and merry!

Part 5

Birth Of The Australian Navy

HMS Encounter moored in Hobart on Regatta Day, January 1912

CHAPTER XXII

I Join HMS Drake

--- ooOoo ---

On the 30th November 1911, I boarded HMS *Drake* and took up my appointment again for Gunnery Instructional Duties. As I have referred to this post quite a number of times in these memoirs, I trust the reader will not have the erroneous impression that gunnery work constituted the whole of my duties in the various ships in which I served. Far from it. For as implied in the Admiralty appointment, my first duty was that of an Officer of the Executive Branch, and as such was available for watch keeping or any other duties at sea or in harbour as and when required. Of course, one could not perform the ordinary seamanship duties on deck and gunnery work at the same time, and since the latter had become so absorbing in the navy, naturally one's time was largely taken up in the constant improvement in the ship's gunnery efficiency.

HMS *Drake* was a class of very fine Armoured Cruisers all completed in the year 1902. The other ships of the class included the *Good Hope*, *Leviathan* and *King Alfredo*. The *Drake* was built at Pembroke and her particulars were as follows:

Displacement	14,000 tons
Length	530 feet (Over all)
Beam	71 feet
Draught	28 feet
Boilers	Belleville type developing 30,000 H.P.
Coal Capacity	2,500 tons
Weight of Armour	2,700 tons
Armament:	Two 9.2-inch B.L. 45 calibre guns
	Sixteen 6-inch B.L. M.K. VII guns
	Fourteen 12-pounder Q.F. guns
	Two 18-inch submerged torpedo tubes.

The *Drake* was altogether superior to the *Aboukir*. For some years she was the fastest ship in the world and in the year 1905, in a race across the Atlantic with ships of nominally equal speed, the *Drake* came in first! In December of 1906, at four fifths boiler power, she averaged 22.5 knots for 30 hours. Moreover, unlike the four-funnelled prototype of cruiser, such as the *Powerful*, the Drake Class were comparatively economic steamers. For an expenditure of only 11 tons of coal per hour, 19 knots would be maintained, and up to the year 1912 these figures had never been beaten in terms of horsepower per ton displacement.

Frederick W Sweetingham

We sailed for Australia in December 1912, calling at Gibraltar, Malta and Port Said through the Suez Canal. The voyage out from Portsmouth was a very pleasant one and I found both Officers and men a jolly lot of fellows. At Port Said we had made the acquaintance of an extraordinary amusing chap - an Egyptian who claimed to have sufficient blood from the Emerald Isle in his veins to call himself "Jim Irish". The likeable Jim very successfully convinced those with any influence on board that he had their ship's interests at heart and would be only too delighted to help anyone in every possible way. Incidentally, Jim was a most successful trader and could produce anything for sale from a needle to a sheet anchor. His record was notorious among Naval men of ships that had passed his way, in that Jim had never been the loser in any deal. Yet he was most popular and was recognized as a factotum in all matters pertaining to the local requirements of a ship passing through the Suez Canal. It was said that in his earlier days Jim had served in the Royal Navy as a cook or steward on board a ship stationed in the Red Sea. There were of course many traders and pedlars of wares who endeavoured to do business with ships between the Mediterranean Sea and the Red Sea, but Jim was a seaman as well as a salesman, and that was the secret of his successful monopoly in trade among the Officers and bluejackets.

In those days ships could not pass each other in the Canal, unless one of them had previously stopped and geared up alongside at selected positions on the bank; thus making sufficient space for the other to proceed on her way. Usually, priority of passing straight through the canal was granted to ships carrying mail or for other important reasons, while tramp steamers and others would be secured to the side of the Canal as required. During this passage, the Canal Authorities required our ship to gear up and this meant that ordinarily our ships boats would have had to be lowered each time to run the hawsers for securing the ship alongside. Jim Irish knew all about this of course, he also knew that the number of traders allowed on board at Port Said for passage through the Canal would be strictly limited. Therefore, very wisely and subject to the recognition of his exclusive right to trade on board Jim had previously arranged to provide his own boats and gangs of natives to do all that was required outside the ship whenever the operation became necessary. This arrangement worked exceedingly well and to the entire satisfaction of the ship's company, who had the simple task of attending to the hawsers at the ship's end, while Jim and his men in their boats very ably secured the outboard ends to the shore.

During the passage through the Canal one was impressed by the disproportionately large staff of attendants Jim had employed on the upper deck which had been assigned for the display of his wares for sale to the ships' company. From further light thrown upon this subject, it transpired that this incomparably sharp seaman and businessman had effectively contrived to run a select passenger service from Port Said to Suez in a British Man-of-War! Doubtless, Jim Irish collected a substantial fare from each one of his privileged passengers and this, together with the profits of sales of his goods, plus a few coils of the best hempen rope and tackles which his boats' crews had purloined from the ship, would be calculated as good business. But, not so by Jim, who boasted that British Naval personnel were the salt of the earth, and that he was ever ready to give them gratuitous service without any monetary remuneration which, literally was perfectly true!

We arrived at Colombo in due course. Here we met my dear old ship the *Powerful* of very many pleasant memories. The *Powerful* had been the flag ship on the Australian Station for several years and how the *Drake* was to succeed her. Accordingly, the Commander-in-Chief, Admiral King Hall, had arranged for the two ships to meet at Colombo and to relieve each other there. Captain D. Johnson commanded the *Drake* during the voyage out to Colombo, while the Flag Captain, Edward Francis Bruen brought the *Powerful* to meet the *Drake*. Here the two Captains exchanged

Birth Of The Australian Navy

Commands and the *Powerful* then continued her voyage home to pay off. This practically ended the sea going career of the good ship *Powerful* for she was removed from the active Navy List soon after her arrival in England.

The Commanders of the two ships also exchanged appointments and Commander Reginald Norton came to us with his Flag Captain. Captain Bruen was an old Gunnery Officer, and was extremely keen and anxious to get his new command on the Australian Station and to bring our ships' company up to a high standard of fighting efficiency. He lost no time in instituting gunnery drills, fire control exercises and so forth throughout the passage to Fremantle. Since a battle practice target was not available, we could not carry out actual gun firing, though intensive training was maintained at all the appliances by day and night.

In January 1912 we arrived at Fremantle and the sighting of the beautiful continent of Australia, for me, marked the beginning of enduring thoughts and joyful memories. The landscape as we entered the harbour appeared to be very similar to that presented by some of the ports of call in South Africa; more especially the sand dunes behind the beaches.

After completing with coal and provisions at Fremantle we made brief calls at Adelaide and Melbourne and proceeded to Sydney. There we met the C-in-C who was staying at Admiralty House and whose flag was hoisted when he came on board. During our short stay in the beautiful harbour of Australia's greatest city, full opportunity was taken by Officers and men to visit the numerous places of interest, including those wonderful beaches of Manly, Bondi and Coogee where picnic and bathing parties were arranged.

Our first days in Sydney were thus truly happy ones. Indeed, the hearty welcome and boundless hospitality which everyone on board received from the kindly people of Australia were almost unbelievable. As I write these words some 34 years later, I am able to thoroughly appreciate the heartfelt gratitude for similar kindly blessings bestowed upon my countrymen of the Royal Navy during World War II; as expressed by many of them and reiterated in a recent address delivered by Admiral Lord Frazer on behalf of the British Pacific Fleet.

The ships of the Australian Squadron were not a formidable lot. In fact, the only vessels of any fighting value were the *Drake* and two cruisers armed with 6-inch guns - the *Encounter* and the *Challenger*. Squadron manoeuvres in the days of which I write were therefore few, and in consequence, the ships were seldom in company. The birth of the Royal Australian Navy as we know it today had not then taken place; though steps had already been taken in this direction, and I am glad to reflect that, in a small way, I was able to contribute to its beginnings. The small Commonwealth naval ships at that time hoisted the blue ensign, but the new R.A.N. ships were to fly the White Ensign similar to ships of the Royal Navy. Actually, a purely Australian Squadron was not formed until nearly two years later (October 1913).

The Australian Squadron of which the *Drake* was flagship was functioning under the naval terms laid down at the Colonial Conference of 1902, which stipulated that normally it should be based on Australian ports, but could be called for service on the bordering Naval Stations of China and the East Indies as directed by the Admiralty. It was realised then, as it proved conclusively during the Great Wars, that the defence of Australia was bound up with that of the South Pacific, Indian Ocean and the South China Seas. Further it was not only a matter of costs, but the personal service of Australian seamen was required to man the ships, no less than the men of the Royal Navy.

We left Sydney and proceeded to Jervis Bay, where we stayed for a considerable time carrying out all manner of ships exercises including gunnery and torpedo battle firings. It was during the intensive training here that I was able in a small way to improve our secondary fire control system in the event of the primary arrangements being shot away or breaking down for some other reason. This was done by the introduction of several small hand operated instruments, which would take the place of the range clock and range transmitters to the guns when put out of action. Six of these instruments were used; one in each 9.2-inch gun turrets and one at each 6-inch gun assigned to control groups of four guns. Thus, if the main fire control communications were cut at any of these stations the use of these range keeping instruments would enable the firing to continue with little delay. I fashioned a rough pattern of this range keeping instrument at first, and instructed the midshipmen in its use. The Captain was so pleased with the results that he ordered a sufficient number of them to be made by the ships mechanics. I am glad to mention here that after some practise, the midshipmen at the various control stations became quite proficient in the use of this device, which was incorporated permanently into the ship's Fire Control System. One morning after the Officers and men had assembled on the Quarter Deck for Revision and Prayers, Captain Bruen, to my surprise and not a little embarrassment, very kindly referred to my efforts towards furtherance of the gunnery efficiency of the ship, and complimented me upon what he described as my ingenuity in introducing the special range keeping instrument.

During this somewhat strenuous shake up of every Officer and man at their fighting stations, I found time to go ashore in Jervis Bay to take long walks and on two occasions to shoot rabbits and wallaby. In the case of the bunnies, we were very successful, but owing to the swift movements of the wallabies during their hops between cover, I'm afraid that the results were disappointing. One had often heard others discussing their successful hunting of the kangaroo and wallaby, but I had no idea until I tried it myself, how very difficult it was to shoot them whilst on the run, and I fear that during our attempts, there existed the more dangerous sport of shooting each other.

Having completed our exercises which were considered sufficient to qualify the ship to take her place as an armoured cruiser in a squadron or single ship action, we next proceeded on a cruise among the Islands of the South Pacific. Our first port of call was at the sea port of Noumea, in the French Island of New Caledonia, belonging to the Polynesian Group. After quite a short stay, which permitted a few afternoons on shore, we proceeded to Suva, the capital of the Fiji Islands. We anchored in the delightfully fine harbour situated on the south coast of Viti Levu, the largest island of the Fiji Group which contains some two hundred smaller islands. Here we stayed for several days and leave was given to the ships company during the afternoons and evenings.

Soon after we arrived, the Captain paid a call on the Governor (Sir Harry Rawson, I believe it was). Although the *Drake* possessed three steam boats, the Captain's six oared galley (or gig) was chosen to convey him to the landing jetty and while this boat was waiting alongside the ship, one noticed several smart little motor boats manned by Fijians had arrived on the scene. In due course, the Captain was piped over the ship's side and as he moved down the gangway to step into his boat, the native motor craft moved nearer and their native crews became excitably interested with the saluting and other incidentals of this pompous little ceremony. Then a very amusing spectacle followed, for shortly afterwards, one could perceive the Captain steering in his boat for the shore and propelled by the oars of six stalwart British seamen in precisely the same manner as Nelson and his forbears did more than a century before. While this was going on the frizzy haired Fijians were speeding beside him in their ultra-modern small motor powered vessels, grinning maliciously as if in a manner to suggest that we should come to the Pacific Islands and be taught to shed our antiquity there!

Birth Of The Australian Navy

In this British Crown Colony there was a large proportion of Indians, and the products of the Islands included coconuts, copra, sugar and yams, while the forests yield valuable timber. During my walks on shore, I also noticed that pig breeding was a very considerable industry. As one passed down the palm groves under the tropical blue sky, along rows of well-kept conically shaped huts, and amidst the curious stares of interested natives and their children; one could not but wonder whether perhaps here was a happier and healthier community than those found among European populations.

Comparisons in travel, as in other subjects, may be odious, but when one visits in the same week two Colonies under the remote rule of two separate European nations; one may perhaps be forgiven for mentioning the contrasts so apparent between this British dependency, and that of the French possession of New Caledonia. To begin with, the natives of Noumea appeared to be an unhappy lot, while those of Fiji seemed most cheerful and contented. The cleanliness and orderliness of the roads and public buildings at Suva, presented a striking relief when compared with the filthy conditions and obnoxious smells that one was forced to contend with at Noumea. Perhaps this loathsomeness was merely a hangover from the days when New Caledonia was a French penal settlement; for one noticed at the time, that there were still unfortunate inmates behind the bars of the dungeons that were open to the public gaze from the street.

It was at Suva that I remember exercising the ship's divers, and contrary to my experiences in diving in other places of the world, one could see the beautiful coral growth at the bottom of the sea, and clearly observe each movement of the divers as they walked about at a depth of several fathoms. The water too was quite warm; truly a diver's paradise when compared with the cold muddy waters of the northern hemisphere where he is hidden from view when only a couple of feet below the surface.

From the Fiji Islands we proceeded due south to New Zealand and called at Auckland in the North Island. Lying on the opposite side of the world to that of the British Isles, I found this country with only one exception (Tasmania) more like England than any I have seen in the world. This is true of the climate and the people of British stock alike. One also found the Maoris intensely pro-British in their outlook and a fascinating people whose loyalty to the Crown is unsurpassed throughout the native races of the Empire. Unlike the aborigines of Australia, who are fast becoming extinct, the Maori population is increasing. Moreover, they have the good will and sympathy of the white New Zealanders. If I remember rightly the native population in the days of which I write (1912) numbered some 40,000, whilst today (1946) it exceeds 80,000, chiefly in the North Island, whilst the total population of the Whites is approximately 1½ million. One noticed the laughing Maori women proudly dressed in their native costumes and their hair hanging long and loose.

During our stay at Auckland, I took the opportunity of visiting Rotorua, a township about 160 miles or so by rail from the port. Here indeed was a wonderfully interesting place in the midst of a country abounding in geysers and lakes of cold and boiling water. Beautiful flowers, ferns and shrubs were in abundance there. A remarkable place which demands a better pen than mine to adequately describe it. Some time ago I well remember listening to a story expounded by a tourist who had visited this beautiful place. He said that his party had found a spot where the fish caught from a lake were swung by the rod and line into a nearby pool of boiling water and thus cooked for luncheon!

After spending such a healthy and interesting time in the North Island, we sailed to Milford Sound in the South Island, situated on the south-west coast near the borders of the provincial districts of Otago and Southland. The day on which we arrived at the entrance to the Sound was perfect, and as we steamed up the still waters under a clear blue sky, one was struck by the beauty and magnificence of the scenery all around. I had already passed up several fiords of Norway and my memory at once recalled them. The water of Milford Sound is very deep and we were so close to the towering cliffs on either side of the ship that it seemed almost possible to touch them with a pole. As we proceeded further, beautiful mountain mists came into view. Some of these started like the bursting of a shell and rose in spirals to hundreds of feet. It was produced of course by the warm air moving up the wet mountain side. Then we came to an islet (I forget its name) and circled slowly around it until the ship headed towards the sea. Moving past such magnificent splendour compelled one to make the most of the experience before the ship passed out at the entrance and left it far astern.

Arrival of the HMS Drake in the Derwent River, Hobart, February 1912

Continuing our cruise, we crossed the Tasman Sea and arrived at Hobart, Tasmania early in March 1912[2]. Of all the places of the world, which I have had the privilege to enter, I do not believe there is one other so lovely and so truly delightful as the pretty sea port of Hobart. From the moment one's ship enters the approaches of the Derwent River until its arrival 12 miles distant near the foot of Mount Wellington upon which the city stands, there is a continuous scene of beauty presented throughout. Then as one's ship is brought to anchor a couple of cables off the Domain, there is indescribable beauty as far beyond as the eye can see. Here indeed we had found a remote spot of dear old England if ever there was one.

On the morning of our arrival, the weather and climate were perfectly salubrious. Under a sunny sky and in calm waters we took up our position, in a beautiful setting almost within a stone's throw from Government House an imposing and beautiful structure, straight ahead, while the

---

[2] An article in the Tasmanian Mail, February 8, 1912, p24 indicates HMS Drake arrived in Hobart in early February.

heart of the city was equally as close on our port beam. It was all so enchanting and the first impulse created in the whole ships' company was to set foot upon this soil. There was plenty of service work before us however, for after what might be described as a pleasure cruise, we resumed further gunnery activities. But during the week-ends, as much leave as possible was granted to Officers and men, who soon found that the kindness and geniality of the people of Tasmania was no less wonderful than their beautiful surroundings. I will refer to this pleasurable phase of our experiences again.

Shortly after our arrival at Hobart, a matter of important world history occurred there. The famous Norwegian explorer, Captain Roald Amundsen entered the harbour in his little ship the *Fram*. It was on March 7th, 1912 that the *Fram* came quietly up the Derwent and anchored near the *Drake*. This was Amundsen's first port of call after he had reached the South Pole on the 16th December 1911. I well remember this eventful occurrence for, on the next day, the great explorer came on board the *Drake* and walked up and down the quarter Deck with Captain Bruen for a considerable time. This truly great seaman was admired by all of us who had the pleasure and privilege of meeting him, for his quiet unassuming manner.

At that time of course, Amundsen had already explored the Arctic Seas and had led a party through the North West Passage about six years earlier. At the time of which I write (1912) he was in the prime of life at forty years of age, but at fifty-six his end came all too soon, when in June 18th 1928, Amundsen left Tromso, in Norway, to search the Arctic region for the wrecked Italian Airship commanded by General Nobile and never returned.

It will be remembered that Captain Robert F. Scott R.N. and Antarctic explorer, who set out from New Zealand in November 1910 in the Whaler *Terra Nova* and finally reached the South Pole on January 17th 1912, only to find that he and his party had been preceded by Amundsen. Those who accompanied Scott in the final dash for the South Pole included Petty Officer Evans, whom I knew quite well. A fine, powerfully built, lovable fellow, whose help in the party was incalculable. It is to be regretted that Scott and Evans together with their brave companions Wilson, Oates and Bowers, were overwhelmed and perished in a blizzard on the return journey at latitude about 80 degrees South.

The fact that Amundsen won the race to the South Pole from Scott was, of course, terrible bad luck for the British Party. It is quite probable however, that, had Scott used dogs for haulage and transport over the ice, as Amundsen had done, instead of depending upon ponies, he would have reached the pole before his competitor, and above all, the lives of his party would have been spared. Apart from other distinct advantages in the employment of dogs instead of ponies, one existed in the fact that dog will eat dog and so ease the position regarding the provision and haulage of food for the animals especially on the homeward journey. To be sure this consideration will appear to be downright callousness to the reader, especially to lovers of the highly intelligent and faithful dog.

A few days after the *Fram* came to Hobart, she was followed by the *Aurora* a little ship engaged on the Australasian Antarctic Expedition at the time under Douglas Mawson - now Sir Douglas Mawson. As the *Aurora*, a small three masted vessel with square rigged sails on the foremast, passed the *Fram* her ships company heartily cheered Captain Amundsen and his gallant men. Afterwards, Amundsen generously presented Mawson's ship with twenty-one of his famous dogs, retaining only a few puppies and the veterans that, had reached the South Pole with him.

The *Aurora* was under the command of Captain James K. Davis, who had returned to Hobart after landing a Polar Expedition under Mawson, already an experienced Antarctic explorer having been on the scientific staff of Sir Ernest Shackleton's Antarctic expedition of 1908. On this occasion, Mawson had selected Adelie Land for his main base. A station was also established in Queen Mary Land under Commander Frank Wild while another small party was stationed at Macquarie Island under G.F. Ainsworth. A Dr Xavier Mertz was also included in Mawson's expedition to whom I shall refer later. It is pleasing to record here that HMS *Drake* was able to assist this expedition in some small way by sending time signals twice a week to the wireless station set up at Macquarie Island. These signals were passed on to Mawson's Depot at Adelie Land by Ainsworth in due course.

The peculiar nature of Polar Expeditions being necessarily such that little outside assistance can be rendered to them once they have left civilized lands. It was gratifying to feel that even so little could be done for those isolated men who were fighting the extreme elements at temperatures reaching 30 - 40° F below zero, while the wind velocity, according to Beaufort Scale, frequently attains 80 miles per hour and more. It is an interesting fact that neither the North Polar Region or any other part of the globe experiences such low mean temperatures or such high wind velocity as those of Antarctica. The reason for this is apparent when it is considered that such a large expanse of land covered with ice circumscribes the South Pole, and that the Antarctic summer occurs when the earth is further from the sun than the Arctic is during its summer.

The exploration of the Polar regions has long since been a subject of much interest to me and I was fortunate in again meeting some of the fine fellows who have sailed in ships to those ice-covered lands. This was many years later, when at the Cape of Good Hope, I had the honour of meeting Sir Douglas Mawson, Captain J.K. Davis and many others who were bound for Antarctica again in the Polar Ship *Discovery*.

--- ooOoo ---

I now come to an episode in my life, which led to an enduring and treasured romance. For it was at Hobart in 1912 that I met a girl of radiant beauty and extraordinary intellect. Some 14 years my junior in age her name is Adelaide Theresa, the only daughter of Mr and Mrs Marshman, who were residing in Hobart at the time. The personality, dignity of carriage, and expression of sweetness in this young lady, made a profound impression upon me, and I am happy and grateful to record that this remarkably charming person has been my beloved wife and helpmate, for some 30 years. On the 5th May, 1914, we were married at the English Church of St Thomas in the parish of Portsmouth, Hants., England.

Through peacetime and war, some fair weather, but mainly through difficult times, in four continents of the globe, providence has vouchsafed to me the companionship of such grace and gentleness, that I dared not hope for at the time of which I write. With an ever-ready smile and grace of movement, she has been adored by everyone who has known her; more especially by our four children and the servants of the home. In the days of trial, whether in official, social or home life, her understanding sympathy and help has been maintained unswervingly and I can but thank God for all the good gifts that have come to me through our blessed union.

--- ooOoo ---

On completion of gunnery firings and other ships exercises we sailed from Hobart to Sydney. Here the ships company carried out musketry on the rifle ranges at Randwick. Once again, my friend Colin E.M. Law was in general charge of the Rifle Companies while the duty of conducting the rifle and revolver shooting at the targets was mine. Upon landing from the ship however, Law came over to me and said, "Sweetingham - where is my white horse?"

To this I replied, "In Malta Sir! - I'm afraid you will have to march or take a tram to Randwick".

It was about this juncture that drastic changes were impending in regard to the constitution of Naval Defence on the Australian Station. As these changes related to the foundation of the Royal Australian Navy as we know it today, and which played such an important part in the two World Wars, let us review the formation of the Naval forces operating in Australian waters from the early days before the Federation of the States into one Commonwealth. In that period Auxiliary Navies as they were then called were formed by separate Colonies in Australia. Though none of these navies possessed any serious fighting value they did constitute potentialities for the future.

The first Australian ship armed with any appreciable gun power was the monitor *Cerberus*. This vessel was built at Jarrow in 1868 for Victoria, together with two sister ships, the *Abyssinia* and *Magdala*, which were sent out from England for the defence of Indian ports. The *Cerberus*, a drill ship in 1912, was of 3,480 tons armed with four 18 ton muzzle loading guns and protected by an armoured belt eight inches thick. The present Gunnery and Torpedo School at Flinders Naval Depot, Crib Point Victoria, bears the name of HMA.S. *Cerberus* in which my daughter Mary and myself served during World War II.

Frederick W Sweetingham

In 1884 Australia's local naval defence was reinforced with four gunboats. Particulars and allocation of these vessels were as follows:

Name	Displacement	Armament	Colony
Protector	920 tons	One 8-inch gun Five 6-inch guns	South Australia
Victoria	530	One 8-inch gun	Western Australia
Eayunda	360	One 8-inch gun One 6-inch gun	Queensland
Paluma	360	One 8-inch gun One 6-inch gun	Queensland

From then onwards a few Australian Officers and men were sent for training in the British Navy and towards the end of the eighties, real interest was taken in Australian Defence matters. In an important order, five cruisers and two torpedo gunboats for local Australian Service were borne on the list of the Royal Navy. This was decided upon at a Conference between the British and Colonial Governments in 1887 and the vessels were built under the Naval Defence Act of 1889. They were renamed and commissioned for this service as indicated hereunder. Five Pallas Class Cruisers of 2,575 tonnes (armed with eight 4.7-inch Q.F. and smaller guns) with a protected deck and a speed of about 18 knots:

Katoomba (ex Pandora); Mildura (ex Pelorus); Ringarooma (ex Pysche); Tanranya (ex Phoenix); and Wallaroo (ex Persian).

In addition there were two Sharpshooter Class Gunboats or Catchers:

Bommerange (ex Whiting) and Karrakatta (ex Wizard).

At the Conference, agreement was made between the British, Australian and New Zealand Governments whereby the Admiralty bound itself to maintain a Squadron of ships, in which the above were included, to be based on Australian Ports for defence service in the Western portion of the South Pacific; but to be available for service anywhere within the bounds of the East Indies and China Stations if required. The cost of the Squadron was divided on a pro rata basis according to population and trade. One half being borne by the United Kingdom, five twelfths by Australia and the remaining one twelfth by New Zealand.

Australian and New Zealand personnel were trained for Naval Service in a number of drill ships stationed at local ports while a branch of the Royal Naval Reserve was instituted in both countries. Further a few cadetships were allotted each year for service in the Royal Navy. Thus provision was made by the British and Colonial governments concerned, for the protection of sea-borne trade in Australian and New Zealand waters before the end of the Nineteenth Century. During the nineties however, Naval ships attached to Victoria and Queensland were put out of commission; so presumably all was not well with the Australian Naval force at that time. This would appear to be confirmed, for according to records, the total Australian Naval personnel did not exceed 1,000 men, a large proportion of whom were engaged on a voluntary basis, and a hundred or so cadets. Had it not been for the untiring efforts of the Naval Commandant in Queensland, Captain William

BIRTH OF THE AUSTRALIAN NAVY

R. Creswell (afterwards Vice Admiral Sir W.R. Creswell), whose energies were directed against the disintegration of the Australian Naval Forces, it is probable that they would not have remained in existence at all. In the course of time, the seagoing warships mentioned above were worn out or eventually recalled, and at the end of 1900 the number of vessels in the Australian Naval Force had been reduced to nine only, constituting a tonnage of not more than 6,000; while the personnel serving permanently to instruct the volunteers for Home Defence numbered less than two hundred.

Such was the naval position when Federation of the Australian Colonies was proclaimed on January 1st 1901, when Earl Hopetown was appointed the first Governor General and Sir Edmond Barton became the first Prime Minister of the Commonwealth of Australia. The Naval Service of Australia then came under the general powers of the Commonwealth Federal Parliament which adopted the policy of self-defence with a fuller partnership in the security measures of the Empire. Coincident with this, Australians revived their interest in Imperial Defence and in 1905-6 Australia, with New Zealand, contributed £240,000 to Imperial Naval Defence and a project was put forward for the building of eight destroyers and four torpedo gunboats for local defence. Scarcely any improvements had been made however, and by 1909, the total tonnage of warships then was approximately the same as in 1901; though the Naval personnel on the permanent list had increased slightly to 242. A poor advance indeed for the first eight years of Federation.

It must be mentioned however, that a year later (1910), two destroyers the *Parramatta* and *Yarra* arrived from England, while a third the *Warrego* was being completed in the Cockatoo Dock at Sydney. As a matter of fact, the whole subject of Dominion and Colonial Navies was somewhat complicated in its relation to the British Navy, particularly as to their liability when required for Imperial needs. For instance, Dominion Navies acting on their own responsibility might create undesirable Imperial complications; for example - Canada with the United States and Australia in these days with Japan. On the other hand, it was thought that little enthusiasm could be expected in the Dominions for their ships which were not always in their home waters, when the strategic need deemed their service elsewhere. New Zealand, however, disregarded the latter theory, when later, she presented the Battle Cruiser *New Zealand* to the British Government as a gift ship. But generally speaking, it is only natural for the people of the Dominions to think first of the defence of their own country.

The two divergent views, nevertheless, were extremely delicate. In 1911 Prime Minister Mr Andrew Fisher and two Cabinet Ministers of the Commonwealth Government, attended an Imperial Conference in London when at last the project of previous years took a more practical shape. The status of Australia's future Navy was definitely settled and put into force. Under the arrangement then made, the Commonwealth Government agreed to furnish an Australian Fleet unit, to be called the Royal Australian Navy. This force to be exclusively under the control of the Australian Government whilst in Australian waters. It was agreed that when a ship of the British Admiralty meets a ship of the Dominion, the Senior Officer will have the right to command in matter of ceremony or international intercourse, or when united action is agreed upon; but will have no power to direct the movements of ships of the other service unless the ships are ordered to co-operate by mutual agreement. The British Admiralty also undertook to lend the Dominion, during the period of development of their Services, under conditions to be agreed upon, such Flag Officers and other Officers and men as may be needed, but they should all be volunteers for the Service.

This was an excellent agreement and an equally satisfactory arrangement was come to regarding the, discipline, training and uniform of the personnel. All were to be interchangeable with that of the Royal Navy and both Officers and ratings were to have equal status and promotion according to seniority. The limits of the Australian Station were clearly defined; they included the waters between longitude 950 E and 1600 E, as far as the Antarctic Circle (including Knox Land, Wilkes Land and King George V Land); and the northern boundary was drawn so as to exclude the Cocos Group and all Dutch East Indies Islands, but including the whole coast of British Papua. The Eastern boundary was extended to include Norfolk Island. Thus, the purely Australian Naval Station touched nothing beyond the shores of Australia itself and its direct dependencies. The limits were altered considerably during the Great Wars.

Regarding the ships and personnel, Admiral Sir Reginald Henderson, who had visited Australia before the Prime Minister left to attend the Imperial Conference in London, further recommended the provision of 52 ships and 15,000 men calculated on a proportional basis of population and overseas trade as compared with that of the United Kingdom. This Fleet of ships was to have been built in about 22 years and by 1918 it was intended that the Australian Fleet would consist of 23 ships and some 4,000 personnel. Accordingly, the following ships were ordered:

One Battle Cruiser of the Indefatigable Class:	HMA.S. *Australia*;
Three protected Cruisers of the Town Class:	*Melbourne*, *Sydney*, and *Brisbane*;
Three Destroyers:	*Huon*, *Torrens* and *Swan*;
Two Submarines:	A.E. 1 and A.E. 2.

Thus, the nucleus of a modern Australian Navy was in the making though the vessels now ordered did not arrive from England until 1913. HMA.S. *Brisbane* was completed in Australia during the War (1916). The administration of this new navy was vested in a body known as the Australian Naval Board. The first members of the Board being:

Chairman:	The Minister for Defence
1st Naval Member:	Rear Admiral W.R. Cresswell R.A.N.
2nd Naval Member:	Captain Gordon. A. Smith R.N.
3rd Engineer:	Captain W. Clarkson C.M.G. R.A.N.

A characteristically democratic system of entering cadets in Australia for Officers of the fleet was adopted. Unlike that which existed in the Royal Navy, cadetships were open to boys regardless of the social position of parents, and were educated and maintained entirely at the Governments expense. A Naval College was built at Jervis Bay, though the first entry of cadets there was not until January 1915. While this establishment was being built, the College at Osborne House, North Geelong in Victoria was used for the instruction of Naval Cadets. The age for entering the College was thirteen years. Regarding the instruction of seamen, a boys' training ship was commissioned at Sydney in 1912. This was HMA.S. *Tingire*. The Officers and Petty Officer Instructors were lent from the Royal Navy, many of whom I knew personally.

About this time the New South Wales ship building yard at Sydney was taken over by the Commonwealth Government and converted into a Naval Dockyard. Further, the Royal Naval Armament Depot at Spectacle Island Sydney was transferred from Admiralty control to the Royal

Australian Administration. Thus were the beginnings and the position of the Royal Australian Navy when we arrived at Sydney in HMS *Drake* in August 1912.

While the *Drake* was at Sydney, important changes were made relative to both British and Australian ships on the Station. HMS *Encounter* one of the ships of the Royal Naval Squadron had paid off was presented to the Australian Government as a sea going cruiser. About the same time a sister ship, HMS *Challenger*, was withdrawn from the Squadron and returned to England. Upon acceptance, the Commonwealth Government commissioned HMA.S. *Encounter* immediately. For this purpose, Captain Betram. M. Chambers R.N. was appointed followed by a Commander and certain other officers of the ship. In this connection some difficulty was experienced, for it had been anticipated that more of the old ship's company would volunteer to recommission the ship for service in the R.A.N. than could be induced to volunteer. However, the vacancies of Officers and ratings were partially filled by R.A.N. personnel and the balance made up from Officers and ratings lent from the Royal Navy. Some of the latter eventually transferred to the R.A.N. permanently.

Accordingly, volunteers were urgently requisitioned from the *Drake*, as it was desired to send the *Encounter* on her first cruise as soon as possible after commissioning. In the circumstances, I volunteered to fill the vacant post of Gunner of HMS *Encounter* and my old friend Lieutenant Colin Law transferred from the *Drake* to take up the post of First Lieutenant. This took place on the 9th September, 1912 and upon boarding my new ship I met the Captain, Commander and Lieutenant Lanslot A. Spooner R.N. the Gunnery Officer, with whom I have had the privilege and pleasure of again serving 30 years later during the Second World War. I was rather loath to leave the *Drake*, but when the true situation came to my knowledge, as explained above, I felt that everyone who was able to assist in the beginnings of such an important service, which seemed to me to be long overdue, should be prepared to do so.

Having taken over charge of the guns, ammunitions and armament stores, I soon settled down and found that this new appointment was very much to my liking. Towards the end of the month, we sailed from Sydney for a cruise to the capital ports of Australia. I thus had the honour of going to sea in the first fighting cruiser of Australia's new Navy. We had rather an important mission to perform at each port of call in the selection of the first term of cadets for entry into the R.A.N. Incidentally, the people of Australia were given the opportunity to inspect their newly acquired Cruiser and to witness the ship flying the White Ensign together with their own Flag on the jackstaff.

Hobart was our first port at which we called and a number of Tasmanian boys came on board with their parents or guardians to be given an oral examination by a Board of Ships Officers presided over by Captain Chambers. I well remember the first batch of boys coming on board, as indeed those to follow at other ports. Unlike the brand of entries into the Royal Navy, it was quite likely that the ancestors of these Australian lads knew nothing about the Naval Service or had had no connection with it whatever. Here was the true novice, with no one to give him an inkling of the nature of the ordeal that lay before him; or to provide him with any idea of the questions that he was expected to answer. Neither was this a written examination where perhaps some of these boys, of only thirteen summers, might have time to study the paper before writing the answers. Having passed a preliminary educational and medical examination on shore, the candidate was brought before the Selection Board to be tested mainly for his intelligence and character, so necessary to fit them for their new vocations. In a calm and quiet atmosphere each boy was received at the first interview when ordinary conversational talk was entered into and interspersed with questions relating to their experiences of the day. For example, the times and method of travel to the ship, games that he plays and sporting events that he is specially interested in or has taken part in. Then the candidate was sent with a verbal message to the Officer of the Watch relating to some routine duty in the ship; such as whether a certain ships boat was away from the ship, and if so in what service? An oral reply was given to the by the O.O.W. describing the type of boat affected including the number of oarsmen and this was transmitted orally to the Board by the candidate. In variation, a simple question on Naval history was introduced and perhaps the gunnery factor of relative velocity e.g. names of famous Admirals and the throwing of a ball straight out of the carriage window of a train travelling any speed, in what position would the ball fall to the ground relative to the thrower? Such questions as these were put, while the Officers of the Board closely observed the general bearing and manners of the boy during the tests. By such means, conducted with total disregard of the social position or influence of the candidate's family, brought about most fair and satisfactory selections of boys possessing the basic qualifications desired.

After a short stay at Hobart, we sailed for Fremantle. This voyage I remember quite well for it was made against one of the most ferocious gales that I have ever experienced. Low barometric pressures were recorded moving from the west, and as we cleared the South West Cape there were ugly signs indicating that we were in for dirty weather. And so it proved, for the following day the wind had increased and heavy seas were met. The *Encounter* was a sturdily built ship, however, and behaved very well, though she laboured heavily and it became necessary to batten down hatches and lash all movable gear stowed on deck. About the third day out we were driving into tremendous seas and a fierce gale and were apparently in a storm centre. Heavy seas were shipped and life lines had to be rigged to enable one to proceed along the Upper Deck. Owing to the limited number of Lieutenants borne for watchkeeping duties, I was glad to take my turn on the bridge and so offered them some relief in addition to my ordinary duties as Gunner of the ship. Incidentally, I had been swotting up some navigation and hand books on the storms in the regions of the Indian Ocean at the time, and during some of these watches I was fortunate in obtaining some useful information on the subject from the Captain as I paced beside him on the bridge. I have often thought of his kindly interest and help in those days. As it happens, the Navigating Officer of the ship was a Lieutenant whose name was Langford, a very able professional Officer who, I believe, had entered the new Australian Navy with that rank direct from the Merchant Service.

During our short stay at Fremantle, I paid a visit to Perth and the beautiful surroundings of the Swan River. I have since been there on several occasions, but even then, one was struck by the wonderful development of this sandy spot on Australian soil, since the first landing of Captain James Stirling of the Frigate *Success* in 1827. Here in Western Australia, as in other parts of the Continent, the ship's company of the *Encounter* were welcomed by the kindly people who visited the ship and afterwards entertained us on shore. It seemed to me, that there was no limit to the beneficence of the inhabitants of this bounteous land.

From Fremantle we went to Albany where our stay was so short that there was little time for leave on shore, after which we proceeded across the Australian Bight to Port Adelaide. Here quite a number of candidates for Naval Cadets came on board and, in consequence, our stay lasted an appreciable time. As in the case of Fremantle and Perth, I have visited Adelaide several times since, but I think my first impression of this capital and trade centre of South Australia should be remarked upon here. This beautiful city of azure skies, standing about seven miles by railway from

Birth Of The Australian Navy

Port Adelaide so named after the Consort of King William IV, possessed wide streets and enormously spacious parks. An extraordinary feature relating to this, is that the parks surround the old, or inner city and consequently are in close proximity to the entire population. The inhabitants of Adelaide have every cause to be thankful to the Municipal Authorities of past years for calling a halt in the continuity of building in the inner city. The usual congestion and slums, peculiar to most other cities, were thus prevented, and a healthy lay-out of the outer buildings was made possible to the perpetual benefit of the citizens of future generations. Furthermore, the broad tree lined avenues of this pleasant city savour of the Boulevards so famous on the Continent of Europe.

As one strolled in these health-giving and lovely areas, one could not help wondering how much suffering in the health of the people had been avoided, as compared with that in the congested towns in England with their miserable patches of so-called recreation grounds. Also, how much saving in the cost of medical services down the ages of this fine city, doubtlessly due to the wisdom and courage of those men in Municipal authority. For doubtless, they had to fight the vested interests and greed of landlords in the endeavour to keep their city clean and habitable equally as much as their contemporaries in England; though the latter had failed deplorably.

While the *Encounter* was lying alongside the wharf at Port Adelaide, one forenoon when I was performing the duty of Officer of the Day, my attention was drawn to a distinguished old gentleman who had been walking up and down the jetty abreast the ship for some considerable time. After a while he approached the Sentry who was posted on the gangway leading to the Quarter Deck and at that moment, I walked over to the brow towards him and asked if I could assist him in any way. He seemed very pleased and told me that he was a retired Master Mariner and wished very much to board Australia's newly acquired Cruiser. Thereupon, I invited him to come on board and instructed a Petty Officer to show him around the Upper Deck and to escort him back to me when they had completed the circuit and reached the Quarter Deck. By that time, I had been relieved from duty for lunch, and then asked our visitor if he could come below to the mess and join me with some refreshments. His name was Osborne, a remarkably versatile man, and despite his 76 years, he appeared quite hale and hearty. He told me that he had commanded several sailing ships in the grain and wool trade between Australia and Britain, and that since his retirement he had become more interested than ever 'in ships that go down to the sea'. We parted great friends and upon his departure he remarked kindly, "Come and see me. You will find Captain Osborne at Osborne House, Osborne. Always at Home!"

I thanked him for his kind invitation, though owing to our short stay at Port Adelaide, I was unable to accept. I can see that fine, upright specimen of humanity now, with his long white flowing beard, whom I afterwards learned was a most prosperous old sea dog living in a fine house with an imposing tower. This tower was equipped with powerful telescopes from which he enjoyed a magnificent view of the outer harbour and the ships that passed by.

From Adelaide we proceeded on our mission to Brisbane. Here a fair number of candidates for Naval Cadets were dealt with and afterwards we sailed for Melbourne. This was early in 1912 and we found our old ship the *Drake* there, also HMS *Torch* a gunboat attached to the Australian Station. Coincidentally the great race for the Melbourne Cup was due to take place within a day or two. Prior to this I had not attended a really first-class Race Meeting, although naturally I had been greatly interested in horse racing, the National Sport of England and the results of the classic races there such as the Derby, Oaks, St Ledger, Ascot, Gold Cup and others. Here then was my first opportunity of being present at a world-famous event at Flemington and I was so glad to avail myself of it.

On the evening of our arrival at Melbourne, I called on board the *Drake* and found that, in accordance with their usual custom of the people of Australia as hosts to ships of the Imperial Navy, my brother Officers of the *Drake* had received kindly invitations to the Flemington race course with complimentary tickets of admission to the Members Enclosure. This friendly gesture however, had not been extended to the *Encounter*, now an Australian ship, for the sole reason one may suppose that according to Australian psychology, the old proverb "Charity begins at home" is as dead as Queen Ann in a country of boundless hospitality for visitors! However, we of the *Encounter* who had now become Bonafide Australians, enjoyed the most delightful race meeting that I have ever since attended - besides backing a few good horses including "Piastre" the winner of the Melbourne Cup!

A few days later the *Drake* sailed for Sydney, and by this time I had become quite attached to the *Encounter* and was giving serious thought of transferring from the Imperial Navy to the Royal Australian Navy. I knew that the Naval Board at the time required the services of Naval Officers belonging to the Gunnery profession and in the circumstances future service in the R.A.N. appeared promising. These meditations however, were abruptly ended by a telegram from the *Drake*, now at Sydney, stating that the Flag Ship had been ordered to sail for England and that I was to return to the *Drake* as soon as possible. Following this, an Officer who had been sent from England for gunnery duties in some other appointment in the R.A.N. was sent on board the *Encounter* as my successor. The work of handing over the armament equipment and my duties relating thereto was completed in a few days, and accordingly I proceeded by railway to join the *Drake* at Sydney.

The journey overland between the two largest cities of the Commonwealth was of absorbing interest to me. I had heard so much of the rolling open spaces in this vast Continent, and was glad to obtain first-hand knowledge of the magnificent countryside, which men of the sea in those days seldom enjoyed. During the course of World War II, I travelled on duty several times between the capital cities of Australia by railway and by air, but somehow in later life it seems that one is not so deeply impressed by the grandeur of the mountain ranges, valleys, rivers and scenery as in those earlier days. I have repeatedly thought of this during my travels and the only reason for it that I can advance, is that it all depends upon the purposes for which the journeys are made. On this first occasion, it was nothing more than a leisurely jaunt, but in all my subsequent passages, some over far greater distances, one was so engrossed in the urgent work at hand, as to overshadow the beatitude of one's surroundings.

Of all the stories that I could tell against myself there are few that I have relished more than the one I must record here. During the latter portion of my journey to Sydney, I was the sole occupant of a compartment of a corridor train. This lonesomeness however, was soon ended by a most congenial fellow who nonchalantly blew in and sat beside me. My new companion was about my own age, who said that he too had been left alone in his compartment and therefore sought company. I gladly invited him to stay, and very soon we were in the throes of an animated discussion, mainly about the race meeting at Melbourne at which we were both present. He said that his luck had been extraordinarily good on the race course, and that he was going on to Sydney to attend a race meeting at Randwick. Like most Australian fellow travellers I have met, he was a most interesting conversationalist and his versatility within the realm of horse racing and sport generally was superb. In fact, our discourse proved quite an education for me for at his suggestion on our arrival at Sydney, I entrusted my friend with a fiver to be placed on a certain horse that actually won! My plausible and sporting associate had planned to meet me at a hotel in Sydney on the night of the race meeting, but I never saw him again or my winnings of several pounds. Though I had with incredulity heard of similar incidents and of the gullibility of man, I would have backed a tenner against the possibility of myself ever being caught in this manner. To this day I have guarded this affair as a strict secret, but feel now, that a place must be found for it in this narrative.

In due course I rejoined HMS *Drake*, and having intimated that I had rather wished to remain in the *Encounter*, the Captain informed me that since hostilities might be encountered during the *Drake*'s passage home, he did not intend to risk a shortage in the ship's complement of Officers. This was a fair indication of naval opinion at the time in regard to foreign affairs which culminated in World War I some nineteen months later.

A few weeks more in Australian waters, then it was good-bye to this wonderful land of sunshine and to your delightful people. To your genuine and sincere hospitality such as I had never experienced before; to your mountains, valleys and waterfalls of rare beauty, and to your incomparably fine harbours; may providence grant my return some fortunate day – "Good-bye!"

Upon leaving Fremantle, the last port of call in Australia, I had seen sufficient of the Continent and its population to enable me to form ideas and opinions which have been considerably strengthened since my residence in this bounteous country during the last twelve years.

It was quite clear to me from the first, that the potentialities of Australia were enormous. It has been said that England's choice of occupants of this fair land constituted a terrible handicap when in 1788 Captain Arthur Phillip, the founder and first Governor in Australia, landed at Sydney Cove. On this point I entirely disagree. At that time civilized life in this new country thousands of miles from home, began with about eleven hundred British convicts together with nearly four hundred soldiers, officers and civilians to form a guard and make and administer the laws of the penal Colony. From this genesis, sprung a free and virile people and perhaps the most vigorous association of men and women on earth. A truly wonderful fellowship and all this in less than four generations!

Now what is the secret of this remarkable achievement! In the first place, it is quite clear that the disability or so-called handicap, never existed at all simply because no drones were included among them. The main points which, in my opinion, have the most important bearing on this subject are:

1) Mostly all of these pioneers had been drawn from British working-class stock, who had hitherto been accustomed to earn their living by manual labour so essential for the development of the colony. Further, no racial or religious differences existed between them: it was therefore entirely free from the most deadly handicap of human progress known in any country.

2) From the very beginning of the settlement, the people of Australia have been blest with one common language; and in all matters concerning the governance of the six states, the English tongue only was spoken.

3) While Australians are fundamentally British, they have not permitted tradition to clog their democratic progress; neither are they slow in showing their dislike of affectation and humbug of any kind. Few of the British leisured class have been seen in Australia and none have resided in the country. In fact, there has been no room for an aristocracy in this vast continent. There has however, been hard work for all the people for all the time. and in consequence, Australia's manhood has maintained its virility through which its greatness has been achieved.

The criticism one hears regarding the tendency of the average Australian to disregard authority, which has been interpreted for lack of discipline, is more than offset by his inborn friendliness, and above all, loyalty to his comrades. He is ever ready to do his job and to sacrifice much in the process, but in no circumstances will he be dragooned.

Regarding the political field, it is quite apparent that the average Australian devotes intellectual study and is interested in his country's affairs far more than the ordinary person in England. The mass mind in politics one has noticed in the old country is substituted here for individuality of thought. In the matter of the Legislature, it might be conceded that twelve state plus two Federal governing bodies appear excessive, but it is difficult to see how this large Continent could be better ruled with a central Parliament. It must be remembered that the present system has worked well, even with comparatively small scattered population which has, for the most part, depended upon the Primary Industry of the country. It is therefore reasonable to expect that with the inevitable increase in population, together with production of the secondary industries, the present Constitution should function smoothly and with relatively less cost per head of population. In this connection however, let us hope that Australia's politically enlightened people, will preserve its democratic strength sufficiently powerful enough to guard against the evils attendant with big business, which has been so manifest in the United States of America.

It was about 9 months after the *Drake* (last Imperial Flag Ship), had been recalled to England, that the people of Australia witnessed with pride their new Royal Australian Squadron led by the magnificent Battle Cruiser *Australia* steamed into Port Jackson in October 1913 to be given an official welcome. When War broke out in August 1914 the Australian Naval Force was made up of the following sea going fighting units:

Battle Cruiser	HMS *Australia*.
Cruisers	*Sydney, Melbourne* and *Encounter*.
Destroyers	*Parramatta, Yarra* and *Warrego*.
Submarines	A.2.1 and A.2.2.

There also existed the old Cruiser *Protector* and other obsolescent vessels, but these no longer possessed fighting qualities to match modern warships.

The seagoing Australian Squadron of ships indicated above, were under the command of Rear Admiral Sir George E. Patey, K.C.V., R.N. with his flag hoisted in the *Australia*. The war efficiency of this small Squadron will be readily appreciated by the fact that a few months it had helped to capture the German Colonies in the Pacific and caused Admiral Von Spee's two Armoured Cruisers *Sharnhorst* and *Gneisenau* to proceed to the safer waters of the Eastern Pacific and South Atlantic. Furthermore, *Sydney* and *Melbourne* with the British Armoured Cruiser *Minataur* formed escorts for a large convoy of 38 transports of Australian and New Zealand troops for service overseas; when on November 9th 1914 HMA.S. *Sydney* left the convoy and destroyed the German Cruiser *Emden* off North Keeling (Cocos) Island.

By February 1915, the Australian Squadron had scattered over many oceans. The *Australia* in the North Sea; *Sydney* and *Melbourne* in the Atlantic; *Encounter* in the Pacific; *Pioneer* on the East Coast of Africa; *Warrego, Parramatta* and *Yarra* in New Guinea and Submarine A.E.2 in the Aegean waters of the Mediterranean. Alas however, her sister ship A.E.1 disappeared without trace on September 14th 1914, while on patrol off Rabaul.

The Cruiser *Brisbane* was laid down in January 1913, but was not commissioned until October 1916, meanwhile HMS *Encounter* was lent by the Admiralty for service with the Australian Squadron until the *Brisbane* was commissioned. The three Destroyers *Huon, Torrens,* and *Swan*, likewise were not completed until after hostilities had commenced when they were commissioned in the December 1915, July and August 1916, respectively. All ships of the Dominion Naval Forces hoisted at the stern the White Ensign (similar to ships of the Royal Navy) as a symbol of the Authority of the Crown; but on the jack staff at the bow, the distinctive flag of the Dominion was flown.

F.W. Sweetingham Esq.

This boomerang is an historic one; it was made by an Aboriginal from La Perouse, Botany Bay, Sydney, N.S.Wales, Australia, & thrown by him in my presence at the Sydney Cricket Ground, during an Aboriginal Display, being part of the Centenary of Australia Celebrations, 28th January 1888.

Please accept it as a parting gift & as a token of our friendship formed during your stay with us in H.M.S. DRAKE the Australian Station

Sincerely Yours
Charles St Julien
Sydney
1st January 1913

During our voyage home to England we called at Aden, that British possession in Arabia, which guards the southern approach to the Red Sea. Here I went on shore for half a day, but cannot say that the experience was as pleasant as that in most other ports. The site of Aden presents an aspect of desolation as one might expect from a position which is nothing more than the remains of an extinct volcano. It was in consideration of its strategic value that Britain is mainly concerned, and being a natural fortress it is easily defended against sea or land forces. At the time Aden was under the Bombay Government for administration. Later, in 1937 the control was transferred from the India Office and Aden became a Crown Colony in its own right. It has an incessant need for fresh water for none can be found from a natural flow anywhere within the town. The Arabs of old however, realising this, built enormous tanks to catch the periodical monsoonal rains which filter through the cracks in the huge masses of rock. With modern amenities including those provided by aircraft, one might perhaps tolerate Aden, but we were very glad to depart from this barren and dreary place.

Except for constant gunnery drills and exercises to keep up the fighting efficiency of the ship the voyage to home was uneventful. We arrived at Portsmouth early in March 1913, and the *Drake* was paid off on the 13th. Though our commission in the good ship *Drake* was of short duration, it occupied one of the most happy and interesting periods of my life. The Officers, Petty Officers and men alike, were a grand lot and I feel that had we been called upon to play our part in hostilities, the *Drake* would have been quite ready.

Chapter XXIII

War Clouds and Political Strife

--- ooOoo ---

Upon paying off, *Drake*'s company was granted foreign service leave. During this holiday period, I visited my elder sister Lucy who was living at Bishop Auckland in Durham, with her husband and family of two daughters. Her husband, Mr W.B. Thirkell, was an official of the North Eastern Railway Company and, one day, he arranged with the local mine Manager for me to visit the coal field and to descend one of the coal mines. My experiences on that day has been indelibly imprinted on me ever since. It is because of the first-hand knowledge that I gained on this occasion, that I am invariably sympathetic towards the coal miners when they are involved in disputes in the coal industry. My guide was an excellent fellow and indeed a most patient one; for in the course of our tour of inspection of several hour's duration, he never seemed to tire of answering my countless questions and of instructing me in the equipment and methods of work at the pit head and in the bowels of the earth hundreds of feet below. Before our descent I was furnished with an overhaul suit, leather gloves and a pair of sea boots, the necessity for the two former articles of wear was quite obvious, but I reminded the Manager that we were many miles from the sea! He laughed and assured me that the requirement of my leg equipment would soon be apparent. Thereupon we entered the lift cage at the top of the mine shaft and began the descent.

The action of the lift, being somewhat similar to the ammunition loading hoists operating between the shell and cartridge stowage in warships, prompted me to ask my companion what would happen if the wire rope supporting the cage from the winch carried away. I explained if this happened on board ship, a safety device would automatically operate and prevent the loading cage from dropping to the bottom of the hoist. But my guide assured me that an arrangement of that nature would be far too costly to instal in a coal mine, so in the event of a break in the wire rope operating our lift the occupants of the lift cage would unfortunately be faced with death.

We seemed quite an appreciable time reaching the bottom of the mine shaft, which was many hundreds of feet below the surface and here I soon found use for my sea boots for water abounded everywhere in the main tunnel, well above the ankles. We then left the cage and by the aid of a miner's lamp waded along a railway track covered with water; passing many broad gauged railway trucks on the way to a railway juncture. From here several small branch tunnels had been cut in various directions leading to the coal face. Each of these branches of the main tunnel was equipped with a railway of narrow gauge, upon which smaller trucks were hauled to and fro to the coal faces by pit ponies with youthful drivers. My companion and guide chose the longest branch of these tunnels to explore. We set out on a seemingly endless tramp in a crouching position still wading through the water and over the railway sleeper, until at last, we reached the mine workers on the coal face. The reader will remember how, in years past, I had the experience of shovelling coal in the bunkers and stokehold of a ship, but that was comparatively easy work compared with the laborious task of those hardy North Countrymen of England getting coal from the seams at the time. Some of them were forced to twist their bodies in various positions of contortion in order to reach their work with picks or other implements in hand. For a quarter of an hour or so, I could see the feet and legs of one miner whose head and shoulders were thrust into a crevice and when he came out from this position, I was amazed to see the large quantity of coal that he had hewn from a seam situated above his face as he lay working on his back. The coal thus procured was then loaded into one of the pony trucks with a token belonging to the miner who promptly returned to his burrow for a further excavation.

I saw other miners gouging coal from strata in almost inaccessible positions and, with a feeling of intense admiration and sympathy for those dour men, I left this scene of Britain's vital industry where the wages for this laborious work and the facilities provided for the men's health were deplorably inadequate.

On the day of leaving the *Drake* (March 12th 1913) I was appointed once again to the Gunnery Instructional Staff of HMS *Excellent*, and took up my work there at the expiration of my Foreign Service Leave. The duty assigned to me was to take charge of the Fire Control and Shooting Battery and I could not have chosen an appointment more to my liking. The Gunnery School was commanded then by Captain Morgan Singer (afterwards Sir Morgan Singer K.C.B. K.C.V.O.), who like all officers selected to command this Senior Gunnery Establishment of the Navy, had qualified in Gunnery as a Lieutenant and had previously served on the instructional staff. The Commander was Olive Backhouse, with whom I had previously served at Whale Island and previously referred to, while Lieutenant Commanders R.G.H. Henderson and Sydney R. Bailey were the Senior Staff Officers, who were leading lights in the Naval Gunnery world at the time.

It was nice to be home again and to receive the greetings of many Staff Commissioned and Warrant Officers. Quite a number of them were close friends of mine and included old shipmates. Among them was my dear old friend Andrew Yule Catto, who was the Inspector of Diving at the time, who kindly arranged a refresher course in diving for me before I took over my new duties. The shooting battery at which I had charge was a singled storied brick building some 150 feet long and was equipped with almost every contrivance for teaching the art of Naval Gunnery existing at the time. A large number of guns were mounted of 6-inch calibre and below and at each gun different types of apparatus were erected in such a manner that motions could be produced on the targets representing the roll and yaw of the ship, also the change of range and bearing of the targets. Each gun with its apparatus was placed under a Petty Officer Gunnery Instructor whose class would number about eight men forming a gun crew. The gun layer whilst using a telescopic sight manipulated an elevating wheel to counteract the rolling motion of the ship and pressed an electrical firing pistol when his sight was on the target, while the trainer operated a training wheel and compensates the change of bearing of the target, due to alteration in the course or yaw of own ship and changes in course of the target ship. The point of aim would be at a miniature warship, and on pressing the firing pistol the result of shot would be registered by a pencil mark operated by an electric magnet, or by a pellet or bullet hole from an air gun or aiming rifle secured to the gun.

A section of the battery was permanently darkened an equipped with a gun and instructional apparatus as described above, together with a search light installation. The appliances attached to the guns were known as Scotts Dotters, Deflection Teachers, and Aiming Teachers. These in addition to the special Loading Teachers and sight-setting appliances, constituted an intensive system of preliminary training of a gun crew for individual firing. In order that each member of the class should become thoroughly acquainted with all functions, a system of changing members of the guns crews was practised.

On completion of examinations in these subjects, sub-calibre and full calibre gun firing tests were carried out in a sea going ship belonging to the Gunnery School; from the results of these firings, qualified men for gun layers and seamen gunners were selected. Officers and seamen thus trained in what is called individual firing are further trained to perform their parts in the collective firing from a ships broadside of guns in action under a system discussed earlier known as Fire Control. In battleships, battle cruisers and armoured cruisers, two fire control systems were installed; one for the larger guns mounted in turrets known as the primary armament, and the other for the smaller guns forming the secondary armament. Some two hundred officers and seamen formed into convenient classes ranging from six to twelve were marched to the shooting battery daily, while the instructional staff worked at full pressure in order to provide sufficient trained personnel to man the vast number of warships being built and commissioned by the navy.

As Director Firing was now coming into general use, a Gun Director was mounted at the east end of the shooting Battery. This apparatus which could be manipulated in exactly the same way as a gun, with instructions given to the director-layer who fired all guns of the salvo by a separate firing pistol when his sights were aligned on the target. Individual firing of guns became only an alternative method in the event of a breakdown of the Director System.

War clouds were now definitely appearing on the horizon, as indeed it seemed since the death of King Edward VII and George V's accession on May 6th 1910 when I was serving in the *Bellerophon*. Affairs in the political and economic sphere at home were no less disturbing than that in the international field.

The People's Budget of the Liberal Government introduced by Mr Lloyd George in 1909, gave rise to bitter political strife. The Chancellor's Bill, had to meet heavy Naval expenditure in addition to Old Age Pensions, which became obligatory the year before, and later to finance National Insurance for sickness and unemployment. Huge sums of money were to be raised by increasing the Income Tax and the imposition of new levies. These included a Super Tax on larger incomes and a substantial addition to the death duties, liquor and licensing duties, tax on land values and on unearned increment in land. The whole budget was fiercely opposed by the Conservative Opposition and was the cause of violent class warfare throughout Britain. Members of the House of Lords were prominent in the attack on the Budget.

I well remember some newspaper articles relating to this controversy, especially after a speech delivered by Mr Lloyd George at Limehouse in support of his Budget. In his statement the Chancellor of the Exchequer pointed out the vast difference between the lives of the poor and the wealthy ducal landlords. This was followed by a personal attack upon the author of the Budget by the entire Opposition and the Press, who accused him of using language more befitting of Billingsgate. Some of the Tory members even declared that the bill infringed on the Eighth Commandment. While the Earl of Rosebery, who had been a Liberal Prime Minister and was still a Liberal Peer, was credited with saying that the socialist policy of the Government would be "the end of all" and that it was the negation of faith, of family, of property, of Monarchy and of Empire. Such lamentations by the wealthiest classes in Britain can scarcely be understood in these days of enormous taxation, though it was a true indication of the selfishness of the aristocratic rulers of the country and of their criminal indifference of the burdens and extreme poverty of the great mass of the working-class population.

But the famous Budget was well supported by the Prime Minister (Mr Asquith) with the Liberals and Labour Party and passed the House of Commons by a substantial majority. But the question now upon everyone's lips was "What will happen to the Finance Bill in the House of Lords ?"

Lord Lansdowne who was the Leader of the Second Chamber commanded an overwhelming majority of Peers, who were bitterly opposed to the measure. The Marquis of Crewe led a tiny force of Liberals in defence of the Bill, and warned their Lordships of the consequences of interfering with the House of Commons right to make laws concerning finance and taxation. Lord Rosebery, probably dreading the consequences refrained from voting against the Bill. But Lord Milner in one of his speeches against it said, "Let those who condemned the Budget prevent its passage and Damn the consequences!"

That is exactly what was done. The House of Lords rejected the Bill and brought upon the country the greatest constitutional crisis of modern times. Mr Asquith faced the challenge immediately, declaring that the Lords had usurped the right of the Commons and had committed a breach of the Constitution. An appeal to the country was made in January 1910, when a fierce election campaign was fought on the issue. Even the Peers delivered innumerable speeches against the Bill in the attempt to justify their action of throwing it out. But Mr Lloyd George and his Budget was well received by the people, despite the supreme effort of the Press, which except for the Morning Leader and a few other newspapers supporting the Government, were overwhelmingly on the Conservative side.

The result of the election was a substantial majority for the Government. The Finance Bill was again submitted and passed through both Houses of Parliament without further delay. The matter however, could not be allowed to rest there for steps were necessary to prevent a repetition of this terrible upheaval and political strife when Governments other than a Conservative one introduced future measures in Parliament. Accordingly, the Prime Minister immediately introduced the "Parliament Bill" as the next issue. The object was to limit the power of the House of Lords. Under this Bill, the Second Chamber could only delay a Money Bill for a short period and an Ordinary Bill, if passed by the Commons in three successive sessions, would become law even if rejected by the Lords. If this measure became law, it would, of course not only have affected the House of Lords, but almost equally the Conservative Party in the House of Commons. For hitherto, the Conservative Governments had always enjoyed an easy passage of their Bill by their sleeping partners in the Second Chamber.

The debate in the House of Commons on the Bill was therefore attended with most discreditable scenes of riot and anger. Mr Asquith suffered terrible discourtesy from Opposition members, while the conservative newspapers made violent attacks upon him and the members of his Government. The ordinary people of the British Isles were again speculating as to what the Lords would do with the Parliament Bill. The Prime Minister, however, was determined to force the measure through, and when questioned by the Opposition as to his plans, he reserved the right to disclose them at his own convenience and answered "Wait and See". The words of this colloquial reply so rankled in the memory of his opponents that they were used against Mr Asquith again and again in later years. At the appropriate time the Prime Minister informed the Leaders of the Unionist Party that the Government, if necessary, would advise the King to exercise his Royal prerogative (to create the required number of Peers) in order to secure the passage of the Parliament Bill as submitted by the Commons. Mr Asquith further stated that his Majesty would act on that advice. This of course had a frightening effect on the Peers for if they rejected the Bill, the House of Lords would then be dominated by Liberal Peers and place the Conservatives for the very first time in the minority!

After the General Election of December 1910 (only ten months later than the previous election) the Liberal Government was again returned to power and presented the Parliament Bill to the House of Lords. A serious political crisis had now arrived and with the threat of creating some hundreds of new Liberal Peers the Conservative Leaders were not in agreement as to their next move. The Marquis of Lansdowne took the moderate view and advised the Conservative Peers to abstain from the vote, and Mr A.J. Balfour, the Leader of the Conservative Party for many years past, supported this advice. But there were many members of the Lords still defiant and dubbed the followers of Lansdowne renegades and hedgers; while Lord Rosebery made it known that he would vote for the Bill though he detested the thing!

The most stubborn of the diehards seemed to be the Earl of Halsbury who was the Lord Chancellor. This great lawyer and 'last ditcher' as he was called, was supported by a large number of Conservative politicians. In the minds of some of them, there was some doubt as to whether a large number of Peers would be created and this encouraged their obstinacy. But all hope of this was definitely shattered by the veteran Liberal Lord Morely, who informed them of the formula to which the King had approved in the matter of exercising His Majesty's Prerogative. Consequently, the Parliament Act was passed and became law on August 8th 1911 and still remains to this day. The memorable Crisis had thus passed without the necessity for the creation of peers.

Following this great constitutional struggle, important changes were made in the Government at Home. Mr Winston Churchill exchanged office with Mr McKenna and became First Lord of the Admiralty. We were indeed fortunate in having this vigorous young man to direct the affairs of our great and growing Navy at such a critical period of Britain's history. An outstanding creation of his was a Naval War Staff, and with Admiral Prince Louis of Battenberg (afterwards a Peer, the 1st Marquess of Milford Haven) forged ahead in the task of putting our Fleet in a state of readiness in case of War against Germany. In this connection, Mr Richard B. Haldane, who had been Secretary for War since 1905, was creating the Territorial Army and getting it in readiness as an Expeditionary Force. Haldane was a fine scholarly statesman and had received some of his education in Germany. On one occasion he stated that his spiritual home was in Germany, a remark that was flung back to him in later days. There is no doubt that the ridicule and treatment he suffered, from the Conservative politicians and Peers was most ungenerous and unmerited. In the Great War that followed, his worth to the nation was proved not only by the fine military Expeditionary Force of his making, but for his timely creation of the Imperial General Staff of the British Army. He was however soon to be succeeded by Colonel Seeley who became the Lord Chancellor and was created a Viscount.

Another important change about this time was in the resignation of Mr A.J. Balfour from the Leadership of the Conservative Party after holding it for 20 years. Mr Bonar Law became his successor. In the closing months of Balfour's leadership there had been intense party strife, though at times, a humorous vein was introduced into the fight by the newspapers. I well remember, a political cartoon appearing in the Daily Express at the time, which followed a speech delivered by the Prime Minister at the Albert Hall. Here were depicted a costermonger dispensing fruit from a street barrow and representing Mr Balfour, while a man selling newspapers obviously intended to be Mr Asquith was passing by. A grotesque picture to be sure with the following dialogue appearing beneath it:

Balfour to Asquith - "Wot abaght it?"

Asquith to Balfour - "Wot abaght wot"?

Balfour to Asquith - "Wot abaght wot you said at the 'Albit 'All"?

Asquith to Balfour - "Well! Wot abaght it"?

There seems to be little doubt that the German Government was well aware of the political strife that was going on in Britain and only too ready to take advantage of the position. They also knew that a considerable number of influential pacifists were in our Government, of whom Mr Lloyd George was credited with being one of the strongest. His true character in this regard however, was shown by his famous intervention in the Agadir crisis, which might have brought about a European War in July 1911.

The year before the incident, some German capitalists had brought land from the Sultan of Morocco, extending over a large portion of the country, and so established a sphere of influence as an offset to that of France. Riots had started at Fez one of the sacred cities of Islam and the northern capital of the Moroccan French zone. While a French force was landed to safeguard their subjects and property, Germany to the surprise of Britain as well as France, sent the gunboat to the port of Agadir to protect German interests. This action was regarded as a threat to our seaborne interests in the Atlantic as well as a challenge to the French Government, while an intimation that Britain could not be disinterested in Morocco was disregarded by the German Government.

The situation became tense and in a timely speech at a dinner at the Mansion House Mr Lloyd George, the Chancellor, declared that Britain could not be ignored and treated as if she were of no account in Morocco. Everyone was surprised that the Foreign Secretary (Mr Grey) had left such a pronouncement to a Minister with pacifist tendencies, though his speech was generally approved in Britain. However, it had the desired effect, despite the indignation in Germany, and in settlement, France ceded to Germany land in the Congo.

In 1911, the great majority of British people were grateful to Mr Lloyd George, who despite the political upheaval that had existed since his Budget of 1909, now introduced the National Insurance Bill, which became law to his lasting credit. This measure covered Health Insurance and Unemployment Insurance for certain classes of workers. Many difficulties were raised by the medical profession and the Friendly Societies over the Health Insurance, also by the well to do classes. Prior to this, unemployment was generally regarded as an unfortunate condition of the workers calling for charitable help. Sometimes funds were raised by public subscription for the sufferers. The Trade Unions that existed gave a small subsistence allowance to their respective unemployed, but this left an enormous number of unemployed who did not belong to unions. Many of the wealthy political opponents of the Government would much rather that the existing system be continued, and Lloyd George again came in for contemptuous ridicule especially for his promise that the Bill would produce "Rare and Refreshing Fruit", also that men insured would receive nine pence for four pence! The contribution of the worker to the Unemployment Insurance was paid in the same manner as that for the Health Insurance. This was four pence only at the time and the employer was required to stamp a card for each employee insured.

To this many society ladies were shocked and declared that they would never lick stamps for that dangerous demagogue (Lloyd George). The political and domestic passions of these Mayfair butterflies however, had no effect upon this great statesman, whose purpose was the emancipation of the poverty-stricken workers who had not the wealthiest politicians, nor the most powerful newspapers in the land to plead their cause. One cannot but recall the part played by the

Conservative press in 1913, in their endeavour to drive Mr Lloyd George entirely out of office. He was then fiercely attacked in connection with certain investments in the American Marconi Company together with Sir Rufus Isaacs, who was then Attorney General. Charges of corruption were levelled against them and both ministers were exposed to relentless calumny that invoked the sympathy of all fair-minded persons. A Parliamentary Committee was instituted to inquire into the matter and its majority report exonerated them.

Though this case was the subject of bitter party-political strife it was gratifying to know that Mr A.J. Balfour still the strongest member of the Opposition, ridiculed the charges of corruption. It is well also to reflect on the sympathy that was felt and expressed with those two men of lowly birth. One who became Britain's Prime Minister and a tower of strength to the Empire during World War I, and the other who started his career as a ships boy rose to be Lord Chief Justice of England and in 1921, Governor General of India.

Since the German Kaiser had declared before the world that the destiny of Germany was upon the sea, he backed this up by a frantic race in warship construction and intensive training of German Naval Personnel. It was a great pity that internal and political unrest still existed at home. Concentration of thought so very necessary by the Government on Foreign and Defence problems to meet the inevitable clash between the two nations must have been seriously affected.

Instead of a tranquil solidarity, Britain was now passing through the most amazing period in her domestic history. Internal convulsions shook the Government to the core. M.C. Haldane had failed in his negotiations, while in Germany, to arrive at an agreeable understanding regarding the expansion of the German Fleet; while Mr Churchill's suggestion of a Naval Holiday was scorned by the Germans. Political and religious passions were aroused inside and outside parliament over the Disestablishment of the English Church in Wales. The Bill was passed finally in 1914, though it did not come into effect until 1920. Simultaneously a prolonged struggle to place before the third reading of the Irish Home Rule Bill was disposed of. This measure for self-government was the culmination of bitter strife ever since 1885 when Mr Gladstone took up the cause, though in the following year his first Home Rule Bill was defeated in the House of Commons. Again in 1893, the Grand Old Man made another attempt and secured a majority for Irish Home Rule, but the Bill was thrown out by the House of Lords.

So here again Mr Asquith was pressing the third Bill forward which contained most seriously inflammable material. The Unionists fiercely opposed its passage over the heads of Peers to the Statute Book while Sir Eduards Carson (Afterwards Lord Carson) the Leader of the Unionists in Ulster, headed the fight against the Bill and raised a voluntary force in Northern Ireland with a view to armed resistance. From 1912 to the outbreak of War in August 1914, Carson led this semi militant organization in Ulster. In this he was assisted by Mr F.E. Smith (afterwards Lord Birkenhead) one of the most prominent members of the Unionist Party. "Galloper" Smith as he was called at the time was Unionist M.P. for Walton Division of Liverpool. Phrases harking back to Gladstone's days were resuscitated such as "Ulster will fight and Ulster will be right" - the impressive words of Lord Randolf Churchill the father of Mr Winston Churchill.

Debates on the Bill in the Commons became most unseemly and the Unionist members in their bitter hatred of the Government used terms of abuse more suitable to the gutter, than the dictums of Parliament. Personal violence was not altogether absent either, for one remembers an incident when a pugnacious Ulsterman picked up a book of some sort and hurled it at the face of the First Lord of the Admiralty. Mr Winston Churchill! I understand however, that Mr Ronald McNeill MP., who was the aggressor offered an apology afterwards which Churchill nobly accepted. All this would have contained a certain amount of humour and amusement to the ordinary person in the street had not the Leader of the Opposition promised his support to these lawless methods of the resisters, which Mr Asquith described as a "Complete grammar of Anarchy".

Then in March 1914 came a most critical military and political disruption. This was started at The Curragh, in County Kildare, Ireland, about 30 miles from Dublin, a place famous for its beautiful turf and race course and had developed into Ireland's Chief Military Centre. This lovely spot had become the scene of grave concern to England.

The trouble commenced with an order for troops to move from Curragh to Ulster for the protection of military establishments. Certain Cavalry Officers protested and flatly stated that they would prefer dismissal from the Army rather than take part in any active operations which, in their opinion, might be ordered by the Government against the opposers of Home Rule in Ulster. Why, the opportunity was given for these military officers to make such a threat, obviously inspired by their political views, one cannot say. But when the rumour of this incident had got abroad, and it was widely understood that the Unionist leaders in Parliament were in sympathy with the behaviour of the Cavalry Officers, the alarm was raised immediately by the Government supporters that Civil War was threatening.

Many of us - in the Navy, felt disgusted with the mutinous conduct of these Army Officers, who we thought should have been court-martialled and dismissed from the Service. Both Liberal and Labour members of Parliament were inflamed by the incident and I well remember a strongly worded speech delivered by Mr John Ward a prominent Labour Member, who later performed such fine work for his country during the first World War, raising many labour battalions so urgently needed. This attempt, he said, of an aristocratic junta of army men to override the Constitution should not be tolerated. He deprecated the attitude of the Opposition in the House of Commons and warned them of what might happen if the common soldier followed their example in the event of future industrial and labour disputes. He added that the time had then arrived for a decision as to whether the people of Britain, through their representatives in Parliament, are to continue its legislative authority without interference from the Army. In the light of these utterances, it is interesting to note that Mr Ward himself had been a navvy and was to become a Colonel in the Army.

Colonel J.E.B. Seely, who was Secretary of State for War at the time, found it necessary to resign owing to some misunderstanding between himself and the Officers at Curragh and Mr H.H. Asquith assumed the post in addition to the Premiership. The resignation of Field Marshall Sir John French (afterwards the Earl of Ypres), Chief of the Imperial General Staff at the time, was also accepted in relation to this incident; though a few months later he commanded the British the British Expeditionary Forces in the Great War.

The Prime Minister throughout this deplorable affair handled the situation with masterly ability and to the satisfaction of all right-minded people of Britain. He summoned the Cavalry Officers, who were responsible, to London and after they had freely stated that they were quite ready to carry out their duties as and when ordered, they returned to their posts in Ireland. This astounding episode closed with an announcement from Mr Asquith after he had taken over the administration of the War Office. He said, "The Army will hear nothing of politics from me, and I expect to hear nothing of politics from the Army!"

The struggle over the Home Rule Bill still continued and even the personal and social relationships between the members of the Government supporters and the Unionists opposition were unpleasant. In the social life of the aristocracy, ladies possessing Unionist sympathies ceased to invite their former Liberal friends to their social functions, and would not attend dinners and events if there were risks of meeting members of the Government and their wives. Indeed, it was said at the time, that even Mrs Asquith the wife of the Prime Minister, was treated in this petulant manner.

Meanwhile the danger of War was becoming very real and a sincere effort was made by the Government to reach an agreement. It proposed that any county in Ulster, if it so desired, could vote itself out of Home Rule for a period of six years. Although the Leaders of the Irish Party gave their consent to this, the Unionists remained adamant; and when War came there was no agreement whatever in this serious national matter. The Home Rule Bill however, was passed into law on September 18th 1914, but owing to the War, the Act was not put into operation. Ireland in fact did not achieve self-government until seven years later.

In early 1914, the great expansion of warship building necessitated the training of more and more officers and seamen to man them. Much difficulty was experienced at the Gunnery School in coping with the ever-increasing number of men that came to us. Several methods were adapted to speed up the work including certain adjustments to the hours of instruction and increasing the numbers of men in each class.

The Gunnery Ship, tenders to HMS *Excellent* were also going at full pressure taking the officers and men from us as soon as we had prepared them for their Firing Tests at sea. The Battleship *Revenge* armed with 12-inch turret guns had been used for a long period as a Battle Practice Ship and was now relieved by the battleships *Albermarle* and *Duncan*, while the Cruisers armed with 6-inch and smaller guns were the *Grafton* and the *Dido*. Destroyers and gunboats were also attached to the gunnery school as seagoing firing and towing target Vessels.

While all these activities were going on at the principal Naval Base at Portsmouth, so too were the Gunnery Schools at Devonport and Chatham; all turning out their quotas of Officers and men for the expanding British Fleet. One of my greatest anxieties at the shooting battery at Whale Island, was the occasional failure due to electrical faults in the functioning of the many and various instruments and appliances. Some of these stoppages would seriously hold up the instruction of a class and disorganize our system of ensuring every man take his operational turn at every appliance included in his course of instruction. To cope with this important matter however, I was fortunate in having an excellent electrical staff who, with the aid of my ordnance artificers, effected the necessary repair and maintenance work with as little delay as possible.

Throughout those days of strenuous work, I seemed never to tire because of the tremendous interest it afforded. As the ships were built and placed in commission, so one had the satisfaction of feeling that one did at least something towards their fighting efficiency before they joined up as a Fleet unit. The more officers and men one could efficiently pass through one's shooting battery the better. It was all grist to the mill so to speak! Despite this, I found ample time for recreation, and one did not have to leave Whale Island for such games as tennis, a little cricket and revolver shooting, while in the Mess there was billiards and cards. The Island too was one of the beauty spots in the south of England and afforded many things of interest as one strolled within its circumference of about one mile.

I have already mentioned Lieutenant Oliver Backhouse as one of the Staff Gunnery Officers in the *Excellent* when I was on the Instructional staff there. He was now the Commander of Whale Island and under his able direction it had been developed into an attractive interesting place for the Naval men to invite their families and friends during the week-ends. In addition to the rose garden created by Commander Chatfield several years before, Commander Backhouse had laid out a fine rockery beside a pool containing water lilies in which gold fish thrived. Nearby and encroaching on the well-kept lawn was an enclosed paddock where kangaroos and wallabies and a couple of Rheas (large running birds from South America like small ostrich in appearance) moved about. At the bottom of a bank leading from this, about 20 feet below, grew the Willow tree obtained from Napoleons grave at St Helena. Here was a lower pool stocked with duck and geese which looked so pretty as they swam around under the drooping branches of the Willow. In order to prevent stagnant, water both pools were connected by pipes and a windmill was fitted to pump the water from the lower to the upper pool. Close to the rockery a very fine aviary was laid out in a setting quite becoming of this altogether delightfully interesting spot.

Early in 1914 the First Lord, Mr Winston Churchill, together with Sir John Jellicoe, the Second Sea Lord, came to Portsmouth and visited HMS *Excellent*. They were accompanied by Admiral Sir Hedworth Meaux who was then the Naval Commander-in-Chief at Portsmouth. As we expected, they came to the Shooting Battery and spent quite a considerable time inspecting the various appliances and watching the classes performing their drills. Mr Churchill appeared to be keenly interested in everything that was going on and was not just content to ask questions and to pass remarks upon Naval Gunnery. He actually mounted the sighting platform of a 6-inch gun and relieved the gunlayer in the task of manipulating the elevating wheel and fired the gun himself. I am pretty sure that this incomparable First Lord was the first Naval Minister to do such a thing. Meanwhile, Admiral Jellicoe revealed a truly knowledgeable interest in the battery by his intricate questions which he personally addressed to me. Admiral Meaux, for the most part however, seemed to display an air of nonchalance and even boredom, so characteristic of certain aristocratic officers who filled the higher commands, and their indifference to purely gunnery matters was legend. I may have been mistaken in thus associating my old captain with the reactionary or conservative type of senior officers who were still in the Service; but for all that I respected him as one of England's gentlemen.

Although Mr Churchill had been at the Admiralty for little more than two years, he had introduced some interesting changes regarding the Naval Personnel. At the time, there was no opportunity whatever for promising young men of the Navy, who had entered as boys of the seaman branch, to obtain commissioned rank except through the long years of service in the Warrant Rank; which typically brought them within a few years of the age for retirement. Furthermore, the necessity for rapid increase in the personnel of the Navy was claiming the attention of the Admiralty as to the best ways and means of inducing the right type of recruits both for seamen and officers. Here Mr Churchill took a hand knowing full well the opposition he would encounter if he encroached upon the existing and very exclusive method of entering and training Cadets for Commissioned Officers.

In order to overcome the shortage of Junior Officers a sort of compromise was arrived at by the introduction of the new rank of Mate. The total number of candidates authorised and ages of entry for this rank was so strictly limited that it became impossible to obtain the best entrants from the personnel of the Lower Deck. The scheme therefore, was as everyone could see at the time, only prosecuted half-heartedly and was killed in its infancy. The rank of Mate was equal to that of Sub-Lieutenant and was generally regarded as a hybrid variety. An alternative proposal put forward at the same time was to promote a substantial number of Warrant Officers, who above the age limit for Mates, had proved their worth as Gunners and Executive Officers and could very well be advanced to the rank of Lieutenants with advantage to the Service. This however, was discarded by their Lordships on the pretext that, if it was approved, the ranks of these officers, of whom there was also an acute shortage, would be seriously depleted, and the replacement of such experienced personnel would involve a considerable number of years. For Warrant Officers not only performed various executive duties in ships of the Fleet, but were also responsible for the custody, care and maintenance of the armaments valued at millions of pounds sterling. Incidentally a considerable number of Warrant Officers at the time were commanding Destroyer, Torpedo Boats and other small vessels. It was thought that the Minister himself would like to have enhanced the position of many of these Officers even though it was necessary for them to continue to serve in their appointments. This, of course, would have provided a tangible inducement to desirable recruits from the seaman branch of the Service. But the social rank of Lieutenant was jealously guarded by nearly all higher naval officers, and they much preferred to rely upon filling the vacancies in the traditional way. Even if the number of Cadets coming forward were too few, they were prepared to recruit volunteers from civilians who had perhaps never been to sea in their lives.

It was said at the time, that Mr Churchill offered one solution to overcome the shortage of Lieutenants of the Executive branch; by giving Paymasters a short course of instruction in seamanship and navigation, so that they could fill vacancies as Officers of Watch at sea. If this astute suggestion had been adopted, it is probable that Doctors and Chaplains might have been roped in next! There was of course much feeling among our fellows regarding this subject. Even to this day, we have yet to see a thoroughly democratic scheme permitting the rightful advancement of deserving men from seamen ratings to Commissioned Officers with the same status as those who are fortunate enough to enter the Service as Officer Cadets.

Whale Island Gunnery School, 1914. Self, 4th Right, Front Row

Frederick W Sweetingham

--- ooOoo ---

In the Spring of 1914, I experienced a happy change in my private life and I became deeply interested in the pleasant anticipation of meeting my future wife to be, who had sailed from Hobart, Tasmania for England on the 21st March on board the P & O Liner *Medina*. On the 1st of May the good ship arrived at the Tilbury Docks in London, and we were married on the 5th May 1914. The marriage ceremony took place at St Thomas' the Parish Church in Portsmouth on a delightfully English sunny day, and was well attended by my brother officers in Naval uniform. Afterwards, we proceeded to London and stayed at the Bolton Mansions, Bolton Gardens, Kensington during our happy honeymoon.

In a previous chapter I have referred to my fiancé, who, throughout the past years has been ever the most lovable wife, with her exquisite feminine beauty and joyously shining eyes, like the Spring sun of an Australian season in which she was born. She is adored by our family of four children and has been the main spring of our home life. Her clear brain and clever fingers have created works of art and beauty which adorn the inside of our home, while cultivating plants and fragrant flowers in their environment is another hobby. Typical of a woman of her nature, she has not spared herself in the endeavour to advance the cause of the Voluntary Aid Movement in Tasmania during the last six years of World War II. In movement and repose alike, I am blessed with the companionship of this loveable person, whom to me is, womanhood personified.

Frederick and Adelaide's Wedding Day May 5th 1914

Among the many wedding gifts we most prize is a magnificent silver Rose Bowl and handsome Android Barometer presented by the Staff Officers, both Commissioned and Warrant, belonging to the Gunnery School of HMS *Excellent*. My enduring gratitude is also due to my dear friend Andrew Yule Catto, who kindly and gently sponsored my fiancé for her absent father in Australia, and to another devoted brother officer James Kelly my admirable groomsman.

Part 6

The Beginnings Of World War I

Chapter XXIV

The First Days of World War I

--- ooOoo ---

The news of the assassination of the Archduke Francis Ferdinand, the heir presumptive to the Crown of Austria Hungary, and his wife on the 28th June, 1914 came as a shock to Europe. It took place at the city of Sarajevo Bosnia, now part of Yugoslavia, and there is no doubt that it precipitated the Great War.

Ever since 1890, when the German Emperor William II dismissed Chancellor Prince Bismarck and became himself the director of Germany's policy, he was convinced that he possessed an invincible army and a powerful navy equalled only by that of Britain. As he pondered on war against Russia, there was reason to believe that the political strife in Britain had divided our people so much as to render them incapable of action. Any hopes of this however, were soon to be shattered.

Regarding the Royal Navy, First Lord Winston Churchill had matters well in hand. After exercises off the West Coast of Scotland the Fleet had dispersed in June 1914; but the ships were ordered to their Home Ports to prepare for a Review at Spithead in July. It should be mentioned here that the Naval Review thus ordered, was a test mobilization and had nothing to do at the time with the European situation. Men of the Naval Reserves were called up for temporary service. These comprised the Royal Fleet Reserve numbering some 27,000 men, the Royal Naval Reserve of 22,000 men and the Royal Naval Volunteer Reserve of 5,000 men. Of all these more than 20,000 responded to the call.

Accordingly on the 18th July, 1914, a huge Fleet had concentrated at Spithead consisting of the greatest number of warships ever seen in history. There were no less than 54 battleships, including 20 Dreadnoughts, 4 battle cruisers, 69 cruisers heavy and light, 149 destroyers and 60 submarines, as well as depot ships and small craft. King George V reviewed the Fleet from his Royal yacht the *Victoria and Albert*, which was anchored in a position off the Nab. On the following day the entire fleet put to sea for manoeuvres. Steaming past the Royal Yacht as they departed, we may be sure that His Majesty had a feeling of pride as those long lines of ships proceeded past the Royal Yacht to seaward, and not the least when the Dreadnought *Collingwood* past with his son Prince Albert then serving as a midshipman on that fine ship. As the *Collingwood* passed the King's Yacht they were 'manned' and three cheers were given for His Majesty the King.

On the afternoon of the 18th July, I had the pleasure of passing up and down the lines of ships in a gunboat with a number of my brother Officers on the Staff of HMS *Excellent*. The Fleet of Warships of unprecedented magnitude extended from the Horse Sand Fort on its eastern extremity for miles to the westward in the vicinity of Cowes on the Isle of Wight. It was on this occasion that my dear wife was first introduced to the British Fleet and she, with many other ladies in company, was enraptured with the magnificence of this grand spectacle that included several of the ships in which I had served.

Five days later, July 23rd, the Austrian Government presented its Note of demand to Servia, the terms of which were so humiliating that no self-respecting sovereign nation could accept. The day after Servia answered Austria's Note and requested further time for consideration of it; and on the 25th Servia forwarded a further answer which was rejected by Austria. Meanwhile the British Foreign Secretary had done all in his power to localise the grave position between the two countries, but without avail. The Tsar of Russia too, made personal representations to the German Emperor William II to use his influence on Austria in the cause of peace. However, at the same time the armies of Russia were mobilised.

Everyone knew that Germany was behind Austria in her impossible demands and, fortified by this assurance, Austria declared war against Servia on the 28th July followed by a bombardment of Belgrade two days later. Russia, answering the role of protector of the Slav races in Eastern Europe, supported Servia against Austria. Hungary and Germany declared War against Russia on August 1st and invaded Luxemburg. The following day, Germany invaded French territory. There is no doubt that the German Kaiser and his Potsdam military clique had been working for this day and at last the die was cast and "Der Tag" had come. Admiral Von Tirpitz, the head of the German Navy, we may be sure, gave his Master assurance as to the efficiency and preparation of the German Fleet for war.

As Russia's ally, France entered the war, and in view of the Entente Cordiale that existed between Britain and France there was much sympathy at home with the French people. It must be remembered however, that there was a Triple Alliance at the time between Germany, Austria and Italy, which was made in 1882 against Russia and France. It seemed inevitable that Britain would now be drawn into the vortex, and in view of the Treaty of Belgium of 1839, which established the status of that country as an independent and neutral Kingdom and to which Germany, as well as our country were signatories; Britain asked the German Government whether she would respect Belgium's neutrality. This inquiry was sent by the Secretary of State for Foreign Affairs on July 31st in the expectation that France would be bound to support Russia in the event of war. And on the 3rd of August Sir Edward Grey announced that England would stand by France in defending the neutrality of Belgium.

Following this, Britain sent an ultimatum to Germany demanding the Belgian neutrality and assured the French Government that the British Fleet would guard the French Channel ports from German attack from the sea. Meanwhile King Albert of the Belgians had appealed to King George V to protect the neutrality of Belgium in accordance with the treaty. Following this, Britain sent an ultimatum to Germany demanding that Belgian neutrality should be respected and requested an affirmative reply by 11 p.m. Greenwich time on August 4th. Heedless of this, Germany invaded Belgium on that day, and by the following day a German force 80,000 strong opened an attack on the industrial city of Liege. There was no answer to the British demand on Germany, and in consequence, Britain declared War against Germany at 11 p.m. on August 4th 1914.

Although the great majority of the British people supported the decision of the Government, there were a considerable number, including certain Cabinet Ministers, who questioned the wisdom of Sir Edward Grey and the policy of the Foreign Office which, in their opinion, had precipitously plunged the nation into the war without sufficient reason. The prominent statesmen of the Liberal Government, Viscount Mosley of Blackburn, the Lord President of the Council and Mr John Burns the Minister of the Board of Trade disagreed entirely with Grey and resigned office. Several other ministers were at first against intervention in the war, but mainly through the influence and tact of the Prime Minister Mr Asquith, and to Germany's violation of the Belgian

The Beginnings Of World War I

Treaty, they were persuaded to withdraw their resignations which they had tendered. The Leader of the Labour Party Mr Ramsay MacDonald strongly criticised the action of the Government, and openly challenged the statement that it would be dishonourable not to declare war in the circumstances.

While admitting that public opinion, even in democratic countries has very little effective influence on Foreign Policy, except in rare cases such as that of the Hoare-Laval pact in more recent years, it is a fact that if the ordinary man in the street, understands the real cause of war, as he did in this case, his support is usually whole hearted. Let us examine this aspect of the situation at the time. In the first place this war was not brought about suddenly, and secondly there were many reasons for it apart from the violation of Belgium neutrality. Power politics had been at work for some considerable time and they are necessarily opportunistic and cynical in character, and in critical situations such as this, ethical principles are usually sacrificed to expediency.

So, the main causes of this war were:

- Serious enmity between Austria and Russia over their disagreement in regard to the Balkan question.

- Bitter hatred of France towards Germany ever since the Franco-Prussian War fought in 1870-71 between France and Prussia assisted by Bavaria and other German states. After the defeat of France, the terms of peace included the loss of Alsace and Lorraine together with the payment of a War indemnity to Germany of £200,000,000.

- Acute industrial competition between Britain and Germany and the tremendous Naval armament race for supremacy between the two countries. Furthermore, it was considered that with the finest army in the world Germany with Austria would have defeated Russia and together with the world's second strongest Navy, France would soon be overwhelmed.

In these circumstances, Britain would have been left to fight alone against the victors on the continent who would have thus become incomparably stronger on land and sea. It might be argued that if Britain had made it clear to Germany sooner, and to all other nations concerned, of her intentions that she would actively support France and Russia if the Belgian Treaty was violated, then war might have been prevented.

Be that as it may, the decision taken by Sir Edward Grey (afterwards Viscount Grey of Falloden) the Foreign Secretary, won the high approval of the great majority of his countrymen in the handling of this most difficult situation. The strain upon him must have been enormous during the days preceding the war. Moreover, his negotiations with the German Government were made all the more difficult by the German Emperor William II - whose reign was marked by a fanatical militarism, while his intense ambition to dominate the Councils of Europe was well known before Germany's mad rush into war.

Though the people of the United Kingdom of Great Britain and Ireland gave solid support to the Government in its resistance to German aggression, there was no jingoism at the time. There was however, a determined spirit throughout the British Isles to see the war through. In the House of Commons, the Government was strongly supported by the Leader of the Opposition Mr Bonar Law, but the most outstanding feature in this connection was the attitude of the Irish Nationalist Party. Mr John Redmond their fine leader, and some eighty members of the Irish political party, had taken part in the bitter strife in order to secure Home Rule for their country, right up to this time of war; and everyone was anxious as to the course they would now take. Would the Nationalists unite with the Ulstermen, sink their differences and join in the common cause with Great Britain in her hour of need? That was the question which, to the profound relief of everyone, was answered by Redmond in an eloquent speech. Liberals, Unionists and Labour members alike joined in a great ovation when the Irish Nationalist Leader declared that his country was wholeheartedly on the side of Great Britain in the coming struggle; adding that the Government could entrust the defence of Ireland to her own sons and withdraw the regular soldiers stationed there.

Mention here should be made of Theobald Von Bethmann Hollweg, who was the German Chancellor and Minister President of Prussia at the time. He was chosen by the Kaiser for this post in 1909, and as the highest official who assisted the Emperor in affairs of State, he possessed an intimate knowledge of the position which led to war. Among his numerous speeches in the Reichstag in defence of the action of Germany he referred to the Belgian Treaty as a "Scrap of Paper" a colloquialism used to this day.

Some of us who lived in the Victorian days had experienced the rigours of lesser wars, but the enormity of the one that we were to enter in 1914 was beyond one's imagination. We have, at the time in which I write, just concluded a still greater world struggle, but the First World War forms a chapter in our political annals with its own profound and lasting memories.

As the war clouds were imminently approaching, Admiralty orders were received for certain Staff Officers serving in HMS *Excellent* whose war appointments were abroad to proceed forthwith and join their ships with all dispatch. Accordingly on the 28th July I received personal instructions to take up an appointment in the Torpedo Boat Flotilla based on Gibraltar. I must here confess that I was not too pleased with this war station which seemed to be a token one to suit the peace time conditions of the appointment I held at the time. My other concern was that the only opportunity of refitting all the Guns Mountings and appliances in the Shooting Battery was on occasion when all men under instruction at Whale Island were absent during mobilization. This of course would give one a free hand as Officers in Charge with my local staff to effect overhauls and repairs as necessary before the classes of men returned from mobilization.

It was true that my previous experience in destroyer flotillas would be invaluable for service in the torpedo boats at Gibraltar, but most of my work and study in the service had been devoted to modern gunnery as indeed my appointment at the time implied. I felt therefore that my services would be put to better use in a capital ship, but the order came so suddenly that there was no hope of changing the position. The following day, I embarked in the P&O liner *Arabia* at Tilbury Dock and sailed the same evening for Gibraltar (S.S. *Arabia* was sunk by torpedo in the Mediterranean on November 16th 1916). During the voyage we were kept well informed of international developments, which were growing more serious every hour and during the forenoon of August 4th we arrived at Gibraltar.

The Senior Naval Officer in charge was Rear Admiral Brock who flew his flag in the Depot Ship HMS *Cormorant* while living in Admiralty House, a fine official residence situated in an imposing position on the Rock of Gibraltar. His duties included that of Superintendent of the Naval Dockyard. Captain John Harvey - a fine buff type of Naval Officer was Chief Staff Officer

The Beginnings Of World War I

and also lived on shore, while Lieutenant Commander Ward Hunt commanded Torpedo Boat No 90 and was Senior Officer of the Torpedo Boat Flotilla, consisting of ten vessels numbered from 88 to 97. All T.B's except No 90 were commanded by Chief Gunners or Gunners each with a nucleus crew and comprised the peace time Naval Defences which were now being brought up to war strength including an Officer Second in Command all of whom had been sent out urgently from home ports.

In less than an hour after my arrival, I reported for instruction on board the *Cormorant* and was directed to join Torpedo Boat No 94 for duty. Leaving the bulk of my luggage at the Depot, I boarded the little vessel early in the afternoon and to my joy I found a dear old friend of mine Solomon Ousely, the Officer in Command, who welcomed me on board. Ousely was a Chief Gunner and had been in command of T.B. 94 for a considerable period. For some reason, he was known as Tim Ousely by his friends and I shall never forget Tim's most hearty and kindly greeting as I boarded his little ship on that memorable day. I had known Tim for years, a remarkably fine seaman, possessing a genial and kindly nature and above all was the embodiment of an efficient Naval Officer. Though older than I, he was unmarried and when in England had made a home in Portsmouth with his aunt whom my wife and I knew very well. Tim was therefore highly delighted to receive direct news from his aunt whom he had loved and revered since he was a small boy.

T.B. 94 was one of the vessels that I have referred to earlier, of 130 tons displacement, speed about 22 knots, and armed with Q.F. 3-pound Hotchkiss guns and two Torpedo Tubes firing 18-inch torpedoes. She had a single screw and the boilers were coal burning. All T.B.s of the Flotilla were equipped for mine-sweeping. The organization of the flotilla was arranged so that 6 boats would operate at sea every night from sunset to sunrise, while three vessels carried on the duty by day.

I soon learnt that T.B. 94 was detailed for duty with the Night Flotilla and by sunset on that evening we proceeded to take up our stations. It was a standing order that our flotilla was to sweep a clear channel against possible enemy mines on leaving the harbour and again upon return after daybreak each morning. The method of sweeping was by paired boats overlapping in echelon formation, so that the channel cleared of mines would be wide enough to permit the controlled traffic of ships entering or leaving the harbour. The mine sweeping equipment of each vessel consisted of a large wooden kite which was towed astern by a wire rope at the depth required. Between the two kites of each pair boats was secured the sweep wire of a convenient length which would engage any mine mooring rope that may happen to be in the path between each paired boat as they advanced. If, during the operation a mine was discovered it would be towed out of the ships way and destroyed.

Having completed our first sweep outwards from Gibraltar harbour the Flotilla was dispersed and each boat then took up its appointed position on a patrol line across the Straits when it was our duty to engage any enemy ships attempting to pass from the Atlantic Ocean to the Mediterranean or vice versa; and to stop and search the merchant ships of neutral countries for contraband cargoes in war. Our patrols were kept with vessels at equal distances apart upon a supposed line extending from Carnero Point in Spain to Apes Hill on the Moroccan coast. It was the shortest distance between Europe and Africa and consequently the most favourable for patrol work.

War with Germany, though expected, had not yet been declared but while steaming up and down our beat I had time to collect my thoughts and to go into matters with Ouseley regarding the personnel of our little ships company, armament, speed and manoeuvrability of T.B. 94.

Normally, as Ouseley's Second in Command, it was my job to assume charge of the vessel's armament. This, of course, was a comparatively simple affair for I well knew its limitations in case we went into action. The effective range of our guns did not exceed a mile and a half, while the maximum speed of our Torpedoes was little more than 30 knots over 4,000 yards range. Depth charges for attacking submarines were not then carried by torpedo boats in the Navy. In addition to the above duties, it was Ouseley's desire that I should normally keep, alternate watches with him at sea, relieving each other on deck as necessary. Further, it was to be my duty to board all Merchant Ships that we stopped in order to ascertain the particulars regarding possible contraband cargoes.

Shortly after 11 p.m. an order was passed down our patrol line that War had been declared against Germany and that hostilities were to commence forthwith. Thereupon our recognition signals were tested and our navigation lights extinguished for the duration of the war. A grim moment to be sure, but despite the vicissitudes which I had passed through during the past days, I felt satisfied and comforted in the knowledge that after all, one was actually at one's war job at the right moment. Above all, both my friend the Commanding Officer and I were fully aware of the real strategic importance of the Straits of Gibraltar; also of the great responsibility that had been vested in our tiny mosquito flotilla to guard a vital sea lane against interference by the foe; to prevent its use by him, and to preserve its safe passage for our own ships and those of neutral countries as they sailed upon their lawful occasions. A sharp look-out had therefore to be kept especially for vessels without lights for we knew that the German Fleet had for years been in training for this hour and was now a highly efficient fighting organization. For aught we knew, any type of enemy fighting ship might loom up in the darkness at any moment, including their submarines of which so little was known at the time.

A list of contraband goods was included in our orders, also a copy of Lloyds Register of Merchant ships belonging to all nationalities, which proved invaluable in our work. Every Merchant Ship belonging to neutral countries were promptly stopped by one of our Torpedo Boats as they passed through the Straits. Then they were boarded and the ship's Manifest showing an itemized statement of the vessels' cargo, the ports of lading, names of consignees, passengers and ships destination were scrutinised. If after this inspection, the vessel appeared to have contraband cargoes or enemy aliens on board as passengers, the Captain of the ship would be informed that he must enter the port. Accordingly, the ship would be escorted into Gibraltar and handed over to the Special Examination Vessel where the matter would be dealt with in accordance with International Law.

I do not know how many ships that T.B. 94 had stopped in this manner during our patrols in this area, but I well remember boarding dozens of them. The captains usually received me with courtesy and rendered every possible assistance while one was engaged in the work involved. If, however, some delay was necessary in the examination and especially when it was followed by an order for the ship to proceed to port, one would invariably find the wrath of the captain not far away. On occasions of very bad weather when it would not be advisable to board the ship at sea, instructions would be given by megaphone to the captain to follow the Torpedo Boat into harbour for the examination.

Another important duty on boarding ships belonging to neutral countries was to check up on their passenger lists and to ensure that enemy personnel were accounted for, and that all males of combatant age were disembarked at Gibraltar and interned. A special watch had to be kept on the Italian liners, for a large number of Germans and Austrians embarked in American ports in these

The Beginnings Of World War I

great ships with the intention of reaching the fatherland through Genoa or other Italian ports. Contraband cargoes containing all kinds of raw and other materials for the manufacture of war weapons, once landed in these ports could be easily transported to enemy countries over the Italian border. While discussing these matters with Ouseley during the first watch, about 10 p.m., our attention was attracted to the indistinct appearance of a vessel approaching on our port bow. Thereupon we made the challenge signal and simultaneously we heard the voice of the Commanding Officer of T.B. No 89 (our neighbouring patrol vessel) blazing out: "Have you seen a torpedo about here?". Naturally everyone on board T.B. 94 were astounded to hear such a question while Ouseley hastened a reply in the negative. The night was pitch dark and we felt most concerned about the matter at the moment with visions of being blown up so early in the War! It transpired that a torpedo fully equipped for war service had accidentally shot out of its tube whilst T.B. 89 was heeling over to a heavy sea and was never seen again! At a Court of Inquiry which was instituted later to investigate the cause of this extraordinary incident, it was revealed that the loss of the torpedo was due to a series of unfortunate coincidences. The safety devices fitted to the firing lever and the Torpedo Tube to prevent such an occurrence became simultaneously ineffective while the whole matter emphasized once again the difficulties and dangers that beset the seamen of the Navy.

Before day break on the next morning our patrol effected the capture of the German Merchant steamer *Emir* while attempting to pass from the Mediterranean Sea to the Atlantic Ocean. The *Emir* was a fine ship bound from the East Coast of Africa to Hamburg with a general cargo. In addition, several wild animals were on board destined for a zoo in Germany. The Captain was not aware that hostilities had commenced at the time, but took the precaution of hugging the Moroccan Coast as closely as possible in order to elude any British Naval Vessels that might be patrolling the Straits. The Captain of the *Emir* was a very disconsolate man and personally one felt sorry for him. He was interned in the Rock of Gibraltar with his German crew and the ship became lawful prize. There was a sad sequel to this event in the early death of the *Emir*'s Captain, who died about a year later from it was said a broken heart. It is probable that the *Emir* was the first German Merchant Ship captured at sea in World War I.

Since the conflict, which had now become worldwide, let us review the position in the early stages of the war. Europe was mainly divided among six great nations - Britain, France, Germany, Austria Hungary, Italy and Russia and for a long time their divergent policies, ambitions and rivalries had fore-shadowed an inevitable explosion. For example: Germany with Austria-Hungary endeavoured to establish predominant influence in the Middle East, while Russia desired to annex Constantinople as an ice-free port giving her access to the Mediterranean Sea. Both these aims ran counter to each other, and to the interests of Britain and France, who wished to maintain a status quo in order to preserve the balance of power, so that no State was greatly preponderant in Europe. In addition, there existed conflicting trade relations between the various countries while their colonial aims were in opposition to each other. In the line-up for war, Europe was divided into two hostile camps. On one side were the Central Powers of Germany and Austria-Hungary, to which Turkey and Bulgaria joined later, and on the other were Britain, France and Russia, who were aided by Belgium, Serbia, Montenegro, Italy, Rumania and Greece. Japan, the United States and several minor countries aided the Triple Entente and their Allies as hostilities progressed.

Having undertaken our work in the first few hours of the war on the western extremity of the Mediterranean, we were naturally interested with the opening naval operations elsewhere. We knew that Germany's formidable Battle Cruisers *Goeben* and *Breslau* with their attendants were somewhere in the Mediterranean, but their actual whereabouts was uncertain. Meanwhile our Flotilla was ordered by the Admiralty to keep a good look out for both these ships as there was anxiety that they would attempt to break out into the Atlantic and raid our Merchant ships on the trade routes. In the Adriatic, Austria had six Battleships, three of which were of Dreadnought type and Italy, a member of the Triple Alliance and a potential enemy at the time, possessed a force including seven Battleships in Italian waters.

Against the enemy force we had the British and French Fleets. The British Mediterranean Fleet consisted of a Battle Cruiser Squadron of three ships, an Armoured Cruiser Squadron of four ships - four Light Cruisers, fourteen Destroyers and six Submarines, three of them being at Gibraltar. Admiral Sir Berkely Milne was Commander-in-Chief of the British Fleet with his flag hoisted in the Battle Cruiser *Inflexible*, while the second in Command was Rear Admiral R.A. Trowbridge commanding the 1st Cruiser Squadron on board HMS *Defence*. The French Fleet had one Battle Squadron of six ships similar to our Lord Nelson Class (immediate pre-Dreadnoughts), and a Second Battle Squadron of six ships including the Dreadnought *Courbet* flying the flag of Admiral de-Lapeyrire, also, two Squadrons of Armoured Cruisers, comprising five ships and twenty-four Destroyers and a few older Battleships, which formed a Reserve Squadron. In comparison with the number of ships indicated above, it would appear that our forces were overwhelmingly superior to those of the enemy. It must be remembered however, that the French had commenced to transport their African Army to France and covering protection had to be given to the troop ships during passage across the Mediterranean. Obviously therefore, these vital matters had to be allowed for, when the British and French Fleets were disposed for action.

CHAPTER XXV

Chasing the Goeben and Breslau in the Mediterranean

--- ooOoo ---

Admiral Milne's instructions from the Admiralty were to watch the Adriatic and shadow enemy cruisers, cover French troop transports, and at the same time avoid action with superior enemy forces.

The German ships *Goeben* and *Breslau* were under the command of Admiral Souchen and at daybreak on the 4th August, Bona in Algeria was bombarded by the *Breslau*, and Phillipsville by the *Goeben*, where troops but for this would have embarked. This of course was before Britain's declaration of war, but Milne was informed about 2 p.m. that the ultimatum had been sent to Germany to expire at midnight. About 5 p.m. on the same day, one of our light cruisers HMS *Dublin* (Captain John D. Kelly) sighted the *Goeben* and *Breslau* and asked permission to engage the *Breslau*. Since the time limit to our ultimatum had not then expired his senior officer answered "No!" and ordered *Dublin* to continue shadowing. This must have been very disappointing to Captain Kelly when he knew that only a few hours separated him from a fight. At 7 p.m. information was received from the Admiralty that Italy had declared her neutrality. This of course was a great relief but handicapped our ships in their endeavour to bring the *Goeben* and *Breslau* into action because the terms of Italy's declaration was that no ship was to approach within 6 miles of her coasts. Since this applied equally to the German ships, it seemed more likely that Admiral Souchen would attempt a dash westward and break through our patrol at Gibraltar into the Atlantic rather than making for the Straits of Messina where he might have hoped to obtain some respite.

It must be mentioned that Admiral de Lampeyrire with his French Fleet was then under orders to seek out the enemy with his whole fleet and also to cover the transit of troops from Africa to France. Though both French and British Admirals had practically the same objectives, it was unfortunate that no co-ordination of their efforts was arranged between them. With the French Squadrons dispersed in Western Mediterranean, the task left for Milne could have been to cut the possible escape of *Goeben* and *Breslau* through the Straits of Gibraltar. Milne's concern for the safety of the French Troop Transports was unnecessary. However, Milne had received no word of Admiral de Lampeyrire's movements, neither had the order to commence hostilities against Germany reached him until 1.15 a.m. on August 5th; even then there was no modification to his general instructions, to cause him to alter the disposition of his Fleet.

Forthwith, Admiral Milne, who had previously disposed his fleet for trapping the enemy at Messina, now ordered the *Indomitable* and *Indefatigable* to steer west towards Biretta (Tunis), while the *Dublin* was to keep in touch with the enemy. Unfortunately, *Dublin* lost the chase about 10 p.m., and received an order to join the *Indomitable* at Biretta the next morning to fill up bunkers with coal. The line of escape for the two enemy ships through the Straits of Messina from the west was thus left open. Milne with *Inflexible* took up a position off Malta with the light cruisers *Chatham* and *Weymouth* guarding the passages to the eastward and on either side of the Island of Pantellaria, while Rear Admiral Trowbridge in the armoured cruiser *Defence*, with *Black Prince*, *Duke of Edinburgh* and *Warrior* was southward of the Adriatic, somewhere between Cephalonia and the heel of Italy. The light cruiser *Gloucester* detached to watch the southern entrance to Messina and the destroyer flotilla was westward of the Greek Coast.

About an hour after Britain's ultimatum expired, Admiral Milne in his flagship together with the *Chatham* and *Weymouth* proceeded westward to join the other two battle cruisers heading for Biretta. After concentration to the west of Sicily, Admiral Milne dispatched the *Dublin* to Malta; the *Inflexible*, *Indefatigable*, *Weymouth*, *Chatham* with a division of destroyers then proceeded to patrol between Birretta and Sardinia.

Then at 3.35 p.m. on the 5th August Captain W.A.H. Kelly of the *Gloucester* signalled that the strength of wireless signals he was intercepting indicated that *Goeben* must be at Messina. This proved correct for she was coaling from an East African liner, the *General*, which had been waiting for her at port in Sicily which was now neutral. Admiral Milne next morning began to sweep eastward in order to sight the *Goeben* if she left Messina by the northern route. Meanwhile, Rear Admiral Trowbridge who was watching the entrance to the Adriatic to prevent the German cruisers from entering, might well have been anxious at the time. Trowbridge regarded the *Goeben* as a superior force to his own, thus, his instructions were not to engage. With a speed of 27 knots and armed with ten 11-inch and twelve 5.9-inch guns it was considered that in action the enemy battle cruiser could have defeated his four armoured cruisers in detail. The speed of his four ships being about 22 knots; the armament of *Defence* was four 9.2-inch and ten 7.5-inch guns, the *Black Prince* and *Duke of Edinburgh* each had six 9.2-inch and ten 6-inch guns. Trowbridge however, intended to engage the *Goeben* at night and hoped that at least one battle cruiser would be sent to him in order to deal with the enemy ship during daylight hours if necessary. This however did not materialise and when *Indomitable* had completed coaling at 7 p.m. on 6th August at Biretta, she was ordered to join Milne who with the other two battle cruisers continued to watch the northern exit of the Messina Straits where he thought it probable that the *Goeben* would emerge to attack the French convoys; their protection still being his first consideration.

Meanwhile the German Admiral had received urgent orders from Berlin to make for the Dardanelles and the *Goeben* followed by the *Breslau* left Messina at 5 p.m. on August 6th. Thereupon Captain Kelly of *Gloucester* signalled that the enemy was coming south and shadowed the two enemy ships taking care to keep clear of the gun range of *Goeben* with the risk of being blown out of the water. The *Gloucester* was a cruiser with a speed of about 25 knots, armed with 6-inch guns and of less than 5,000 tons displacement. At 7.40 p.m. the Admiralty ordered Milne to chase through the Straits if the enemy went south but unfortunately the signal did not get through to the *Inflexible* until midnight when it was too late to modify her movements. Incidentally, it was Milne's idea that Trowbridge with his cruiser and eight destroyers would be strong enough to sail up the Adriatic while there was still a possibility of the German cruisers making back westward. He, of course, knew nothing about Admiral Souchen's order to make for the Dardenelles.

In the meantime, the *Gloucester* gallantly held on to the *Goeben* and at midnight, in spite of *Goeben*'s efforts to jam his wireless, reported her going south-east and that she was probably making for the Eastern Mediterranean. About 1 a.m. on the 7th, Captain John Kelly of *Dublin* in the brilliant moonlight saw smoke in the distance, and from signals that he was receiving from *Gloucester*, he hoped with his two destroyers to attack *Goeben* later. Opportunity however, did not occur and *Dublin* made for a rendezvous according to previous instructions. At the same time Trowbridge, being then off Zante in the Ionian Isles, also gave chase with the intention to engage *Goeben* if he could make contact before 6 a.m. That was his only chance otherwise the full daylight would enable the enemy with superior speed and gunpower to choose his distance and outrange him. When at 6 a.m. Trowbridge found it impossible to engage the enemy and slowed down in expectation that the *Indomitable* and *Indefatigable* would now be sent to him with instructions for concerted action. Alas they did not come and about 10 a.m. on 7th August *Goeben* had passed ahead of him, escaping to the east.

Captain Kelly in *Gloucester* was left to carry on the chase alone and, despite Milne's signal to him to drop astern so as to avoid capture, he chose to take the message as permissive and held on tenaciously. At 1.35 p.m. he engaged *Breslau* astern of *Goeben* with the intention of either forcing *Breslau* too close to her flagship or delaying *Goeben*'s progress by bringing the flagship back to protect her. The *Gloucester*'s armament was superior to the *Breslau* 4 and the engagement lasted 15 minutes at ranges from 11,500 to 10,000 yards. Kelly had achieved his objective for the *Goeben* turned sixteen points and came back and though far out of range she opened fire. Kelly then broke off action and *Goeben* turned eastward again. When the signal reporting this action was received by the C-in-C Milne, he was getting anxious knowing the *Gloucester* must be short of coal. He sent her orders not to chase farther than Cape Matapan but to join Trowbridge. But no other cruiser was sent to take *Gloucester*'s place, and at 4.40 p.m. on the 7th August, the *Goeben* and *Breslau* could be seen on an easterly course and Kelly gave up the chase.

At 2.30 p.m. on the 8th, Milne was about half way to Matapan when he received an Admiralty telegram stating that hostilities had commenced against Austria. He thereupon proceeded to a position about 200 miles south of the Adriatic in order to prevent the Austrian Fleet cutting him off from his base at Malta and ordered Trowbridge to join him. Later however, came a telegram from Admiralty to say that we were not at war with Austria and that he was to resume the chase of German cruisers! Accordingly, leaving Trowbridge to watch the Adriatic, he proceeded southeast with his three battle cruisers, ordering *Dublin* and *Chatham* to follow. On the 10th, Milne rounded Cape Malea and entered the Aegean Sea heading north-east some 60 hours after Souchen had arrived there. Milne was without information as to the enemy's whereabouts but they were only about 150 miles from the British battle cruisers who were on a course that was rapidly closing on the *Goeben*.

The German ships had coaled from a collier at a pre-arranged rendezvous at Denusa and about 6 a.m. on the 10th, Souchen put to sea and made for the Dardanelles. Without knowing, Milne had actually reached a position little more than 100 miles to the west of the German cruisers while he continued his sweep among the Grecian Archipelago. But before noon on the 11th August he heard from Malta that the *Goeben* and *Breslau* had entered the Dardanelles at 8.30 p.m. the previous night.

So, this unhappy affair had come to an end in so far as Admiral Milne and his fleet was concerned. The one highlight, however, was the brilliant performance of HMS *Gloucester* and her gallant Captain who had kept up the chase while sending accurate reports regarding the movements of the German ships for nearly 24 hours before the ship was called off. The *Goeben* could have caught and sunk the *Gloucester* if Admiral Souchen had wished and, in just recognition of his masterly conduct, Captain Kelly received the honour of Companionship of the Bath.

The failure of Admiral Sir Berkely Milne to destroy the *Goeben* and *Breslau* and their escape to Constantinople, as was seen later, had far reaching effects on the course of the war. The burst of public euphoria at home that the German ships were so soon driven out of the Mediterranean to suffer an ignominious internment in a neutral port turned out a poor consolation indeed for the nation.

At the time, the British relations with Turkey were seriously strained owing to the fact that on the day before war was declared, we commandeered two Dreadnoughts (*Sultan Osman I* - 27,500 tons and *Sultan Recard V* - 23,000 tons) which were just completing for her in our shipbuilding yards. The delivery of these battleships, armed with fourteen 12-inch and ten 13.5-inch guns respectively, was prevented just at the time when Turkey mobilized and when the German Military Mission was taking charge of her army. Incidentally, it was also known that the Dardanelles was mined, supposedly against all belligerents. In these circumstances we might well appreciate that the German powers of cajolery succeeded at Constantinople, as the Turkish Government allowed *Goeben* and *Breslau* to be piloted safely through the minefields of the Dardanelles. Furthermore, the presence of these two modern fighting ships at the Golden Horn, obviously had a bearing upon Turkey's aid to the Central Powers which led to our declaration of war against Turkey less than three months later.

It was thought that with more initiative on the part of Admiral Milne, the enemy ships might well have been brought to action with at least one of his battle cruisers and destroyed with the support of the armoured cruisers under the command of Trowbridge. Milne was ordered to return to England to attend a Board of Inquiry. However, he was exonerated from all blame.

After Milne's departure the Command of the Mediterranean was reorganized. Trowbridge was given command of the British seagoing ships and Admiral Carden was appointed the Senior Naval Officer at Malta and on the 18th August, Admiral de Lapeyrere who had then completed the transportation of the Algerian Army to France, became the Commander-in-Chief of the Combined Fleets in the Mediterranean.

I well remember the night Milne passed through the Straits of Gibraltar in the *Inflexible* on his way home. T.B. 94 with three other boats were, as usual, out on the patrol line guarding the Straits with special orders to keep a good look out for the battle cruiser passing from the Mediterranean into the Atlantic. Sure enough, about midnight the great form of the ship loomed up and passed through the centre of the straits between our boat and the next one on the African side of the patrol line. We were quite sure that it was the *Inflexible* and allowed her to pass unmolested in accordance with previous instructions. Then a few minutes later when the ship had faded out of sight, and to our great surprise we saw a searchlight on the *Inflexible* and what appeared to be one of our torpedo boats doing her best to stop the great ship, followed by the sound of a blast from the little vessel's 3-pounder gun. Nothing daunted, however, the great Flagship sped on and the torpedo boat, realising that it was all a mistake gave up the chase. Though the reason for this regrettable incident was due to an entire misunderstanding on the part of the Officer concerned, we felt that our humble apologies were justly due to the Admiral and the Ship's Company for their magnanimity shown towards our delinquent flotilla.

CHAPTER XXVI

The Navy's Part in Home Waters

--- ooOoo ---

Whilst I was involved in operations in the Mediterranean, rapid developments were taking place in Home Waters. The appointment of Admiral Sir John Rushworth Jellicoe as Commander-in-Chief of the Home Fleet, now known as the Grand Fleet, in succession to Admiral Sir James Callaghan was most gratifying to the Naval personnel generally and to those of us who had previously served with him as I have earlier recorded. Like Lord Fisher and Sir Percy Scott, Jellicoe possessed an intimate knowledge of all the changes that the advance of science and mechanics had rendered necessary in warship construction, their armament equipment and the training of naval personnel. He had also a profound knowledge as to the best use a fleet and doubtless saw the necessity for vital changes in naval strategy and tactics at the time. He was a great choice to take command of Britain's Grand Fleet in War and he hoisted his flag in HMS *Iron Duke* (a Dreadnought Battleship) as the Fleet flagship.

The composition of the Fleet comprising three Battle Squadrons was:

Dreadnought Battleships -	20
King Edward Battleships –	8
Duncan Class Battleships -	4
Battle Cruisers	4
Armoured Cruisers	4
Cruisers	4
Light Cruisers	6

In addition, there were 65 destroyers forming flotillas based at Cromarty, Firth of Forth, Humber, Harwich, The Nore, Dover, Portsmouth, Portland and Devonport.

In the same manner as Admiral Milne in the Mediterranean, Jellicoe was at sea on August 4th when he received notice of the British ultimatum. It was about 5 p.m. and the German Naval Authorities were then trying to locate the Grand Fleet by using fishing trawlers in various parts of the North Sea. German mines were laid with immediate effect by the minelayer *Konigen Luise*. Mines were laid off the Suffolk coast in the fairway and before she could return to her base the *Konigin Luise* was caught by our cruiser *Amphion* and sunk. Unfortunately, in the early morning of the 6th August, the *Amphion* was blown up. One Officer and 150 men perished as well as some prisoners taken from the *Konigin Luise* who had laid the mines.

From the very start of hostilities, the utter disregard for neutral ships and German ruthlessness by mining international waters without warning was quite apparent. German submarines were also active at the outbreak of war, and as early as August 7th, U 15 was sunk by HMS *Birmingham*. This was the Navy's first experience of submarine warfare and afforded a certain measure of confidence at that time that this new weapon could be defeated if attacked with vigour.

It seems incredible, but was nevertheless true, that when Jellicoe took over the command there was no safe harbour available for his new fleet. This must have been the cause of great anxiety for Scapa Flow in the Orkneys was the only harbour in the North Sea large enough to accommodate the Grand Fleet. Scapa Flow had three entrances at the time, but none of them were equipped with boom defence, and his entire fleet was therefore exposed to torpedo attack from enemy submarines. This harbour into which Jellicoe took his fleet was, curiously enough, not a Naval Base at all! It was not equipped with a dockyard and no facilities existed for even minor ship repairs. In these circumstances a determined attack by enemy submarines might have had disastrous effects.

The layman might ask: Why then did Jellicoe use such a dangerous anchorage as his base? True there were other ports on the East coast of England and Scotland such as the Naval Bases at Chatham and Sheerness but they were totally inadequate in size; while the Scottish ports of Rosyth, Firth of Forth and Cromarty were just as undefended as Scapa Flow. These are astounding facts observing that for years we had been preparing for a probable war against Germany. But the reason for this was in the realm of Politics which one must leave at that!

In contrast, what a vast difference existed in regard to the German High Sea Fleet commanded by Admiral von Pahl. His great Battle Fleet was tucked away securely in the protected harbours at Wilhelmshaven or Kiel; equipped with docks, ship building and repair plants equal to that of our greatest Naval Base at Portsmouth. As the Japanese had carried out a successful attack on the Russian Fleet at Port Arthur in Manchuria 10 years before, so the Germans expected a surprise attack from the British Fleet. In this connection the Germans believed that from the geographical view all the strategical advantages were with the British Fleet, and that the British Isles laid like a great boom across the North Sea. They constituted merely inmost corner of the Heligoland Bight, the gate of egress of the German Fleet, as a strategical defence line.

The primary task of the British Fleet was to secure the life nerve of the British Isles, namely her overseas trade and a decisive battle for supremacy of the sea was necessary only if the pressure exerted by the German Fleet became so rigorous as to impede the conduct of the War for the Allies, or if our shipping to and from Britain was endangered.

In the political sphere, the support of all parties for the Asquith Government and his Liberal Ministers would be needed to undertake the enormous task that laid before them in formidable political conditions. Field Marshall Lord Kitchener came home from Egypt at the outbreak of War and joined the Cabinet as Secretary of State for War. This office was taken over from the Prime Minister himself, and Lord Kitchener's work in building up the Army won universal admiration; whilst his great personality added prestige to the Government.

On August 6th troop movements began with the despatch of six Infantry Divisions. Thus, the Navy commenced its huge task of escorting troop transports as well as the protection of overseas commerce. The chief port of embarkation for troops in England was Southampton, from Scotland was Glasgow, while the ports of Dublin, Queenstown and Belfast were used in Ireland. The sea routes had, of course, been decided upon prior to the War and all of them were safely covered by the British Fleet. For this purpose, three Battle Squadrons were formed into a Channel Fleet, comprising nineteen pre-Dreadnought Battleships with attendant Light Cruisers, Destroyers and Submarines. The Battle Squadron took up its position in the English Channel and elsewhere in order to deal with any enemy ships that might come through the Straits of Dover with the intention

The Beginnings Of World War I

of molesting the great armada of troop transports. Meanwhile, Jellicoe with his Grand Fleet watched ceaselessly for any movement of the German High Sea Fleet should they emerge from their bases. In addition to the protection of our commerce, the enormous task of conducting the passage of our Expeditionary Force to France placed a burden of great magnitude upon the C-in-C of the Grand Fleet. In the first 6 weeks of the War no less than 150,000 British troops were transported across the English Channel to the Continent.

After the *Birmingham* had sunk the German submarine U 15, Jellicoe decided to move the Grand Fleet westward of Scapa Flow as soon as the great troop movement to France was completed. Meanwhile he was compelled to use Scapa Flow temporarily, though for some inexplicable reason the German High Sea Fleet refused to come out as expected. There was a need to guard against the possibility of Germany sending out heavy ships northward into the Atlantic, for once there, much devastation on our commerce would undoubtedly be wrought.

Towards the end of August when the main portion of our troops had been landed in France, a Battle Squadron was released from convoy work and came out to Gibraltar to support our ships that had been sent into the Atlantic to protect our commerce. This Force was under the command of Admiral de Robeck on a station between Finistere and Cape St Vincent.

To give the reader some idea of the risk Jellicoe was taking by holding on to Scapa Flow as a base for his Fleet, it may be interesting to mention that on the 1st September about 6 p.m. when the Grand Fleet was moored there, the *Falmouth* of the 1st Light Cruiser Squadron reported that the periscope of a Submarine was in sight inside the Flow. The Cruiser immediately fired at the supposed object and the alarm was raised throughout the Grand Fleet. Jellicoe ordered torpedo defence nets to be fixed on by ships equipped with them and battle storeships to be placed alongside certain ships without nets. Destroyers and other small vessels got under way immediately and steamed about the harbour with searchlights switched on in their endeavour to locate the enemy submarine. In the meantime, other ships had reported that they had seen the periscope of a submarine. The C-in-C then ordered the Grand Fleet to weigh anchors and afterwards led the ships out of Scapa Flow, leaving a Flotilla of Destroyers to continue the search and destroy the enemy if found.

The anxiety of everyone concerned was heightened by a perilously dense fog which prevailed during the passage of the ships through the Pentland Firth, always a difficult pilotage at night even in clear weather. However, by midnight the whole Fleet had cleared out of Scapa and from there Jellicoe proceeded to the North of Ireland and moored the Grand Fleet at Lough Swilly. The continued search by the destroyers at Scapa for enemy submarines proved abortive and it was afterwards considered that the whole incident arose from a false alarm.

Whether the alarm was false or not, one must agree that it was most timely and brought about the much-needed defences of this important naval base. It cost the nation however, one of our finest Super Dreadnought Battleships, *Audacious*, completed for service only the year before, was sunk by striking a mine off the north coast of Ireland on October 27th 1914. It was impossible to keep this serious matter a secret even for a short period, because the liner *Olympic* was present and went to the aid of the *Audacious*. American passengers were on board the liner, and very soon the enemy, and indeed all the world were informed of this very material loss to our navy. It was only a couple of months before the incident that I called on board the *Audacious* to see my dear old shipmate and friend Paddy Flynn, who was the commissioned Boatswain of the ship, a similar appointment to that which he held when we were serving together in HMS *Drake*. I took the opportunity then of congratulating him on his splendid fighting ship and expressed a wish that I could be shipmates again with him if war should come.

An important change was affected at the Admiralty on October 29th, by the appointment of Admiral of the Fleet Lord Fisher as First Sea Lord in succession to Admiral Prince Louis of Battenberg (who later took the name of Mountbatten, and was created the Marquess of Milford Haven). There is a most unsavoury story attached to the removal of Prince Louis from his posts, about which most of us in the Navy were disgusted. For that great and loyal seaman was subjected to unjustifiable calumny of the worst kind by a miserable section of the people and the press in England. Lord Fisher, as we have already seen was the First Sea Lord from 1904-10 and the creator of the Dreadnought type of battleship, and apart from the regrettable circumstances which caused this vacancy was, despite his 73 years, generally considered the ablest man to again occupy this important post.

CHAPTER XXVII

Deployment of the British Army

--- ooOoo ---

While we were keeping our long vigil in the great sea-lane off Gibraltar, news came to us regarding the formation of the British Expeditionary Force under the command of Sir John French.

In a previous chapter I have referred to Sir John's departure from Ladysmith just before the siege in the early days of the South African War. Soon after General French had left us, I was interested to learn from one of his cavalrymen who had remained with us, that Sir John himself, had entered the Navy as a boy in the days of sailing ships. Naturally I asked the reason why he had left our service, and was informed that owing to his inability to endure the height when aloft in a masted ship he was transferred to a Cavalry Regiment. And so, this fine Cavalry Officer who had served in the Boer War with such brilliant success, eventually became Chief of the Imperial General Staff, a post that he resigned in May 1914 following the resignation of Colonel Seely the Secretary of State for War, as a result of the Irish Home Rule crisis at the Curragh.

The Kaiser of course, no less his General Staff, knew of our "contemptuous little army" but they had no idea as to when it would cross the Channel to the Continent. It which was transported by the navy without mishap in less than 2 weeks in August.

Then came news of the great German drive with no less than seven armies, extending from Alsace-Lorraine to Belgium and the northern flank of these millions of German soldiers swinging around through Belgium, threatening to envelope the French Army and to occupy Paris with one swoop. But this was not to be, for we now heard of the timely advance of the French and British Forces across the Marne and through a gap between the northern German Armies; while the French Armies held the remainder of the line some 250 miles long. The French victory at the Marne was largely due to the genius of General Ferdinand Foch, who had commandeered all possible transport, including outmoded motor vehicles, in order to rush troops from Paris to the sagging French front. This great French soldier and military Professor was a Corps Commander at the time; but before the end of the war, he was appointed Generalissimo of the Allied Forces on the Western Front.

With the German line thus broken their northern armies were then brought up with a round turn and retreated some thirty miles to the Ainse. There they entrenched themselves for practically the duration of the war. As a result of this momentous check of the enemy's advance, the German High Command received the shock of their lives, and soon realised the sterling worth of the gallant little British Army which they were won't to ridicule. The Chief of the Imperial German Staff Von Moltke had deadly reason to remember them when owing to this failure to capture Paris, he was dismissed and superseded by General Von Falkenhayn.

The removal of the seat of the Belgian Government from Antwerp to Ostend on October 7th brought grave apprehension as to the Belgian ports. Then came the German rush to the Belgian Coast which despite the efforts of the Allied Armies could not be stopped. The seizure of Ostend and Zeebrugge proved of incalculable value to the enemy, who promptly fortified and used them as submarine bases to the discomfiture of the British Navy for the remainder of the War. Had the Allied Army Commands foreseen the grave importance of retaining the Belgian ports in our possession, there is no doubt that greater effort would have been made by them to prevent the strategic loss of these ports. It was of grave concern to the navy and it was thought that at least some attempt should be made to re-occupy the Belgian coast before the Germans had time to convert Ostend and Zeebrugge into fortified naval bases.

The decision not to do so should have rested equally with the naval as well as the army authorities, for these fortified bases not only became a threat to the northern flank of our army in a purely military sense, but also constituted a serious menace to our shipping and food supplies to Britain. A well-planned combined operation by both Services together with Naval bombardment might well have succeeded in driving the Germans from the Belgian Coast and would thus have prevented the enemy from establishing that deadly submarine and destroyer base at Zeebrugge from which many thousands of tons of British, Allied and neutral shipping were ultimately destroyed. It is true that we would still have suffered losses by German U Boats, but their submarine bases would then have been pushed back into Germany, several hundred miles further from our shipping lanes.

What of the Eastern front? In those early days of the War, when Russian Armies at first advanced victoriously, all sorts of rumours were abroad regarding the huge manpower of our ally and the proverbial 'Russian Steam Roller' which, it was said, nothing could survive its advance. Indeed, it was said that thousands of the Tsar's soldiers were on their way to the French ports to reinforce the Allies on the Western Front. These fantasies soon faded from one's mind when news came that the German Forces in East Prussia had defeated the Russians so disastrously at the Battle of Tannenberg.

This disastrous defeat sustained by our Ally, was by no means due to the lack of valour on the part of the common Russian soldier. On the contrary, they were very badly equipped compared with the Prussian Army. Indeed, it was said that the men in support and reserve on the battle fields were short of boots and were not even provided with rifles and ammunition. The latter were obtained by these men from their comrades in the fighting line as they became casualties. The tragic defeat of the Russians after they had invaded German territory in the North was, indeed, bad news for the Allies, while it heartened the German people after the failure of the tremendous attack of their armies in France and Belgium. Thenceforth Hindenburg, who was 67 years of age, became the Colossus of Germany, and with his Chief Lieutenant Ludendorff, were idols of the German nation!

It was generally anticipated at first that the duration of the war would be rather short. But the failure of Russia on the Eastern Front and the declaration of war by Turkey against the Allies in October 1914, had now definitely threatened our security in Egypt including the vital hold on the Suez Canal. In consequence the whole outlook had now changed and the end of the war appeared to be a long way off.

It may be interesting here to comment on the beginnings of aircraft warfare as it occurred at this time. In August 1914 until the end of the year there were four British Squadrons of the Royal Flying Corps attached to the Army Head Quarters in France. These were employed on reconnaissance duties only, and these pioneer airmen in this early war work proved themselves so valuable that urgent and rapid expansion of this Service was put into operation. New machines were manufactured and equipped for use as fighters and bombers and the training of the new personnel was speeded up for both Army and Naval Services. Actual long-range bombing did not take place until November 1914, when the Royal Naval Air Service successfully bombed and destroyed a Zeppelin at the Friedrichshafen Airship Base in Germany. Though the distance covered for the return journey was less than 300 miles and the weight of the bombs used only 20 pounds it was considered a fine achievement in those days.

CHAPTER XXVIII

Naval Action off Heligoland

--- ooOoo ---

The first naval engagement of the war in the North Sea involving a considerable number of British and German warships and took place off Heligoland on August 28th, 1914. This followed observations reported by our submarines that it was the practice every evening for enemy destroyers led by light cruisers to come out into the North Sea and rendezvous the next morning about 20 miles north west of Heligoland.

A drive was therefore planned by our forces to intercept them upon their return from their morning manoeuvres. Our attacking force belonged to the Grand Fleet and consisted of the 1st and 3rd Destroyer Flotillas, supported by a Squadron of six light cruisers and five battle cruisers under the command of Vice Admiral Sir David Beatty flying his flag in HMS *Lion*. In all about 50 British fighting ships and vessels were involved including 6 E class submarines.

At 7 a.m. on August 28th a German destroyer was sighted, when a chase began and soon after ten more enemy destroyers were sighted and became engaged with our 3rd Flotilla led by Commodore Tyrwhitt in the light cruiser *Arethusa*. About 8 a.m. two German light cruisers - the *Stettin* and *Franenlob*, were sighted coming up from the north of Heligoland and engaged the *Arethusa*. Tyrwhitt's ship came under the concentrated fire of both enemy cruisers and was hit many times at ranges between 6,000 and 3,500 yards until about 8.15 a.m. when our 1st Destroyer Flotilla led by HMS *Fearless* engaged the *Stettin* and chased her eastward towards Heligoland, leaving *Arethusa* and *Franenlob* in a running fight down the west.

The *Arethusa* was armed with two 6-inch and six 4-inch guns and many of these were put out of action and her position became serious. But she still continued her engagement with *Frannlob* until 8.25 a.m. when only one 6-inch gun remained active. By that time *Frannlob* had had enough and made for Heligoland where she received the protection of German land batteries. The enemy guns on the island also compelled the *Fearless* to turn away from *Strettin* ending the first phase of the action.

About 8.30 a.m. four of our destroyers engaged the German Destroyer *V 187* at 6,000 yards and soon afterwards she was punished severely by two of our light cruisers and four more destroyers. It seems incredible how *V 187* stood up to the battle so long, for at one time she was engaged at no more than 600 yards, and by 8.50 a.m. her engines had become disabled and she was almost stopped. She continued to fire her guns however, and badly damaged our destroyer the *Goshawk* at point-blank range, just before she went down with her colours flying at 9.10 a.m. The second phase of this action was accompanied by much confusion, some destroyer mistook our own cruisers for those of the enemy and one of our light cruisers, the *Southampton* flying the broad pendant of Commodore Goodenough, attempted to ram our submarine *E.6*. Happily, no harm was caused by these mistakes, though without the skilful handling of *E.6*. by her commander, the submarine would have surely been sunk.

The Beginnings Of World War I

At 10.20 a.m. more enemy was in sight whilst all of our ships were steering west and the *Arethusa* was able to use both of her guns again, though her speed had been reduced to only 10 knots. Ten minutes later the German light cruiser *Stratsund* was sighted and opened fire on the *Arethusa*. The First Destroyer Flotilla led by *Fearless* (Captain Blunt) delivered an attack on the *Stratsund* and when she sheared off, Commodore Trywhitt called off our ship and his force resumed their course westward. Later the *Arethusa* and *Fearless* both became engaged with the *Stettin* once more and also the enemy light cruiser *Mainz*. By 11.30 a.m. *Arethusa* was in such a bad way that Trywhitt signalled an urgent call to Beatty for assistance. Thereupon Commodore Goodenough was sent to assist with his light cruiser squadron. Meanwhile the German light cruisers *Koln* and *Ariadne* had joined *Stettin* and *Mainz* in the engagement. Soon after, Goodenough arrived upon the scene with *Southampton* and three other cruisers; and Beatty himself came up in the *Lion* leading the other four battle cruisers of his force. The *Mainz* was sunk at 1.08 p.m. and by 1.35 p.m. the *Ariadne* and *Koln* (the German Flagship) had been sunk by our battle cruisers. However, *Stettin* got away, and owing to the possibility of the enemy battleships coming out to support her, Beatty decided not to pursue the *Stettin* but to keep his force intact.

Our destroyers endeavoured to rescue the German survivors, but succeeded only in picking up one stoker of the *Koln*, while the German Admiral and 380 men perished. The *Lurcher* however rescued 348 officers and men from the *Mainz*, including 60 wounded. The Germans thus lost three light cruisers and one destroyer, while their total casualties in men killed and wounded were about 1,250 including nearly 400 prisoners of war. On our side only the *Arethusa* suffered severely and was towed back to port by HMS *Hogue*. Our losses were 35 killed and 40 wounded. Considering the comparatively large number of British ships engaged, this first action on this side of the North Sea brought us only a small victory. But the morale effect was good and it demonstrated to the enemy that ships of the Grand Fleet were ready and eager to seek out and destroy their vessels of the High Sea Fleet even in the German Bight!

On reflection, the *Arethusa*'s was a lightly armoured cruiser of an entirely new type with a nominal speed of 30 knots and there were questions surrounding why she was unfortunately disabled so soon in the engagement. The reason may be due to the fact that the ship had been in commission for only a week or two and was certainly not in a condition to fight at sea against an enemy ship with well-trained crews. During the *Arethusa*'s trials her maximum speed was much less than the 30 knots estimated, and her Q.F. 4-inch semi-automatic guns gave much trouble and jammed after they were fired.

Ultimately, the *Arethusa* came to grief on a mine laid by German V.C. Boats from Zeebrugge planted in the approaches to Harwich on February 11th 1916. The explosion killed 11 men in one of her boiler rooms. A south-easterly gale was blowing at the time with a nasty sea and though destroyers tried to take the ship in tow, the hawsers parted. She eventually drifted ashore on the South Cutler Shoal off Felistowe where she broke her back and settled down - a total loss.

In a previous chapter I have given some details of HMS *Aboukir* an armoured cruiser in which I had served during 1910-11 in the Mediterranean, also of the *Hogue* as having towed the disabled *Arethusa* to port. I will now describe the loss of these two ships together with their sister HMS *Cressy*. They were all armoured editions of my old ship the *Powerful* and belonged to the Southern Patrol Force in the North Sea engaged in the protection of our troop transports operating in that region early in the war. Admiral A.H. Christian (with whom I had previously served in HMS *Excellent*) commanded the Patrol Force, and flew his flag in HMS *Euralus* (another cruiser of the Cressy class). The 1st and 3rd Destroyer Flotillas which had previously taken part in the action off

Heligoland also patrolled this area, one off the Dogger Bank and the other in the Broad Fourteens. The armoured cruiser *Bacchante* and the light cruiser *Amethyst* in which my brother Albert was serving was also attached to the Southern Patrol Force.

On the 19th September 1914, the weather in the North Sea was so bad that Admiral Christian ordered the two destroyer flotillas back to the harbour at Harwich, while the *Euryalus*, *Hogue* and *Aboukir* carried on their patrol duties in the Dogger Bank area. In the early morning of the 20th however, the *Cressy* joined the Squadron and the Admiral in *Euryalus* left to embark coal, leaving Captain Drummond of *Aboukir* in command. It was still too rough to permit the destroyers on patrol, therefore the three cruisers were left to maintain their watch without a Flotilla screen to protect them from the danger from enemy submarine attack, still possible during the gale. These conditions continued throughout the day of the 21st, but during that night the weather had moderated and Commodore Trywhitt, who now flew his broad pendant in the light cruiser *Lowestoft*, set out for the broad fourteens with 8 destroyers.

He was well on the way, early on the 22nd, when the Admiralty sent out repeated wireless signals that *Aboukir* and *Hogue* were sinking in position Latitude 52°18' N, Longitude 30°41' E, about 30 miles west by south from Ymuiden in Holland. Eight more destroyers were then immediately ordered to join Commodore Tryhwitt and Admiral Christian made for the scene in the *Amethyst* at the utmost speed. But before they could arrive one of the greatest tragedies of the war with loss of valuable lives had happened.

Just before 6.30 a.m. on the 22nd September, the poor old *Aboukir* was torpedoed; she heeled over to 20 degrees and the order was given to abandon ship, but only one sea boat was available and there was no steam with which to hoist out the boom boats. Twenty-five minutes later the ship turned over and floated bottom upwards, then all hands took to the water while she sank. Captain Drummond who believed his ship had been mined, signalled to the other two ships to close in order to pick up survivors of *Aboukir*, and when the *Hogue* closed, she was struck by two torpedoes and immediately afterwards an enemy submarine on the surface on her port quarter. The *Hogue* promptly trained their guns and opened fire on the enemy, but in minutes the ship's decks were awash, and 10 minutes after she was torpedoed, the *Hogue* went down. At 7.17 a.m. Captain R.W. Johnson of the *Cressy* began calling for help, while his boats with those of the *Hogue* were picking up survivors of the *Aboukiri*. Then a periscope came in sight on *Cressy*'s starboard quarter only two cables (400 yards) distant and the track of a torpedo coming towards the ship was visible. Full speed ahead both engines was the order of the next instant, but before she could gather way the *Cressy* was hit abreast the aft funnel; a second torpedo just cleared her stern; then a third hit the ship just before the forebridge. The *Cressy* turned over on her beam ends, laid there for about 15 minutes and then disappeared.

The circumstances attending the *Cressy* were most extraordinary, in that all her boats were away and filled with the survivors of the other two ships. Commodore Tyrhwitt was still 50 miles away and it was not until 10.45 a.m. that he was able to make the distance. However, a couple of Dutch trawlers were near and effected some rescues, but the loss of life was very great. Whilst 60 officers and 1,777 men were saved, 60 officers and 1,400 ratings were drowned. Despite these appalling losses, the men displayed admirable discipline and conduct beyond all praise, both before and after their ships went down.

At first it was thought that no less than five enemy submarines had attacked our ships, and when the Germans announced that only one U Boat (the U9) was involved it seemed incredible. It is probably a record in the annals of naval warfare that so great destruction had been achieved by so little means. This also necessitated a great change in the future handling of our ships in relation to the deadly submarine, the importance of which had been disregarded with astounding credulity. Following this disaster an Admiralty order was issued to all commanding officers to the effect that if one of several ships in company was torpedoed by a submarine or struck by a mine she must be left to her fate and the other ships were to clear out of the dangerous area calling up minor vessels to render assistance.

CHAPTER XXIX

Capture at Sea and Contraband Cargoes

--- ooOoo ---

The incidents such as our capture of the German Merchant Ship *Emir* in the first hours of the war, and our search of neutral vessels for contraband merchandise which were promptly seized when found had revived an old question which has been the subject of much controversy regarding the treatment of shipping and commerce in war even to this day.

According to International Law on maritime rights, Contraband of War is anything furnished by a neutral country to a belligerent that is by the Laws of War subject to seizure. Arms and military supplies are classed as "Absolute Contraband"; grain, horses and so forth are "Occasional Contraband", while goods consigned to a neutral country which may be transferred to a belligerent, or to a belligerent country which may be used by its armed forces constitute "Conditional Contraband".

The Declaration of London 1909, had maintained the right of *Capture at Sea* and included a formal presentation of neutral and belligerent rights etc., which were submitted to the Great Powers. This was adopted in Britain by an order in Council on August 20th 1914 and additions to the list of contraband were made from time to time, but the Order was rescinded on July 18th 1914. The view held in certain quarters was that radical changes were needed in dealing with International shipping in war and among the reasons advanced in this connection were:

- Wars are always decided by the operation of land or air forces, while *Capture at Sea* cannot bring about a decision.

- *Freedom of the Seas* for neutral shipping is necessary and action against this policy, invariably finds new enemies among the nations whose sea borne trade has been interfered with, and who would otherwise have remained neutral.

- The expenditure in peacetime upon armament by Maritime Nations for the protection of commerce in war, would be obviated under a policy of Freedom of the Seas, while the money and effort could be more usefully employed on land and air forces.

- If two or more nations choose to settle their differences by fighting, they have no right to inflict losses or delays on the shipping of other nations who are in no way connected with the quarrel. Moreover, Commerce at Sea being private property should be regarded as immune from seizure and confiscation similar to that on land.

The Beginnings Of World War I

- Whereas Britain is an Island and entirely dependent upon overseas trade, and Continental nations have alternative inlets and outlets for food and other essential goods over their land frontiers; it appears that in her opposition to freedom of movements by the sea, Britain prefers to retain a weapon which can destroy herself while, at the most, can only injure an opponent.

These and other arguments were put up against *Capture at Sea* - which in effect meant that the cutting of sea communications of an enemy people, or even of an enemy army and air force is wrong!

Now let us consider the other side of the argument, particularly as it affected the British Empire at war in 1914. The offensive measures by which Germany or any enemy nation can be subjected to pressure are invariably two in number:

- depriving it of essential supplies without which it cannot exist or its territory may be occupied and the lives and liberty of the people placed in jeopardy.
- depriving it of food or means of movement.

Enforcing the surrender of a nation is the object of every war and in these two measures lie the only methods of possible success for the victor, and the right to employ them has never been questioned in International Law. Why then should it be considered wrong to cut off supplies for the enemy at sea, when it is agreed by everyone that the destruction of his railways, bridges and other means of transport, by bombardment from the sea, land or air is not wrongful? Merchant vessels discharging or loading cargoes at an enemy port are, considered to be perfectly correct war objectives; then why not those self-same ships when at sea?

Here we see an unreasonable lack of consistency on the part of those who advocate *freedom of the seas*, for a neutral country is equally injured if the territory with which he trades is bombarded or occupied by armed forces, because all commerce thereby ceases. Moreover, his business premises and employees suffer by the attack, though curiously enough this is not considered sufficient reason to protect against such bombardment or occupation by attack. The only inference that may be drawn from this is that, apparently a neutral country may suffer injury from loss of property or trade only on land but it should be prohibited at sea! So long as he shall be able to make huge profits, which the distress of other people affords, the neutral is to be quite free to transport by sea and to sell munitions of war to belligerents in war. He can thus sustain both sides in the fighting by prolonging the fight until he feels it will no longer be profitable to himself! One may ask who could defend this new doctrine upon any degree of morality at all!

In all past wars, history has shown that it is morally right to bring about the surrender of an enemy by cutting his supplies and communications. This has never been questioned and in fact was our experience in the Defence of Ladysmith during the Boer War. Included in our besieged garrison was an Army in the field and a comparatively large number of civilian inhabitants, who though useless in the defence of the town, had to be fed from the common stock of food. General Joubert, the commander of the besieging town refused to allow this civilian population to be evacuated and so relieve the food situation for the fighting units, and so far as I am aware, no one condemned him upon moral grounds. The Boer General's reason for such a refusal obviously being that there existed the alternative of surrendering, with food to follow for the whole garrison.

Nations advocating the new maritime doctrine certainly do not suggest any alteration in this, but they claim that the infliction of sufferings such as these is quite immoral if they are imposed on the salt sea! They declare that capture of contraband in ships plying the oceans should be abolished. Therefore, they mean that war weapons and all warlike stores, foods etc., which they admit may be captured legitimately on land, have merely to be loaded and carried to neutral or enemy countries in satisfaction of their new doctrine of *Freedom of the Seas* and abolition of the age-old *Blockade from the Sea*. The rights of neutrals during war time must of course be respected by belligerents, as far as possible, but to concede the above demands would mean that the profits and interests of financiers in neutral countries are of greater importance than the lives of people of nations at war. Although the Declaration of London was adopted on August 20th 1914, the measure was rejected by the House of Lords in 1911 and strong objection to Britain's maritime policy was raised by the American Government.

The restrictions placed upon German overseas commerce at the time was often referred to as the 'British Blockade', though Britain in fact never declared an actual blockade against Germany. The object of a blockade is to completely stop an enemy country from all commercial intercourse with the outside world and cutting off its supplies of munitions and food. This, of course, was quite impracticable against a country like Germany with its small coast line, while it could receive supplies over its land borders from the neutral countries of Holland, Denmark and Italy and from Norway and Sweden across the narrow waters of the Baltic. In Maritime Law, moreover, a Blockade is really an act of War. Britain therefore could not legally close the ports of the above neutral countries when trading with Germany. The great British Fleet in this regard was quite impotent; but it was certain that unless it could stop the flow of munitions and other essential materials of war destined for Germany through neutral ports, we would surely lose the war.

What then was the British Fleet to do in this most desperate struggle in the country's history, and at the same time remain on friendly terms with that great industrial and agricultural English-speaking nation across the Atlantic and with other neutral countries, particularly Italy who had refused to join in the war against the Allies. This was a very serious and delicate question for the British Foreign Minister Sir Edward Grey to handle observing that German influence in the United States was very strongly backed by American industrial magnates, cotton men, and Chicago meat packers who insisted upon trading with Germany through neutral ports.

In this connection, I well remember in the early days of the war, great Italian liners and other neutral ships, laden with cotton (one of the principal materials used in the manufacture of explosives), and stopped by us when passing through the Straits of Gibraltar bound for Genoa. Everyone knew that the ultimate destination of these cargoes was Germany, but after the ship had been through its examination and the matter reported to the Admiralty, the Foreign Office decision to allow the ships to proceed would invariably prevail. Sir Edward Grey met with great unpopularity in our own country and particularly in the House of Commons. He was charged with being subservient to the interests of American trade and thereby losing the war for Britain. They declared that in order to please America he was hamstringing the British Fleet. Admiral Lord Charles Beresford, the Conservative Member for Portsmouth, was particularly outspoken in Parliament and stated that the Navy was not allowed to act and that the Foreign Office was constantly interfering with its operation. It was correctly said that the Naval Patrols were bringing in suspicious cargoes only to witness the Foreign Office orders to release them.

But Grey, obviously unhappy about the question kept to his main purpose of maintaining good relations with neutrals and more particularly with the United States of America. It must be

The Beginnings Of World War I

remembered that there were powerful influences operating on behalf of the cotton, copper and other interests, and certain American Congressmen and Senators were actively and openly against Britain. Therefore, the Foreign Secretary, being well aware of this, was most careful lest an embargo might be placed upon the shipment of munitions to Britain, or even worse of creating the necessity for the United States to convoy their merchant ships with American Cruisers which might lead us to war between the two countries.

Even a British steamer was stopped by us when on passage from the United States to Genoa, and when searched some 2,000 tons of copper ingots were found to be consigned to Genoa "to order". This meant to order of the German Government of course! Within 6 months from the beginning of the war, thousands of tons of such precious metal required for war manufacture could be seen stacked on the breakwater moles at Gibraltar. It was to be expected that the strongest objections to our method of search and restrictions of cargoes would come from the greatest neutral trading country – America; curiously enough Britain was only following a precedent adopted by herself during the American Civil War.

During that war Britain sent arms and other warlike weapons to the West Indies and Mexico ostensibly in the performance of trade between Neutrals just as America was sending war materials to Italy, Holland, Denmark and Scandinavia at the time of which I write. Yet, in both cases, this trading was obviously not neutral at all. For the cargoes from Britain were intended for the use of the armies of the League of Southern States of the American Union (Confederate States) that sought to become independent in 1861-65; just as the warlike freights from America were destined for Germany in 1914. As the cargoes in the former case were reshipped to the Southern States, the American Government seized both ships and cargoes and condemned them as lawful prize.

Following this, America created a new law of sea warfare under the names of *Continuous Voyage* or *Ultimate Destination*. In this connection America insisted that neutral ships could be stopped and searched anywhere on the high seas, even if they were trading between neutral ports, and cargoes of contraband seized if determined that its' ultimate destination was enemy ports. The so-called neutral shippers were thus foiled in every way and the British Government, doubtless with an eye to the future, raised no official objection to this reasonable policy which has since been recognized in International Law.

There still remained however, the controversial question as to what articles should constitute Contraband, as apart from those under a Blockade, where everything besides guns, ammunition and other necessities of war. As I have previously mentioned, Britain had not declared a blockade on Germany for the obvious reason that we could not enforce it effectively; but we did adopt the right of search and capture upon the high seas in combination with the policy of Continuous Voyage or Ultimate Destination.

Though International lawyers were busy fighting for the cause of neutral trades in contraband goods, the American Government acquiesced with our Foreign Office in the matter as Britain had done in the American Civil War. But there was disagreement as to certain items of commodities included in the list of "Conditional Contraband". Food for Germany was figured on our list; though it was declared officially in America that the stoppage and seizure of foodstuffs from entering a neutral port was tantamount to a blockade, and as such an act of war against the neutral country concerned. Some Americans even denied our right to include copper on the list of contraband.

But the British Foreign Office in its determination to prevent food supplies to enter Germany from overseas as far as possible, cast about for an effective reply to this and found one on the grounds of reprisals against the illegal submarine warfare. Early in February 1915, Germany had declared her submarine warfare in allied and neutral shipping and, in reply, Britain announced her intention of preventing commodities of any nature from entering Germany. The British Foreign Office justified this procedure as a retaliatory measure and cleverly brought the French Government in its support in the following announcement, "As a retaliation for the illegal warfare which Germany had declared on Merchant shipping, both that of enemy and neutrals, the British and French Governments hold themselves free to detain, and take into port ships carrying goods of presumed enemy destination, ownership and origin".

And so, this very important service was carried on by armed Merchant Cruisers in the Atlantic Ocean, and by our Torpedo Boats, armed Boarding Vessels and other small war vessels by day and by night.

The ruthless conduct of the German U Boat campaign soon led the United States Government and people to appreciate the British and French announcement. But despite the "Blockade" Germany drew enormous quantities of food supplies from America, mainly through Scandinavian countries and the Baltic. Nevertheless, we learnt from General Ludendorff and others after the war, how very near the Central Powers were to collapse due to want of all kinds of material for the manufacture of guns, mountings and other weapons, and food for their armies and people.

When we consider that our enemies might well have collapsed entirely in 1917, and the lives and suffering of millions thus saved, but for the so-called moral restrictions placed upon the British Navy in our endeavour to completely isolate the Central Powers from the rest of the world, it makes one's blood boil! This could have been accomplished if it had not been for the trading interests of the neutral countries mainly America. The powerful industrialists and speculators simply would not forgo their ever-increasing profits and insisted upon further depths of disaster in their claim of moral right! Never in the history of the whole world had so many been held to ransom for the personal gain of so few. And while I live, I shall always be grateful for the privilege granted to me of serving in HM Torpedo Boat No 94. For it was in the flotilla, of which we were one unit, that we were mainly engaged in the service of alleviating the sufferings of the enormous majority of mankind by limiting the enemy's sinews of war and thus shortening the struggle.

The activity of Maritime Capture was most humane, affecting the seizure of property only. It took no lives, shed no blood and imperilled no household, as in the case of bombardment from the sea or land warfare. It dealt only with persons in the trade and their cargoes, voluntarily embarked in the changes and chances of war solely for the purpose of private gain, while great insurance companies supported them.

CHAPTER XXX

Exploits of the German Raider Emden

--- ooOoo ---

Since the Germans for the most part, adopted a ruthless and dastardly method of undersea warfare against allied and neutral shipping, it seems proper to record here at some length the exploits of one of the few German ships that observed the humane international code of capture at sea. I refer to the German light cruiser *Emden* of 3,592 tons armed with ten 4.1-inch guns, two torpedo tubes and a speed of 24 knots. This comparatively small warship with her intrepid Captain Von Miller and crew formed a unit of the German Pacific Squadron commanded by Vice Admiral Graf von Spee who flew his flag in the larger armoured cruiser *Sharnhorst*. The other ships of this squadron were the *Gniesnau*, sister to *Sharnhorst*, and two cruisers similar to the *Emden* making five ships in all.

It was on September 14th, the day after Rabaul was captured from the Germans, that an important wireless message was received at Calcutta from S.S. *City of Rangoon* that a German Cruiser was operating off the Hooghli. This proved to be the *Emden*, which till then was thought to be with Von Spee's Squadron. Her sudden appearance in the Bay of Bengal came as a disagreeable surprise to all concerned. She had already captured a large Greek Collier the *Pontoporos* laden with 6,000 tons of coal, and had used her as a coaling tender while proceeding towards Calcutta. When the *Emden* was in a position about 250 miles south-east of Madras she sank our transport ship the *Indies* bound for Bombay, though fortunately with no troops on board. The following day the *Emden* sank another empty transport, the *Lovat* also bound for Bombay. Both the *Indies* and the *Lovat* were sunk by gun fire after the crews of both vessels had been transferred to a large tender - the *Markomannia* which had accompanied the *Emden* from the China Seas. On September 13th whilst still on the Colombo - Calcutta course in the Bay of Bengal, the *Emden* captured and sank the S.S. *Killin* with a cargo of coal for Colombo and the next day Muller transferred her crew to another vessel by the name *Kabinga* which he had captured with an American cargo, and had kept in his company. Then the *Emden* came across the S.S. *Diplomat*, a splendid ship of about 7,000 tons carrying a most valuable cargo including 30,000 cases of Indian tea!

It seems incredible that in spite of Admiralty instructions to the contrary, all these ships were captured whilst steering along the normal trade routes with navigation lights exhibited at night as if in normal peace time. To make their capture all the more easy, it was said that the ships approached the German Cruiser believing that she was a British Man of War! Luckily however, this comfortable method of capture ended with the next ship that Von Miller stopped, the neutral Italian S.S. *Loredanow*, whose Captain was asked to take over the crews of the other captured ships. This request was refused and the *Loredanow* was allowed to proceed to Hooghli where, the Italian Captain, named Giacopolo, met the *City of Rangoon* who promptly reported the matter. His splendid action saved the *City of Rangoon* together with her valuable cargo worth more than £500,000. Furthermore, a general alarm was raised by wireless to all ships ready to sail in the East Indies, which were held in port until the Naval Authorities had dealt with the situation. The Naval hunt began for the marauder. The British cruiser *Hampshire* with the light cruiser *Yarmouth* were dispatched from Singapore, while the powerful Japanese armoured cruiser *Ibuki* was sent to the Cocos Island and our Armoured Cruiser *Minotaur* to the coast of Sumatra to intercept the *Emden* if she turned up in there.

Again, on the 14th September, the *Emden* sank the S.S *Trabbock* bound for Calcutta and on that day Von Muller learned from intercepted wireless messages of the alarm caused by his presence in the Bay of Bengal. Thereupon he released the *Kabinga* with all the captured crews which then proceeded to Calcutta. He then met and sank S.S. *Clan Matheson*, and on the 18th, when *Emden* was only 20 miles from Rangoon, Von Miller handed over the crew of the *Clan Matheson* to a Norwegian S.S. the *Dovre*.

The Bay of Bengal was now getting too warm for Captain Von Miller and he learned that the *Hampshire* was coming up on his track past the Nicabar Islands through intercepted messages between the latter ship and the Indian Authority. He knew therefore that several British Cruisers were searching for him and successfully escaped from the Bay of Bengal.

Nothing more was heard or seen of the *Emden* until 22nd September when she was back again into the Bay of Bengal and bombarded the Burma Company's Oil storage tanks at Madras. Two tanks, containing half a million gallons of kerosene, were set on fire and consumed, a few shells fell in the town killing and wounding several people. During this attack the *Hampshire* was about 300 miles northward of the *Emden* while the Japanese light cruiser *Chikuma*, who had also joined in the search, was about 290 miles southward. The *Emden* was therefore in a somewhat uncomfortable position. At 6 a.m. on the 23rd she was reported off Cuddalore when the *Chikuma* was off Trincomalee about 200 miles distant. During these last days in the Bay of Bengal the *Emden* sank seven more ships and the trade routes had to be closed once again.

At this time the New Zealand Government was preparing to embark troops for overseas and were anxious about the safe passage of the transport ships. The *Minotaur* and the Japanese Cruiser *Ibuki* were therefore ordered to proceed to Wellington to escort the New Zealand convoy to Fremantle where the Australian Transports would join them enroute to Aden. This, of course, necessitated the withdrawal of these ships from the Cocos Islands and Sumatra where they had been watching out for the *Emden*. During their voyage towards Wellington, however, the New Zealand Government, hearing that Von Spee with *Sharnhorst* and *Gneisenau* was near Tahiti, where he had bombarded the French port of Papeete and sank a French gunboat, decided to sail the New Zealand Transports without delay and meet the *Minotaur* and *Ibuki* at sea.

On 25th September, the *Emden* captured and sank the S.S. *King Lud* about 25 miles south of Ceylon and later Von Miller stopped and destroyed the S.S. *Tymerie* some 50 miles out from Colombo. Both these ships were sunk by explosive charges in order to save the ammunition of the *Emden*'s guns. The German Raider then worked northwards towards Cape Cormaria and on the conveying tracks from Colombo, Bombay and Aden she captured the S.S. *Gryfervale* and kept her in company. Three more ships were fated to be sunk by *Emden* - the Steam Ships *Buresk*, *Robera*, and *Foyle*. Sinking the two latter ships in the usual economic way (explosive charges), Von Miller had no intention of treating the *Buresk* in the same manner for she had a precious cargo of some 4,000 tons of Welsh coal. What a lucky capture this was to be sure, and right on the trade route! Here was an abundance of the best class of steaming coal from which he could fill the bunkers of the *Emden* to his heart's content, so the ship was promptly commandeered and the enemy's depredation was thus prolonged materially. Captain Von Miller then released the *Gryfevale* and the ship reached Colombo on 29th September.

Meanwhile the *Hampshire* was still searching in the Bay of Bengal with the *Chikuma* who entered Colombo the same day as the *Gryfevale*. Both *Hampshire* and the Japanese Cruiser had experienced very bad luck in their fruitless hunt for the German raider. On October 9th, Von Miller went into Diego Garcia to coal from the *Buresk*. This British Island in the Indian Ocean was such a lonely spot that the inhabitants were still unaware that war existed. In the circumstances Miller took the opportunity to clean the ships bottom as well as to embark coal. The *Emden* sailed again the next day, 10th October, and during the next ten days she had captured six more ships including the *Exford* an Admiralty Collier with a cargo of about 6,000 tons of Welsh Coal, for the British Fleet at Hong Kong. This was another valuable prize which enabled the *Emden* to obtain a further lease of life. Among the other prizes was the Blue Funnel Line S.S. *Troilus* a vessel of 7,500 tons homeward bound with a cargo insured for no less than £130,000. All except the *Exford* and a ship carrying a neutral cargo, the *Eghert*, were sunk, the latter being released with the prisoners from the other ships.

On the 20th October the *Emden* just escaped the *Hampshire* once again about the latitude of Colombo whilst steering South. But for the slow speed the *Buresk* and *Exford* in company with the *Emden*, the British and German Cruisers would certainly have met. At one time the *Hampshire* passed across the enemy's course only about 15 miles ahead of him, but owing to the bad weather the *Emden* was not sighted. Captain Von Muller then sent the *Exford* to a rendezvous north of Cocos Island; but went on with the *Buresk* to Nankowy Harbour in the Nicobar Islands arriving there on the 25th October.

Three days later at 5 a.m. the *Emden* disguised with a dummy funnel and flying a flag that was taken for the White Ensign, entered the harbour of Penang. Here she passed the patrol boat, while the Russian Light Cruiser *Zhemchug* also anchored there, remained in her position as all appeared well until the *Emden* arrived within half a mile of her. Then the enemy suddenly displayed the German Ensign and fired a torpedo at the *Zhemchug* and opened fire with her guns at close range. The French destroyer *Mousquet* was also present, but she and the Russian cruiser, completely surprised and unready for such an attack, were both sunk. The *Emden* then rescued survivors from the *Mousquet* and made off in a northerly direction. The *Zhemchug* was an old cruiser and of a total complement 340, there were 200 killed and wounded. A daring and brilliant achievement on the part of the *Emden* to be sure.

Soon however, these incredible successes of so small a cruiser were to be ended. On November 8th the *Emden* rejoined the *Exford* at the rendezvous off the Cocos Island where she had been waiting. Von Muller Miller was not then aware that Admiral Jerram, who had been directing our ships searching for the *Emden* had expected him in this vicinity, and he was also ignorant of the convoy of Australian and New Zealand troops that had left Fremantle and were on their way northwards towards him. Presumably feeling safe therefore, he went close to Direction Island and landed a party of 60 men with a machine gun with orders to raid the Cocos Cable Station which was the focal point of the cable centre of the Eastern Telegraph Company. This was at 6 a.m. on the 9th November and the Station Staff of the E.T.C. then sent out an S.O.S. calling up *Minotaur* and told her that a strange ship was entering the harbour. Though the message was jammed, they managed to get it through to Admiral Jerram as the German party made for the shore.

During the previous night the convoy had passed 40 miles east of the Cocos Islands and was about 55 miles north of them, when at 7 a.m. HMA.S. *Melbourne* got the warning. The *Melbourne* could not leave the convoy because of a possible attack so she remained with it, together with the Japanese cruiser *Ibuki*, but detached H.M.A.S. *Sydney* one of the convoy escorts. Accordingly, with all dispatch away went the *Sydney* commanded by Captain Glossop, leaving the *Melbourne* and *Ibuki* to look after the convoy. In the meantime, the German landing party destroyed the telegraph instruments and the wireless installations, but before they could cut the cable leading to Perth, smoke on the horizon could be seen by the *Emden* and they were recalled to the Raider. The smoke came from the *Sydney*'s funnels as she raced to the scene at the utmost speed. So rapidly was she coming from the north-east, that Von Miller was compelled to put to sea in order to prepare for action, before his men on shore could return to the ship.

I have previously mentioned the displacement, speed and armament of the *Emden* and one may be sure Captain Von Muller now hoped that the British warship coming towards him might be one of the small light cruisers. In this he was deceived, for the *Sydney* displaced nearly 2,000 tons more than the *Emden*, possessed a superior speed, was built five years later and armed with eight 6-inch guns which fired shells about three times the weight of those fired from the guns of her opponent.

However, it was Von Muller's intention to fight and he headed his ship northward and as the two ships crossed in opposite directions, the *Sydney* turned northward on a parallel course to that of *Emden*. Soon after, at 9.40 a.m., the *Emden* opened fire at a range of 9,500 yards and the engagement began. The visibility was excellent in the clear morning sky and the shells from the enemy guns straddled the *Sydney* immediately. The *Sydney* replied, but her estimation of the range was in error and the 6- inch projectiles fell far over the target. According to the German report, a straddle was not obtained until the twelfth salvo when hits were registered on the *Emden*. The enemy's shells however did little damage to the *Sydney*. The advantage in regard to speed and manoeuvre, as well as gun range was definitely held by the *Sydney* and therefore Captain Glossop could choose and maintain his range and relative position as he pleased. About 10 minutes after the action began the *Emden* had been hit repeatedly, and altered course eastward. Her firing became less accurate and one of her funnels and the foremast were shot away. Moreover, her steering gear was put out of action and she could steer by her engines only.

The *Emden* was now in a bad way and as the fire from her guns slackened, the 100 pound lyddite shells from the British cruiser created havoc on board the German cruiser. Some of her guns were put out of action and their crews were swept away. No doubt the shortage of guns' crews was serious owing to the necessity for leaving the landing party on shore. But in spite of the devastating fire, *Emden* gamely continued the fight. The *Sydney* manoeuvred closer to a range of about 5,500 yards and fired a torpedo which missed, turned away and opened the range again. Parallel courses were thus resumed and the firing continued. The action had now lasted 40 minutes and both fire control positions in the *Emden* and her two remaining funnels were shot away. She had shot holes in galore, fires raged fiercely fore and aft and she became obscured in smoke. But she appeared again on an easterly course parallel to that of the *Sydney* till then turned away to starboard and doubled back sixteen points on a north-westerly course heading for the North Keeling Island. Captain Glossop quickly made a similar turn and continued his gun fire at about 7,000 yards range. The *Emden* still kept firing with the guns she had left though her fight now had become feeble. At 11.20 a.m. it became apparent that Captain Von Muller intended to beach his vessel on the Island. Captain Glossop then increased to full speed to cut her off, but it was too late and the *Emden* with her flag still flying ran on the southern shore of North Keeling Island. For 2 hours the *Emden* had thus put up a gallant fight against a superior force in every respect.

The Beginnings Of World War I

Captain Glossop then chased the *Buresk* which could be seen making off in a northerly direction. But when she was stopped, it was found that the Germans on board, had opened her inlet valves and damaged them so that the ship could not be saved. Thereupon the German crew were taken on board the *Sydney* and about 4 p.m. she returned to the *Emden* to find that the German flag was still flying in her. Captain Glossop ordered the *Emden* to surrender and no reply came. After repeating the signal, the *Sydney* opened fire on the wreck and it was not until the helpless ship had been reduced to a shambles that the *Emden* displayed white flags and a man was sent aloft to haul down her colours. It seemed a horrible and perhaps unnecessary procedure to again open fire in such circumstances, but the evening was closing and Captain Glossop had to leave the enemy's ship in time to reach the Cocos Island some 12 miles southward before dark in order to deal with the German landing party who had wrecked the Cable Station there. On the way however, the *Sydney* stopped to pick up men belonging to the *Emden* who had been blown into the water, and owing to the delay, nightfall came upon them and the German party escaped in darkness from Cocos in a small sailing vessel.

The *Sydney* then returned to the North Keeling Island and rescued the remaining survivors of the *Emden*. This was no easy task considering the terrible state of the ship and the large number of wounded men to be got on board the *Sydney*. Captain Von Miller was among those saved and he stated that the German dead numbered 7 officers and 108 men. The prisoners taken on board were 20 officers and 191 men, of whom 3 officers and 53 men were wounded. The damage to the *Sydney* was very slight, and the casualties among the men were few. She lost only 4 killed and 12 wounded.

On the morning of November 11th every available man was on board and the *Sydney* then followed the convoy to Colombo. In the crowded decks, little could be done for the prisoners, 4 of whom died of wounds. Luckily however, much relief came about midnight when the S.S. *Empress of Russia* met the *Sydney* and all the Germans, except the most dangerously wounded who could not be moved, were transferred to the Merchant vessel.

Sometime later I had the opportunity of discussing this action with Mr Salter the Gunner of the *Sydney*. He was the first to board the *Emden* after the action and found the officers and crew dazed amid a perfect shambles. For a small cruiser of less than 4,000 tons, it might well be conceded that the exploits of the *Emden* and her gallant captain and crew, were perhaps, the most successful of any other single warship throughout World War I. The economic losses caused by this vessel and the strategical importance of them were of considerable dimensions. The skill, boldness and resourcefulness of Captain Von Muller, who conducted his duty with true chivalry and humanity, brought for him the admiration of friend and foe alike.

CHAPTER XXXI

Ongoing Patrol Work at Gibraltar

--- ooOoo ---

Our patrol work in the T.B. Flotilla continued every night with little variation. Life on board in fine weather was rather pleasant and the work was comparatively easy, as compared to that when the wind and seas were more disturbing. Until my experience in T.B. 94, I had always regarded the waters of the Straits of Gibraltar as a haven of calm and restfulness. Perhaps this was due to serving in large ships when in this region, or that fine weather had prevailed on those occasions. However, in our tiny vessel we were soon to realise that furious gales with heavy seas were common in that vicinity. Though the Straits open to the stormy Atlantic to westward, I well remember these dirty easterly gales coming with tremendous force from the Mediterranean Sea. It was no mean task on these occasions to run up alongside the merchant vessels and to jump on to the sea gangway in the process of boarding them for examination. In the matter of recreation, the ships companies of the Torpedo Boats on night duty were perhaps better off than those engaged by day. True the time available to us for pastime and relaxation was very short, observing that it was usually about 10 a.m. before we had completed coaling and any refitting necessary, and at 5 p.m. or thereabouts, we departed to sweep the channel for mines outwards from Gibraltar and take up our positions on the patrol lines.

Within these day periods I usually managed a shave followed by ablutions in our tiny India rubber bath, and after dressing in the rig of the day I would stroll out into the main road and spend an hour or so in the Alemeda Gardens and take in the pungently refreshing aroma there under a sunny sky. Here one could read letters received from home, and meditate in peace and tranquillity. After a rough night at sea our little ship had been washed down fore and aft, so everything was damp and fuggy in the Wardroom below, in contrast to the delightfully refreshing ozone produced in this sunny spot.

After several months of unceasing patrol work, it was only to be expected that the stability of the Torpedo Boats making up the Flotilla would occasionally be seriously affected. The comparative high speed used in all weathers in these frail hulls soon exposed the weakness of construction in many boats, necessitating overhauls and repairs by the dockyard. With only a few vessels to carry on the ever-increasing work of the Flotilla we could ill afford to spare even one boat for a few days absence thus created. It was our main endeavour to keep our place in the running Flotilla at all costs. In this, Torpedo Boat No 94 was most fortunate in that our Chief Engine Room Artificer was a man of considerable experience in small vessels and no matter what trouble arose in the engine and boiler rooms, or any other compartment for that matter, he would never admit that it was beyond repair by ships staff; which really meant himself and a few of his trained stokers. Through the masterly way in which Ousely handled the vessel, particularly when going up alongside the numerous ships that we boarded, together with our Chiefie's (Cera's) incomparable industry and ability, it was the pride of us all in T.B. 94 that, not once were we absent from the patrols throughout the period in which I served in the Flotilla, due to mishap or other humanly avoidable reason.

Nevertheless, as the months passed the routine became distinctly monotonous, and personally, I hoped for exciting episodes which came all too sparsely. During the winter months the nights were cold on deck, but the duffle suit with hood, in which Ousely and I robed ourselves, kept us tolerably warm as the gales roared in dirty weather. As I have previously mentioned, Ousely desired that on ordinary look out patrols we should keep watch, and this arrangement was strictly adhered to when the exigences of the service required only one of us on deck. But sleep during the watch off was of a scrappy nature and we usually chose to remain on deck rather than lie down in one's bunk, especially in bad weather, when owing to certain causes, there was always a rattle going on over one's head. For instance: the rudder chains passed through the wardroom over the bunk in each side, while the steering engine was situated in an adjacent compartment to the head of my particular bunk. In bad weather the helm was seldom still and one can imagine the rattle of the chains above and the thump of the steering engine permitted no sleep whatever, and in consequence, it was far more comfortable to spend the time on deck.

During the early months of the war the great Italian and other liners belonging to neutral countries passing through the Straits afforded considerable interest that helped to pass away the weary hours. These fine ships exhibited their navigation lights and were lit up fore and aft as in peace time. Veritable towns they appeared to us coming up at a fast speed. It was quite simple therefore to lie in wait for them with our lights always out. As soon as they crossed our patrol line our method of approach was to run up alongside at full speed, then switch on our searchlight and blare through the megaphone an order for the ship to stop engines. This often brought to my mind the two characters of dignity and impudence as the bridge of the great ship towered above the top of our mast. Certainly, the merchant captain in the first instance regarded us as somewhat insolent and from his position of eminence he would usually stand with a superior type of megaphone in hand and bellow through it some indignant sounds of protest. Then the long rope ladder (or sea gangway) would be dropped over the ships' side, simultaneously with the audible clanging of the engine room telegraph for the engines of the great ship to stop and go astern. Then we knew that the captain had decided to comply to our will. Ousely would then place our little vessel alongside the ladder and in a jiffy, I would scamper up the ships side.

Upon reaching the top rung a deck Officer was usually there to receive and conduct one to the Navigating Bridge. If this occurred early in the night all the passengers usually lined up along the ships side as interested spectators. If the Captain happened to be of the angry and boisterous type, I approached him with caution, but curiously enough this kind of person had invariably cooled down by the time one reached him and upon acquaintance became 'Mine Perfect Host'. In these circumstances, I was always anxious to clear the ships as soon as possible. So, with the usual questions having been satisfactorily answered and the ships papers found in order, I would take leave and return to T.B. 94. The searchlight was then switched off and the captain allowed to proceed.

As we expected, the captains of these passenger liners complained to their shipping companies as to this manner of holding up their ships in the Straits of Gibraltar and in due course representations were made to the British Foreign Office. The Italian Government, a signatory to the Triple Alliance but still neutral, were particularly concerned in this affair just at the time when the British Foreign Secretary, Sir Edward Grey, was doing all he could to induce Italy to join us in the war against the other two members of the Alliance - Germany and Austria. Thus, in the early stages of the war cross currents were manifest though we of the Navy continued our work until a better arrangement could be made between the British Admiralty and the Foreign Office. I have often thought that our method of action was rather crude and that a less arbitrary and more amicable procedure might have been resorted to.

In the matter of passengers, it was well known by us that many German and Austrian nationals were included in Italian ships, homeward bound from America, and upon their arrival at an Italian port they had little difficulty in joining the enemy military or naval forces as required. This matter became acute as time went on and an agreement was arrived at by the Authorities concerned that so long as the number of enemy nationals did not exceed twelve and that Italian ships were cleared in respect to cargoes, they were to be allowed to proceed to Italian ports without interference on our part. Though we respected this order implicitly everyone knew that it constituted a large hole in our net for precisely twelve enemy nationals figured on the passenger lists thereafter who were free to join the fighting services of the enemy.

CHAPTER XXXII

Battles of the South American Station

--- ooOoo ---

Early in November 1914 news came to us of the Naval Battle of Coronel off the coast of central Chile. Fought on the 1st of that month, it resulted in the defeat of the British South American Squadron under the command of Rear Admiral Sir Christopher Craddock by the German China Squadron commanded by Admiral Von Spee.

Shortly after Japan had declared war on the side of the Allies, and a considerable time before the Japanese had captured Tsingtao a town of North East China in the German territory of Kiao-Chau (November 7th 1914), Admiral von Spee had apparently considered that the China Station would not be a healthy one for him to remain on. In any case, he decided to make for South American waters where, incidentally, our Naval Force was comparatively weak. Von Spee's Squadron then consisted of his flag ship, the armoured cruiser *Sharnhorst* and her sister ship the *Gneisenau*, also the light cruisers *Dresden*, Leipzig and *Nuremberg*. Both *Sharnhorst* and *Gneisenau* were armed each with six 8-inch guns while the light cruisers mounted ten 4.1-inch guns.

The British Squadron on the station at the time was Admiral Craddock's flagship the armoured cruiser *Good Hope*, a 14,000 ton vessel of the Drake Class, the *Monmouth*, a 9,800 ton armoured cruiser of the County Class, and the *Glasgow* a protected cruiser 4,820 tons. In addition, the 14,900 ton battleship *Canopus* armed with 12-inch guns, and the armed merchant cruiser *Otranto* was also attached to Craddocks' command.

On the 1st November 1914, Admiral Craddock's force was cruising off the Coronel seaport in the South East Pacific when he met the German squadron commanded by Admiral Von Spee. A battle ensued in which the *Good Hope* was sunk in less than an hour and the *Monmouth* was put out of action and sunk by the *Nuremberg* sometime later. But the *Glasgow*, having a speed of 25 knots, escaped. Not a soul from our two ships was saved due to the heavy seas; 1,500 men were lost, while the German ships received little damage and less than half a dozen of their men were wounded.

The news of the disaster came as a shock, but on analysis of all the circumstances the defeat was more easily understood. In the first place, the German Squadron was manned by long service men with an excellent gunnery shooting record on the China Station. Secondly, the *Sharnhorst* and *Gneisenau* were both able to stand up to the heavy weather and use their 8-inch guns throughout the engagement as they were mounted on the upper deck. Thirdly, Von Spee's squadron possessed a speed of about 20 knots and superior to that of Cradocks'. The enemy could therefore choose the range and the tactical position during the fight. There was almost a gale blowing at the time and in consequence, most of the 6-inch guns of the *Good Hope* and *Monmouth* (which were mounted in casemates on either side of the messdecks) could not be run out to their fighting positions or used at all. It is true that the *Good Hope* was armed with a 9.2-inch gun mounted at each end of the upper deck, but it must be remembered that against the highly trained guns crews of the German armoured cruisers, the British guns were manned, for the most part, with men from the Naval Reserve whose gunnery efficiency was doubtless very poor. Unfortunately, the only British ship which could have stood up to the German cruisers, the *Canopus,* with two 12-inch guns in turrets at each end of the upper deck, was not present during the action. This battleship was coming up behind Admiral Craddock at a maximum speed of no more than 15 knots, some 300 miles astern.

In all these circumstances, which it must be assumed were known to the British Admiral at the time, it is most regrettable that Admiral Craddock failed to take the advantage of the support that the *Canopus* could have given him by leading Von Spee's Squadron back to the battleship before the British Squadron became seriously involved in the fight. In extenuation, it was advanced at the time in certain quarters, that Sir Christopher had applied the Nelson touch in this engagement. We may be sure however, that the great victor of the Battles of the Nile and Trafalgar, would not have been caught in this manner. Happily, however, British prestige suffered but a brief spell as a result of this misfortune thanks to the master mind of Lord Fisher, the First Sea Lord of the Admiralty.

Now it so happened that Admiral Von Spee's victorious squadron was making for the British Crown Colony at the Falkland Islands in the South Atlantic at the time, for the purpose of capturing and converting it into a German Naval Base.

Without delay, the battle cruiser *Invincible*, flying the flag of Rear Admiral Sir Doveton Sturdee, and the *Inflexible* were dispatched with the utmost speed from Home Waters to the South American Station, arriving at the Falkland Islands on December 7th 1914. Early the next morning while our battle cruisers were coaling, the *Gneisenau* and *Nuremberg* sighted the tripod masts of our battle cruisers and immediately turned and steamed back to their main squadron, which had been coming up behind them. When Admiral Sturdee sighted the *Gneisenau* and her consort, he gave the order to cease coaling at once and got his squadron under weigh and pursued the enemy.

Our two battle cruisers had been reinforced and Sturdee's Squadron now included the light cruisers *Glasgow* and *Bristol* and the Armoured Cruisers *Carnarvon*, *Cornwall* and *Kent* all of about 10,000 tons, well-armed and possessing a speed of about 22 knots. Sturdee's flag ship and the *Inflexible* were splendid ships of 17,250 tons, with 25 knot speed and each were armed with eight 12-inch guns mounted in turrets. A formidable squadron indeed, and the battle which followed resulted in the most complete British Naval victory of World War I.

Admiral Sturdee knew that his squadron was overwhelmingly superior to that of Von Spee's, both in speed and in gun fire. He therefore chased the enemy with complacency and entirely without panic or hurry. Indeed, before the action commenced, he ordered the ships' companies to dinner and informed them that the fight would begin afterwards!

At 12.35 p.m. the *Invincible* opened fire at 17,000 yards range and the *Inflexible* commenced firing about 20 minutes later, while both squadrons were steering on a south-easterly course. The choice of range, of course, rested with Sturdee and a long-ranged action continued without a reply from the enemy's guns until 1.30 p.m. when the opposing ships had closed to about 10,000 yards. The enemy's salvoes straddled our ships after which Sturdee opened the range to between 13,000 and 15,000 yards. During the firing Von Spee altered course on several occasions only to be followed by the British ships who relentlessly pursued him the whole time, but outside the effective range of the enemy's guns. At 4.17 p.m. the *Sharnhorst* was sunk, but the *Gneisenau* continued to fire her guns until she was sunk at about 6.15 p.m. The *Nuremberg* was chased and sunk by the *Kent* at 7.30 p.m. and the *Leipzig* was destroyed by the *Cornwall* and *Glasgow* at about 9 p.m., but the German Cruiser *Dresden* escaped. Admiral Von Spee perished with about 1,800 officers and men of his Squadron including two of the Admiral's sons who were serving with him. About 200 men belonging to the German ships were saved. The British casualties numbered about 30 only while the damage to our ships was negligible.

So, Admiral Craddock's defeat at the Battle of Coronal was avenged. Both these actions proved that with good visibility, the Squadrons possessing superior gun power and speed might be expected to destroy an opponent without serious damage to the victor. This conclusion however, should not be regarded as infallible. In the changes and chances of naval combat lucky hits in the vitals of ships, especially in the early stages of a fight, might well change the whole situation as we were to learn from naval actions yet to be fought.

Soon after this battle, the *Inflexible* came to Gibraltar and during her short refit, many of us serving in the T.B. flotilla visited the ship and got first hand news of the famous fight. Several personal friends of mine took part in the engagement, and, among them, was the Chief Gunner of the *Invincible* whose name was George Hunt. To his intimate friends he was usually known as "Froggie" Hunt for what reason I know not. During a most interesting talk with Froggie, he related to me an extraordinary incident which occurred while the fight was going on. A full rigged merchant ship was in the vicinity during the afternoon and her crew were close spectators of the battle for a considerable time. Hunt said:

"There she was with her white sails set - presenting a lovely peaceful and beautiful sight. She crossed the track of the battle cruisers about 3 p.m., when only a few cables distant, and doubtless the merchant sailors could clearly see the huge splashes caused by the fall of shots as the battle raged."

I have since often wished that I could have been on board that fine ship sailing the seas upon her lawful occasion, while our squadron of warships were demonstrating so realistically the Might, Majesty, Dominion and Power of the British Naval Arm.

German raid on the English coast, original drawing by Author

Part 7

Naval Action In Home Waters

CHAPTER XXXIII

The Dover Patrol and the North Sea Strategy

--- ooOoo ---

With the destruction of Admiral von Spee's squadron the enemy navy was weakened towards the close of 1914. But there still remained on the wide oceans however, several German warships that required watching closely. For instance, the light cruiser *Dresden* which luckily escaped from the hands of Admiral Sturdee; also the light cruisers *Karlshrue* and the *Konigsbergh* which had battered and disabled HMS *Pegasus* in Penang harbour in addition to destroying sixteen allied merchant ships with their cargoes of great value. Then there were some German armed liners in American and other neutral ports and the armed merchant cruisers *Prince Eitel Fredrich* and the *Kronprinz Wilhelm*, still out on the oceans. To cope with this threat, it was necessary to maintain a considerable force of British warships in the Atlantic and the South Pacific Oceans.

The position in our home waters however, was very different. Here we had so-called 'Command of the Sea', in that Britain was able to move her Fleet at will, transport her troops with safety and maintain her overseas trade. But our shipping losses in the approaches to the home ports from enemy submarine attacks were considerable. Incidentally, the endurance, speed and destructive power of the U boats were steadily increasing and this, together with the enemy's mines laid on our coasts, enabled their submarines to spread their activities further afield. This menace to Britain's vital needs from overseas had to be countered by the quickest possible means, for it was now realised that unless some drastic and unprecedented measures were taken, the country's life blood would be throttled, despite the existence of our greatest Navy in the world.

Here was a task mainly for small craft in great numbers, manned by men of the sea who could stand up to all weathers while waging warfare against this new menace. Very fortunately for our Empire, Britain possessed the exact material and men required. Providentially, there existed at the time those sturdy little vessels of the fishing fleets, already manned by the hardiest seamen in the world. From Grimsby, Yarmouth, Stornaway and elsewhere, some hundreds of Trawlers and Drifters were accordingly commandeered for Naval Service, armed with guns and fitted out with mine sweeping equipment. Their men were given short courses of training in the use of their guns, minesweeps, and explosive charges in order to deal with the new peril. Flotillas of these submarine defence vessels were placed under the Command of the C-in-C Grand Fleet and other Senior Officers around the British Isles.

I have often thought since of the wonderful service rendered by these deep-sea fishermen. Their vessels were never intended for war service though they were admirably designed to stand rough usage and for riding the seas in foul or fine weather. Theirs's was indeed a hard task and happily they came in the nick of time when our destroyers and torpedo boats were being seriously overworked in the defence of our traffic lines by day and night. It is my firm belief that the Royal Navy, as it was then constituted, could not have overcome the German menace to our merchant shipping, as soon as we did, if at all, without the aid of these great fishers of the sea. The manifold duties performed by them during the War can hardly be described in these memoirs, but the few which I mention hereunder will suffice for the reader to comprehend the importance of them:

- General Patrol and protection of local traffic routes.
- Laying out and operating drift nets, and moored mine nets to prevent enemy mine laying in our navigable waters.
- Sweeping for mines and the destruction of enemy minefields when found.
- Defence and maintenance of permanent net defences against enemy torpedoes.
- Local convoy of merchant shipping.
- Life Saving Service including the rescue of crews of merchant ships torpedoed or mined.

Drift nets consisted of steel wire nets having ten to twelve feet mesh; they were 100 yards wide and varying in depth between 30 and 100 feet, to suit the depth of water in which they were to be used. The nets were floated by hollow glass balls.

These operations would go on continuously through the days and nights in the hope of arresting enemy submarines and when one was caught and dragged the net through the water its position would be continuously indicated by a buoy or some other device attached to the net suitable for day or night operations, when a Destroyer or other vessel available would be attracted by it and rush to the kill. An improvement on this method of destroying the catch was introduced later by securing mines to the net which automatically exploded when contact was made with the hull of the submarine with almost certain destruction soon after its envelopment in the net. There were of course, occasional false alarms before the mines were introduced and when the nets were fouled by a large fish or some obstruction other than a submarine. This would invariably bring all the Destroyers in the vicinity searching for the mark buoy or float which would indicate the position of a hoped-for submarine in order to destroy it. But these spasms of excitement, though abortive really, put everyone on their toes and provided at least a good form of submarine drill for the participants!

Throughout the ages, centuries before the Christian era to this day, wars have called for the services of the finest manhood in every country. For this purpose, sporting games of a definitely unproductive and wasteful nature, were fostered and pursued mainly in the production of athletes ready for battle when called upon. However, in retrospect of this aspect of World War I, an entirely new feature comes to view. For here were those incomparable toilers of the deep sea, taken directly from their normal and extremely economic vocations, in which they had spent their entire youth and manhood in the useful production of food for their fellowmen. These men were strong, physically fit and ready to serve their country strenuously in war with a few weeks training. One therefore wonders why the countless millions of men in the past ages could not have received their training for athletics and war concurrently, with some such useful employment as our British fishermen whose health and fitness in mind and body were equal to their forbears and perhaps built up on a sounder basis than that obtained from conventional sport!

At the close of the first year of the War, patrol areas were established all around the British Isles and no less than twenty ports were used as bases for these areas. They extended from Dover to the Shetland Islands past the east coast of Great Britain, thence south-westward to the Hebrides and Lough Swilly, and down the west coast of Ireland to Berehaven, thence up the English Channel to Dover past Plymouth and Portsmouth. In consideration of these great distances, one has some idea of the enormous number of Destroyer, Torpedo Boats, Trawlers, Drifters and other small vessels that were engaged on this defensive Patrol Service. Meanwhile, our Grand Fleet was supreme in our home waters, though it was "contained" continuously by the German High Sea Fleet, which was predominant in the Baltic Sea. Admiral Von Ingenohl commanding this great Fleet, did not venture beyond German waters but permitted a sortie into the North Sea occasionally by his Battle Cruiser Squadron, under the command of Admiral Von Hipper.

For many years the veteran Admiral Von Tirpitz had been the head of the Prussian Navy, and ever since 1892, when he was appointed Chief of Staff to the Naval High Command, he had been studying and developing the strategic and tactical questions relating to the employment of the German Fleet. He was a powerful personality when the war broke out, well versed in naval history and a strict disciplinarian. It was mainly due to Von Tirpitz that, although the German Navy was comparatively young in 1914, it entered the war with a Dreadnought fleet, admirably constructed, well-armed and manned by thoroughly trained seamen. It must be remembered that the introduction of the Dreadnought battleship in 1905 produced a distinct bearing on the rapid development of the German Fleet. Only 9 years before the war, our huge fleet of pre-dreadnoughts was thereby rendered all but obsolete and in consequence the Germans were given a completely fresh start in the building of ships that really mattered. Also their light cruisers and destroyers were being handled in an amazingly skilful manner.

In these circumstances there was no need for the Grand Fleet to attack, so long as the High Sea Fleet remained in the Heligoland Bight or other home waters. Admiral Jellicoe therefore showed a remarkably clear vision of the situation when he maintained his fleet at Scapa Flow and at Scottish ports, rather than at the southern naval bases, for at the northern harbours he was able to thoroughly train his fleet in every detail, while holding it in readiness to attack whenever necessary.

German Naval Officers, with whom I later discussed this matter, admitted that Jellicoe had displayed a surprisingly strategic insight. The German Naval Authorities knew that their High Sea Fleet was inferior in numbers and strength to ours and recognized that the Grand Fleet controlled the traffic in the North Sea and except for a few sporadic raids upon our Eastern coast, Britain was immune from invasion. While the Germans adopted the role of defence with readiness to attack, we were clearing the wide oceans of enemy cruisers and transporting our troops wherever they were required on the Continent or to occupy the German Colonies abroad.

It must not be supposed however that the Grand Fleet was idle in the North Sea areas while the enemy fleet was sheltering snugly behind their defences waiting at their chosen moment to come forth and strike. No one knew better than Jellicoe that Von Tirpitz and his higher commands were perfectly free to make their plans and choose their day to send the High Sea Fleet out for a trial of strength with his Battle Fleet, with the certainty that every German battleship would be fully equipped with coal, clean bottoms, trained crews and attended by their destroyers, submarines and even airships to complete the organization to its greatest efficiency for attack. Meanwhile the enemy would have laid his minefields as required for his particular plan of action. Admiral Jellicoe in contrast, though admittedly commanding a superior force, had to be quite ready every day, month in and out, to combat the High Sea Fleet of the enemy at his chosen date, and at the same time keep a large number of his vessels, especially the ubiquitous destroyers, continuously upon other essential work or otherwise undergoing refits and repairs in the dockyards in order to combat the enemy's war of attrition. In consequence, Jellicoe could be caught with his main fleet actually inferior to that of the German Fleet as a whole, when the enemy issued forth to give battle.

So far as the German surface ships were concerned, they were well bottled up in the southern exit from the North Sea to the English Channel by the establishment of the highly important Dover Command. Here efficient Patrols were carried on by Destroyers, Trawlers and Drifters and an effective minefield and net defences. In this measure the passage of German Submarines through the Straits of Dover was also prevented. The functions of the Dover Patrol were manifold and of vital importance to the successful conduct of the War. By it, the transport of our troops with their equipment and stores across the Channel was safeguarded and thousands of Merchant ships were given refuge and protection as they passed the Straits of Dover from the English Channel to the London Docks and East Coast ports. This providing food and other essential supplies to the population of London and other great centres for distribution.

The work of this Patrol increased immeasurably after the enemy had occupied the Belgian coast and established bases for destroyers and U Boats at Zeebrugge and Ostend. Both these bases were less than 70 miles from Dover, and the enemy forces there, constituted a direct threat of attack upon our shipping concentrated in the Downs, the anchorage which had been selected for the examination of all ships as they passed up or down the English Channel. The large number of vessels in their scattered positions on the patrol lines were continually open to attack.

The Northern exit from the North Sea was, of course, an entirely different and more difficult proposition to close off enemy traffic than the Dover Straits. The passage between Scotland and Norway is no less than 250 miles of deep water with an average depth of 100 fathoms. With our meagre patrols that could be afforded in these early months of the war, German submarines had little or no difficulty in spotting our surface ships when passing outwards or homewards and therefore eluding them with ease. Neither was it possible to prevent German surface ships from passing out into the Atlantic Ocean during low visibility caused by fog or darkness. However, the British Patrols in this region were doing a fine job especially in regard to capture and seizure of contraband cargoes of neutral ships for enemy destination.

CHAPTER XXXIV

German Raids on the East Coast of England

--- ooOoo ---

One of the most experienced and capable German Admirals of the High Sea Fleet was Franz Von Hipper. He commanded the enemy Battle Cruiser Force, under the C-in-C Admiral Von Pohl, a similar command to that held by Vice Admiral Beatty in the Grand Fleet under Admiral Jellicoe.

According to information which came to us later, Von Hipper was bitterly disappointed with the German naval strategy of attrition adopted by the German High Sea Fleet and felt that he should be given the opportunity to take a more aggressive part with his fine squadron in the North Sea. Von Hipper's battle cruiser force consisted of his flag ship the *Seydlitz*, with the *Moltke*, *Von-der Tann* and *Blucher*, together with attendant light cruisers and destroyers. On November 2nd 1914, with this force he made his first dash into English waters. At 6 a.m. on the 3rd he entered Yarmouth Roads and then sighted our torpedo gunboat *Halcyon*. The four German battle cruisers opened fire but the *Halcyon* managed to escape. The bombardment of Yarmouth then took place and afterwards Von Hipper's force made for home and was safely anchored in the Jade the same night. This event, naturally caused a stir at Home. Although Jellicoe had arranged sweeps at irregular intervals across the North Sea in the endeavour to intercept possible enemy raids, unfortunately Von Hipper's force was not brought to action.

Heartened by his success Von Hipper left the Jade on December 15th for a raid on the coast of Yorkshire and Durham. This time his Battle Cruiser Squadron was strengthened by the addition of the *Derfflyer* a new ship just completed. Four light cruisers and a destroyer flotilla were also included in his force. On this occasion, the German Battle Fleet came as far as the eastern fringe of the Dogger Bank (about 100 miles from the English coast) in support of Von Hipper's Squadron, but early in the morning of the 16th his vanguard came in contact with our destroyers. Von Ingenohl turned the supporting Battle Fleet about to avoid an engagement with our Battle Squadron. Admiral Jellicoe was well aware of the movements of the enemy Fleet and had made the necessary positions of the Grand Fleet against this enemy advance, and to bring them to action if possible. When contact was made, fire was opened between Admiral Beatty's destroyers and those of the enemy and the *Lynx* and *Ambuscade* were put out of action and returned to port.

It was most probable that had the High Sea Fleet held on its course, the first battle fleet action of the war would have been fought, for our 2nd Battle Squadron of six Dreadnoughts, commanded by Vice Admiral Sir George Warrender, had come down from Scapa Flow and had reached a rendezvous east of the Dogger Bank that morning, ready to join Beatty's Battle Cruiser's force. But on this morning of the 16th December, only a portion of Jellicoe's battleship strength would have met the German battleships in superior numbers and thus Von Ingenohl lost a golden opportunity when he turned back.

Meanwhile, Hipper's Battle Cruiser Squadron had proceeded towards their objective, through a gap between two large minefields laid by the Germans covering the approaches to the Tyne and

Humber to the north and south of Whitby. A third enemy minefield was laid off the East Coast of England which extended from Lowestoft to Harwich. The *Von-der-Tann* and *Derfflinger* with the light cruiser *Kolberg* reached a position off Scarborough about 8.30 a.m. on the 16th. While the battle cruisers bombarded the town, the *Kolberg* laid mines in that vicinity. Afterwards the *Von-der-Tann* and *Derfflinger* appeared off Whitby and fired about fifty rounds at the Signal Station in the town. Scarborough and Whitby were undefended towns and the shelling of them was contrary to the terms of the Hague Convention.

Almost simultaneously Von Hipper in the *Seydlitz* led the *Moltke* and *Blucher* north, sighted Hartlepool and about 8.20 a.m. bombarded this seaport of Durham causing much destruction to the docks and ship building yards. But four of our destroyers went out to attack the enemy while our shore batteries returned their fire and before the bombardment was over, our guns had scored four hits on the *Blucher* three hits on the *Seydlitz* and one on the *Moltke*. At 8.55 a.m. the Admiralty informed Admirals Warrender and Beatty of the bombardment and by 11.30 a.m. the two groups of enemy ships had now reformed as one Squadron under Von Hipper who steamed on a homeward course. The German Admiral must now have realised that the German main fleet had returned home and he was now left in a critical position with an overwhelming British Force barring his way back to the Jade.

Both Warrender and Beatty had disposed their Squadrons in order to intercept Hipper's force to the best of their ability, and consistent with their instructions received from Jellicoe. Their aim was to intercept Von Hipper's battle cruisers as they returned through the gap between the mine fields and to bring them to action. About 12.30 p.m. contact was made between Beatty's light forces and Hipper's scouting cruisers and destroyers. Later Warrender had himself sighted them when they were about 70 miles east of the German Battle Cruisers. Still, as luck would have it, aided by poor visibility at times, Hipper's large ships managed to elude action and got clear away. Hipper brought this about by turning north as soon as he cleared the mine gap avoiding all of our battle ships, battle cruisers and four armoured cruisers of the Devonshire class barring his way only 30 miles eastward. This was about 12.45 p.m. and standing on his northward course until 2.30 p.m.; Hipper then turned eastward on his homeward course on the northern fringe of the Dogger Bank.

During that afternoon two British trawlers sighted them when Warrender's battleships were only 20 miles further south steering towards their wake while Beatty's battle cruisers were about twice that distance from the enemy. The search continued until 3.30 p.m. when Warrender evidently believing that the enemy's battle cruisers had got away and signalled to Beatty to discontinue the search.

Von Hipper maintained his homeward course and ran into the Jade at 7.30 a.m. on December 17th. He was extremely fortunate when his retreat began to have obtained information from his light cruisers, as early as 9.15 a.m., that our heavy ships were waiting for him eastward of the mine gap. This was the reason for his turn North at 12.45 p.m. which enabled him to make his escape by the only means open to him. Being an extremely religious man Von Hipper noted in his diary: "Here again God helped me".

The military damage caused by the enemy bombardment was slight though the civilian casualties in the towns was considerable. They included 86 killed and 424 wounded while over 300 dwelling houses and other buildings were damaged or destroyed. The effect of these bombardments, following so closely upon the shelling of Yarmouth, naturally caused indignation in England and there was much criticism of Admiral Jellicoe for the failure of the Grand Fleet to prevent these so called "tip and run" sorties.

These critical remarks were pronounced just at a time when the C-in-C of the Grand Fleet was experiencing most seriously anxious moments, for on December 27th 1914, two of his Super-Dreadnought Battleships collided while in the Pentland Firth – it was on a very dark night in a heavy sea that the *Conqueror* rammed the *Monarch*, her next ahead, as they were entering Scapa Flow. Much damage was done to the both ships and the 2nd Battle Squadron, which had also lost *Audacious*, was reduced from eight to five ships. This serious loss was aggravated further by the sinking of still another battleship four days later (December 31st 1914) when the pre-dreadnought *Formidable* commanded by Captain A.N. Loxley was torpedoed and sunk.

Many of us who knew Captain Loxley, a beloved Gunnery Officer with whom I served in HMS *Excellent*, deplored his loss to the Navy when he went down in his ship with 34 Officers and 512 men out of a gallant ships company of 780 all told. The 5th Battle Squadron of which the *Formidable* was a unit had left Sheerness for Portland under Admiral Sir Lewis Bayley to carry out battle practice firings, and after passing through the Dover Straits as far as Folkstone, the destroyer screen attending the Battle Squadron was sent back to rejoin its flotilla at Harwich, leaving only two light cruisers, the *Diamond* and *Topaz* in company. Early on the morning of the 30th December the 5th Battle Squadron had arrived safely off Portland where the Admiral exercised Squadron manoeuvres off the Bill, followed by a cruise up and down the English Channel until the early hours of the 31st. Then at 2.20 a.m. the *Formidable* was struck by a torpedo fired by the German Submarine U 24 which had followed the Squadron unseen for many hours waiting an opportunity to make its attack. The crippled ship turned out of the line and was again torpedoed and later at 4.45 a.m. she sank.

Cruising in such a manner without any adequate screen of destroyers to ward off enemy submarine attack was a risky operation. After a subsequent Enquiry held by the Admiralty, Admiral Bayley was superseded in his Command by Vice Admiral, the Hon. Sir Alexander Bethell. Later however, Admiral Bayley was appointed to Command at Queenstown on the coast of Ireland.

Towards the close of 1914, a considerable number of merchant ships were armed with heavy guns up to 6-inch calibre, and fitted with a modified system of fire control. These fine vessels were taken from the Passenger Services and after fitting out were known as "Armoured Merchant Cruisers". Several of them came into Gibraltar on occasions and on my visits to their gunnery Officers, I was glad to be of some assistance to them in making suggestions for the improvement of their fire control and other matters relating to their armament equipment. Unfortunately, these great ships with tremendous freeboards offered fine targets for enemy ships; but on the other hand, their sea keeping qualities were admirably suited for patrolling the oceans for long periods in all weathers without refuelling.

Admiral Jellicoe must have felt relieved at the time of his serious losses of battleships when a large number of Armoured Merchant Cruisers were commissioned as the 10th Cruiser Squadron. Under the command of Rear Admiral Dudley R.S. De Chair, who flew his flag in the *Alsation*, this force of about twenty ships was organized into four divisions, each assigned to guard the egress and ingress to the North Sea from the Atlantic, from a position North of the Faroe Islands to the Shetlands, thence to Cape Wrath and the Hebrides. The work of this patrol was most effective from the beginning for no less than twenty ships were intercepted by them in the first week of January 1915, and sent into port with crews for examination.

Chapter XXXV

The Battle of Dogger Bank

--- ooOoo ---

In view of the success that the German Battle Cruisers had in their bombardment on the East Coast of England, there was ample reason to believe that the enemy would attempt further raids on our territory. Further the German Naval Authority hoped that one day some portion of Jellicoe's Battle Fleet, sent out to cover such possible raids, would be exposed to their superior fleet, or even to the guns of Heligoland, and so materially weaken our naval strength and reduce our number of Dreadnoughts to equality with their own.

In this connection Admiral Von Tirpitz firmly believed that German Naval personnel were equal to, and their fighting ships in many ways were superior to the British. Moreover, the enemy was well aware of our recent losses which left Jellicoe with a fighting strength at the time of 18 Dreadnoughts against 17 Dreadnoughts belonging to the enemy. We were, of course, superior in pre-dreadnought battleship power and several of our Dreadnoughts were in dockyard hands. Also, the *Invincible* was at Gibraltar, and the *Inflexible* in the Mediterranean, leaving Beatty with five Battle Cruisers against Hipper's four. So, we see that at the time, the power of the Grand Fleet ships of the line as compared to that of the Germans was not overwhelming. In support of this fact, it was Jellicoe's view at the end of the war, that the German Fleet had its best chance of success in the first months of the war, and that after April 1915 their prospects steadily decreased.

It was not surprising therefore when reports reached the Grand Fleet that unusual activity was going on in the German Naval Bases, and that on January 23rd, their Battle Cruisers had left the Jade once again. Rear Admiral Von Hipper sailed at 5.15 p.m. on that day with a force of 27 vessels including the *Seydlitz Moltke*, *Derfflinger* and *Blucher*, the light cruisers *Grandeur*, *Rostock*, *Stralsund* and *Kolburg*, and nineteen destroyers in two flotillas. The German Battle Cruiser *Von-der-Tann* was absent in dock. The Commander-in-Chief of High Seas Fleet, Von Ingenohe, had previously approved of a plan to attack the British forces whose presence had been repeatedly reported by his scouting group of light cruisers and destroyers.

Admiral Jellicoe became aware of the German ship movements and planned a countermove accordingly, and at 7.15 a.m. the next day (24th January) our light cruiser *Aurora*, belonging to Commodore Tyrwhitt's force based on Harwich, came into contact with the enemy. This was the *Kolburg* in a position just North of the Dogger Bank; the two ships opened gun-fire and the *Aurora* scored hits above and below the waterline of her opponent and she withdrew eastward. This was reported to Admiral Beatty and soon afterwards, the German Battle Cruisers and Light Cruisers were sighted by our light cruiser *Southampton* (Goodenough). Then Beatty in the *Lion* leading the other battle cruisers *Tiger*, *Princess Royal*, *New Zealand* and *Indomitable* sighted the enemy ships himself at 7.50 a.m. Hipper now decided to return towards the Heligoland Bight and turned his ship eastward while Beatty gave chase with the enemy about 14 miles distant.

Naval Action In Home Waters

By 8.30 a.m. our battle cruisers had worked up to a speed of 26 knots and were gaining fast in the race. At 8.45 a.m. Jellicoe received a report on Beatty's pursuit. Jellicoe and was 150 miles north-north-west of Beatty, with three Dreadnought Battle Squadrons with cruisers and destroyers with him. He ordered the 3rd Battle Squadron to proceed eastward to bar the enemy's escape, while he steered a south-easterly course in the hope of intercepting the enemy if they came northward. Beatty, in the *Lion* with *Tiger* and *Princess Royal*, all armed with eight 13.5-inch guns, increased speed to about 29 knots, though the older Battle Cruisers *Indomitable* and *New Zealand* could not keep up. When the *Lion* reached 20,000 yards of Hipper's rear ship (the *Blucher*), she opened fire on her, whilst still closing the range. Then the *Tiger* and *Princess Royal* opened fire as they drew within the range and by 9.15 a.m. our ships had obtained hits on the *Blucher* and the enemy returned the fire. About 9.30 a.m. the *Lion* was hit on the waterline and the enemy's shell penetrated her coal bunkers, but the damage was soon repaired. Soon afterwards the *New Zealand* came up and with her 12-inch guns, engaged the *Blucher*. The *Lion* then engaged the enemy flagship, the *Seydlitz*, and Beatty signalled his four ships to take on their respective opposite numbers in Hipper's line. The *Indomitable* was not yet within gun range at 9.35 a.m., more than 17,000 yards away.

At 9.40 a.m. the *Seydlitz* was struck aft by a 13.5-inch shell from the *Lion*. The projectile penetrated the armour in the aft turret and the explosion ignited a charge in a waiting position for loading into the gun. Flames shot up into the gun house and down into the ammunition chamber and passed through to the ammunition stowage in the next turret. The gas thus created compelled the abandonment of the aft engine room while the magazines affected were flooded to save the ship. Thus, the four aft 11-inch guns of the *Seydlitz* were put out of action for the remainder of the engagement, and almost the entire guns crews of both turrets perished in the flames.

When the *New Zealand* had joined in the fight, after Beatty's signal for each ship to engage their opposite number in the enemy's line, there was some confusion with the order, which unfortunately left the *Moltke* (second ship of Hippers line) quite free from British fire. This was brought about by a mistake on the part of the *Tiger* who, believing that the *Indomitable* was firing at the *Blucher*, and that the *New Zealand* was engaged with the *Defflinger* and the *Princess Royal* was firing at the *Moltke*, continued his fire on the *Seydlitz* with the *Lion*. This would have been perfectly correct, if the *Indomitable* had caught up and was firing at the *Blucher*. Incidentally, in accordance with an old tactical order dating back to sailing ships of the line, it was far more important to put the vanguard of the line out of action when sailing in a wind, and so bring about confusion in the enemy line. Since quite properly, the *Princess Royal* had shifted her fire from *Moltke* to *Defflinger* in obedience to the signal, this error of leaving the *Moltke*, armed with her ten long ranged 11-inch guns, quite unmolested by the fire from our ships was a matter of far graver concern than the above tactical instructions.

About 9.50 a.m. a heavy shell struck the roof of the *Lion*'s foremost turret and disabled one of the two guns and 10 minutes later she was hit again by a shell from the *Seydlitz* which penetrated the *Lion* armour. Sea water damaged the switchboard, also disabled two dynamos and put the aft fire control system out of order. At 10.18 a.m. the range between the opposing forces was still more than 17,000 yards and about this time the *Lion* was hit again by two more shells. One projectile struck the armour below the waterline and drove several plates through the wooden backing, causing a flood in the foremost coal bunker on the port side. The other shell pierced the armour on the waterline forward and exploded in the torpedo body room, and in a few minutes all the adjacent compartments were flooded up to the main deck. The enemy's fire was devastating, but only the *Lion* and *Tiger* had been hit. In fact, the other British ships were not hit at all throughout the engagement! By 10.30 a.m. all the enemy ships showed clear signs of heavy punishment and it seemed then that victory was assured providing our ships could maintain their speed which had now been reduced to about 24 knots to enable the Squadron to keep up.

An enemy's smoke screen made by his destroyers now reduced visibility and under it their formation was changed from line ahead to line abreast, to which Beatty responded by a similar movement. Fire however, was hampered by the smoke. Then the *Blucher* was straddled by a salvo which set her on fire amidships and disabled her engines and she gradually fell astern. Von Hipper tried to cover the crippled ship by ordering his destroyers to the attack, while he turned his Squadron southward, but having failed in this, he recalled his destroyers, and with his flagship full of water, aft and two turrets out of action, he abandoned the *Blucher* about 11.10 a.m. and steamed a south-east course for home.

Meanwhile the enemy's firing was very accurate and the *Lion* was hit once more, her armour was pierced in the foremost turret and more coal bunkers were flooded. It was evident that the enemy had concentrated their fire on the British flagship and were determined to put her out of action at all costs. And in this Von Hipper succeeded, for about 11.00 a.m. the *Lion* received a tremendous blow by a shell that drove in the armour on her waterline, disabled the feed tanks in the port engine room, which in turn stopped the engine. In addition, No.1 dynamo was thrown off by a short-circuit and the electric lighting and power failed. Further, the ships list to port which had previously been taken was now increased to about $10°$. The *Tiger* then steered to pass between the *Lion* and the German ships who concentrated their fire upon her. It was bad luck for Beatty when his ship was put out of action and consequently dropped astern. But the remaining ships of the opposing squadrons were still four to three in favour of the British, while only the *Tiger* on our side had been hit; a result demonstrating very clearly that the enemy's fire had been concentrated on the British Vanguard.

Then followed the crucial moment of the engagement, for submarines were reported on the starboard bow of the *Lion* and Beatty signalled all ships to turn eight points to port in order to avoid the supposed submarines. From all later reports no submarines were present. Unfortunately, however, this made the course North by East while Hipper's three ships were racing homeward on an easterly course almost at right angles, and the British ships were losing the chase. But Beatty realising this, and of the danger of encountering mines in the wake of the enemy if he continued on the new course, signalled course north-east a few minutes after the eight-point turn. This was sufficient to avoid the danger of mines and incidentally enabled the remainder of his Squadron to cut off the *Blucher* from the German Squadrons and thus induce Hipper to turn back to her succour. But as we have seen, Hipper had made an effort by ordering his destroyers to attack while altering his course southward.

While these manoeuvres were going on however, much confusion had prevailed and the enemy battle cruisers, except the *Blucher* were, for the most part, out of gun range, which in fact, was never regained. When the *Lion* had dropped so far astern as to render Beatty's control impossible, Rear Admiral Moore flying his flag in the *New Zealand*, took charge of the Squadron. This was just after the eight-point turn to the north and two further signals had been made by Beatty. They were:

1. "Attack the enemy's rear"

2. "Keep closer to the enemy".

Shades of Admiral Lord Nelson at Trafalgar!

Naval Action In Home Waters

Then Admiral Moore's difficulties began, for the flags became obscured as they blew end-on to the leading ship, and the first of the two signals was apparently hoisted before the compass signal course "North East" had been hauled down. Moore therefore concluded that Beatty had ordered his leading ships to concentrate their attack on the *Blucher*. Accordingly, the *Tiger* and *Princess Royal* ceased their fire on the fleeing enemy ships. Beatty's intention really was to keep closer to the other three more powerful ships and concentrate their gun fire upon them. In the chances of war, incredible happenings occur, and unfortunately, our battle cruisers did not take in Beatty's second signal. Their attention was therefore given to the *Blucher*, the weakest of the enemy battle cruisers. The other three ships were mercifully spared punishment and eventually escaped altogether. A most costly lesson in Naval Signals.

A word here in praise of the *Blucher* and her gallant crew seems not out of place. For about 3 hours they stood up to severe punishment. The *Blucher* had been attacked not only by our battle cruisers, but also by our light cruisers and destroyers, and fought back gamely against them all, until finally she was torpedoed at 11.45 a.m. and sank half an hour later. The *Blucher* was a much less powerful ship than her consorts and was with twelve guns of 8.2-inch calibre only (the weight of one 8.2-inch shell was less than half that of the *Lion*'s 13.5-inch projectile), but during the engagement her fire was so accurate that she drove off our light cruisers on two occasions. Truly one of the most remarkable feats of courage and fighting efficiency in the annals of naval warfare.

By 11.30 a.m. our battle cruisers had circled to the north east of the *Blucher* at comparatively close range, and when he was sure that she was doomed Admiral Moore ceased fire and resumed the chase after Hipper's three Battle Cruisers. But Hipper's Squadron was over 12 miles to the south east and making good progress towards home. It would be a considerable time before he could hope to get within effective gun range once more, and observing that by then the enemy would be close to Heligoland and near the High Sea Fleet which he had now heard was coming out, Moore decided to stop the chase about 11.45 a.m. and retire in the direction of the *Lion*.

Beatty however, believing that the chase was still on called a destroyer alongside the *Lion* and at 11.50 a.m. embarked and proceeded in order to transfer his flag to the *Princess Royal*. But it was too late, the enemy battle cruisers had got away in their damaged conditions and there was nothing more to do. The *Lion* was afterwards towed into Rosyth by the *Indomitable*, arriving there early on the morning of the 26th January escorted by a screen of light cruisers and destroyers.

Our losses in personnel were comparatively slight, four men were killed and two were wounded in the destroyer *Meteor*, which was damaged and towed to the Humber by the *Liberty*. The casualties on board the *Lion* were eleven wounded and on board the *Tiger* were killed and eight wounded. There was no British ship lost. According to German accounts their losses were substantial. Of *Blucher*'s crew of 1,026 - 792 were killed or drowned and 45 wounded. The remaining 189 were picked up by Commodore Tryhwitt in the *Arethusa*. The *Sydlitz* lost 59 killed and suffered 33 wounded and the *Kolberg*'s casualties were - three killed and two wounded.

The Dogger Bank encounter was the first ever between capital ships of the Dreadnought type, and several lessons were learnt:

- In the first instance it proved that only completely efficient ships with equal speed and gun power preferably should take part in such a battle.
- The penetrating power of modern naval artillery demanded the very best armour protection of the vitals of all ships engaged.

- Pre-dreadnought ships would have fallen an easy prey to modern dreadnoughts (as in the case of the *Blucher*).
- An enemy submarine attack, though not made, was possible in such a stern chase; therefore destroyers to form a screen during the advance of the attacking force is necessary.
- Admiral Fisher's foresight regarding the advantage of preponderance of gun-fire and speed of each unit was fully justified. The effect of single shots at extreme range can be of great importance or even decisive.
- Beatty commanding superior speed, with the armour of his ships perhaps inferior to that of the enemy's, was quite right in maintaining an extreme range during the action.
- After the flagship *Lion* had been disabled and put out of action, an unfortunate misunderstanding occurred over Beatty's signals, which doubtless robbed our battle cruisers of greater success.
- The experience on board the *Seylitz* early in the battle when at 9.15 a.m. her aft turret was penetrated by a shell from the *Lion* was an extremely important lesson which only the Germans learnt at the time. The ignition of gun ammunition in the waiting position might well have led to the destruction of the ship (just as three of our battle cruisers were later lost at Jutland).
- As the Dogger Bank was only 80 miles from the Yorkshire coast and about 220 miles from the German Naval Base at Wilhelmshaven, it was proved that Hipper's tactics in deciding upon a stern chase engagement were correct. It also proved that unless superiority of ships were ensured, future actions such as this should be brought about nearer one's base.

The return of the entire German battle cruiser force to its base except the *Blucher* showed the masterly way in which its leader, Von Hipper, conducted its tactics. Thereafter it was generally thought that future offensive operations by the German Fleet would most likely be in the form of similar sorties by their battle cruisers and with this in view the Grand Fleet was divided into two forces.

Admiral Jellicoe retained under his immediate Command, four Battle Squadrons comprising three squadrons of Dreadnought battleships based on Scapa Flow and one of battleships of the King Edward Class based at Rosyth. With Jellicoe's Battle Fleet was a cruiser force of the 1st, 2nd, 3rd and 7th Cruiser Squadrons. The duties of these cruisers also included the reinforcement and cover of the 10th Cruiser Squadron (armed Merchant Cruisers). Admiral Beatty commanded a Battle Cruiser Fleet comprising ten Battle Cruisers in three Squadrons with *Lion* as Fleet Flagship, the others being *Tiger, Princess Royal, Indomitable, New Zealand, Australia, Queen Mary, Invincible*, (and later in June the *Inflexible*). One Light Cruiser Squadron was attached to each Battle Cruiser Squadron, with *Fearless, Commodore D* and 1st D Flotilla moved up to Rosyth from Harwich.

Chapter XXXVI

The War on Commerce

--- ooOoo ---

Considerable interest was current about the time of which I write, in an incident that caused tension in Great Britain's relations to America. In the cotton districts of the Southern States, the need for oversea merchant tonnage had become serious, and to provide more shipping, a bill was being passed to authorize the purchase by the Americans of German ships that had been interned in American ports. Valuable ships indeed, but they dare not sail under the German flag for fear of capture. This procedure, for a neutral in time of war, was obviously not approved of by Britain and France.

However, a German merchant ship named *Dacia* had already been sold to a New York firm and was registered as an American ship for the transport of cotton to Germany. This act was against the terms of the Declaration of London, but it constituted a test case for future sales, if no notice was taken of it. The matter was apparently settled between the British and American Governments for the time being, on the understanding that if we captured the *Dacia* and seized her contraband cargo the shippers in America would be paid the price that the enemy was willing to pay.

The deftness with which our obligation had been avoided in this matter was soon realized when it was announced that on February 27th that the *Dacia* had been captured by a French Cruiser and the arrangements that the British had made with the Americans could not bind France!

On the 18th February 1915, the Germans adopted a new scheme in their sea warfare on commerce, by the declaration of a War Zone round the British Isles. It was quite unlawful, for the Germans had not sufficient means to carry out an effective blockade under the maritime rules contained in the Declaration of Paris. Admiral Von Tirpitz, the German Minister, knew very well that he could only blockade by his submarines, of which he had comparatively few, and that the German declaration was practically meaningless if the laws of sea warfare were still to be observed. But there was something more deadly in the purpose of this new policy that marked the beginning of their degradation at sea.

So far, Germany with a few exceptions, had conformed to the laws of humanity in war, as manifested by the German Cruiser *Emden*, though in the waters nearer the British Isles, British ships had been sunk by U Boats without warning, including the Hospital Ship *Asturias*. Up to February 18th, 1915, German submarines had sunk 12 British and Allied Merchant Ships. Of these, four were torpedoed without warning. Germany had also laid mines by which 18 British fishing vessels and 38 Merchant ships were sunk. Many of the mines were in the open seas, the laying of which was against international law.

But now when our Navy had swept their surface ships from the seas and their overseas trade was paralysed, Germany suddenly discarded her mask of toleration and issued the following official declaration, "All waters surrounding Great Britain and Ireland, including the whole of the English Channel, are hereby declared to be a War Zone".

This meant that from February 18th onwards, every enemy merchant vessel found within this war zone will be destroyed without it being always possible to avoid danger to the crews and passengers. A paragraph added to this was, "It is impossible to avoid attacks being made on neutral ships in mistake for those of the enemy".

The reason given for this was that Britain had been waging war against their commerce and had added to the list of contraband certain goods not of military value. Also, unlawfully searching German property carried by neutral vessels and removing from neutral ships German subjects liable to military service and making them prisoners of war. It is true that most of these things, we of the Gibraltar Torpedo Boat Flotilla had done. But compared with the torpedoing of ships without warning, the world could judge which acts were the most humane, if not strictly according to law which one is not.

Regarding the movements of German merchant ships, except within the Baltic Sea, their whole fleet had now been swept from the seas by our naval patrol vessels. This struck hard at German military strength and the economic life calculated to starve the population into surrender. One of the German excuses for torpedoing Allied merchant ships on sight was that it was quite impracticable to board and search our ships on the high seas as our merchantmen were now armed. Moreover, their submarines were the only means they had left to execute their orders. The real reason for the declaration was clearly pointed out in a further German statement that our blockade was not only paralysing German overseas trade, but also that of neutrals. The direct threat to neutral shipping in the German announcement would naturally affect America more than any other country, and the Government at Washington promptly protested against it.

In its Note to Germany, Washington claimed that the right of belligerents was limited to visit and search for contraband (unless blockade could be effectively maintained, which was impossible for Germany to do); but to claim the right to attack and destroy any neutral vessel entering any prescribed area without search or establishing the nature of her cargo, would be an act that would be very hard to reconcile with a continuation of friendly relations between the two countries. In their reply, Germany insisted that while neutrals submitted to British interference with the importation of their food, they intended to prevent the contraband trade with the British Isles by every means in their power. One of Germanys chief complaints was our attempt to starve the German people into surrender by the prevention of foodstuffs from being delivered to them by non-belligerent countries through neutral ports.

In this, America protested against our methods of dealing with foodstuffs shipped to neutral ports on the-mere assumption that they were intended to reach the enemy. But in the British Foreign Office reply, it was explained that such foodstuffs were not treated as other contraband, or dealt with through the prize court, but upon agreement with the shippers that payment made in full for cargoes diverted to British ports, and so that neutrals concerned would suffer no loss. A reasonable quantity of foodstuffs from overseas, of course, was permitted to enter the ports of neutral countries in order to feed their populations.

Earlier, on January 25th 1915, the German Government announced that as from February 1st it would take over the control of all foodstuffs. In consequence, this entitled us to seize all such cargoes as contraband to be dealt with by the Prize Court.

An interesting incident occurred about this time when the American ship *Wilhelmina* was seized at Falmouth with a cargo of wheat consigned directly to an American agency in Hamburg. The

Naval Action In Home Waters

American Government protested at this act, claiming that the foodstuffs were for the consumption of the civilian population of an unfortified German city. In our Foreign Office reply, it was pointed out that Hamburg was no less a fortified place than Scarborough, which the German battle cruisers had bombarded only two months before. Moreover, it was asserted that the time had come for Britain to treat all foodstuffs as contraband cargoes, in view of the repeated breaches of International Maritime Law by Germany.

As anticipated, the enemy soon carried out her threat, by torpedoing several of our merchant ships without warning and we were now up against the grim fact of further and increasing losses. Acute submarine defence measures were therefore seriously considered to meet this new menace, for at all costs our merchant shipping must go on, to and from all ports in the British Isles, despite the worst that Germany could do in their declared war zone.

Neither our shipping companies nor their brave captains and crews were daunted in this effort and, accordingly the Admiralty, took counter action in their aid without delay. Measures were taken to increase patrols in certain areas, large number of trawlers were requisitioned and equipped with gun armaments for this service, while our defences against attack by enemy submarines on the eastern side of the Straits of Dover were further strengthened by the laying of an additional minefield. Patrol yachts and other small craft armed with guns and explosive sweeps were pressed into this anti-submarine service, also a large number of Indicator nets laid out and operated by a number of new fishing drifts. These defence measures were instituted at various ports on the East Coast of England and Scotland, the English Channel ports, also ports in the St Georges and North channels as well as others on the east and west coasts of Ireland.

Hitherto, only merchant ships engaged on overseas trade had been defensively armed with one gun in the aft part of the ship, but now, vessels engaged in home waters only, were also equipped with gun armaments with two naval ratings included in the gun crew. The production, manning and equipment of all these vessels and the provision of miles of indicator nets was a tremendous task, but it was carried out without interference with the strategical position of the Main Fleet, though it was necessary to withdraw from it, several destroyers for the escort of certain naval ships and large merchant vessels entering or leaving our home ports, in addition to those detailed hitherto for transports carrying troops and munitions to France and elsewhere.

Special anti-submarine warfare instructions were also issued to captains of merchant ships as to the best means of dealing with enemy submarines as soon as they were sighted. The advice was given confidentially, and of course, varied according to the distance bearing and other circumstances that might arise. Obviously, much thought and care were given in order that the instructions avoided the suggestion that these ships might no longer be regarded as non-combatants, and that their duty was to elude a submarine attack if possible in self-defence only. Doubtless the Germans were on the look-out for such instructions as could possibly be used in favour of the devilish work of their U-Boats, by claiming merchant ships were attacking rather than defending.

The general instructions issued therefore were that if a submarine was sighted at a reasonable distance, the captain should turn his ship's stern towards it and increase to utmost speed; if shoal water was in the vicinity he should make for it if possible. If, however, a U-Boat was seen within torpedo range ahead, and by turning to run away it his ship would present a better target, he should then steer directly towards her and force the submarine to dive. Having passed over the enemy in this manner he would be brought astern and so allow the ship to proceed as previously directed. This was as far as the instructions could go, though the reader will appreciate, that if the submarine had not sufficient time in which to dive to a depth below the draught of the ship, it would most probably be rammed and sunk!

A case similar to this happened on February 28th 1915 when Captain Bell of the S.S. *Thordis* whilst streaming down the English Channel off Beachy Head sighted the periscope of a submarine on his starboard bow. It was crossing his course at the time and upon reaching a position less than 50 yards distant on the *Thordis* port beam, the submarine fired a torpedo, without the slightest warning, but missed the ship. When Captain Bell saw the wake of the torpedo, which indicated that it had passed under his ship, he put his helm hard over and steered straight for the enemy. Then followed a crash and when the *Thordis* was subsequently docked, it was found that she had lost a blade from her propeller and that the keel plate had been damaged. Surely one would imagine that this impact would have sunk the enemy U-Boat! But it was not so, for later it was known that she was the German Submarine *U6* and though suffering much damage, she reached a homeport safely.

I would here mention that less than a month later, the famous German U Boat Commander Otto Weddigen, of *U-29,* who had sunk four of our cruisers, the *Greasy, Rogue, Aboukir* and the *Hawks*, was rammed and sank with all hands by *HMS Dreadnought* on the morning of March 18th 1915. This occurred when Admiral Jellicoe was exercising his Grand Fleet Battle Squadrons east of Scapa Flow, and while Admiral Sturdee was leading the 4th Battle Squadron in the *Dreadnought*. A submarine had been sighted and an enemy torpedo had just missed the *Neptune*. Then after spotting the periscope on the port bow of the *Dreadnought*, her Captain increased speed and made straight for it, and in a few minutes, the great battleship struck the submarine a crushing blow that sent her to the bottom. There was no doubt whatever as to the identity of the victim, for as the bows of the U-Boat came out of the water, just before she sank, her number 29 was clearly read on board the battleship.

This success, in addition to avenging our great losses in men and cruisers, marked a fitting end of the first month of Germany's lawless warfare in their declared war zone. Our losses during this short period however were considerable, and foreshadowed the grim struggle to come in the Navy's task of keeping the sea lanes open for our great armies and the ports of the United Kingdom for overseas trade. In all about 45 ships had been attacked and of these, 21 vessels were lost while the remainder escaped. Three enemy submarines were known to have been destroyed in the same period; one of these, the *U-12* was hunted down by destroyers and armed trawlers on patrol in Scottish waters on March 10th. Ten survivors of her crew were rescued.

To continue reading the rest of this memoir, please see:

Volume II of My Destiny the Sea

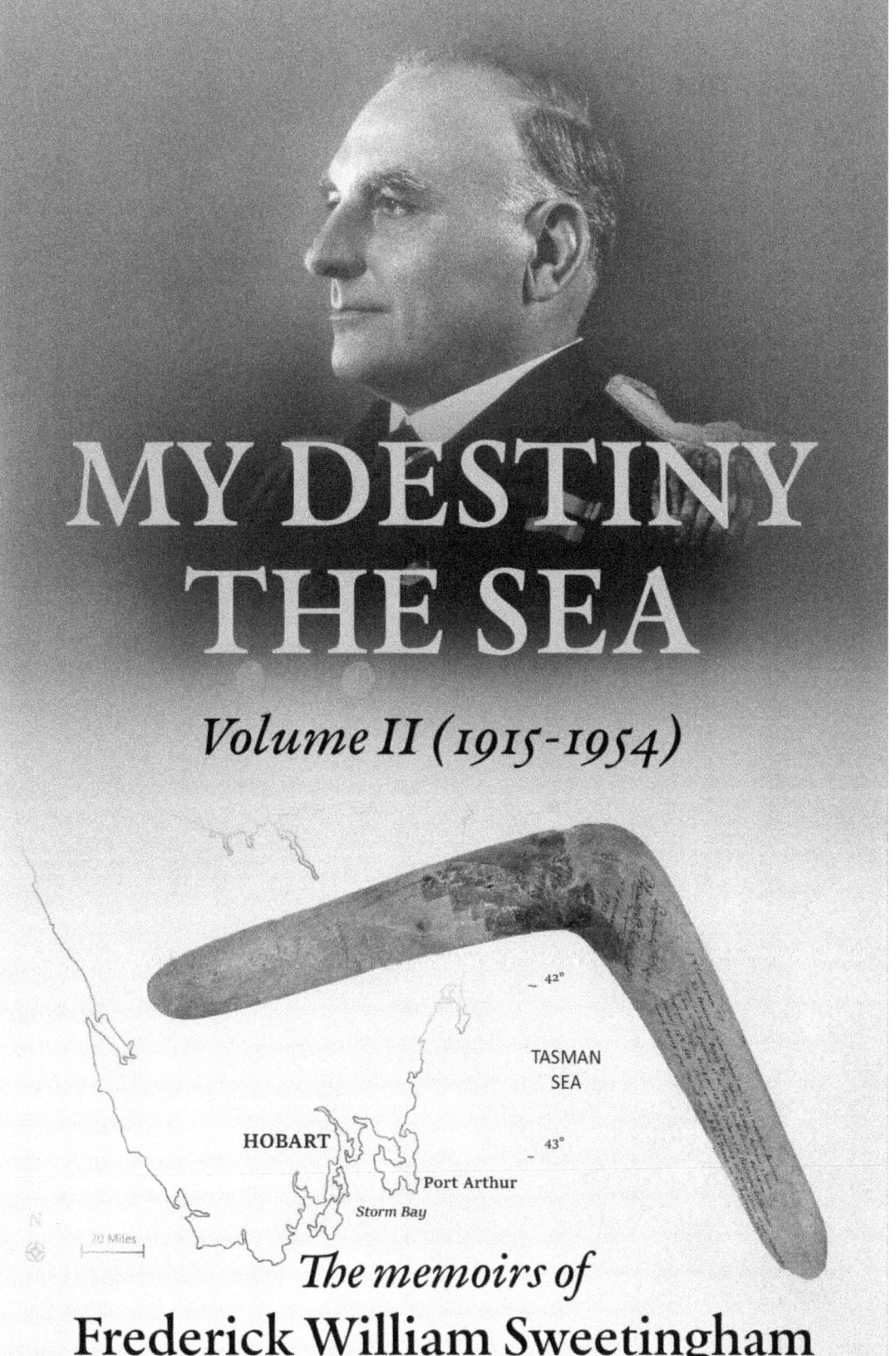

MY DESTINY THE SEA

Volume II (1915-1954)

The memoirs of
Frederick William Sweetingham

www.ingramcontent.com/pod-product-compliance
Lightning Source LLC
Chambersburg PA
CBHW061409070526
44584CB00032B/4199